# Nondual Chakra Awakening

*A HERO'S JOURNEY TO HEALING*

*RELATIONSHIP INJURY*

*IN SEVEN HOLOGRAPHIC STAGES*

Yoga Meets Attachment Psychology

By Zeb Lancaster, Ph.D.

Copyright Page

Published by Whole Being Books

## Dedication

I dedicate this book to helping us learn to live from a deep center of wholeness and unity, so we can become more authentically human and realize the potential of our created existence.

The "whole-being-embrace" approach presented here, democratizes our life in relationship, in that both dual and nondual dimensions of self, mutually co-exist. This allows for a spirituality that is a matter of the heart, rather than the awareness or mind alone. We learn to re-feel and reshape our reality and our destiny so we can live by the spontaneously arising opulence of our authentic self.

## Acknowledgment

I owe the bulk of my acknowledgment and gratitude to Teresa Neptune. She listened to and advised me every step of the way. The presence and understanding she brought to the process were tremendously insightful, and the way she did this was engaging (non-abandoning) and respectful (non-invasive). In this light, she expressed the deepest principles underlying the healing process espoused in this book. As a result, I have experienced a personal transformation that has enabled me to share with others the heart of this approach much more effectively.

I thank Richard Freeman for guiding me through his profound teachings in Ashtanga yoga. His *satsang* gatherings and yoga training have shaped my life and therapeutic work with other people. I thank Judith Blackstone for her development of the Realization Process® meditation method. Judith's approach has greatly influenced my yoga, my counseling practice, and my life. I thank Peter Levine for his brilliant insights into trauma and the psyche. His work has been very influential in informing my orientation to the healing process. I thank Ilia Delio for her astute insights and for providing a perspective that has helped refine my own. I thank Rodrigo Inostroza for lending his talent to the graphics in this book. I give honor and respect to my children Miranda and Devon, for their unwavering support and love.

## A Word About Words

In this book I present an alternative view of "self" that includes the duality-based, constantly changing "evolving-self," and the nondual innate "unchanging-self." The relationship between the two is significant in that neither dimension of self is eliminated or collapsed into the other. For this reason, I generally refer to "self" as a distinct entity and separate the word self from other words. So "myself" becomes "my self," "yourself" becomes "your self," and ourself becomes "our self." This expression is deliberate and not a typo.

In an attempt to clarify the concepts discussed, descriptive Sanskrit terms (in brackets) are included to refer to the terminology used in the school of thought involved. Reference to the "sutras" always implies the *Yoga Sutras* of Patanjali, unless otherwise indicated.

There are so many ways of describing the nature of existence and the spiritual dimension, that we are often left wondering if different authors on the subject are even discussing the same principles. Several factors contribute to this confusion. Sacred spiritual texts are conventionally written in a "twilight language" (Bucknell, Stuart-Fox, 1986), a secret language we cannot un-riddle without guidance.

Moreover, because spiritual traditions use similar terms to mean different things, and different words to mean the same thing, an attempt to interpret the meaning of the keywords used, is provided. Sanskrit words have multiple meanings depending on their doctrinal context and sometimes mean different things in different traditions.

Furthermore, nondual experiences are holistic in nature so expressing them in the linear dualistic structure of language can often result in statements that sound paradoxical or nonsensical. Adapting descriptions of nondual experience to the relativistic and constructivist views of contemporary clinical psychology can be challenging. An attempt has been made here to describe the realization of nonduality at the level of experience. Yet keep in mind that any claims about the nature of being, the nature of reality, or metaphysical import, are simply inferences. The accuracy of these suggestions cannot be ascertained based on experience alone, yet experience is often our best tool. Using experience as our guide is a "heuristic" approach to self-discovery in that it is a practical method, not guaranteed to be optimal, perfect, or purely rational. Yet, it allows us to understand the nature of existence immediately.

# Table of Contents

*Dedication & Acknowledgment* ......................................................... 3

*A Word About Words* ...................................................................... 4

**Introduction** ............................................................................... 8

**CHAPTER ONE: EVERYTHING, EVERYWHERE, ALL AT ONCE** ..................... 1

*UNCHANGING PRESENCE-OF-BEING AS A BODY EXPERIENCE* .......... 1

*WHAT IS TRANSCENDENCE* ............................................................ 6

*THE BODY'S ALTERNATIVE TO TRANSCENDENCE* ............................ 12

*THE TWO IN ONE & ONE IN TWO PARADOX OF QUANTUM* ........... 18

*THE QUANTUM BODY* ................................................................... 23

*DUAL & NONDUAL EMBODIMENT* ................................................. 24

*FIVE LAYERS OF SELF (PANCHA KOSHA) AS BLISS* ........................... 26

*UNCOVERING & AWAKENING THE BLISS LAYER* ............................ 30

*THE NEED FOR PARADOX* .............................................................. 30

**CHAPTER TWO: QUANTUM EVOLUTION** ............................................ 33

*HISTORY IN THE MAKING* .............................................................. 33

*THE QUEST FOR WHOLENESS & THE RISE OF QUANTUM* ............... 37

*PERENNIAL PSYCHOLOGY OF THE HERO'S JOURNEY* ...................... 40

Three-Phases of Energy ........................................................ 47

Seven Stages .......................................................................... 53

*THE INTERRUPTED ENERGY CYCLE* ................................................ 57

*THE SUCCESSFUL RETURN "HOME"* ............................................... 59

*THE HOLOGRAPHIC APPROACH TO SOCIAL CHANGE* ..................... 61

**CHAPTER THREE: AS ABOVE SO BELOW** .......................................... 65

*YOGA AS A DIRECT & INDIRECT-PATH TO AUTONOMY* .................. 65

*NONDUAL-QUALITIES & THE CHAKRAS* ......................................... 70

*NONDUAL-QUALITIES & UNCONDITIONAL LOVE* ........................... 72

*THE CHAKRAS & THE CENTRAL-CHANNEL* ..................................... 74

*CHAKRAS & 7 STAGES OF CHILD DEVELOPMENT* .......................... 77

*ASPECTS OF WHOLE-BEING-EMBRACE HEALING* ........................... 82

*ENERGY OBSTRUCTION & CHAKRAS & STAGES OF GROWTH* ......... 89

**CHAPTER FOUR: MEETING PRESENT MOMENT** ................................ 92

*WHOLE-BEING-EMBRACE & NONDUAL MIRRORING* ...................... 92

*THE UNIFYING EFFECT OF WHOLENESS* ......................................... 96

*REFINING THE SENSES & ATTUNEMENT* ......................................... 97

*UNIFYING THE SENSES* ................................................................ 106

*REVIEW OF NERVOUS SYSTEM'S 7 RESPONSES TO THREAT* ......... 108

**CHAPTER FIVE: CHAKRAS AS A HERO'S JOURNEY** ............................ 112

*UNBALANCED CHAKRA & CHILD DEVELOPMENT STRUGGLES* ...... 112
*FIRST CHAKRA/STAGE - CALL TO ADVENTURE* ............................ 117
*SECOND CHAKRA/STAGE: CALL TO COMMITMENT* ..................... 129
*THIRD CHAKRA/STAGE - RISE TO ACTION* ................................ 144
*FOURTH CHAKRA/STAGE: DEATH & REBIRTH* ............................. 157
*FIFTH CHAKRA/STAGE: THE ROAD TO SATISFACTION* .................. 178
*SIXTH CHAKRA/STAGE: COMPLETION & RESURRECTION* ............. 199
*SEVENTH CHAKRA/STAGE: HOME AGAIN* ................................. 222

**CHAPTER SIX: AWAKENING THE CENTRAL-CHANNEL** ......................... 242

*THE SUBTLE CORE & THE APPLE OF KNOWLEDGE* ..................... 242
*TRILOGY & CADUCEUS AS OUR DEATH-REBIRTH CYCLE* ............. 243
*HOW THE PHASE-STAGE CYCLES RELATE TO THE CHAKRAS* ........ 246
*IDA, PINHALA, SUSHUMNA NADI* ........................................... 249
*DIAPHRAGMS AS GROUNDING FOUNDATION* ........................... 252
*OPENING INTO NONDUALITY BY FINDING "APANA"* ................... 261
*THE UPWARD CURRENT OF PRANA* ........................................ 263

**CHAPTER SEVEN: WHAT IT IS** .................................................... 268

*FROM CONTROL & SEPARATION TO NOURISHMENT* .................. 268
*WISDOM* ........................................................................... 271
*EXISTENTIAL TRUST, ACCEPTANCE, & SMELLING ROSES* ............... 272
*FROM CREATIVITY TO SPONTANEITY* ...................................... 274
*RETURNING FROM TRANSCENDENCE TO SAVE THE PLANET* ........ 278

**CONCLUSION** ........................................................................ 283

**APPENDIX ONE: NERVOUS SYSTEM'S SEVEN STAGES OF HEALING** ..... 293

*THE SEVEN STAGES OF HEALING TRAUMA* ............................... 296
*SEVEN STAGES TO RECOVERY WITH EMBODIED NONDUALITY* .... 299

**APPENDIX TWO: INTEGRAL APPROACH TO PATANJALI'S YOGA** ......... 321

*YOGA'S FIRST STAGES OF PRACTICE (limbs 1-2)* ......................... 323
*YOGA'S SECOND STAGE (Limb 3)* .......................................... 327
*YOGA'S THIRD STATE (Limb 4)* ............................................. 329
*YOGA'S FOURTH STAGE (Limb 5):* .......................................... 335
*YOGA'S FIFTH STAGE (Limb 6)* .............................................. 339
*YOGA'S STAGE SIX (limb 7)* ................................................. 340
*YOGA'S SEVENTH STAGE (Limb 8)* ......................................... 344

**BIBLIOGRAPHY** ..................................................................... 347

# Introduction

After completing my last book, *From Trauma to Wholeness: Embodied Nondual Meditation, Yoga Therapy, and Somatic Psychology*, I needed a break from writing. However, after only a month, I realized I was not finished and had a compelling "story" to share. It addresses the heart of personal and social change to a new paradigm for relationship healing and enlightenment.

In this new work, I invite you on a journey to a new paradigm where the unified (nondual) nature of your chakras help guide you to freedom from limiting relationship injuries. You will discover the support from each chakra as an innate, unified ground-of-being, in embrace with your injured evolving-self. In this relational approach, you will heal rather than "bypass" or transcend the injuries and messages found in your body, that are there to lead you back to self-love, and your deepest personal truth. It is a method that enables you to find the nondual-qualities in each of your chakras that support you to live authentically and joyfully, in wholeness.

This book offers an alternative approach to the self-transcendent orientation of separating from our emotions by submerging them into unified consciousness (all is one), or claiming that emotions are not real (no self). I offer a healing encounter, called "whole-being-embrace," between the dual and nondual dimensions of our existence. This approach is congruent with the quantum physics claim that both aspects of existence can be found within the nature of energy, in an entangled endless feedback cycle. I propose how this endless feedback cycle is represented in the three-phases of energy (charge, discharge, balance), as seen in our nervous system.

When our body experience of balance is clear, energy moves freely and authentically through each of the charge-discharge phases. As we refine our senses, within this balanced state we perceive the unified nature of our existence become more prominent. We can feel how our experience of unity is the source of the most profound contact with our self* (*see Word About Words), with other people, and with our environment. This experience of unified consciousness has been called by many different names, such as Buddha-Nature, Christ-consciousness,

8

*Ishta-Devata*, and *saguna Brahman*; I call this essence the "unchanging-self."

In meditation, I came to realize how the three-phases of energy (charge, discharge, balance) have seven sub-stages that are holographic in nature. They manifest in the seven stages of child development, the seven stages of the nervous system's response to challenge, the seven stages of adult relationships, and the seven primary chakras. How we move through the challenges in these stages represent, what Joseph Campbell described as the "Hero's Journey." This is a journey from injury, back to authenticity and wholeness-of-being, where we are nurtured in whole-being-embrace.

My discovery of whole-being-embrace reminded me of the entangled nature of all of life, and reaffirmed the sacred bond between my dual and nondual self. It was an "I" to "I" experience, much like the Rastafarian "I and I" expression. This was an internal inter-abiding, in mutuality, of duality and nonduality. Whole-being-embrace helped me expand beyond my experiences in yoga practice that were based on transcendent separation via disregard, disidentification, or dispassion towards my emotions and disturbing thoughts. The emotional injuries that I harbored in my body were now embraced and healed, as a natural part of my spiritual path. This had profound implications for my life. I have come to see this as part of a leap in consciousness toward a more inclusive spiritual paradigm that is emerging today.

This is a leap that is built on embodying a more expansive understanding of the nature of self, providing solutions for our collective future. As we awaken to embodied nondual consciousness, the immaterial nature of unity consciousness becomes tangible and relational. This allows us to make the leap from a spirituality, based on separation from duality, to embracing duality with unity consciousness, thereby transforming both the physical and metaphysical planes of our life.

In this book I highlight the role our body plays in our healing and in our spiritual life. By spiritual I mean self-aware (aware that we are aware) unified consciousness. When this is experienced as a dimension of our own existence, spirituality gives us access to our most fundamental, innate, ground-of-being. Like the moon reflecting the sun, it is in the reflection of the body that we recognize and awaken to our self-aware, nondual divine being. This is the basis of an embodied spiritual experience.

The body is also where we feel our unresolved emotional injuries and trauma. Personal and social change require a fundamental shift, in not only how we view spirituality, but also in how we relate to the human body. This inner relationship influences all other relationships. Our body experience of unified consciousness, as an expression of self, allows us to simultaneously be in an alchemical relationship with our emotional injuries.

This understanding is a paradigm shift away from what Karl Jaspers (1966) called the "Axial Age," an era based on mind-over-body, and thinking of existence in mechanistic terms, where life is composed of separate interrelated parts (explored in the first part of *chapter two*). The new paradigm of spirituality and healing is mirrored in the shift from mechanical physics to quantum physics.

Quantum physics upholds the understanding that our evolution and spiritual awakening is an entanglement of energy and consciousness (as explored in the second half of *chapter two* and all of *chapter three*). As I discovered, this is reflected in three-phases of energy (charge-discharge-balance) that have seven sub-stages representing both our unified ground of being, as found in the seven primary chakras, and the seven stages of child development (our evolution). This entanglement is our human odyssey, in seven archetypal and holographic stages of our "Hero's Journey," that is reflected in every aspect of our life.

As a result of my own inquiry, as well as my work with clients and students, I have developed a method of attending to our deepest injuries and awakening to the most fundamental expression of our existence (spiritual awakening), in a nurturing communion of whole-being-embrace. When we understand the primary challenges of our own Hero's Journey, and where we were interrupted in this seven-stage sequence of growth, we reveal what we need to heal in order to mature and awaken our consciousness. We discern which chakra can provide the most support for us, and tailor our contemplative practice for the most effective results.

This book combines Eastern and Western philosophy, psychology, and provides a roadmap for contemplative practice to heal injuries and awaken to our whole-self. The journey towards emotional maturity, recovery from injury, and spiritual awakening, have a direct influence on how we engage with every aspect of our life, most specifically, on our relationship with our self and others.[1]

---

[1] Dualistic devotional traditions of Hinduism (Dvaita Vedanta) claim the individual human Self and Brahman/God are two different realities. Loving devotion to Brahman (Vishnu, Krishna) releases us from suffering (*saṃsāra*), and with the deity's grace we experience spiritual liberation. Nondual traditions (Advaita Vedanta) claim that the individual human Self and Brahman are identical, and transcending (or neutral witnessing of) our evolving-self is the proposed solution. The path to liberation proposed in this book, also claims that the individual human self and Brahman are identical. Yet, to achieve liberation in this life (*jivamukti*), instead of liberation from suffering only through transcendence, we emphasize awakening unified consciousness as a body experience of our "unchanging-self." This allows us to honor our emotions rather than transcend them. With relationship trauma, transcendence alone too easily leads to a spiritual bypass.

# CHAPTER ONE: EVERYTHING, EVERYWHERE, ALL AT ONCE

UNCHANGING PRESENCE-OF-BEING AS A BODY EXPERIENCE

Eastern and Western traditions have a guiding principle based on separation as opposed to one of inclusion espoused in this book. Eastern spiritual traditions are guided by the ideal that the ultimate aim of human existence is transcendence of the earthly realm. This is based on various means of distancing or separating from our body and emotions while abiding in pure nondual consciousness (*atman*). In meditation, we are guided to objectify and minimize our humanness by either being dispassionate toward (simply witnessing), discounting, distancing, or disidentifying from what makes us human.

Western traditions separate us from nonduality by simply not recognizing its existence (with a few exceptions). Instead, we are informed by our rational mind and our sense of being a separate, unique individual. Psychology's most powerful resources for overcoming our deepest emotional injuries and trauma, including all the leading trauma therapies today,[2] are entirely focused on the evolving nature of "our self"* (*see "A Word about Words"). There is little or no understanding of our innate unified consciousness, and the healing power of wholeness. Moreover, the West is under the influence of monotheistic religions that separate human nature from God's divine nature.

Both Eastern and Western traditions lack the essential elements of human connection and wholeness that we need to heal and awaken as individuals and as a society. We are in need of a new collective paradigm that is guided by unified consciousness in a nourishing relationship with our suffering "evolving-self." In this book, I explore how this experience of unified consciousness, as our most profound source of support, can be found in each of the chakra centers of energy and consciousness. I emphasize that as we refine our senses, we can

---

[2] Leading trauma therapies today include forms of talk therapy, cognitive behavioral therapy, somatic experiencing, emotionally focused therapy, and EMDR.

uncover and awaken a body experience of the unified (nondual) nature of the chakras, as an expression of our self. This essence has been called by many different names, such as Buddha-Nature, Christ-consciousness, *saguna Brahman, and ishta-devata*; I call this essence of our being the "unchanging-self."

When we uncover and awaken to our unchanging-self within our body, we have a spiritual experience. By the term "spiritual," I mean the experience of unified consciousness. When this universal, pervasive, unchanging, timeless unity is experienced as a dimension of our own existence, spirituality gives us access to our most fundamental, innate, ground-of-being. It also gives us access to a ground-of-being in other people and our environment. This spirituality is enlivening and enriching. It has a ripple effect on society and fundamentally transforms our relationship to all life on Earth. The consequences of how this changes our relationship with our evolving-self, other people, and our environment, is the primary subject of this book.

What we discover is that, unlike transcendent states, when unified consciousness is a body experience it is relational in nature. The relationship between our evolving-self (as duality) and our unchanging-self (nonduality), goes beyond normal relationships. Yet, the maxim "injuries happen in relationship, so it is our experience of healthy relationship that heals," is an organizing principle. We give primacy to the body-felt sense of "presence," in a heart-felt inner relationship. This enhances our capacity for meaningful intra-personal (internal) contact and healing. This experience is especially important when we consider the current tendency to objectify our self, others, and the planet.

These tendencies are only made worse with the cultural shift that has altered how people communicate. Inter-personal contact has become progressively more digitized, objectified, and delivered in virtual platforms to the extent that we can no longer agree on the facts or truth of what is being communicated. While we may feel more connected than ever, it seems we are actually becoming more isolated and disconnected from authentic human contact. With the most sophisticated information technology in history, we are still losing the ability to speak with one another.

2

Authentic contact with others starts from within, intra-personally. If we are not in authentic contact with ourselves, it is impossible to be authentic with other people. Intra-personal contact is also a powerful way to reverse our externally focused and reactive fixations that result from relational injury and trauma. The philosopher Martin Buber's understanding of an authentic relationship as an "encounter," or I–Thou meeting, has new meaning when it involves an internal encounter between two dimensions of our own existence. This new meaning is captured in the Jamaican Patois words "I and I," expressing how we exist as the same One Love. The total is greater than the sum of the parts. Our inner relationship between our evolving-self and our unchanging-self, becomes greater than the individual contributions each dimension of existence offers alone. It is a divine entanglement that goes beyond the interconnectedness of separate individuals, to include the unified nature of our existence.

This internal "I–Thou," or "I and I" relationship, is informed by mutuality, directness, unified presence, and ineffability. In contemplation, our evolving-self can feel how communion with our unchanging-self is a relationship based on inclusion and oneness. It is in this relationship that we become fully human. Both dimensions meet in mutuality, where our essence as unity is acknowledged without obscuring our uniqueness and separateness. The relatedness that is shared is an I–Thou, I and I experience, that I call "whole-being-embrace."

The whole-being-embrace relationship is a foundation of therapeutic growth. In its healing capacity, it is fundamentally affirming of authentic human connection, validation, and participation with each other. Deep participation with our essential ground-of-being reveals our innate capacity to affirm and accept our evolving-self and transform our relationship with others despite their differences. In our own small sphere of influence as individuals, we feed into global collective consciousness, promoting a more compassionate and humanized world.

To be confirmed and affirmed in our own evolving uniqueness by the essential unified ground-of-being, is the source of our compassion for our self and humanity. The self-realization that grows within every human being, can be actualized in its most authentic form, only when our evolving-self is fully received in the presence of the most fundamental manifestation of our existence, our unchanging-self. This confirmation is at the heart of the whole-being-embrace communion that promotes self-love, healing, and flourishing.

This confirmation does not create or impose "conditions of worth" in the relationship. We acknowledge our unified "essence" as an unconditional potentiality, and affirm the authenticity that we become. For example, a child experiences the tension between growth and fear along each step of the developmental path. Our unchanging-self, as experienced in each of the chakras, embraces this struggle in the moment, and provides affirming support for us to take the next step on our developmental path. At all ages, in whole-being-embrace, we thrive as humans in these continual moments of recognition of our uninjured, innate unified essence and potentiality. In this book, I point out how each stage of child development (that is repeated as an adult) correlates with each of the primary chakras of our unchanging-self, in a way that is inherently healing.

When we refine our senses and awaken to this unified ground of our existence as an adult, we experience the wholeness and unconditional love we always wanted from a healthy parent. As we struggle with making the "growth choice" or the "fear choice" when we experience the intensity of our life, our unchanging-self allows for an inner-communion that supports us in our relationships. For instance, instead of sacrificing our authenticity in hopes of preserving our attachment to others, we feel confirmed and profoundly supported in our uniqueness from an unbiased source, our unchanging-self. This allows us to make the make the most healthy, authentic choices for our self (healthy relationship boundaries).

In embodied nondual meditation, the ways we stay hidden from ourselves and others in self-protection, dissolve as we progressively open to our essential ground-of-being. This I–Thou, I and I encounter, is a relational event that is co-created. It does not fully reside in our evolving-self alone (psychology), or nondual consciousness alone (transcendence). Our ability to mine the riches of whole-being-embrace, while more deeply opening to our relationships in the immediate moment, is an experience of inclusion that helps heal our relationship injuries.

With this understanding, we experience our evolving-self, and others, with more than empathy; we experience a sense of inclusion that emerges from realizing our divine entanglement. This alternative paradigm, which is based on whole-being-embrace between both dimension of our existence, rather than separation, is congruent with the basic tenets of quantum physics. Quantum physics explains that within the solid nature of the world, we find a unified dimension of existence. From this understanding, matter cannot be considered apart from unified consciousness, and both aspects of existence can be found within the nature of energy.

As the physicist David Bohm explains, the movement from nonduality into duality, is an endless feedback cycle, entangled as we are in whole-being-embrace. In this book, I emphasize how this endless feedback cycle is represented in the three-phases of energy (charge, discharge, balance) as seen in our nervous system and all of nature.

When we refine our senses in embodied nondual meditation, we experience that unified consciousness is fundamental to the energy that composes our body, embedded within its tissues. We experience how the energetic nature of the material dimension of existence, as found in our thoughts, emotions, and sensations, seems to spontaneously arise out of the immaterial nature of unified consciousness. When unified consciousness is a body experience, we can feel how both states co-exist in a whole-being-embrace that heals our suffering heart and PTSD.

Moreover, in meditation, we feel that the energy within us has a charge-discharge-balance cycle, and notice when we become fixated in the charge-discharge states. We experience that the more energy flows freely and authentically through each of these phases, the more balance, integration, and unity we have in our body-mind system. When energy moves freely, the unified nature of our existence becomes more prominent. When we recognize that we exist as unified consciousness within our body, nothing obstructs the flow of energy through each of its three phases and authenticity prevails.

In this book, I point out how the three-phases have seven sub-stages. These seven stages are holographic in that they are fractal in nature. They manifest in the seven stages of child development, the seven stages of our nervous system's response to challenge, the seven stages of adult relationships, and the seven primary chakras. This three-phase, seven sub-stage pattern, bridges cultural boundaries and represents, what Joseph Campbell described as archetypal stages of the "Hero's Journey." A journey from injury, back to authenticity and wholeness-of-being.[3]

I reference this archetypal, holographic journey in each of the seven stages of our growth. As a result, this book is not only deeply philosophical and psychological; it is also explicitly practical as a means of healing relationship injuries and awakening authenticity. Specific contemplative practices are suggested that can be tailored to address the particular stage in which you experienced injury. Enjoy the journey, and let me know how it turns out for you.

WHAT IS TRANSCENDENCE

Understanding how the guiding principle based on separation is found in Eastern nondual spiritual traditions, can help us clarify why a more inclusive alternative is important. Eastern spiritual traditions generally help us overcome our suffering by guiding us toward the bliss found beyond our evolving nature of self in a transcendent state. It is often presented in light of defining what "true" reality or "true self" is. This is the foundation of most ancient mystic traditions, including Hindu Vedanta, Hebraic traditions, and Christianity. The transcendent state is the end goal and *raison d'etre* of most forms of yoga.

---

[3] It is also congruent with Ken Wilber's integral model of the spectrum of consciousness and stages of development. I do not emphasize Wilber's model, primarily for simplicity's sake. If you are informed by his integral model, the associations will be clear.

The transcendent approach is also found in the tendency to separate God from the body and psyche, or its claim that the ultimate destination of evolution is a transcendent state of unity beyond, other, or above the evolving process (thoughts, emotions, and sensations). In most popular forms of meditation, when we transcend what we experience, our evolving-self has no value in our healing and becomes insignificant to our spiritual awakening. In this state, the "evolving-self" and its injuries are perceived to be an illusion (*mayavada*).

In yoga, this transcendent nondual consciousness, beyond body experience is called *"nirguna Brahman,"* meaning nonduality without qualities. With this approach, we either attempt to focus beyond the plurality of what we experience (duality, our evolving-self), so all is simply one (Advaita Vedanta). Or, we abandon the evolving-self by relating to it as "not real" (*anatta*, Buddhism). Both forms of transcendence eliminate the entire problem that arises with the self-other evolving nature of life.[4]

As mentioned, in Eastern spirituality, the transcendent approach is based on a state that I call "pure nondual consciousness only," or in Sanskrit, *"atman." Atman* is a state of unified consciousness where we abide purely as the transcendental state "without qualities." There is no trace of ego because it is completely replaced by nondual consciousness. This can be described as a "hypo-egoic" state of de-individuation. In Hinduism and Buddhism, our evolving-self, or ego, is thought to keep us on the perpetual hamster wheel of life (*samsara*), filled with habits of mind and body that are the source of all suffering. We become entangled and straddled somewhere between ever-changing, unbearable sorrows and unbelievable joys.

In the transcendent state, subject and object become one and we become the tree we are hugging. We are completely submerged in the condition of unqualified unity (a*samprajnata*

---

[4] This also is found in the Christian belief that Christ draws all things into Himself, where the evolving-self ultimately merges with God, leading to our Christo-genesis. One view of this means we thereby lose our unique identity as a limited individual. (Note, this understanding varies, depending on the tradition.)

*samadhi*). We are not aware of being in a unified state, because we are unified. We submerge the evolving-self back to its ultimate source as "pure nondual consciousness." This means we have no self-reflection that "I am having an experience of unity."[5] There is no trinity of thinker, thinking process, and thought, and there is no experiencer, process of experiencing, and object of experience. It is all one. In this sense, pure nondual consciousness is "dormant" or not self-aware, or a felt experience at all. As Swami Srvapiyananda says, this is because "we are the sunlight."

In transcendent meditation, we can experience this unified state to be non-local or global, in that we feel at-one with all that is, and we have no specific location in space.[6] In practice, our meditation often becomes oriented around discerning hierarchies and polarities, such as higher from lower, right from wrong attention, or real from unreal.

**Eastern Mind Over Body**

Neutral witnessing (*sakshi*) or "bare perception," as a form of transcendence, deserves elaboration because it is so common today. While neutral witnessing is an important skill to have, meditation teachers who emphasize neutral witnessing often believe that all we need to do is perceive all experiences clearly and grow awareness. However, awareness alone does not necessarily grow our capacity for experiencing, and expressing emotionally and physically.

Neutral witnessing too often means we fine-tune the mental capacity for perceptual awareness by focusing the mind without opening all the capacities of our being. It is approached in the same way as the practice of becoming "present." Presence is commonly considered to be about being mentally aware, rather

---

[5] Self-reflection or reflexivity is a property of consciousness that is able to know itself to be conscious. Self-reflection can be a conceptual ordinary consciousness, or non-conceptual, as when we have a body experience of unified consciousness.

[6] "Atman is naturally unconscious...The flow of consciousness in Atman occurs in a specific condition while Atman comes into contact with the mind, sense and intellect, then Atman becomes conscious." Chauhan Kr & Kumar (Journal of Natural & Ayurvedic Medicine.)

than a subtle body-felt experience. Awareness alone can too easily play right into our cultural tendency to prioritize the mind over emotion and sensation. It is not an experience of wholeness, since wholeness contains all aspects of our self and existence.

In the practice of neutral witnessing, we perceive our emotional life through the lens of awareness and sensation without emotional elaborations that distort (often called the state of *turiya*). It is a form of mental training where we manage overwhelming experiences by narrowing our attention to simply being aware of sensations associated with our emotions. We simply witness the associations we attach to the sensations (such as our projections). As a result of this attentive indifference, our changing experiences become objects without relevant, meaningful content. This separates or distances us from the intensity of emotions and provides autonomy that sets us free.

This transcendent distancing orientation allows us to remain present with the experience without becoming overwhelmed. We learn to stay more relaxed and less reactive to certain overwhelming experiences (Seigel; Lutz, Dunne, Davidson). As we often discover from personal experience, withdrawing or holding our self apart from any relationship can put us back in charge. On an individual level, withdrawing from a relationship with the content of our senses by objectifying perceptions is a valuable way to put us back in control of our habits of mind and body, especially in times of emergency. As an initial practice, transcendence (*turiya*) can be very valuable, but when relied upon solely, it is limiting.

Transcendence alone can create a reductionist state where all our projections, emotions, and beliefs are considered to not have meaning, nor inherent value for a spiritual life. This does not establish a relationship with the emotional life that supports us to fully resolve our injuries. We need to be very discerning when objectifying our experiences. It can too easily result in a "spiritual bypass" where we discount the personal truth of what we feel, a truth that informs what we need to learn to be in relationship skillfully. We can grow detached from our emotions, and in doing so, cannot develop a deep understanding of our feelings and lose touch with the information it takes to navigate the nuances of relationship. Important psychological issues and opportunities for growth are transcended, rather than understood and refined. Associating autonomy from our injuries using these practices of separation through dispassion, can lead our body-mind system to equate freedom with objectifying and being dispassionate toward our experiences.

When we have unresolved injuries, neutral witnessing too often plays into the common parental message to not trust our sensory body experience, and instead trust the parent. Parental childrearing practices can overrule our ability to perceive, discern, understand, respect, and even love the injured part of our self. This is particularly possible when we suffer from relationship trauma, low self-esteem, and when we live in a culture that values mind over emotions while discounting the body as a source of wisdom, and our inherent divinity. In the long run, this strategy becomes integral to our basic approach to life.

When we devalue our emotions, sensory life, and physical nature, it is easier to objectify or devalue others and the planet. We can objectify or ignore our wounded inner-child, and our evolving-self becomes less important in a hierarchy that devalues our worldly experience as an integral part of awakening spiritually. The feeling that if we were sufficiently spiritual, we would not be feeling these emotions, is an easy step to make. Introducing a transcendent orientation (where the non-local awareness trumps our local existence) is particularly problematic in a Judeo-Christian society, that is guided by the notion that the afterlife is our liberation. This influences society's collective consciousness to believe that otherworldliness is better than being of this world.

Because trauma (self-objectification, depersonalization, disembodied experiences) so often disconnects us from direct perception of the reality of our lived experience, we too easily end up being guided by our mind alone. Striving to intentionally add self-compassion can compensate for the transcendent state of dispassion. However, it is too often a contrived, mentally generated intention (top-down), rather than an authentic expression that spontaneously arises from wholeness (bottom-up).[7] This spontaneous arising becomes possible on the direct-path to awakening unified consciousness as a body experience of self (*turiyatita*). Being nonjudgmental towards what we experience can happen without intending it, and allows self-acceptance to arise on its own, naturally.

This said, as described above in "What is Transcendence," there is much we can learn from transcendent consciousness. It can be a valuable supportive resource to draw upon to gain autonomy from overwhelming emotions. It also gives us access to a broad perspective that can help us process deep existential concerns. We all have our own path to liberation from suffering and it is important to respect this. Whatever path we take, I believe it is important that it help us awaken to the realization that fundamentally we are goodness and divinity, and we are also in the process of evolving. Moreover, our path needs to help us understand how the limitations inherent to our body and emotional life, can be a part of our healing and spiritual awakening. In this book, I emphasize an embodied nondual approach as a clarion call to our own divine entanglement.

The objectifying way of maintaining and reinforcing our freedom from suffering through strategies of separation is not new. As we shall see, it seems to go back to the mentality of what the philosopher Karl Jaspers called the "Axial Age," which brought a major shift in the mainstream of our cultural evolution. In *chapter two*, I link the transcendent approach to this broader trend in history.

---

[7] Cultivating the attitude of kindness, tenderness, or gentleness towards what we experience counters the tendency to become indifferent or emotionally numb towards our evolving-self's process. Yet, developing empathetic meditative presence requires a healthy emotional development at least at the level of a seven- or eight-year-old child (Bentzen, 2020). If we experienced relationship trauma before this age, which most of us have, emotional and empathetic presence may not be as available to us. Therefore, when we try to conjure up compassion, we generally imagine it, and are just in our head trying to have more compassion than we do.

Upon spending time with the yogi T.K.V. Desikachar and reading his books, I was exposed to the alternative experience that "everything is real" (*satvada*). The very nature of existence, including my self, existed in duality and nonduality. I came to call this expression of self, the "whole-self." This understanding is unfamiliar to most spiritual communities. Yet, when it comes to spiritual awakening and healing our deepest injuries, it makes all the difference. After all, how we regard our evolving-self in its relationship to unified consciousness, dramatically influences our attitude toward our own emotions, sensations, and thoughts. Attending to them as if they are real and matter, often requires a shift in the orientation of our contemplative practice.

At this point, I became intensely interested in the pursuit of my own wholeness-of-being and my desire to have a deeply contactful life. In meditation and increasingly at other unexpected times, I experienced the unified field of consciousness as the unchanging part of my self that I was born with. This was not an idea I had of my self. It was a tangible, direct, and present experience of my innate, ineffable presence-of-being.

This presence-of-being was an "isness" or a palpable "thereness," that was not based on one expression or another, like that of my body or of an emotion. It was a new category of experience. It was entirely outside my normal identity; yet it felt familiar. I felt as though I was remembering something, or coming home after being gone for a long time. This essence of my consciousness was a deeply soothing presence. It gave me an inner-sense of being oriented and at home, where I belong, on Earth. As I refined my senses, I could also feel how this same essence of my existence was in my environment at the same time.

The sense of belonging and connectedness that accompanied these experiences helped me face and heal my deepest emotional injuries. These were the injuries that resulted from how I was related to as a child and had such a destructive influence on my adult relational life. I recognized that this unified presence-of-being came before and lay beyond the projections of my evolving-self (ego) (which focused mostly on people, tasks, and objects I could grasp and manipulate). I felt this unwavering presence as an alert, relaxed, and open feeling of wholeness-of-being that allowed me to live my life in a richer and more empowered way.

Upon reflection, I realized that when the evolving-self is not included, we cannot locate what is divine in our experience of human existence in the body. Unified consciousness and even God are relegated to the supernatural or other-worldly cosmic consciousness, rather than recognizing our own human divine depths. Consequently, our evolving-self, much like the planet, gets objectified and loses its rightful place and true value.

It became evident to me that "real" is the experience that appears in the moment of direct perception of our experience of it. All things are known to be just as they present themselves. The illusion (*maya*) is the ignorance that makes us believe that either duality (Western psychology) or transcendent nonduality (*turiya*) is all there is. The deeper truth is that both dimensions of self co-exist in mutual relationship (*turiyatita, One Taste*). The final step of including our evolving-self's process leads to a co-emergence of the two dimensions of self, the whole-self. In embodied nondual meditation, we experience this as co-existence and communion between both dimensions, rather than completely collapsing our evolving-self's ego into a state of unity so unity is all that exists.

The transcendent approach to nondual consciousness that claims that duality is an illusion (*mayavada*), is often confusing to the beginning student. This is because it is only true from a transcendent perspective (*turiya*). What is also true is that "everything is real" (*satvada*), even experiences of impermanence and delusion. Both realities are true. Based on the premise that everything is real, there is no need to disappear the evolving-self back into its source (as spiritual teachers so often advise us to do). When it comes to healing injuries, this is crucial.

In meditation, I discovered that the embodiment (*devata*) of my unchanging-self allows the duality-based, changing nature of my evolving-self, to exist in its most authentic form. This authenticity is experienced as the free-flowing energy that underlies mental, emotional, and physical life. When unified consciousness does not transcend the relationship dynamics inherent to my evolving-self, my experience of nondual consciousness becomes self-reflective, and I am aware that I exist as unity and the sense of wholeness that results.

In a sense, nonduality finds completion in the relationship it has with our evolving-self's duality-based, eternally changing, and creative nature. This completion occurs when transcendent nonduality (beyond body experience) becomes awakened as "self-aware nonduality," because it is a body experience. It is "awakened" as self-aware because we directly know that we are aware, in a way that is not mediated by our concepts and emotions that structure our experience as a self-other, subject-object duality.[8] This is when we are "the moon," a reflection of unity experience in the body and not the sun itself. In self-reflective unified consciousness, the mind remains identified with the object of meditation, our unchanging-self.

This self-aware nonduality can have a relationship with our evolving-self (creation), so both exist concurrently. Our evolving-self's consciousness is based on concepts and symbols that have a dualistic nature (subject-object). We are aware of our evolving-self via the changing nature of our thoughts and emotions (making it an indirect awareness). When we recognize that we exist as self-aware nonduality, it allows for a form of nondual consciousness that is a "relational holism" (Delio). Being unified and relational is counterintuitive, yet when it comes to nonduality as a body experience, paradox reigns.

Our evolving-self (with its unresolved injuries) benefits from being aware that we also exist as unity and wholeness. Wholeness has an integrating and unifying influence upon us. Since they exist as body experiences, they seem to transform unresolved injuries in a way that directly communicates to our mind-body physiology. In my years guiding clients and in my own contemplative practice, this understanding has resulted in a most

---

[8]. The term "self-aware" is here used to refer to knowing our self to be conscious, rather than their common use in psychology and neuroscience to mean "thinking about our thinking."

profound healing and spiritual awakening. When nondual consciousness became "self-aware" due to its relationship with my evolving-self, it introduced a radical shift that can only be described as divine.

My understanding of quantum physics seemed to back up this body experience of unified consciousness. It exposed me to the notion that there is an "event horizon" between two dimensions of consciousness, the dual and nondual (local and nonlocal). This aligned with my experience in the embodied nondual state, where all things are known as they are experienced. Both dimensions of self appear; one has a shifting diversity and obstruction (duality), and the other has unity, stillness, and unobstructed consciousness (nonduality).

The broader perspective of unity as an experience of stillness and unobstructed consciousness, is gained not by simply going beyond the evolving-self. It is gained by attending closely to each of its expressions (projection, trauma) without losing our attunement to the deeper, unchanging, unified essence of our existence. I found that in this attentive contact between both dimensions of existence, I had access to states of wholeness that offered me the profound connectedness and breathing room, so vital for overcoming my deepest injuries. I came to feel how the profound communion between the residual trauma in my system and the nondual-essence of my being, is a solution to what Western psychology lacks, and what Eastern spirituality discounts. I now call this communion "whole-being-embrace."

My discovery that we have a presence-of-being common to us all, that never changes, fundamentally altered my approach to healing my unresolved relationship trauma. It also gave me a new approach to a spiritual life. One could say my discovery was a "spiritual" experience that is synonymous with "transpersonal" awakening. But psychology differentiates the terms transpersonal from spiritual to avoid confusing it with religion. To clarify, in this book, the terms "spiritual," "spirituality," and "divine" refer to our fundamental nature. It lies beneath our passing thoughts, emotions, and sensations that distort direct perception of our experience. It involves a clear attunement to a body experience of the most subtle sense of self as an

15

unchanging, unified presence-of-being. This experience of unified consciousness uncovers wholeness and unites us with the world around us, allowing our most authentic self-expression to arise.

This "presence-of-being" is the basis of our experience of what we commonly call "unified," "divine," and "deity." It also has been referred to as "ishta-devata" (i.e., "inner deity of choice" in the classical yoga of Ashtanga), "saguna Brahman" (Vedanta), Buddha nature (Mahayana Buddhism), Christ consciousness, (Christianity), and "*saguna Brahman*" (nonduality with qualities, Vedanta). Western mystical thinkers such as Jung, Teilhard, and Tillich have described this universal divine eminence as the "ground-of-being." "Ground" can mean the Earth that we stand upon, but it also can mean the nature of our own inborn essence, our own divine nature. In Christian mystic understanding, in contrast to the "nunc fluens" (the flowing present), the ground of being is the "nunc stans" (unchanging present).

This "presence-of-being" can also be considered to be an expression of Tibetan Buddhism's "One Taste," or Vedanta's "*turiyatita*," in that we are timeless unity as well as all of existence. Yet, as I explain more later, our body experience of "presence-of-being" is self-reflective "consciousness as such." That is, we are aware that we are aware and yet we paradoxically exist as unity at the same time. In contrast to transcendent nondual consciousness (*turiya*), which provides *freedom from* what we experience through separation (simply aware as witness), this is when we are *oneness with* all experience (while paradoxically remaining self-reflective). Our existence is not so much a state of consciousness as it is an ever-present condition.

Our mystical union with the unified nature of the divine, becomes available most profoundly when we recognize this nondual ground of our being is an expression of our unchanging-self. This divine eminence underlies our body experience of our own divinity. This is why, here, I call it our "unchanging-self" because this is how it feels. It is an experience of existence that is paradoxically both personal and universal, subjective and objective. We feel our body is the location where the eternal divine and our ever-changing humanity coincide.

This book is a result of my years of intrigue with this universal eminence, and recovering this deepest essence (of all beings) as an experience of my own divinity or deity in the flesh. I have found that when we abide in the nondual ground-of-being, as an expression of our self within the body, we live from a center that is simultaneously unified with our environment.[9] The mystery in this paradox prevails and yet becomes clear as day, in meditation and with practice, in our whole life.

Knowing our self from the inside, while feeling the connection to the greater unity of consciousness, transforms us from the bottom-up, in that the body experience informs the mind.[10] It also transforms us from the inside out, in that it is self-referent rather than an externally located source of information. It is conscious presence that is an experience of wholeness-of-being, that we all have. We can experience it most clearly in the subtle centers of consciousness within the body, collectively called "chakras."

In the following chapters, we will explore how each chakra, when fully balanced, is the infinite ground of our unified nature. The chakras are points, much like the acupuncture points in

---

[9] Gurumai explains that "Even though we feel it is an out-of-body experience, it is within this body. When you have this experience, you become aware of how this body is not a barrier, not an obstacle." (Gurumayi Chidvilasananda, quoted in Peter Hayes. The Supreme Adventure: The Yoga of Perfection).

[10] A "bottom-up" method is the most effective and profound way we can actually transform trauma (Kolk, Levine, Ogden). Cognitive-behavioral and exposure-based interventions are the most common way to treat post-traumatic stress disorder (PSTD). However, cognitive-behavioral and exposure-based interventions often do not help clients reduce their PTSD symptoms (e.g. Corrigan & Hull, 2015). Mental understanding that trickles down to our body and the nervous system becomes limited when we are injured, especially when our primary mode of learning is kinesthetic in nature. Plus, cognitive, language-based interventions need a lot of mental processing. But when we suffer from traumatic experiences, cognitive functioning is impaired due to the increased negative emotions and thoughts (Van der Kolk, 2016). Moreover, exposure-based interventions lead to high drop-out rates because of its confrontational and aversive nature (Lewis, Roberts, Gibson, & Bisson, 2020; Wald & Taylor, 2008). When what we feel is not our primary guide, it is much harder to stay within our window of tolerance and not get overwhelmed.

Chinese medicine, that exist along subtle channels that form a network in the body. These points are locations of subtle energy and consciousness. Seven primary energy and consciousness points are situated along a central-channel (*sushumna*) of the body's torso, each expressing important aspects of our being.

This understanding of the nondual ground of our universal eminence, as an expression of our self found in the body, is not a common perspective in the West nor the East. The mechanistic mentality of the West has shaped religion, science, and psychology, elevating the rational, objective, and mechanical functions of life. This is a limited guide for overcoming our deepest emotional injuries (and the habits of mind and body that result.)

The Greek metaphysics that underlies Western religions continues to discount the existence of our body experience of self as unified divine consciousness. The transcendent orientation of most spiritual traditions today, too often stifles our ability to experience wholeness and unity consciousness as our body's expression of our self. These spiritual traditions, that are now adopted by the most progressive aspects of Western psychology, commonly strive to transcend our body experience of nondual consciousness. In this book, I offer a distinctly different approach that I believe offers a healthy, more inclusive alternative.


THE TWO IN ONE & ONE IN TWO PARADOX OF QUANTUM

The notion that when we refine our senses, we can uncover the innate nondual dimension of existence, within the duality dimension of our evolving-self, is counterintuitive. In meditation and then in our everyday life, we experience that the unified presence of our own being, reflects everything it permeates. The stillness of our embodied experience of unity and wholeness feels as if it contains, and reveals, the movement of our evolving-self's thoughts, emotions, and sensations within it. As we deepen into our practice of embodying the opposing and paradoxically interdependent qualities of our whole-self (dual and nondual), it feels like an "Earthing" of spirit and a spiritualizing of the Earth.

This parallels the Chinese Taoist philosophy of yin and yang, where yang contains the seed of yin, and yin contains the seed of yang. Opposites include one another. From this view, the duality nature of our body contains the essence of nonduality, and nonduality contains the seed of duality in a synchronistic, intimate, "sacred marriage" of opposites. In fact, without duality, there can be no actual experience of nonduality.

It is interesting how the emergence of quantum physics can help us understand the infinite regress of duality and nonduality in their entanglement. Einstein developed the theory of general relativity in 1905, which proposed a new concept of space and time. His insights led to an appreciation for the ever-changing, elastic nature of the universe. The unfolding nature of space-time motivated Einstein to consider that gravity was not a substance, but instead was a curvature of space-time due to the influence of matter. He realized that the heaviness of matter not only stretches or shrinks distances, but also seems to slow down or dilate the flow of time. In other words, gravity acts to structure space.

Einstein's realization changed our understanding of matter and energy. Instead of perceiving them as separate properties, mass was understood to be a property of energy, and energy was a property of mass. Because mass and energy were now understood as two forms of the same thing, matter could be transformed into energy and energy into matter. No wonder self-regulation of the energy in our body, mind, and emotions is a central focus of somatic psychology and yoga. Yet, since yoga refines our senses more than somatic psychology (via body, breath, sound, and visual experiences), it gives us the potential to have access to a very refined state of balance. Most significantly, we gain access to a sense of the unified consciousness buried within the energy that composes our body.

Understanding the energetic nature of the material plane has significance when it comes to meditation practice. We come to feel how energy forms the basis of all experience. We can feel how our evolving-self's ego identity, our mind, and our body are all composed of energy. We recognize that everything we think or feel has an energetic nature to it. So, when we want to heal our deepest psychological injuries, we must deal with the fundamental nature of energy.

What we find as we refine our senses, is that energy has three primary phases: charge (*rajas*), discharge (*tamas*), and balance (*sattva*). (In yoga, they are collectively called "*gunas.*") These expressions of energy are felt to directly correlate with the three primary states of our nervous system: sympathetic (charge), parasympathetic (discharge), and homeostasis (balance). Our experience of energy also has a multi-dimensional nature to it (dual and nondual). It turns out that science has an explanation for this too.

Einstein's theory of special relativity ($E=mc^2$) led to Broglie's "double slit" experiment, which opened up a whole new meaning of matter. In 1924, Louis Broglie took Einstein's theory a step further by proposing that light waves could behave as particles and particles could behave like waves. This shifts our view that matter is simply a composite of atoms (particles). We recognize that atoms are composed of electrons and that electrons are both waves and particles at the same time. Importantly, much like nondual consciousness, the wavelike aspects of atoms do not have a defined shape as the particle does.

Finding the wavelike aspects of atoms within the nature of energy, which composes the duality consciousness of our body, mind, and emotions, broadens our understanding of reality. Waves and particles actually co-exist within energy. While the elementary particles of matter are governed by the same forces as the material things that they create, they also exist in a realm of possibilities (the Uncertainty Principle). The electrons come into an existential relationship that is entangled, in that their inner properties (mass, charge, and spin) become indistinguishable. They seem to have an enmeshed relationship between them. Each of the properties within an electron is influenced by the relationship because they cease to be separate things and become a unified part of a whole. This is an internal relationship that is a relational holism, relational yet unified.

This understanding reflects what happens in embodied nondual meditation when we focus inward and recognize that we have access to both dimensions of existence. We can experience being a part of the whole that is not an isolated fragment (nonduality/wave), and also being a part of a collection of experiences that exist independently from one another in time and space (duality/particle). We can perceive how unified consciousness acts from within, at the core of each of our evolving-self's expressions, and illuminates us from within. Every aspect of our evolving-self bears within it unified consciousness, that is both within and beyond our evolving-self at the same time. This is the awe-inspiring experience of the dual and nondual dimensions of our self together. This "the two that are one and the one that is two" experience, allows us to reach beyond the Newtonian mechanistic view of life.

In meditation, quantum reality becomes an embodied nondual experience. It seems that we experience an expression of the multi-dimensional nature of the electron (wave-particle duality). Depending on where we place our attention (evolving-self or unchanging-self), our electrons show up as duality-based perception-response experiences, or as nondual wholeness (uncertainty principle), or both at the same time. [11]

When we are limited to feeling we exist only as our evolving self, the underlying original unified state of our electrons (quantum waves) appear as separate particles. Our electrons express as a multitude of individual particles that form specific thoughts, emotions, and sensations. When we broaden our awareness to feel that we exist as our unchanging-self, our electrons maintain their original state of unity (waves). Our body experience of unified consciousness as wholeness, effectively allows for an internal wave-state of unity to occur.

This unified field is what allows us to feel as if we are in a "non-local relationship" with our environment, without leaving our

---

[11] Atoms are composed of protons, neutrons, and electrons. When an electron wave overlaps other waves, existence becomes more unified. When we attune to our body experience of nondual consciousness, it seems we cause more electron waves to overlap as our experience of unity begins to emerge. Our perception shifts from experiencing individual expressions (particle), to experiencing the underlying unified essence of existence (wave). We are able to feel the essence of this aspect of our self as potentialities, out of which individual expressions arise.

body. From any one location within our body, we have access to an experience of wholeness and are open to the unified field of consciousness that pervades us and our environment. Plus, even though we are separated by large distances, we can respond as if we are connected as one (entanglement, non-local relationship). We can experience that the movement of our evolving-self becomes unified (discontinuous in cause and effect). In a unified state, the energy and consciousness underlying our thoughts, emotions, and sensations are entangled with all that is. We have access to all consciousness, without going through an exchange from one place to another (everything, everywhere, all at once).

In embodied nondual meditation, these two features of quantum theory (local-non-local, particle-wave duality) become an experience, making it possible to feel connected with the entire universe as an unbroken whole. Each element of that whole has qualities or properties that pervade the overall environment as a unity. David Bohn called the unbroken wholeness the "implicate order." His way of explaining divine entanglement is that enfolded within the movement of electromagnetic fields, sound waves, and other aspects of the changing nature of existence (body, emotion, and mind) is a unified field of consciousness.

As we refine our senses in embodied nondual meditation, we find that within each experience, deeper than anything that changes, is stuck or solid, there exists a conscious space that is an unwavering presence-of-being. This can be described to be a quality-rich, full-emptiness. When our body experience of this paradox becomes a stable presence, the implicate order and the undivided wholeness of the universe become available to us on an ongoing basis.

The separate parts of our evolving-self and of existence, can be overwhelming to experience if we do not bring in the broader perspective that unified consciousness, as an experience of wholeness, provides. Without unified consciousness, the body is often experienced as a location of pain, pleasure, stuckness, and/or fluid movement. Unresolved emotional injuries are felt as patterns of constriction that are frozen, numb, and collapsed. These sensations can make it uncomfortable to live in the body.

They most certainly make it challenging to feel that the body is a location of divinity.

Without an embodied sense of wholeness, we are too easily pulled into the vortex of our human suffering. We can so easily be held hostage by our past experience of injury, and the resulting thoughts that stir up emotions that flood us with intense sensations (or vice versa). We become caught in the arrest, orient, fight, flight, freeze, and collapse survival modes of operating. We can end up "fragmenting" and defensively acting out our deepest fears in relationship in ways we eventually regret.

It is vital for us to understand the cause, and the way out of our injury or trauma symptoms, that trigger us to fragment. This means we need to become familiar with the nature of the injury, and what stage in our life the injury happened. We also need to become familiar with our particular symptoms of fragmentation. With this information, the way out of fragmentation, and the kind of self-support we need becomes apparent. Yet, without an embodied sense of wholeness this discovery process can be extremely challenging.

Wholeness can express itself and be experienced in many different ways. Each particular expression of wholeness, such as each chakra or five layers of self, is a fractal part of a larger wholeness. As we come into whole-being-embrace with the chakra that addresses our particular relationship injury, we feel how the wholeness that accompanies unity, actually exists within the duality of our suffering. We also feel that the fundamental experience that we are made of a single presence of wholeness, transforms all our relationships, including the one we have with our own injuries.

THE QUANTUM BODY

Similar to nondual spiritual traditions, quantum physics claims that all objects, including our evolving-self, seem to begin with the immaterial nature of consciousness. What we usually think of as empty space and the solidness of the material dimension of existence, is now understood to have a background consciousness. Consciousness is fundamental to matter and the energy that matter is composed of (including our body and mind). In a sense, consciousness reflects everything, and everything reflects consciousness.

When nondual consciousness is a body experience, it becomes a self-aware luminous presence (aware that we are aware). In this way, embodied nondual consciousness is unlike the transcendent state that lies beyond the material plane of existence and body experience. The transcendent "nondual consciousness only" state of *atman,* becomes aware of itself in the presence of our material form (duality). In its reflection, we incarnate as self-aware, nondual divine beings. Our body is the mirror of unified consciousness.

This understanding highlights how our body, and all its experiences, serve as a medium that allows our experience of spirituality and the divine to exist. The quality-rich full-emptiness of our body experience of unity, seems to pervade and illuminate everything we experience. We can feel that we become more open to life. The feeling of openness within our own physical form, allows us to experience intimate contact and live as a unity of self and other. We feel the continuity of the space within and outside the body as the undivided wholeness of all that is.

The preeminent role the material plane plays in revealing unified consciousness, is a theme throughout this book. This understanding shifts the common view that our body is a part of nature that corrupts, or is inferior to the mind and spirit. Instead, the body is revealed to be the vessel, the Holy Chalice or Grail, to our divinity. It is through this foundational understanding of the body that we acquire the building blocks for shifting our paradigm from one based on strategies of separation, to one based on inclusion.


DUAL & NONDUAL EMBODIMENT

The body experience that we exist as the evolving-self and/or the unchanging-self is called embodiment. When we are embodied as our evolving-self, we experience the changing nature of our thoughts, emotions, and sensations. The changing nature of these experiences can include the injuries and fixations of our unhealthy ego, and the supportive, comfortable, relaxed, and settled nature of our healthy ego.

Embodiment on a nondual level is an experience of the unified essential ground-of-being. Nondual embodiment is an experience of wholeness, inherent to the nondual-qualities of our self, as found in the five layers of self and the chakras. Each nondual-quality of wholeness is a fractal of a larger wholeness. This means that each of the chakras and five layers of self can be experienced in a variety of ways, such as emptiness, transparency, balance, stillness, pervasiveness, and as universal. Each one is experienced as nondual embodiment. Wholeness can be experienced as sensory (subtle), motor (stillness), spatial (unified), temporal (timelessness).

Uncovering and awakening to the subtlety, depth, and breadth of our existence in these ways is profound. They convey a sense of belonging, choice, confidence, love, existential truth, and knowing that is fundamentally benevolent. Each of these experiences of embodiment give us access to our own innocence and goodness.

These experiences of nondual embodiment provide a felt sense of having an actual location (thus a container or sorts) for our unified ground-of-being. In this body location we have a sense of "I AM," with a timeless truth or knowing. When we feel embodied as this unchanging-self, fundamental existential questions such as, "Who am I and how do I interact with other people?" disappear. We recognize there is nowhere to go, and begin to realize that we are already home in our nondual nature.

The embodiment of our healthy evolving-self (authenticity) and our unchanging-self (wholeness) provides the support we need to overcome obstacles to our spiritual enlightenment and well-being. When we can maintain our experience of this support as we face our unhealthy ego and deepest injuries, we feel safe. We can feel our suffering and learn how to release it from our system. However, if we transcend, dissociate, repress, or interrupt our experience, it often lasts much longer on an unconscious level.

## FIVE LAYERS OF SELF (PANCHA KOSHA) AS BLISS

As we refine our senses, we gain access to experiences that the Western scientist, philosopher, or psychologist does not generally acknowledge. With this refinement, we experience deeper understanding and sense of being, and recognize subtle nondual aspects of existence.

Normally, when we tune-in to our body experience, we feel the physical, mental, and emotional layers of self. When we refine our senses, we recognize two crucial additional layers of self: wisdom and bliss. This recognition is congruent with one of the earliest human metaphysical conceptualizations found in Hinduism (Taittiriya Upanishad). This metaphysics is an expression of the Great Chain of Being, a philosophy of the levels of being (ontology) and levels of knowing (epistemology) that has existed in different forms throughout history. This progression usually is portrayed as: matter, body, mind, soul, spirit. In Hinduism, all experience is perceived through five layers of awareness: physical, emotional, mental, wisdom, and bliss (i.e.,*anna, prana, mana, vijnana, ananda*).[12]

Transcendent pure nondual consciousness, *"atman"* (*asamprajnata samadhi* or *nirguna Brahman*), lies at the center of these five layers and is beyond the most subtle expressions of existence (Image #1). In this model, the bliss layer of self is our quality rich body experience of nondual consciousness, our unchanging-self ("consciousness-as-such"). [13]

---

[12] The "emotional" layer here is associated with energy layer (*prana kosha*). Traditionally, emotions are associated with the mental layer (*mano kosha*). The energy layer is the elan vital aspect of existence.

[13] In the following diagram, the layers of self are illustrated. Note that the Sanskrit names for each aspect of self, include the word "*maya*," which means illusion. This is based on the Vedantic notion that all of manifestation is an illusion or a fragmentation of the pure transcendent unity of *atman* (*mayavada*). When we ascribe to the notion that all of existence is real, even its distortions and projections (*satvada*), the names for the aspects of self do not have the term *maya* in them.

## Image #1: The Five Layers of Self & Transcendent Consciousness

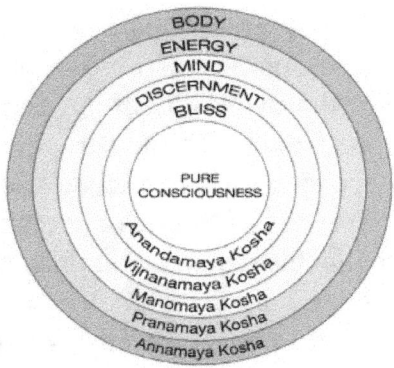

The traditional Western, dualistic, three-part-self approach (physical, emotional, mental) to overcoming our injuries is limited. The two additional aspects of self (wisdom and bliss) are important resources for overcoming our injuries and limiting habits. With the five-layers-of-self model/ontology, we can understand our self more holistically and heal more effectively.

Much like the chakras, the five aspects of our self can be understood as a sequential progression ranging from the most dense, to the least dense expression of our existence. In this case, our physical form is the most dense, and the bliss layer is the least dense (from particle to wave). This progression has also been depicted to represent our process of evolution, where we attend to our physical needs, emotional needs, then mental needs, and so on, until we evolve to finally reach the unified state of bliss. This sequential process is the "indirect-path" to awakening unified consciousness. With this approach, we need to create balance on the denser levels of our being, before we can progress to the less dense levels of our being.

Yet, embodied nondual meditation is informed by a fractal or "holographic perspective." It primarily adheres to the "direct-path" to unified consciousness, with the recognition that we are already whole. As Great Chain theorists claim, unity is woven intrinsically into each manifestation. Consequently, Plato explained that the natural world is a "visible, sensible God." Discovering this expression of unity as an experience involves refining our senses so we can directly attune to the nondual-qualities of self. We directly experience the essential ground of each of the chakras and five aspects of self in their waveform, as nondual potential or essence-of-being.

At this depth and subtlety of perception, it feels as if we experience each of the five layers of our self as an unchanging unity, that is also part of a larger holographic, fractal unity. This level of subtlety becomes available to us when we uncover and awaken the bliss layer of self through direct attunement.

Embodied nondual bliss is an experience of our unchanging-self.[14] When we refine our senses enough to directly access the bliss layer of our self (*ananda kosha*), we recognize that this entanglement exists with each of the five aspects of self. As we embody the "bliss" layer of self, all other aspects of self can be perceived as a nondual expression of unity and wholeness. When we awaken to this nondual experience of our existence, the most common description of what we feel is the delightful well-being of bliss. [15]

---

[14] This is also different from the bliss we feel from transcendent nondual awareness, which is the result of transcendence and the experience of the infinite beyond the body and self of any kind. This state of pure nondual consciousness, (here called "*atman*" or "*nirguna Brahman*," nonduality *without* qualities) is blissful, much like the bliss we feel when we access the bliss layer of self, but not the same.

The bliss we experience in transcended states is a result of complete absorption to the point where the evolving-self becomes an insignificant object of occurrence. Whereas the bliss of our body experience of nondual consciousness as an expression of self, saguna Brahman, the evolving-self is not insignificant. Everything is still there, and yet we have let go of our grip upon it. In other words, our emotional and mental life is still significant, and yet we do not lose our sense of wholeness and unity. When in this state, all our desires and aversions are still there but we relate to them within the context of our sense of feeling that we exist as unity and wholeness. *Saguna Brahman* is a nondual presence-of-being that is luminous and blissful but not transcendent.

[15] This perspective is congruent with the early understanding of the five kosha layers of self as discussed in the most ancient text, Tattiriya Upanishad. Even though the bliss layer is where we feel unified consciousness as a body experience most clearly, this understanding was later replaced by the transcendent Vedantic view. It claimed the bliss layer of self is always inherently dense and duality-based and, therefore, must be transcended to achieve "pure nondual consciousness," *atman*.

It is in the bliss layer that we can recognize that depending on what we attune to, we can access consciousness based on duality and/or nonduality. The energy that composes the material dimension of existence has the potential to be infinite, just as nondual consciousness is infinite. This can be felt in embodied nondual meditation when, for example, we access the experience that the densest aspect of our existence, our physical form, is also an expression of the unified essential ground-of-being. We recognize we have a divinely entangled body, the finite, with the experience of the infinite. This is an experience that right here in our flesh is the true location of our divine-genesis, our Buddha-genesis, and our Christo-genesis.

The experience of our five layers of self in meditation is not only healing, it can also be a diagnostic tool, and a source of spiritual awakening. When a layer is unbalanced, it shows up as an aspect of our evolving-self with specific developmental injuries to resolve and heal. Discerning which aspect of our evolving-self is unbalanced is important information for tailoring our contemplative healing practice. When a layer is balanced, it shows up as an aspect of our unchanging-self's existence. Discerning which layer of our unchanging-self can address our suffering, refines our practice. When each of the five aspects of self can be experienced as both dual and nondual, it greatly expands our choices for how we might tailor our contemplative practice to heal the aspects of our self that are most injured and fragmented.

When we attune to the nondual dimension of our self as a body experience in meditation, we can feel how, much like the chakras, each layer of self is also a means of mutual and unified contact with other human beings. This body-felt experience can render contact with the people we are most intimate with quite exquisite, and render contact with challenging people, painless. We can feel the connectedness of unity with other people, and the breathing-room of unlimited space. This communicates directly to our relationship injuries. We feel the stillness and timelessness of this essential ground that transforms fear and touches the core of our hearts. Our evolving-self experiences a profound sense of our unbreakable, uninjured, inherently benevolent (non-abandoning, non-invasive) nature. This naturally heals our deepest wounds.

## UNCOVERING & AWAKENING THE BLISS LAYER

All the practices explored in embodied nondual meditation, help us uncover and awaken the nondual bliss aspect of our self. The bliss layer is where we encounter the frontiers of psychology and spirituality today: As we attune to this level of depth and subtlety, we expose that even the densest expressions of existence can be perceived as the bliss aspect of existence.

This essence of existence, which cannot be detected by the ordinary range of our senses, is a subtle general felt-sense or feeling-tone. By refining our attunement to this inborn essential ground-of-being, our senses become more adept at perceiving this unified dimension of existence. They reveal the radiance, fluidity, and spacious stillness that exists within each aspect of existence. As our senses become more refined, under or deeper than the variations of density and solidity in our body, we begin to feel conscious space that is a unified presence of our existence.

We shift from feeling as though we are a solid physical object with sensations and constrictions, to feeling that we exist as a subtle unchanging feeling-tone of physicality. Or better said, we seem to exist as the innate essence of our physical nature. This unified ground of physicality is empty of our psychological process. Therefore, paradoxically, it is a "content-free," conscious stillness, out of which all our evolving-self's particular, individual, physical experiences and expressions arise.

We can experience each layer of our self (physical, emotional, mental, and wisdom) as an embodied nondual ground-of-being. When this is an enduring experience, our individual expressions of each layer, emerge in their most authentic form. This is the key to our ultimate freedom from suffering.

## THE NEED FOR PARADOX

I believe integrating the entangled existential nonduality-duality dichotomy of our existence, is crucial for healing and spirituality to emerge. This requires a psychology and spirituality that recognizes the need for paradox. This is a form of spirituality that cultivates the ability to be emotionally available, engage with, and be fully open to the rawness and intensity of each moment (duality). It is a psychology and spirituality that allows us access to the larger awareness of being unbound by conditioned existence (nonduality). This means living consciously in the juncture of both dimensions of self, dual and nondual. It is at this "event horizon," the liminal edge of both dimensions (as a particle-wave duality), that healing and awakening to our embodied divinity happens most clearly.

As we embody the experience of unified wholeness and engage with the present moment, we can actually feel how duality is an expression of the nonduality, out of which it eternally arises and into which it ultimately returns. But rather than setting up a division between nonduality and duality (which creates a duality in itself), or collapsing duality into nonduality, we recognize how opposite truths can be viable at the same time. There is no hierarchy that pits one over the other. There is only a co-arising and interdependence between the two dimensions, much like the wave in the ocean. In the form of a wave, we are a dynamic, unique individual. In the form of the ocean, we are all a part of one reality since both are water. Both what changes and what does not change, are two dimensions of one whole-self.

A body experience of our nondual unchanging-self, helps the Hero in us to tame the "dragon" (our ego's sabotaging habits of mind and body), rather than slay it using strategies based on separating from it. In this scenario, we can experience the transparency and bliss of nonduality while experiencing the meaning we associate with all our painful thoughts, emotions, and sensations. This results in a true nonduality, where unity (*purusa, Shiva*) and evolving experience (*prakriti, Shakti*) become one awakened wholeness pervading our body and mind and everything around us at the same time.

What we begin to witness is how the very nature of the present moment reveals our own nondual-essence. We discover that our body's most subtle sensory life is the source of awareness that allows us to look with fresh eyes and listen with open ears. We penetrate beyond the mundane ego state of our evolving-self and access the "pure ego" (*ahanta*) familiar to Kashmiri Shaivism. "Pure ego" is a naturally radiant and ceaselessly, spontaneously responsive to the experience of our unchanging-self in communion with our evolving-self. This communion becomes our inner "Guru."

All the "nondual-qualities," such as the five aspects of self and the chakra qualities, have the inherently benevolent nature of wholeness. We often experience wholeness most clearly as an experience of unconditional love. Yet, this changes depending on the nature of our injury. Since our deepest injuries involve the loss of love, we may have too many negative associations with the experience of love and need to access unity through other nondual-qualities of self. It is important for us to discover and awaken the expression of wholeness that most effectively integrates our state of fragmentation. The nondual-qualities of self that provide us with the clearest experience of wholeness and unity, have the most powerful healing influence on our body and unifying effect on our psyche.

# CHAPTER TWO: QUANTUM EVOLUTION

## HISTORY IN THE MAKING

It is often our suffering in life that makes us ask the questions, "What is life all about", "What gives life significance, meaning, and purpose?", "What caused me to respond the way I did", "How do I want to I live my life?", "Where am I headed and why?". Understanding where we have been and what has motivated us can help us gain insight into these profound questions.

The psychiatrist and philosopher Karl Jaspers (1966) referred to a model of history that describes how we have an ongoing progression of consciousness toward increasing levels of complexity. He explains that this progression towards complexity results in a new sense of our self in relation to other people, the environment, and to the cosmos. In this book, I maintain that our evolution ultimately leads to the most simple, subtle, and unified dimension of our existence, our unchanging-self. This dimension of self is not based on evolution since it is an experience of unity.

The experience of our self as unity introduces a deeper and broader sense of our self in relation to other people, the environment, and to the cosmos. This depth and breadth provides our complex evolving-self with more choices, which is healing and escalates the rate of our evolution. Embodied nondual meditation provides a means of directly uncovering this state of unity and bringing it into intimate contact with the diversity of our injuries. This is a path towards whole-being-embrace. History can inform us of the head winds we face on this transformational journey.

Jaspers explains that the spiritual foundations of modern humanity were established during the Axial Age, which occurred between 800 BCE and 200 BCE (Wilber's Mythic stage). This was when the spiritual and moral foundations of humanity were laid across ancient China, India, the Middle East, and Northern Mediterranean Europe. Before this time, we were governed initially by the mystical mind of ancient civilizations, followed by organized religion. Up until 3000 years ago, tribal communities had a type of consciousness that psychologist Julian Jaynes (1976) called the "bicameral mind" (Wilber's Archaic stage). This was a time when our mind's cognitive functions were divided between the part of the brain oriented towards our ability to "speak", or the part which listens and obeys. In this way, the brain supported the cosmic orientation of religion at the time. The two chambered mind had one half generating commands that the other part perceived to be the voice of Gods. Only until 3000 years ago did this mystical perspective change due to the evolution of a more complex physiology (Wilbers's "Magical" stage).

This brings us to the late pre-history of ancient tribally oriented Greeks (1200 BC – c. 600 AD), which continues to influence Western society. One important influence of ancient Greece was the belief that our emotions and desires originate from the actions of Gods who are external to us, rather than our own mind. In effect, the understanding of self in relationship was externally oriented in that it was guided by the collective consciousness of tribal society. Our individual personal identity in relation to others (society) was determined by beliefs about the cosmic nature of the Gods. (You can imagine how this is a set up for injury.)

Our externally oriented style of being in relationship was perpetuated in other ways as well. Ancient societies were guided by the belief that we can only maintain our connection to spiritual sources of meaning through an imaginal conduit. This conduit served as a bridge between the duality consciousness of our everyday mind, and the consciousness of the omnipresent and omniscient Gods. Mircea Eliade (1950) called this imaginal conduit the "axis mundi." The symbolic representation of this conduit is commonly depicted as a vertical axis with a path of ascent and descent between humans and the Gods. This understanding became implicitly present in religious rituals. The mythical thinking involved was informed by direct experience, but it was also influenced by projection, fantasy, and wish fulfillment.

34

By contrast, yoga (especially contemplative yoga, *antaranga*) offers a more internally oriented path. It is the art and science of direct experience as a means of overcoming our tendency towards the projections of our imagination. Yoga, like Tai Chi and the Sefirot in Kabbalism, uses the body as a form of axis mundi. The yoga practice of awakening the chakras via the central-channel (*sushumna*) in the subtle-core of the body is explored in *chapter six*. The chakra system also has a vertical axis with a path of "ascent" and "descent" (*ida, pingala*) and a place where the two become one (*sushumna,* and sixth chakra).

Interestingly, the way we reach this center is often as important as arriving there. We can do this in a transcendent way, where the duality of everything we experience (thoughts, emotions, sensations) collapses into a state of unity. Or, we can do this with embodied nondual consciousness, where both dimensions of self (our evolving-self and our unchanging-self) co-exist. As explored in this book, the path we choose has a significant influence on how we relate to our sense of self and others. Yet, both paths can complement one another.

In physics, there have also been two divergent approaches. One was based on principles of unity (quantum) and the other was based on principles of separation (Newtonian). Quantum physics recognizes that electrons, inherent to the energy that underlies the material expression of existence, is composed of both waves and particles. The wave functions have a unified field comparable to the nature of nondual consciousness. Moreover, the particle and wave are understood to be two variations of one field, where paradoxically, both particle and wave can exist simultaneously (particle-wave duality). This simultaneous existence of both dimensions mirrors the inclusivity we experience in the "mutually co-existent" approach to wholeness, where both our evolving-self and unchanging-self are in reciprocal co-existence.

By contrast, Newtonian physics only recognizes the electron's particles as entirely separate. The particles function according to the laws of duality where every action of a particle causes a reaction. In this paradigm, matter was the basis of all existence and was composed of a multitude of separate objects that were organized like a giant machine. This prevents us from considering how the particle and wave are two variations of one field that paradoxically can exist simultaneously (particle-wave duality). Instead, it is based on the separation of parts.

The distinction between quantum and Newtonian physics tells a story that is similar to the ways we arrive at unified consciousness in meditation. The transcendent approach to meditation is based on becoming autonomous from our evolving-self using strategies of creating distance and separation. It can be understood to be an expression of Axial Age mentality (after 800 BCE; Wilber's "Mythic" stage) because it separates the duality consciousness of our evolving-self from nondual consciousness.

This transcendent orientation seems to have been largely motivated by a desire to return to an unblemished, pristine state prior to suffering on Earth. This is still the guiding premise of most spirituality today.[16] The emphasis is on transcending the messiness of the material plane of existence (including our emotions) by denying its importance and bypassing the depth of meaning found in our lived experience. This basis of separation between dimensions of existence found in spirituality is comparable to how the Newtonian physics mechanistic principles are based on separation between parts. When this is the only solution to our suffering, we limit our sense of self in life and in relationship. It also limits our ability to overcome emotional injuries.

By contrast, the mutually co-existent approach of embodied unified consciousness, is an example of post-Axial principles. It allows for the simultaneous existence of both dimensions (dual and nondual). This post-Axial approach found in embodied nondual meditation, based on mutuality and co-existence, is an amalgam. It has some pre-Axial mythical experience in feeling the

---

[16] George Feuerstein explains that the Aryan aspects of the Hindu Vedic view understood the ultimate aim of human existence is transcendence of the earthly realm. This can also be found in the Christian focus on always trying to return to the Garden of Eden or the Kingdom of Heaven after we die. We forget there's also the biblical saying that we seek first the kingdom of heaven within, and all else will be added unto us. This is much more sound spiritual guidance because the Kingdom of Heaven within is our own divinity.

connectedness between dimensions of existence (Wilber's Magic stage). Yet, our embodied experience of unity is also supported by post-Axial quantum physics principles, in its recognition of the mutual existence of both dimensions (called "particle-wave duality"; Wilber's 3rd-tier of consciousness).

## THE QUEST FOR WHOLENESS & THE RISE OF QUANTUM

I now realize that I have lived my whole life searching for wholeness, belonging, and a sense of connection with something greater. My youthful ventures into drugs, sex, and rock and roll were early expressions of this longing. Now, as an adult, I can find myself in search of a better version of myself. Only in the last fifteen years have I realized that what I'm looking for is right here, right now, all the time, and in every place. This recognition has allowed me to relax, let go, settle down, and be open to the nurturing nature of wholeness. I am not alone in my quest for wholeness-of-being.

The quest for wholeness and connection with something larger than our self lies at the heart of religion and spirituality. This quest is the spark of our inborn spirituality, which Carl Jung called "transcendent function." Jung felt that our transcendent function is the unifying force that allows for communication between the conscious and unconscious aspects of the psyche. It does not necessarily involve transcending the psyche and leaving it behind, but it serves to draw together and unify the various parts of our self. We can experience this in embodied nondual meditation when our evolving-self comes into contact with our unchanging-self, without transcending our body's experiences.

Access to the unchanging-self's sense of unity and wholeness is exactly what twentieth-century Western religion tried to gain when it emphasized the cosmic unified nature of God. This ideology served as a psychological "umbilical cord" to the experience of wholeness. The quest for wholeness can be seen in the sixth century BCE, when Western Axial thinkers began to speculate about a "divine spark" within the soul that animates us toward transcendence. Plato (427-347 BCE) and neo-Platonic traditions emphasized the concept of "the one."[17] With the rise of science in the Age of Enlightenment (Wilber's Rational stage), the mystical experience of divine wholeness, as proposed by religion's understanding of God, was discounted.

Yet, as I've suggested, science was also motivated by a transcendent function of sorts, in its belief that logic and reason would be our salvation. Biology contributed to the understanding that nature dynamically recreates, transcends, and evolves into more complex interconnected forms of life. More recently, quantum physics took the quest for wholeness even further in discovering "wave-particle duality," where both duality and nonduality co-exist. Reality as we know it is fundamentally composed of an endless series of "part/wholes," particles and waves, or duality and nonduality. Quantum physics added to this theory of wholeness when it identified that in the act of choosing to observe an experience, the observer of experience affects what is being observed. This implies an entangled relationship between the duality consciousness that chooses to observe, and what we observe.

The discovery that energy contains both particle (duality) and wave (nonduality) implies that the intrinsic property of matter must include unified consciousness. This scientific insight helps reverse mechanistic Axial Age thinking of existence in mechanistic terms. It also sets the stage for us to move past the view that in order to experience unified consciousness, it must be transcendent, pure consciousness only, beyond sensory perception (*atman*).

Unified consciousness can be a body experience, and depending on how we observe our body experience, we can access duality or nonduality, or both simultaneously. Quantum theory supports the experience that within the matter of our body and environment, we can uncover the essential unified nature of existence. This book is an exploration of how we can

---

[17] Plato talked about an immortal soul as a divine spark and later Plotinus concurred in proposing "the One" was beyond every limitation and existed in all things as the source from which all things emanate.

experience this in each of the chakras in order to heal and awaken spiritually.

These discoveries about wholeness and unity from science and spiritual traditions have introduced a new social network and intersubjectivity (connection between parts) that has promoted collective, global consciousness. They also take us beyond the view that we are an intersubjective network (which is a series of distinct entities in relationship). We gain access to a body experience of self as unity and divine entanglement. Embodied nondual experience is a prime example of this. This body experience of nondual consciousness runs counter to the common notion of spirituality as an intangible, celestial awareness that lies beyond worldly existence, that is only available to a few of us after years of practice.

I believe this understanding of a body experience of unified consciousness is being acknowledged by more and more people today. The heart of cutting-edge psychology and spirituality is directly experiencing the ultimate wholeness that is available in each moment, by contemplatively connecting our mind and body to a seamless unity. A body experience of unified consciousness is a form of relational holism (unity that is paradoxically relational) that introduces a new paradigm of consciousness. It is much better suited to reflect the plasticity of nature and the complexity of our biological system as we evolve. From this foundation, we can overcome our injuries, clarify our healthy boundaries in relationship, and flourish as humans. We can discover the invaluable role that meaningful connection and unconditional love have in orienting us toward a fulfilling future.

The spiritual traditions of the world that are exclusive and polarizing in orientation (by only embracing the non-material, other-worldly dimension of life) are an old paradigm. We are discovering that contemplative and spiritual practices can include our body experience and that the body itself is divine. This gives us depth of meaning and purpose. Our evolving-self bonds with our experience of unity and wholeness, and thereby gains access to its authenticity. This communion is an experience of whole-being-embrace that gives us the authenticity we need to relate to the challenges of life on Earth. It sets us free by inviting the sacred to embrace the mundane and even the "profane."

While the pre-Axial mystical sense of collective consciousness and Axial Age principles of separation and reason were necessary to survive the rigors of life a long time ago, today, we need a new form of relational holism. We no longer need an external "imaginal conduit" (axis mundi) to bridge between the dimensions of duality and nonduality. Many of us are ready to realize that our body is a literal location for both dimensions to co-exist in communion. Just as the caterpillar forms a chrysalis to transform into a butterfly, whole-being-embrace is our medium of personal transformation and metamorphosis into our own enlightenment.

Our "axis mundi," as a bridge to access an experience of wholeness, is within us instead of only outside of us as an imaginal experience. Our "whole-self" is actually composed of the evolving-self's duality and of our unchanging-self's nonduality. We simply need to refine our senses so that we can uncover and perceive this whole-body divine axis. As discussed in *chapter six*, we find this axis most clearly within the central-channel (*sushumna*) of the body where all the chakras live. Without this inner experience of our self as wholeness and unity, no aspect of life can survive because our authenticity turns into protective defensiveness with the tendency to polarize existence and create hierarchies in life.

Just as religion and science have played an important role in giving us access to our sense of wholeness, we now need to become more internally referent and reclaim our own authority. We must realize that wholeness lies within the tissues of the body and within the very nature of our environment on this planet. The purpose of this book is to provide an illuminating roadmap for this paradigm shift.

PERENNIAL PSYCHOLOGY OF THE HERO'S JOURNEY

Current-day psychology generally overlooks how relatively available a body experience of unified consciousness is. It fails to include the deepest expression of our self and how it can contribute to overcoming our most profound emotional injuries. Yet, as we refine our senses in meditation, we find that each of us has a ground-of-being, or an essential nature, that is identical to the divine reality of nondual consciousness. Our body experience of this essential nature offers solutions that psychology can only dream of.

As a way to include unity consciousness in order to heal emotional injuries in a way that is not transcendent, I propose a recurring (perennial) psychology and model of spirituality that is entangled. This model is based on the most fundamental aspects of our existence: energy and consciousness. In considering the nature of energy and consciousness, it becomes possible to understand how they are entangled and influence our evolution. This understanding provides a roadmap for our contemplative practice to heal our unresolved relationship injuries and to live joyously in wholeness. As we shall see, their entanglement underlies the cycle of birth and death inherent to all life.

In *chapter five* and the Appendix, I elaborate on how six models/ontologies of thought, or traditions listed below, share a single metaphysical or psychological pattern that has three-phases with seven sub-stages. The "three-phases" describe the nature of energy as having a charge-discharge-balance sequence. We need to successfully pass through each of these phases in order for our evolving-self to respond to what we experience authentically. Since energy is what composes our mental, emotional, and sensory life, the three-phases underlies our psychological journey toward awakening and overcoming suffering.

The "seven-stages" represent subdivision, or a more detailed expression of the emotional dynamics we need to deal with in order to make it through the three-phases of energy. As we shall see, with each successful progression through these phases and stages, we become more integrated and unified.

A brief preliminary look at the six models/traditions included in the holographic pattern discussed in this book will help orient us:

1. **NERVOUS SYSTEM**: I describe the stages the nervous system goes through in responding to challenge or danger. Each stage, as described in chapter five, begins with a brief description of what the nervous system is doing. For an overview of the nervous system, you can go to Appendix One, which offers a detailed description of the dynamics involved in recovery from trauma. It is no coincidence that this recovery also involves seven primary stages.

2. **CHILD DEVELOPMENT**: The learning processes we go through as children is called "development." Margaret Mahler, a leader in Object Relations psychology, describes five primary stages of child development. The emotional issues involved in each stage play a role in all the models discussed in *chapter five*. However, because psychology is based on duality consciousness (perception-response, self-other), it is limited. It also fails to recognize two additional stages that are more subtle expressions of our evolution: wisdom and bliss.

3. **ADULT RELATIONSHIP**: As adults, we naturally change over time and progress through a series of predictable developmental stages that parallel stages of child development. The skills that we bring to the challenges we face along the way can be predicted based on how successfully we progressed through our developmental stages as a child. How we relate to our self and others is a reflection of this. Our unresolved psychological injuries interrupt our energy and consciousness, and sabotage our Hero's Journey as an adult.

4. **CHAKRAS**: The "chakras" are the subtle energy centers in our body, as found in Tantra yoga. The chakra centers are where we can find the clearest experience of our nondual-qualities of being. *Chakra* means "wheel" or "disc" in Sanskrit. The seven primary chakras are located in the central-channel of the torso (*sushumna*). Chakras have a special role in healing injuries because they manifest in both dimensions. When a chakra is unbalanced, it becomes an expression of our

evolving-self's process. When a chakra is balanced, it becomes an expression of the unchanging-self's nondual-qualities of experience. In this sense, the chakras are psycho-spiritual expression of existence, both dual and nondual. I describe how inhabiting each balanced chakra can be used to tailor our meditation practice to address the specific stage where we experienced injury in order to heal and awaken spiritually.

5. **STAGES OF RECOVERY FROM TRAUMA:** This model is described in Appendix One, for those who want to dive more deeply (but is not necessary for an overall understanding of the book). Peter Levine uses nine therapeutic steps to help us renegotiate trauma symptoms, such as fear, to shift back into a more regulated state. I propose that two of Levine's nine stages can be combined with adjoining stages and become seven primary stages. Consolidating Levine's nine stages into seven becomes possible because two of the stages have the same principles to adjoining stages. I emphasize how this consolidation also makes more sense when we uncover a body experience of our existence as a unified field of consciousness. This leaves us with seven primary stages to recovery, which correlates with the seven stages of the Hero's Journey.

6. **CLASSICAL YOGA OF ASHTANGA:** This model is found in the Appendix Two for those interested in the details of how classical yoga might align with embodied nondual meditation. Classical yoga, called "Ashtanga" or "Raja" yoga, has eight stages called "limbs." Each stage represents an aspect of what most people on a spiritual path practice, in one form or another. I propose an embodied nondual alternative approach (*samprajnata samadhi*) to the traditional transcendent approach (*asamprajnata samadhi*). The first two limbs of Ashtanga original eight limbs/stages are combined because they both are based on the same principle: how to manage relationship issues. This leaves us

the seven basic stages, congruent with the holographic, archetypal model presented in this book.

The above six models provide a view of personal growth and spiritual awakening as a holographic (in their nondual expression) archetypal (they reflect collective consciousness) perennial (they have a common ground) psychology. In this chapter I describe how all these models mirror each other in terms of the underlying energetic three-phases (building, releasing, and balancing the energy underlying our thought, emotion, sensation - see Image #2 on page 51) with its seven sub-stages (see Image #4 on page 62).

As mentioned, both the three-phases and seven sub-stages are schemas that help us understand the energetic and psychological process involved in our evolution and the entangled nature of unified consciousness. As curious students of human nature, it is helpful to be familiar with the "common ground" in each model. The common principles involved provide important information that supports us on our personal path or Hero's Journey toward personal growth and spiritual awakening. The details of how this journey relates to the chakras will all be explained in *chapter five*.

**The Hero's Journey**
The Hero's Journey was introduced by the mythologist, Joseph Campbell (1949). He describes the common archetypal template underlying the soulful adventure a person goes on, to face the most profound challenges and return home transformed. Our "Hero's Journey" is a different version of "Hero" in that, this expression is not one that divides and conquers but instead, one that communicates, integrates, and unifies. There is a common psychological pattern behind the three-phases and seven sub-stages involved in the "Hero's Journey." This pattern reflects our approach to overcoming the habits of mind and body that result from the unresolved injuries and trauma we carry within us.

The obstacles the Hero overcomes along the way, are different lessons that each of us must face and learn from. With each stage we grow our skills and self-awareness. With each skill that we learn, we acquire the ability to face our deepest injuries and evolve into a better version of our self. In the version of the journey I present here, when we "arrive home," we ultimately become able to sustain an enlightened state of grace. We thereby understand and deal with life, while maintaining our sense of wholeness-of-being.

The three fundamental phases in this journey involve: 1) embarking on a journey to overcome an obstacle, 2) slaying a monster and recovering a precious artifact, and 3) returning home having saved the world and our self from destruction. It can be said that the three-phases of energy reflect how we relate to what we experience, and how we are oriented as we move through life. (The seven stages also reflect this, but in much more detail). As mentioned, each stage has its unknown challenge and outcome. Joseph Campbell describes these phases of the Hero's Journey as: 1) *Departure*; 2) *Initiation*; 3) *Return*.

**Departure:** Departure is the creative act of committing to a plan of action. As a Hero, we live in the ordinary world and receive a call to go on an adventure. This adventure can be any new beginning, the one found in each moment, our birth, or the beginning of a relationship. It is a wake-up call that implores us to overcome the outdated habits of mind and body that sabotage us, and cause suffering. We can be reluctant to follow through with the call to act, but we are helped by a mentor figure. The mentor is often our own inner wisdom, the discerning part of our self, or any supportive experience that helps us realize we have what it takes to start the journey.

**Initiation:** In the initiation phase, we face the challenge, which upon completion, allows us to begin the journey home. This phase begins with us as the Hero who traverses the threshold to the unknown. This unknown represents a challenge in any relationship with our self or others. We face tasks or trials with the assistance of supportive resources ("mentor figure"), such as our yoga self-regulation practices or embodied nondual meditation.

On the journey, we then reach "the innermost cave." This represents where we find a challenge of any kind. This can be the main habitual way we respond to life, due to the relationship fears that sabotage us. Here, we undergo "the ordeal" where we overcome the main obstacle. When we deal with the challenge successfully, we gain a reward (a "treasure" or "elixir"). In this book, this means our consciousness does not dissociate, and our energy flows freely without obstruction. We overcome our limitations and regain our sense of well-being. As the Hero, we then begin our return to the world with the "reward." At this point, we may be pursued by our outdated habits of mind and body. This is depicted in myth as the "guardians" trying to reclaim the treasure.

**Return**: We return home to the ordinary world with the benefits of having successfully met the challenge of our habits and injuries in a skillful way. We are empowered with new skills, a broader perspective, and a sense of success. We are more emotionally autonomous due to having the "treasure" or "elixir" we gained from successfully facing the challenge at hand. On this path, we are transformed by the adventure and gain wisdom or spiritual "power" with both dual and nondual dimensions of self. With each adventure, we come closer to overcoming core habits of mind, body, and emotion, with a sense of inner peace and wholeness-of-being.

**Image #2: Three-phases of the Hero's Journey**

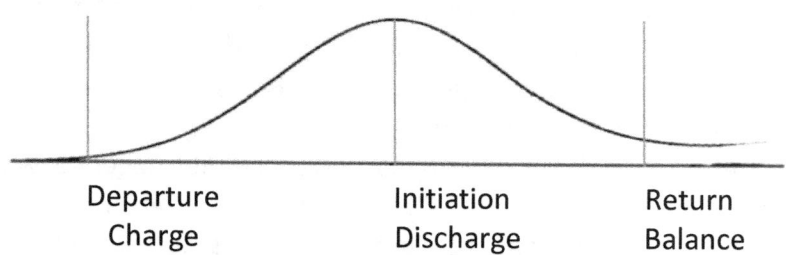

| Departure | Initiation | Return |
|-----------|------------|--------|
| Charge | Discharge | Balance |

The Hero's Journey sequence is graphically depicted as a bell curve, representing the relationship between our phases of energy, consciousness, and our challenges in life.

These three-phases are archetypal and holographic in nature, because the sequence manifests on the macro and micro levels, over time, in our life.[18] The phases refer to our own psychological personal growth process. Most of us tend to struggle with one or two of the seven sub-stages (within the three phases), due to our unresolved injuries and traumas.

## Three-Phases of Energy

Experience is comprised of thoughts, emotions, and body sensations. All experiences are composed of energy, and all energy is based on variations of three phases: charge, discharge, and balance. These three ingredients are inherent to duality consciousness. Duality consciousness is based on the cause-and-effect of our perceptions and responses involved in our everyday thoughts, emotions, and sensations. The charge phase is a buildup of energy; the discharge phase is a time of "rest and digest"; the balance phase is a time of homeostasis and stillness. In yoga these three phases are collectively called "*gunas*."

While there are some minor discrepancies, the three-phases of energy (*gunas*) correlate with the Hero's Journey (departure, initiation, return). The "departure" phase correlates with the "charge" phase of energy, because it is when we gather the energy to embark on the journey. The "initiation" phase is when we apply the skills we learned in the charge phase to succeed and begin our return home. The return phase relates to the full discharge of energy, in that it involves a resolution and integration process. This allows us to return to well-being and wholeness. In this light, these three-phases are a holographic template that replays over and over with every experience we have. It also plays out over the course of a lifetime.

Classical yoga (Patanjali), somatic psychology (Wilhelm Reich), and neuroscience (Porges) all recognize the charge-discharge-balance cycle as a fundamental, innate nature of energy. As mentioned, like the "*guna*" energy tendencies, on a very basic

---

[18] My understanding is that conceptually the universe is a hologram, but physically it is a fractal. Here I choose the term "holographic" rather than "fractal" since, as nondual spiritual traditions explain, all of physical existence arises from a unified source of nondual consciousness.

level, the three-phases of the Hero's Journey are the primary expressions of energy (charge, discharge, balance) that underlie our developing and changing sense of self as we mature. It also shows up in every aspect of life.

The basic pulsation of all life is an expression of the three phases of energy, no matter how complex or simple. It is the sequence found in our heart as well as the movement of a worm. In daily life, unless we are fixated by trauma, with every experience we have, we normally progress through the three-phases. We experience this sequence with every breath; inhale, exhale, and pause.

Another common example is how our arousal in the sexual act builds until we reach climax, flows into a release, and returns back to inner-peace that has a more stable and expansive feeling of equilibrium. If we have a full-body orgasm, we may experience what Freud called the "little death" (which leads to a temporary loss of our self-reflective ego awareness). Without the ability to build an energetic charge and then fully release it, we cannot experience satisfaction and well-being.

We continually go through beginnings and endings in every moment, one mini-lifetime after another. Every moment has a beginning, an experience, and an end. The end of a moment includes a gap before the beginning of the next moment. This gap can be our most balanced state and where we find completeness, openness, and unlimited potential. It is a pregnant space from which spontaneous energy arises, allowing what will arise next. In meditation we learn to slow down enough to notice these-phases as the subtle movement of life, with gaps where our state of balance grows.

In Buddhism the three-phases are described as the "three *kayas*" (*kaya* means body). Sambhogakaya is the beginning of energy manifesting. Nirmanakaya is the experience of the moment. Dharmakaya is the space to which all form returns, and from which all energy-forms arise. These three levels of reality are considered to be three opportunities for awakening to unified consciousness that repeat themselves moment to moment.

## Three-Phases as Three Deities

The same fundamental three-phase nature of existence is personified in the Hindu myth of the *Trideva* (meaning the "three deities," or divine trinity). As deities, they exemplify energy and consciousness in their three primary forms as the three fundamental forces (*gunas*) that cyclically create, maintain, and destroy the universe (charge/rajas-discharge/tamas-balance/sattva). In this eternal birth-death cycle, Brahman is the creator (charge), Shiva is the destroyer (discharge), and Vishnu is the preserver (balance).[19]

The word "destroyer" does not feel similar to the word "discharge." It implies the destruction of our attachments and habits of mind and body that accompany what interrupts the three phases. When this happens, our attachments (limiting habits) are overcome or released. This naturally gives us access to an experience of balance, and our consciousness becomes increasingly unified. Vishnu, in the role of "preserver," restores the cosmic order and protects *dharma* (living authentically in alliance with our nature).

Whenever the world is threatened by humanity's sabotaging habits of mind and body, Vishnu is called upon with his ten primary "powers" (*dashavatara*). Discernment of these "powers" came from ancient sages in deep states of meditation. The most important of the powers are Rama and Krishna (states of energy and consciousness). Their nature depicts the attributes we access when in a balanced state, and what is needed to preserve our balanced state.

Both Rama and Krishna are deities that are depicted as having many different natures, depending upon the tradition of Hinduism. On the simplest level, the root of the word *Rama* is *ram-* which means "stop - stand still – rest – rejoice - be pleased."

---

[19] Traditionally, Trideva are most commonly depicted as male deities. This highlights the absurdity of Axial Age consciousness, which is under the belief that creation has nothing to do with the role women have on Earth (alternately see Tridevi). This triptych is also associated with Christianity's Holy Trinity: Father, Son, and Holy Ghost. Like the Holy Trinity, the Trideva are different forms or manifestations of one consciousness (three in one).

Other Indo-European languages describe *Ram* to mean "support - make still." Krishna is associated with protection, compassion, tenderness, and love. These experiences associated with Rama and Krishna help preserve the state of balance. In embodied nondual meditation, we learn to allow protection, compassion, tenderness, and love to arise spontaneously out of our embodiment of wholeness and unity. Whenever our life is threatened by sabotaging habits, contemplation upon these expressions helps us maintain a state of balance and unity.

### Three-Phases as Found in the Nervous System

As mentioned, the charge-discharge-balance cycle is the fundamental innate nature of energy, yet it is also expressed in our autonomic nervous system. The autonomic nervous system regulates our involuntary physiology, such as heart rate, blood pressure, respiration, digestion, and sexual arousal. It is composed of three anatomically distinct divisions: sympathetic, parasympathetic, and enteric.

This involuntary system is made up of the sympathetic (charge) and parasympathetic (discharge) aspects of the nervous system. Activation of the sympathetic nervous system innervates nearly every living tissue in the body. It gives us a general sense of arousal, and/or increased heart rate, alertness, and is involved in our flight, fight, and freeze survival responses. The parasympathetic nervous system, however, innervates only the head, viscera/organs, and genitalia. We experience it as relaxation, resting, digesting, slow heart rate, and is involved in our freeze and collapse survival response.

The enteric nervous system is an extensive, web-like structure that involves the vagus nerve. The vagus nerve oversees control of our moods, immune response, digestion, and heart rate. It connects the brain and the gastrointestinal tract and sends information about the state of the inner organs to the brain. In this way, it activates what Porges (2003) calls the "social engagement system," which gives us a sense of safety, receptivity, and openness to social contact.

The social engagement system results from the nervous system in a state of "dynamic equilibrium" (balance). Dynamic equilibrium happens when we have a shifting range of arousal and can build an energy charge and then release it in a kind of seesaw action. This seesaw allows us to sustain homeostasis and balance. When we can go about our life flowing through charge and discharge phases freely, we have increasing levels of residual balance in our body-mind system.

The commonality of the three-phases of energy in each model, (the nervous system, yoga philosophy, and Hindu mythology) are depicted below:

**Image #3: Different Models Abiding by Three-phases:**

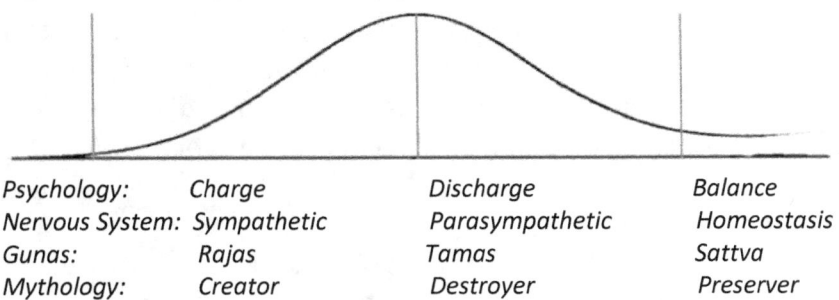

| Psychology: | Charge | Discharge | Balance |
| Nervous System: | Sympathetic | Parasympathetic | Homeostasis |
| Gunas: | Rajas | Tamas | Sattva |
| Mythology: | Creator | Destroyer | Preserver |

The stages in the holographic pattern of the models mentioned above, reflect our energy and our consciousness. The three-phases are graphically depicted as a bell curve showing the rise, fall, and balance of energy. When this "birth-life-death" sequence happens freely, consciousness becomes more integrated and unified.

When we refine our experience of being an unobstructed three-phase system (free from habitual constrictions), we find full completion and access a progressively more refined state of balance. This state gives us access to a new dimension of our sense of self. In embodied nondual meditation, we experience this as wholeness and the feeling we exist as a unified state of balance itself.[20]

---

[20] This is in alignment with the understanding that all binary systems naturally seek completion and balance. We are in an interplay of two polarities, here called charge and discharge, that brings forth a third mediating or reconciling force called balance. Balance is a third force that emerges as a necessary mediation of the charge-discharge opposites. Balance, as the third ingredient,

Our emotional growth depends on how we manage our energy and consciousness in each of the three-phases. When energy and consciousness are obstructed due to emotional injury and relationship trauma, we express our self defensively, automatically, and habitually, due to our underlying fear. When it is not obstructed, we are able to express our self authentically and evolve. Unobstructed energy allows us to express our self in the most authentic way. We can express, breathe, create, and even orgasm, fully and successfully.

Moreover, when energy flows through each of the phases without obstruction, we also gain access to the most balanced, relaxed state, that provides an open and unified inner experience. The more balanced our energy is, the more we gain access to the stillness and simplicity of an embodied nondual experience of our existence. The charge and discharge find completion, and we gain access to a new dimension of unity.

## Desire & Aversion

The pattern of energy and consciousness becomes obstructed when our sense of self fragments into pieces due to overwhelm, fear, unresolved injuries, and trauma. Our mind is disconnected from our body and emotions, or our emotions are disconnected from our mind and body. This disconnected state becomes obvious to those of us harboring injuries and trauma in our body and mind. Our original injuries, that most of us have not fully recovered from, began with how we were related to as a child. Psychology and yoga agree on the source of what fragments us.

Yoga recognizes that what interrupts our energy and consciousness most is some version of desire (*raja*) and aversion (*dvesha*) (*Yoga Sutra*, 1-24). Buddhism says desire (as greed), aversion (as hatred), and delusion (wrong view of reality) are the three poisons.[21] Western psychology understands these

---

not only opens opposites to reconciliation but also makes possible a whole new level of consciousness. Balance is the resolution of a dialectic that creates a new realm of possibility.

[21] Integrating the fundamental forces of our desire and aversion as expressed in our yearning for an experience of union (desire) and emotional independence (often felt as an aversion to being imposed upon) was also fully

inclinations as the desire for contact and aversion to contact (Bowlby, Ainsworth, Mahler, Bowen). Variations of desire for, and aversion to contact (with others or an experience) result from our relationship injuries, and are acted out in our life.

Psychologically, the forces of desire and aversion that result from how we were related to as a child, are often understood in terms of the quality and quantity of love we received ("healthy mirroring"). But the underlying issues involve feelings of being emotionally abandoned or imposed upon, and the desires and aversions that result. How we negotiate these basic emotions determine our style of being in relationship, and how we come to terms with our unresolved injuries. It also determines how we progress through each of the three phases of the holographic Hero's Journey. This is a journey towards awakening to our evolving-self's authenticity and also our innate nondual nature as wholeness and unity.

Many traditions of healing our suffering, focus almost entirely on finding ways to re-balance our energy (here called the indirect-path). Yet, when the initial emotional cause of our loss of balance is not explored as an important part of the healing process, the beneficial results are often short-lived. Our body and mind may learn from having our energy re-balanced, but too often, our emotional life throws us into an unbalanced state again, if it is not attended to with care.


*Seven Stages*

As a part of gaining a broader perspective, in this book, I emphasize the holographic psychology that connects six models. I point out how each of the six models is an expression of our Hero's Journey (based on Joseph Campbell's book, *The Hero with a Thousand Faces*) to overcome our deepest injuries and awaken spiritually. I propose that the recurring nature of this journey has seven primary stages, which are superimposed upon the three phases of the nature of energy (charge, discharge, and balance).

---

acknowledged by the traditional Hindu Shaiva tantra yoga practice of balancing and awakening the seven primary chakras.

53

The seven stages reflect the primary psychological issues of dealing with experience. Interestingly, the number seven allows for perfect symmetry of three, with a center, and then another three (as found in the chakras). Synchronistically, the number seven historically is associated with "completeness." (This is most likely related to the lunar calendar of moon cycles and the understanding that our path in life has seven primary stages. Yet, completeness is somewhat similar to the "wholeness" associated with the seventh chakra.) This understanding of seven is common in spiritual traditions.[22]

Each of the six models discussed above, (and in more detail in *chapter five* and Appendices), can be understood to have a common seven-stage pattern. Each model has a different name for each stage, depending on the tradition, yet the same basic underlying principles are involved. By dividing up the three-phases into seven stages, we can discern specific emotional issues that get in the way of our successful Hero's Journey in life.

The seven stages found within the three-phases of energy, form the basis of a predictable sequence of developmental milestones expressed in all aspects of life. Each stage is holographic. For instance, how we deal with each stage can be expressed in how we inhabit our body and even breathe. I have found that the exact place where we obstruct our inhale or exhale has a direct correlation with how we manage our energy

---

[22] The Old Testament describes how the world was created in six days, and God rested on the seventh. This correlates with the seven-day-week we use to this day. The Bible tells us that God created order out of chaos in the first six days, and on the seventh day, there is a culminating ideal that concludes with a day of rest, completion, and wholeness (In Hebrew, the word "seven" has the same consonants as the word completeness or wholeness.) The New Testament considers the number seven to be related to the unity of the four corners of the earth with the Holy Trinity. The Book of Revelation draws upon the number seven (seven churches, seven angels, seven seals, seven trumpets, and seven stars). The Koran depicts seven heavens and how Muslim pilgrims walk around Islam's most sacred site (the Kaaba in Mecca) seven times. The Puranas of Hinduism describe seven higher worlds and seven underworlds. Buddhism depicts that the newborn Gautama Buddha took seven steps upon being born, where each step except for the past represents how he would transcend suffering.

in our whole body physically, emotionally, and mentally. Also, our posture, the segment of the body that is less open, and how we move through life reflects our obstructions of energy and consciousness. This influences how we manage each stage and is reflected in how we approach relationships in general.

Each of us has more difficulty with one or two of the stages, due to our system being sensitive to being re-injured. Each stage involves different challenges that we must face in life (due to the desires and aversions created by experiences of emotional abandonment and/or invasion). The degree of support we receive as children in each stage, as well as the strengths and weaknesses this leads to, is expressed in every aspect of our life. For example, one notable way it manifests, pertains to the seven stages of adult relationships:

The *first stage* involves "self-awareness," which is about how we become familiar with a new situation. We assess whether a new relationship (person, situation, ideology, substance, etc.) is dangerous or safe and whether we belong or not. Self-awareness can be a time of developing intimacy in relationship, as we come to understand our self in the relationship. In the *second stage*, "desire," involves clarity about our interests and needs in relation to the other person's interests and needs. We learn about how we want to proceed. The *third stage*, "approach," is about putting our interests into action. We gather the information and skills we need to manifest our desires, which can involve negotiating our personal needs in relation to others.

In the *fourth stage*, "release," we find what it takes to successfully manifest our interests in relationship, such as our need for mutuality, connection, and autonomy. In the *fifth stage*, "satisfaction," we accept our new view of our self in relation to others. In the *sixth stage*, "completion," we integrate and learn to live with the new reality. In the *seventh stage* we open to a new level of intimacy that ideally includes wholeness and unity in our body mind system. How we progress through each stage and manage our desires and aversions, determines our distinct personality as an individual, and how we relate to our injuries.

In *chapter four* ("Review of Nervous System's 7 Responses to Threat") and in *chapter five* I describe how our nervous system also follows this general seven-stage pattern. How we respond to threat, and what happens when we experience injury and trauma, have a similar pattern to how we engage with challenges in relationships. (In this sense, how we live is how we die, how we love is how we live, etc.).

## The Entanglement of Energy & Consciousness

The entangled relationship between energy and consciousness is reflected in the degree of balance we have in our body-mind system. As we refine our senses in meditation, we find that the more balance we experience in our body-mind system, the more we also gain access to unified consciousness. With more balance and unity, our energy flows more freely. We simultaneously gain more access to our evolving-self's authenticity, and to the nonduality of our unchanging-self.

The seven holographic stages in all the models, can be understood to represent the degree to which we are being influenced by dual or nondual consciousness. When energy is not free-flowing, we not only become unable to authentically express our self, but we also lose access to our sense of wholeness.

Since energy and consciousness are entangled, this dynamic can be depicted in the following bell-curve image. This manifests in a variety of timelines, ranging from the how we negotiate the present moment, to how we live our life:

**Image #4: Energy Divided into Seven Sub-Stages:**

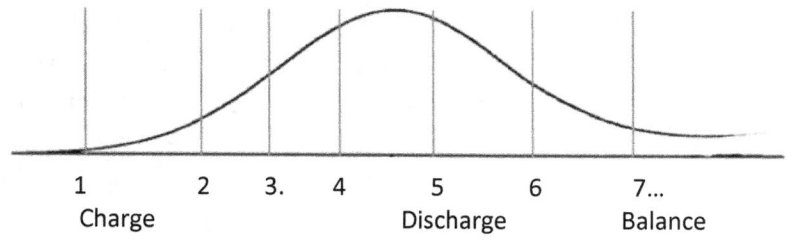

|  1    |   2   | 3. | 4 |    5     | 6 |  7...   |
| Charge |  |  |  | Discharge |  | Balance |

It is valuable to understand that the three-phases overlap the seven-stages. For example, in the charge phase, the psychological stages of our adult relationship that build are: 1) "self-awareness," 2) "desire," 3) "approach." In the discharge phase, we let go with: 4) release, 5) Satisfaction. In the balance phase, we experience: 6) completion, and 7) wholeness. The three-phases and seven sub-stages of each of the six models overlap in the same way.

Understanding how energy and consciousness are entangled, lays a foundation for healing our deepest injuries that may exist in each of the seven stages, using the seven nondual-qualities of the chakras. Before embarking on the journey to understand how balance and unity are healing, we will now take a look at what happens when we become unbalanced.


THE INTERRUPTED ENERGY CYCLE

As the transpersonal theorist Ken Wilber describes, each stage (of consciousness) remains with us even as we move forward, and newer stages come into ascendance. Each stage goes beyond but includes the previous one, and in the process brings forth new and emergent truths. When we become overwhelmed, we tend to unravel and regress. As we meltdown, we go through a deconstructive collapse of the leading-edge of our growth in order to find a sturdier base. We make self-corrective readjustments as we attempt to find this base and begin to organize once again.

Our unresolved injuries and relationship trauma cause our energy's three-phase cycle to become obstructed. If our energy is obstructed, it becomes fixated in either a charge (sympathetic, *rajas*) or discharge (parasympathetic, *tamas*) phase. If what causes these fixations is an enduring condition that leaves us with unresolved injuries, we become creatures-of-habit that sabotage us. We constantly act out these habits in relationship to our self and others.

So, for instance, when we have a strong emotion, or if our boss or friend does, we become overwhelmed and resort to habitual, automatic survival responses (flight, fight, freeze, collapse) in order to cope. This condition robs us of choice, interfering with our energetic balance (homeostasis, *sattva*), and limits the breadth and depth of our consciousness. We also develop limiting habits of mind and body that show up in each of the six models described here.

Fixation in the charge phase leads to symptoms such as anxiety (fight or flight), panic, hyperactivity, inability to relax, restlessness, hyper-vigilance, digestive problems, emotional flooding, chronic pain, and sleeplessness. If our fixation is in the discharge phase, it leads to depression, numbness, flat affect, lethargy, disorientation, disconnection, dissociation, and poor digestion. We can also experience fixations in both charge and discharge at the same time, which causes us to freeze.

The two most common kinds of unresolved relationship injuries that lead to fixations, are emotional abandonment and/or invasion. When we experience emotional abandonment as a child (unappreciated, discounted, unwanted, etc.), we may have unresolved injuries that lead to excessive desire for contact with other (person, job, food, etc.). We may feel the absence of a sense of belonging and have a lingering feeling that something is missing. Because we did not get the meaningful feeling of connectedness we needed as a child, we are left with low self-esteem, which fosters self-doubt and perfectionism, while making us our own worst critic. As a result, we may constantly look for signs of other people's appreciation of our intelligence, talents, kindness, or physical beauty. Our low self-esteem causes us to overreact when we do not feel appreciated, and in turn is acted out in our relationship conflicts and internal struggles. This interrupts the successful completion of any one of the seven stages, causing our corresponding chakra to become unbalanced.

Likewise, when we experience emotional invasion as a child (imposed upon, criticized, smothered), we have an aversion to other people's desire for our attention. We become fixated on the feeling that others are criticizing us, or pressuring us with an imposing agenda. We may respond by dampening our sensory awareness (numbing) and emotional availability (low affect). We may also subdue our expressions of open-hearted interest in other's experiences. We become unable to soften and open, to receive the full experience of being in relationship. Our sense of being imposed upon can sabotage the successful completion of any of the seven stages.

58

## Image #5: Interrupted Energy & Consciousness

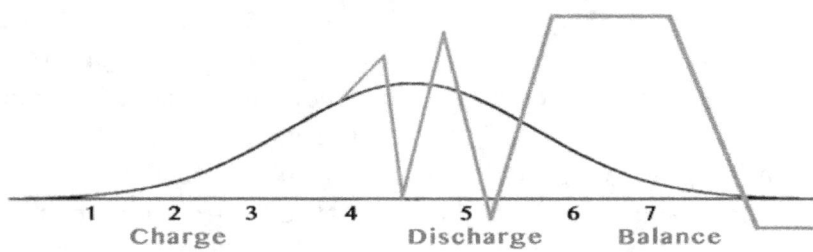

|   |   |   |   |   |   |   |
|---|---|---|---|---|---|---|
| 1 | 2 | 3 | 4 | 5 | 6 | 7 |
|   | Charge |   |   | Discharge |   | Balance |

In this image, we see the effects of being fixated in a charge (sympathetic) or discharge (parasympathetic) state, which interrupts the flow of energy and limits consciousness.

Most of us have a combination of both abandonment and invasion injuries. With these kinds of relationship injury and trauma in our system, we more easily become overwhelmed and fragment our sense of integration between our mind, body, and emotion. This fragmentation can continue subconsciously on an ongoing basis at a low-grade level. Our fragmentation often becomes most evident with important people in our life, that we either like or dislike.

In meditation, we learn to recognize how interruptions to our energy's three-phase, seven-stage cycle, represent the ways we have not yet recovered from our childhood injuries. We begin to notice the way we encounter each present moment, is reflected in how we engage and disengage with every aspect of our life. Yet, we gather this information while attuned to unified consciousness, so our discovery process is not overwhelming.

THE SUCCESSFUL RETURN "HOME"

In embodied nondual meditation, as we face the challenges that show up, we learn to perceive them on the most subtle level, through simple practices that refine our senses (see next chapter). Our experience of the present moment reveals how well we are doing on our Hero's Journey through the three phases and seven stages.

As mentioned, if we manage each of the habit-forming forces in our life well, we increase our chances of not becoming fixated on energy's charge and/or discharge phase, or fixated on the psychological issues associated with each of the seven stages. This enhances our safe "return" to the experiences of balance (*sattva*). We encounter the present and successfully progress through energy's three-phase cycle without sabotaging our energy and consciousness. When this happens, we become increasingly integrated. It liberates us from our attachments and unwanted habits of mind and body (that result from relationship trauma).

When this three-phase process is repeated successfully, we cultivate an increased level of balance in our body-mind system. This is illustrated by the bell curve not returning to the baseline (see arrow). I refer to this increased level of balance as "The Gap."

**Image #6: The Gap** (arrow at the end of the curve)

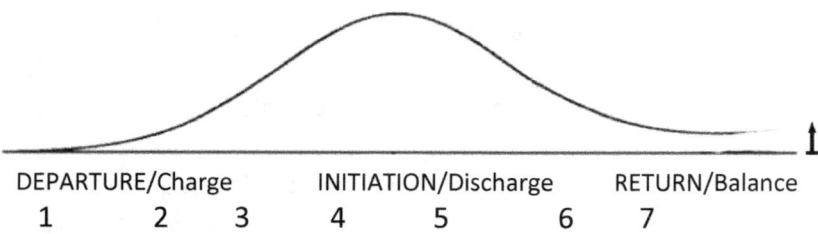

| DEPARTURE/Charge | | | INITIATION/Discharge | | | RETURN/Balance | |
|---|---|---|---|---|---|---|---|
| 1 | 2 | 3 | 4 | 5 | 6 | 7 | |

Increased levels of balance in our system not only give us more relaxed-alertness and robust resilience in life, it also gives us what yoga refers to as the inner heat of "*tapas*." In yoga, *tapas* is the energy and heat that is released in our body-mind system as a result of letting go of any limiting and sabotaging habit (thought, emotions, and behavior) (Desikachar, 1995). When we heal a limiting habit, such as a pattern of physical tension, negative self-talk, panic, rage, or our tendency towards eating for emotional reasons, we increasingly feel great relief, relaxation, and a surge of inspiration and vitality (*ojas*). This is the moment when our energy flows more authentically, and our consciousness broadens and deepens.

We feel an ongoing sense that whatever we experience, we have a secure home base, within the body. We feel that we belong and are safe. This correlates with the post-trauma state that Levine describes where we begin to feel new excitement and joy as we engage with the present moment. We may feel fascination with what we experience and have an enduring sense of the wonder of "newness." This is when colors become vibrant and shapes and textures come to life, as if for the first time. Our capacity to remain present and be in "the here and now" with what we experience, grows. Our actions of thought, emotion, and sensation spontaneously arise from an un-premeditated, un-conditioned nondual source.

Recognizing the three-phase cycle in each aspect of our life helps make our life meaningful, and transform each experience into a path of awakening. The past is bygone, the future hasn't happened yet, and the present is where all of this happens and where the living experience exists. With practice, we start getting the feeling of being in a life that flows through these phases and is always beginning, happening, and ending.

This is a practice of embodied awareness where the end of one moment is always the rebirth of the next. In the process, we deepen our perception of our most balanced state at the culmination of our return home. We may experience this as a moment of stillness or a gap between these cycles. When this state of balance is a stable body experience, it becomes an ongoing, pervasive reality throughout each phase. We perceive that within this balanced state lies a vast potential for healing and personal transformation.

THE HOLOGRAPHIC APPROACH TO SOCIAL CHANGE

Because the Hero's Journey is holographic in nature, it is both personal and transpersonal. Our personal growth has a collective effect. We begin to experience this in meditation when we tap into a deeper, more expansive awareness that goes beyond our personal experiences, and connects us to something greater than ourselves.

On one level, this is similar to Carl Jung's understanding that our "collective consciousness" gives us access to a reservoir of shared experiences. This reservoir is expressed as archetypal symbols. Collective consciousness reflects the combined thoughts, beliefs, and values (conscious and unconscious) that shape our shared experience as a society or community. Similarly, experiencing unity allows us to tap into a collective experience that goes beyond the limitations of the individual self.

Collective consciousness is an interconnectedness of parts that are expressed in archetypal symbols. Each particular action has a ripple effect that eventually influences the collective. By contrast, unified consciousness is based on unity of the parts. Each particular action simultaneously affects everything, everywhere, all the time, all at once. Collective unconscious evolves and nondual consciousness does not.

Every experience of unity each of us has, feeds into the collective unconscious so it can include our relationship to unity, but it does not encompass nonduality. Whatever we experience of nonduality as individuals becomes a part of the collective unconsciousness of society. Understanding this difference can give us insights into how our personal experiences of unity and wholeness influence the collective consciousness of society.

Embodied nondual experience allows us to learn in a holographic way. It activates a holographic, quantum, mind-body-emotion unified understanding. This reflects recent research that suggests that, in more ways than expected, the brain is wired for unity and functions in a holographic fashion. Each part is replicated everywhere else in the brain, leading to holographic transformations (Josipovic, discussion; Bohm). When we attune to our body experience of nondual consciousness, we access this holographic way of functioning. Unity consciousness is applied to every part of our being, not only the brain. Consequently, when we embody the attributes of nondual experience, healing occurs to our whole-being at once, mind, body, and emotion simultaneously. This influences our whole-being more than the slower, piecemeal, cause-and-effect learning, based on our ever-changing evolving-self.

Since all the layers of our being function on a quantum level as a hologram, where all parts contain all other parts, once we learn how to experience a different way of physically responding to what we experience, we simultaneously respond differently mentally and emotionally. At this depth of perception, each aspect of self is informed by, and contains, the other layers of

62

self. Each aspect of our self awakens into wholeness simultaneously. This means that once we heal our emotional habits, using embodied nondual meditation, our mental and physical habits follow suit, and vice versa.

Plus, the quantum healing effect that happens when we attune to an embodied nondual experience is self-perpetuating. It is motivated by the present-moment experience of wholeness and unity, rather than a memory of the past or projection into the future. This allows our new learning to not be extinguished easily. Our responses can now be spontaneous rather than preconceived. The actuality of our emotional experience (anxiety, depression, anger) does not interrupt our body's experience of unified consciousness. Rather, our emotions are embraced by wholeness, and our self-limiting patterns begin to heal.

As these expressions of wholeness and unity pervade us, we are increasingly liberated from our conditioned mind and body. This form of quantum learning dramatically increases our ability to learn more effective ways of responding to life. Quantum learning also applies to how we learn as a society. When an individual accesses the holographic reality of nondual consciousness as a body experience, society collectively gains access to a broader perspective as well.

We discover nondual consciousness as a body experience, not by expanding outward away from what we feel inside our body, even though it is paradoxically non-local. Because nondual consciousness is holographic in nature, it exists everywhere. We do not have to leave our body experience to access transpersonal unity and a sense of oneness with all beings. With this subtlety and depth of experience, we can feel the relationship between our sense of a collective cultural awareness (archetypal) and our sense of unified consciousness (holographic). We can feel the difference between a societal belief, and an authentic personal truth accessed directly from unity consciousness.

When personal insights arise spontaneously out of our sense of wholeness and unity, they have a direct and immediate influence on our sense of collective awareness. As we experience our self as a unified field of consciousness, and broaden our perspective, we expose our evolving-self to insights and outlooks that shift the collective narrative. Each individual experience becomes a catalyst for social change when we feel we are all one and that our expressions are holographic in nature. This supports us to spontaneously act with compassion and thereby enhance personal and collective well-being.

It is well known that meditation increases our brain's gray matter density, and increases our abilities in areas associated with emotional regulation, empathy, and self-awareness. It is less acknowledged that meditation also has the quantum effect of facilitating nondual experiences that enhance our connection to collective consciousness. It is as if, when we embody nondual consciousness, we activate the wave aspect of the electron and commune with all of us. This is important because it alleviates our worry that our personal meditation practice is a form of self-absorbed navel-gazing.

Our personal meditation practice communicates to our global condition and introduces a synergistic broader perspective that fosters nonjudgement, compassion, harmony, and peace. This new paradigm for understanding ourselves and our relationship with the world, is how thinking globally and acting locally can work. It helps us see beyond our differences and paves the way for societal norms to shift toward more inclusive and sustainable ways of living and relating to one another.

# CHAPTER THREE: AS ABOVE SO BELOW

## YOGA AS A DIRECT & INDIRECT-PATH TO AUTONOMY

Yoga is experientially based and intentionally guides us towards the realization of nondual consciousness. The word yoga is derived from the Sanskrit word "*yuj*" which means to yoke (as in the yoke placed on oxen), to unite or integrate. It is the process of integrating the fragmented mental, emotional, and physical aspects of our evolving-self, so they become balanced and unified.

### Indirect-path

In yoga practice, the "yoking" practices of self-regulating or balancing our energy is the "means," and unity or nondual consciousness is the "goal." In this sense, yoga is a method, and yoga, as a state of unity, is also the goal. It is helpful to discern if our yoga and contemplative practice is focused on the "means" or the "goal." When practice involves the means, it is an "indirect-path" to unity through "yoking" or self-regulating our energy underlying our experiences (mental, emotional, sensory), so we can eventually achieve a balanced state.

Yoga (contemplation, meditation) as a "means" offers ways to self-regulate our subjective body-mind perceptions and impulses. This self-regulation of our energy (balancing) is an indirect-path because we have to do the practices that create balance, to realize it. We often spend years exploring how a particular yoga posture, breathing style, or mantra chant activates a particular part of the body and mind to induce balance. Most spiritual traditions inform us that we may get a glimpse of the fully balanced state of nondual consciousness, only after years of dedicated practice.

Meditation is often based on the "indirect-path" of achieving balance through self-regulation. It does this through the practice of trying to keep the mind quiet and wakeful so that we can be totally present to what we are doing (*citta vrtti nirodha*). The indirect approach can also be found in Tantra yoga. Shaiva Siddhanta form of Tantra yoga uses extensive mind and body practices (e.g., pranayama/conscious breathing, mantra/sacred sound, yantra/sacred visualization, asana/posture or mudra) to create conducive conditions for the transcendent state of "pure nondual consciousness only" to eventually arise. (Yet some forms of Tantra yoga mostly embrace the free flow of Shakti energy as an expression of the divine.)

Psychology's methods of restoring our mental health, also help us develop the ability to self-regulate states of imbalance. But the goal is manifestation of our evolving-self's authenticity, rather than unified consciousness. Freud emphasized psychology's approach with his "hydraulic model" of regulating the energies of the psyche, much like Reich did. Jung focused on balancing energies underlying the male and female unconscious.

On a basic physiological level, when we self-regulate energy underlying our mental, emotional, and sensory life, we balance the charge/sympathetic and discharge/parasympathetic tendencies of our energy (*gunas*). This influences our ability to maintain homeostasis and optimal activation of the nervous system. Identifying and tracking what interrupts and obstructs our energy, and what allows it to flow freely, is an important part of self-regulation. Only when energy is unobstructed by habitual constrictions, collapse, or dissociation can we have access to the unfragmented sense of our authentic evolving-self. (Of course, Jung was an exception in his quest for the even more refined state of primordial unity, "*unus mundus*.")

The sage Patanjali's injunction (1.2) to "still the fluctuations of the mind" is not the only way to experience nondual consciousness, and it certainly is not the easiest. Most of us cannot actually restrain or suppress our ever-arising thoughts and emotions, especially when we carry unresolved injuries. Some of us manage to still the mind after years of very committed practice.

In contrast to yoga as a means, yoga as a goal can be a "direct-path" to the realization of the nondual dimension of our self and the environment. This happens when we attune directly to the nondual state of consciousness with minimal self-regulation of mind-body energies (via asana, pranayama, mantra, yantra, etc.).

### Direct-path

When we focus our yoga practice on the goal, we take a "direct-path" to accessing a state of "union" (nondual consciousness). The direct-path is recognized by "immediatist gurus" (Versluis, 2014) who are spiritual teachers that emphasize instant enlightenment and liberation (Eckhart Tolle, Ram Dass, Adi Da, Andrew Cohen). This allows us to have spontaneous, direct, unmediated spiritual insight into reality with little or no prior training. The goal of these spiritual guides is transcendence through complete absorption into unified consciousness and complete surrender of our ego. This direct-path to awakening nondual consciousness is much quicker than the indirect-path and gives us freedom from our ego's suffering, by distancing our self from it.

When we spontaneously experience unity on the direct-path it can feel mysterious. When it is not something we deliberately do, it can feel like grace. We feel we have gone out into the cosmos to access non-local consciousness and have downloaded unity from "out there" or "above." We may feel we have been chosen or that we have been touched by an angel or "God." This external orientation can leave us feeling less empowered, not quite knowing how we got there, and at the mercy of some outside influence. Our evolving-self is not helpful or involved in the process.

In contrast to the "immediatist guru" orientation, the approach to the direct-path emphasized in this book, is a body experience of the unified consciousness, the unchanging-self. This approach also gives us direct, unmediated spiritual insight accessible to anyone who meditates. Yet, the spiritual insight we access is different, because it is an internal embodied experience of our own divinity, rather than transcendent "pure nondual consciousness only." The understanding that non-local consciousness is happening in the body, as an expression of our self, is a paradigm change requiring new semantics.

The alternative "direct-path" in this book initially involves some degree of self-regulating as we learn to refine our senses. But fairly quickly, we begin to recognize our unchanging-self's nondual-qualities (such as a sense of wholeness, unconditional love, emptiness, unchanging presence, balance, stillness, spaciousness, unity, chakras, etc.). We recognize these inborn essential qualities are the ground of our being and not something separate from us, and yet they exist in our environment as well. As we learn to perceive, at this depth and subtlety, we feel that our own being is continuous with everything around us. We recognize this as a unified, spiritual dimension of life. As we awaken to this unbreakable ground-of-being, it transforms how we relate to our self and other (people, situations, ideologies, substances, etc.).

When nondual consciousness is a body experience, what becomes evident is that it is fairly easy to access. When we know how to recognize this experience, it is right there, right under the surface of our ever-changing thoughts, emotions, and sensations. Learning to uncover and awaken to the nondual-qualities of self is much like learning a language. It becomes easier with repetition (*abhyasa; sutra 1:13*) and familiarity. This expression of the direct-path offers a supportive resource that is not often recognized in Eastern spirituality (Vedanta), Western psychology, or by Christian mystics (like Delio, Teilhard, and Bonaventure).

The direct-path recognizes that we can access unified consciousness at any time, even though we still need to evolve for it to become a stable presence in our life. The indirect-path, in the absence of the direct-path, is a much slower process that historically has required the support of an ashram or a monastery. It can occur over the span of a lifetime, or be an expression of the long evolution of consciousness on Earth. When it is a part of contemplative practices, it can take tremendous effort and discipline to eventually experience unified consciousness. With trauma in our body and mind system, few of us can achieve this.

For this reason, the direct-path is a powerful resource to include in our meditation practice. In embodied nondual meditation, both paths occur at the same time. The indirect-path of learning to self-regulate and evolve, occurs within the context of our direct experience of our unchanging-self. Both the direct and indirect-paths can be integral to our contemplative yoga practice.

The whole-being-embrace communion empowers us to engage with our injuries and projections, and we come to understand why they are there. It gives us the information we need to more readily and easily express the personal truth of what we need in relationship to feel safe and supported. As we embody our sense of unity and wholeness, our authentic expressions arise spontaneously out of our wholeness. Understanding when we are using indirect and direct methods in our contemplative practice can help orient us in our psychological healing and spiritual awakening.

Our state of consciousness does not reflect how evolved we are. Most meditative states of consciousness (gross, subtle, causal, nonduality/*turiya*, nondual wholeness/*turiyatita*) are variations of natural states we can have at any stage of development. We do not have to evolve through each stage before we can have a direct spiritual experience of unified consciousness. We simply interpret the experience through the lens of our developmental stage. We can be quite spiritually adept at accessing refined states of consciousness and yet still have a very conformist, conventional, xenophobic, and/or ethnocentric mentality. Accessing a unified state of consciousness through meditation does not always help us grow up emotionally. This explains why so many spiritual teachers have been found acting out their unresolved injuries.

Consequently, it is important to learn to maintain unified consciousness while re-experiencing each stage of our development. To do this requires that we become intimately familiar with the stages of development in which we experienced emotional injury as a child, along with the coping strategies and the symptoms of fragmentation this leads to. Recognizing how these same dynamics continue to influence us as an adult is important. This sets the stage for learning how the state of unified consciousness not only gives us access to the peak experiences so clearly described by spiritual teachers, but actually enables us to evolve to the next stage of emotional development.[23]

## NONDUAL-QUALITIES & THE CHAKRAS

When transcendence is our goal, we strive to learn to become familiar with all pervasive groundlessness and emptiness. The experience of this groundlessness is a valuable one to have. It is a state where we leave our suffering behind completely. Yet, as mentioned, this goal is not an easy path, partly because it involves learning to come to terms with groundlessness and the uncertainty, vulnerability, and insecurity this faces us with.

Christian mystics describe how groundlessness can feel like we are plunging into the depth of darkness or experiencing "the burning love of the crucified." In Eastern spirituality groundlessness arises when our evolving-self is either consumed by nonduality or we are selfless. The emptying our self of ego to find our "true" self can feel like a plunge into the dark-night of

---

[23] To clarify the states of consciousness that most spiritual traditions recognize, a little description can be orienting. The "gross state" is our conventional waking state governed by ego consciousness, which is the direct cause of the suffering inherent to the human condition. The "subtle state" is our subtle personality, or soul. The "causal state" can be described as formless awareness itself. The "nondual state" (called *turiya* in Advaita Vedanta), is consciousness without objects like thought and emotions. It is the timeless sense of "I Amness" that is ever-present consciousness. Yet, here ego's duality consciousness is excluded and all that exists is nondual consciousness (which makes it dualistic). This is what here is referred to as "transcendent."

The "nondual wholeness state" (called *turiyatita* in Advaita Vedanta, or One Taste in Buddhism), is when the ego's duality consciousness seamlessly unites with nondual consciousness. Form (*samsara*) and formlessness (*nirvana*) become two different aspects of an underlying nonduality. Mahayana Buddhism's Heart Sutra describes this as, "That which is Emptiness is not other than Form, that which is Form is not other than Emptiness." In this state, Emptiness is not split from Form but includes all Form, allowing for nondual wholeness. This is the view adopted by Tantra in its outlook that sex and spirit are not different, but are two aspects of an underlying whole. In this way, absolutely nothing is excluded. Here, I call this state "whole-self." When unified consciousness is a body experience of self, we are able to experience both aspects of the underlying whole at the same time, in co-existence.

70

the soul. Groundlessness can feel like we are plodding though darkness stripped of our senses and emotions.

By contrast, when our goal is embodied unified consciousness, what we encounter is a quality rich emptiness that profoundly nourishes us with wholeness-of-being. It also has the attributes of being vast, indestructible, and full of potential for life to manifest. Moreover, for the spiritually inclined person, usually with a little practice this experience is readily available, just under the surface of our ever-changing perceptions. It is an on-going feeling that pervades every moment of our life, all the time, everywhere, all at once.

While this embodied state of unity does not exclude suffering, our suffering becomes a valuable tool for growth. The experience that we exist as unified consciousness allows us to relate to our sabotaging habits in a different way. This allows us to appreciate the rich turbulent life we are living now as an essential part of our spiritual path toward inner-peace.

A central attribute of how we experience unified consciousness in the body is a sense of wholeness-of-being. Wholeness can be experienced in a variety of ways. These are collectively called "nondual-qualities" of our unchanging-self. Uncovering and awakening a body experience of the nondual-qualities can be felt as: stillness, balance, emptiness (of psychological content), unity, and universality, each of the layers of self -physical, emotional, mental, wisdom, bliss- and each of the chakra qualities of self, including unconditional love.

Each embodied nondual-quality of our unchanging-self offers our relationship-injury an alternative sensory (subtle), motor (stillness), temporal (timeless), and spatial (unified) reality. Wholeness is governed by the holographic principle that all of the parts, or expressions of them, contain all of the other parts. Each nondual-quality is much like Arthur Koestler's understanding of "holons." Each nondual-quality is fractal. It is both a unity on its own, as an expression of wholeness, that is also a part of a larger unity. In this sense, they are able to maintain their "wholeness" and also their "part-ness." The paradox that each nondual-quality is a subdivision of unity, is best understood through experience rather than logic.

The alternative perspective each expression of wholeness provides our injured self, can be transformative emotionally and spiritually. Having access to many different expressions of wholeness greatly expands the options we have in supporting our self-other relationship injuries. Depending on the stage in our life we were injured and the nature of the relationship injury, a particular nondual-quality of wholeness may support us more than another expression of wholeness.

The experience of wholeness that accompanies unified consciousness expresses itself clearly in each of the seven primary chakra qualities of self. Each of the nondual chakras relates to the psychological stages of development we go through as children. The stages that we had the most difficulty dealing with as a child, tend to be repeated most dramatically in all our adult relationships (with other people and the relationship we have with our self). Each stage of our development as a child is a time in life when we have specific vulnerabilities and potential for trauma. This is when we first establish our emotional attitudes and beliefs about our self and the world, which become fixed in the body and mind.

In order to recover from the injuries that happen as a child, it is important to reexamine each of these critical times in life. Awakening the nondual chakra qualities of self as a body experience that correlates with the stage in which we experienced injury, can have a transformative effect. This becomes integrated into the fabric of our sense of self and how we relate to others. *Chapter five* offers a detailed description of each stage of development, and how the chakra can help heal the specific relationship injuries we still harbor. While each injury is supported most by a particular expression of wholeness, perhaps the most influential nondual-quality of wholeness is unconditional love.

## NONDUAL-QUALITIES & UNCONDITIONAL LOVE

In embodied nondual meditation, the nondual-qualities become apparent as an unchanging presence in the space that pervades our body. We can feel how this conscious space lies deeper than anything solid in the body. When we attune to the space pervading our body, we can feel the space is not an empty void, but rather, has a fully awake presence or luminous stillness. These ineffable qualities of our existence are an inborn wholeness-of-being and unity. We can also recognize how the nondual-qualities of our nature, support us in feeling whole within our self and unified with our surroundings.

The seven primary chakras are the subtle energy centers along the vertical core of the body. Each chakra quality is a wholeness that pervades everywhere and exists as a spectrum rather than clearly divided aspects of our self. We can attune to each part of the spectrum as having a particular quality that can be most clearly felt in a particular part of our body. Yet all the qualities pervade everywhere in the body and environment as a unified blend of our wholeness.

Inherent to each of these qualities is the "nondual pleasure" (*ananda kosha*) that is often called "bliss." Because we confuse bliss with the duality-based state of bliss and ecstasy, I sometimes call this layer by other names, like "contentment," "pure," or "unconditional love." This is not a particular love for somebody but an open, tender essence at the heart of our nature that can feel like bliss. As described in detail in the *chapter five's* fourth chakra, unconditional love goes to the heart of whole-being-embrace. Since all injuries involve the loss of love unconditional love is the most powerfully healing experience we can have. It allows us to forgive and re-parent our self. We reestablish our own fundamental innocence and innate self-worth.[24]

As we deepen our attunement to the nondual-qualities in our self, how we perceive and respond to life and our sense of contact with other people, gain depth and breath. They become authentic, richer, more complex (interrelated), simpler (more unified), and we can have a broader range of experiences. We experience a fundamental, unified dimension of consciousness

---

[24] Integral to this nondual bliss or unconditional love, is the "happiness" and "knowledge" (of unity) that the Bhagavad Gita tells us accompanies our attunement to the bliss layer (*kosha*) of self.

that connects us with other people through all sensory pathways at once, with our whole body and mind.


## THE CHAKRAS & THE CENTRAL-CHANNEL

As mentioned, yoga delineates the qualities of our unchanging-self into seven primary expressions of energy and consciousness, as found in the chakras (or "mini-brains," Pert). When we attune to, and embody, each of the chakra nondual-qualities as separate expressions of our wholeness, we can recognize and release the specific defenses and injuries related to each of them with precision.

The chakras exist along the body's pathways of subtle energy and consciousness throughout the body. As we have learned, the most important pathway is the central-channel or subtle core (*sushumna*), which runs vertically along the central core of the body, from the center of the top of the head to the center of the bottom of the torso.

Many yoga traditions have a different understanding of the essential nature of chakra qualities of our being. My interpretation of the seven chakra nondual-qualities of self is as follows:

1. Existence
2. Creativity
3. Power/Inner-strength
4. Love
5. Expression
6. Knowing
7. Wholeness-of-being

As shown in the following diagram, each of these chakra locations of subtle energy and consciousness, are situated deep within the subtle core of the body along the central-channel.

**Image #8: Chakras Along the Central-channel**

The chakras are psycho-spiritual centers (psycho = duality, spiritual = nonduality), so they can exist in a balanced or unbalanced state. When fully balanced they manifest as seven nondual healing qualities of our unchanging-self. In that the chakras can be expressed as both the duality-based evolving-self, and the nondual unchanging-self, they are a bridge between the two dimensions of existence. Practices that help us attune to the sense of contact between these two expressions of self are profoundly healing. This is the orientation underlying the "whole-being-embrace" between our evolving-self and our unchanging-self.

When the chakras manifest in an unbalanced way, they express the evolving-self's psychological distortions in each stage of our development. These distortions are based on how our evolving-self's duality consciousness becomes fragmented when we are overwhelmed and injured. This causes our energy's natural charge and discharge cycle, to become obstructed and not return to a balanced state. We develop fixations in the charge or discharge state and become attached to habitual tendencies that can be sabotaging.

In my experience, the most common relationship dynamics that throw the chakras off balance involve relationship bonding or attachment injuries, which is also the cause of our most severe relationship trauma. These are experiences that leave us feeling unfulfilled desire, due to emotional abandonment, and aversion, due to experiences of being imposed upon (invasion). So many of our responses and behaviors are governed by fear associated with these influences in each stage of growth. We act out these fears in relationships in distorted and sabotaging ways. These attachment injuries fragment our evolving-self in specific ways and create a pattern of imbalance in the seven chakra centers.

A first chakra imbalance, for instance, can be the feeling that we are emotionally unappreciated and abandoned, or that we are being imposed upon. As a first chakra experience, this feels like a threat to our sense of safety and belonging. When a chakra is imbalanced and fixated in a charged state, we often constrict and energetically lift the chakra center location up higher from its true location (all fear makes us constrict and lift away from the ground). We hear a common reference to this with the Heart chakra when people say, "my heart is in my throat." Plus, when a chakra is imbalanced in a discharged state, we often collapse and energetically press the chakra center location down lower from its true location. We experience what is commonly described as a "heavy heart."

In terms of how this influences our nervous system, each of the chakras can become imbalanced in either a hyper-active or hypo-active way. Depending on the stage of growth in which we experienced emotional injury, the correlating chakra will become imbalanced and fixated in either a hyper or hypo state.

For example, emotional imbalances of the first or "Root" chakra, include feeling insecure and overwhelmed with our basic survival needs. In reaction, we may fixate on sympathetic, flight-fight panic responses (and become excessively focused on making sure we have full control of these areas of our life). Or, we may fixate on parasympathetic immobility responses (which include dissociation and shutting down). When injured in our first chakra, these responses may cause us to become either, 1) Hypo-fixate, and we become incapable of managing issues concerning money, shelter, and food. We also may be unable to provide for life's necessities that involve establishing a bond in relationship. Or, 2) Hyper-fixate, and we obsess over these issues and excel in these areas of our life due to fear. We may also cling to the bond in relationship like there is no tomorrow. This is discussed in detail with each chakra in *chapter five*.

Each chakra has its own particular expression of hyper and hypo imbalance. In embodied nondual meditation, we become familiar with our own fixations so we can refine our self-regulation skills (balancing practices) and directly attune to the appropriate nondual chakra quality of self.


## CHAKRAS & 7 STAGES OF CHILD DEVELOPMENT

In my experience as a student, yoga teacher, psychotherapist, and spiritual guide, there is a direct correlation between the chakras and our process of maturing. The first five primary chakra qualities of nondual consciousness, correlate with the five primary stages of our maturing sense of self as a child (as recognized in Object Relations psychology). This correlation elegantly allows for our state of unified consciousness to mature our stage of development. Central to this process is the whole-being-embrace experience.

This is important because Eastern spiritual traditions do not recognize the psychodynamic of defenses that result from injury in each of our stages of development. How the state of unity can facilitate emotional growth in each stage is a relatively recent consideration. And as I've pointed out, the trending transcendent orientation of meditation has potential limitations, particularly at certain stages of development. This still has not been resolved, and only the most informed meditation teachers understand the issues. (For more, see *From Trauma to Wholeness, 2023.*)

Sigmund Freud hypothesized many theories about childhood experiences that caused mental health issues later in life. Fortunately, Margaret Mahler added significantly to the field by actually observing children's behavior in relationship to the parent. She observed mothers interact with their young children and noticed that children went through similar developmental changes at roughly similar times. From this observation, she formulated a theory about our stages of separation-individuation. Each stage requires us to accomplish certain abilities to avoid pathologies from developing. From this factual basis, she described the psychological birth and maturation of an infant's sense of self.

In Mahler's view , separation involves an internal process of recognizing and accepting that we are separate from the (m)other; and individuation involves the process of developing a self-concept of who we are, as a unique individual. Both understanding our separateness and ownership of our uniqueness are central to our emotional growth. The health of our separation and individuation process determines our ability to establish a stable bond in relationship to our caretakers. Healthy separation and individuation lead to non-abandoning or non-invasive interactions. These supportive interactions determine our ability to form a healthy bond with our self, (grow self-awareness, self-care, self-love, etc.) as well as with others.

This healthy bond determines how we connect and form a secure attachment, and how we separate and take breathing-room to explore personal interests. Later on in life, this is expressed in how we focus on self-needs, or maintain an individual sense of self, distinct from others, allowing us to be in relationship without losing clarity about our personal truth. Emotional issues around these concerns are expressed differently in each stage of growth. Recognizing these emotional issues can help us orient our contemplative practice toward the most relevant nondual chakra quality of self, that can heal us most effectively.

The primary cause of relationship injuries and trauma, happens as a child, when our attempts to establish and maintain optimal levels of contact and breathing-room are shut down. This means our ability to express our personal truth about our honest feelings, becomes ineffective. When our personal truth, which forms our healthy boundaries, fails, we adopt defensive boundaries and styles of relating that protect us from injury.

The stage in which our personal truth was shut down most severely, is where we become injured and fixated. Our lifelong relationship skills (how we relate to our self and other) are primarily a result of these kinds of early dynamics with our parents. How we pass through each of the primary stages of development has a tremendous influence on how we relate to our self and other people in our current life.

Mahler proposed five basic stages that we progress through on our journey toward establishing a clear mental, emotional, and physical sense of our evolving-self.[25] As shown below, I include two more stages that become available when we refine our senses. These two stages depict subtler levels of self than are commonly recognized in Western psychology. (Although, a more recent understanding of the sixth chakra stage has been described in some psychological methods, Hart et al, 2019; Bentzen, 2020, Marcher, 2010). The last two stages of development presented in this book (wisdom and bliss), become available to us most often with the more refined growth that results from experiences that arise in yoga, or other contemplative practices.

Each stage is a sensitive time when we begin to include new abilities and awareness. Our success at dealing with challenges that arise in each stage, plays a large role in determining the degree to which the associated chakra is balanced and unified, or unbalanced and fragmented. The process of learning to cope and surmount the challenges in each stage, relates to the Hero's Journey as described in *chapter five*.

1. The first stage is "Symbiosis" (0-5 months), where we believe we are one undifferentiated being with the parent. As infants, we experience overwhelming anxiety when we are prematurely separated from our caregivers. (Today, child psychologists do not believe the infant is entirely merged, but only have a rudimentary sense of being different from others).

2. The second stage is "Differentiation" (5-9 months), when we go through stages of separation and individuation, where we begin to "hatch," and realize that we are different than our parent.

3. In the "Practicing" stage (9-14 months), we become mobile and begin leaving the parent to explore the world.

---

[25] Freud originally came up with a psychosexual theory of five stages of human development based on observing adults: oral, anal, phallic, latency, and genital. Mahler's observations of children in relationship led to the five aspects of development discussed in this book. Issues of emotional abandonment and invasion underlie how we connect or separate from a parent and how we form our individual sense of self (Ainsworth).

We develop a sense of separation and practice skills that contribute to a sense of independence. This empowers us to engage in the relational nature of the next stage.

4. In the "Rapprochement" stage (18-24 months), we feel a need to be near a parent, yet also have independence and autonomy. Initially, this can be confusing and lead us to express ambivalent emotions, but in time, we learn to become autonomous while remaining connected to our caregivers.

5. "Object constancy" (24 months plus) emerges when we internalize our parents, so we can maintain an internal sense of their presence when they are not around. This allows us to be comforted when alone, or when our needs are not met. This supports us to function independently and pursue our own personal interests. We gain the ability to integrate good and bad experiences, which supports a more realistic understanding of our self and of others.

6. "Completion" (seven years or later) emerges as we gain an understanding and clear knowing of our sense of self. We begin to recognize that we are multi-dimensional beings. We gain intuition and wisdom while bridging duality and nondual consciousness.

7. "Wholeness" emerges when we uncover and awaken the essential ground-of-being-unity and wholeness, as a body experience of self. While each stage manifests as a nondual-quality of wholeness when fully balanced, in the seventh stage, wholeness becomes a stable presence. We are able to transmute our evolving-self's experience of struggle, so it no longer feels like suffering. We feel unified with our environment and oneness with other people. We perceive bellow the external façade, to the essential ground-of-being.

This transforms the functioning of our senses so that they no longer harbor conditioning. Each of our senses is washed clean of their constrictions and gains access to "direct" or "bare" perception" of what we experience. As a result, our responses to experience are not only authentic, they are uncaused responses that are informed by knowing the deeper truth of our wholeness.

In holographic fashion, as with the other models, the three-phases of energy and consciousness, contain the above sequence of seven sub-stages. This sequence occurs with varying timelines, from how we encounter each experience in the moment, to the span of our entire lifetime. With each successful passage through the stages, the energy underlying our mental, emotional, and physical life evolves toward increasing levels of integration. Our consciousness becomes broader and more unified. As mentioned, the progressive increase of integration and unity in our body-mind system is here referred to as "The Gap." The seven-stage journey is shown here in relation to the human body and the chakra system:

**Image #9: The Seven-Stage Journey & the Body**

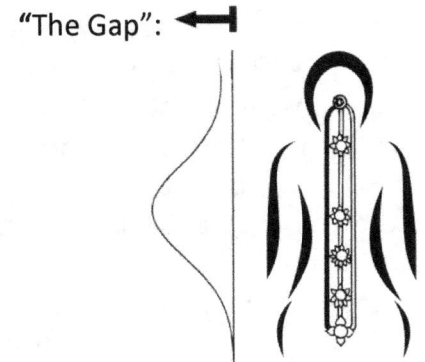

This image depicts a vertical bell curve on the left. The central-channel is shown to have three components (*ida, pingala, sushumna*).

In the following list, the chakra's name in English, is listed on the left. Next to it, "in quotes," are descriptions of how we experience this chakra nondual-quality, as an expression of our self. The list on the right contains the names of our developmental stages. The first five are based on Mahler's view of child development, and the last two are more refined developmental stages.

| **YOGA CHAKRA** | **PSYCHOLOGY** |
|---|---|
| 1. Root chakra: "Existence" | Symbiotic (& Autistic) |
| 2. Pelvic chakra: "Creativity" | Differentiation |
| 3. Solar plexus chakra: "Power" | Latency |
| 4. Heart chakra: "Love" | Rapprochement |
| 5. Throat chakra: "Expression" | Object Constancy |
| 6. Head chakra: "Knowing" | Completion |
| 7. Crown chakra: "Wholeness" | Wholeness-of-being |

## ASPECTS OF WHOLE-BEING-EMBRACE HEALING

Balancing the chakras involves dealing with the challenges in each chakra/stage of development. If we recognize our unresolved injury is related to a particular chakra, we must deal with the cause of the injury at that chakra/stage. This means we must come to terms with the unresolved emotions associated with the particular challenge at that chakra/stage. Coming to terms with an unresolved emotion is a journey itself. This means, in holographic fashion, each chakra stage also has its own seven-stage sequence (see image #10 below). The following example is a roadmap for resolving specific emotions associated with the challenges we face in life. Resolving any emotion, at any stage, can benefit from the following roadmap.

For instance, in the first chakra, we face relationship issues that involve our safety and the sense of belonging. This means that as we engage with our fears around the issue of safety and belonging. This involves progressing through the following stages of healing:

1) Intimacy: We start with self-awareness (thought, emotion, sensation) in relationship to the experience. We develop self-awareness and get to know the emotional issue we are dealing with, such as our sense of belonging. We discover what our fragmentation symptoms are and the story we attach to our fears.

2) Desire: This self-awareness inspires a desire to pursue what draws our attention. We want to have the choice to follow our most attractive interests, so we can feel safe and be able

to create what feels true for us. We orient, and develop a sense of what is important to us, our interests, preferences, and our discernment of the choices we have in relation to our emotion (such as the sense of safety and belonging).

3) Approach: As our interests become clear, we harness the energy to hone our ability to manifest these interests. We develop skills at manifesting our interests, preferences, and choices regarding our emotion. We thereby learn to more skillfully manage our emotion, such as rejection. We may draw upon, for instance, whole-being-embrace with unconditional love; or it may involve clarifying the personal truth we need to honor (to feel safe and that we belong).

4) Release: This empowers us to face the challenge each experience presents us with. We release upon successfully applying skills (to access an experience of safety and belonging).

5) Satisfaction: where we begin to relax and receive a sense of satisfaction from a job well done. We learn to integrate and receive a sense of well-being (safety and belonging).

6) Completion: We feel a sense of completion and come to a deeper and broader understanding of life (our self and other). We fully understand and integrate the new reality (of safety and belonging).

7) Wholeness/Intimacy: we gain an intimate contact with, and understanding of, the emotion (safety and belonging), and use this to enhance our relationship with our self and others. This enhances our wholeness-of-being and inner peace.

When we succeed at resolving an emotion, we access more integration and wholeness in that particular chakra/stage. We can do this process with each chakra/stage. If we have fewer unresolved emotions associated with the other stages, we go through the above roadmap with much more ease. The depiction of this in the following image, illustrates how the three phases of energy and seven sub-stages, relate to our human body:

## Image #10: Phases & Stages Within Phases & Stages

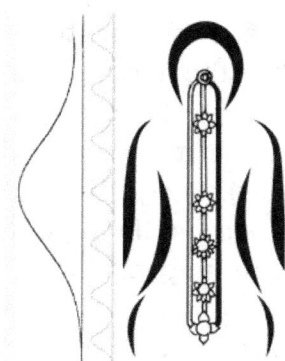

Here we see the progression through the stages and phases relating to our body in general, and we also see the same pattern occur in each of the chakras individually.

Whole-being-embrace involves communion with a particular aspect of wholeness that feels the most nurturing and supportive to us. The sense of wholeness that we get from attuning to, and embodying a particular chakra quality of self, communicates directly to the injuries we have in the associated stage of development, and heals us. *Chapter five* has a detailed description of suggestions for whole-being-embrace practices. To help orient this, the following general overview is provided.

Below on the left, is a list of the nondual chakra qualities ("Nondual-essence") associated with each of our seven stages of development. On the right, is the list of some of the main "Emotional Benefits" the injured part of us experiences as a result of whole-being embrace with the nondual-essence. For instance, in *the roadmap to healing emotions* described above, we can begin the process of embrace in stage three of "Approach." The Emotional Benefits help heal the attachment injury we may have at each stage of our development:

**Nondual-essence**        **Emotional Benefits**
1) Existence ......................(belonging, safety)
2) Creative nature.............(choice, pleasure, sexuality)
3) Power/ Inner-strength...(endurance, competence, pride)
4) Love................................(compassion, acceptance, self-love)

5) Expression……………(personal truth, authenticity, satisfaction)
6) Knowing……(completion, understanding, intuition, wisdom)
7) Wholeness……….(bliss, self-love, connection–breathing-room)

It is rare that we have challenges with only one stage of growth, so we most likely need to embody several nondual chakra qualities. We need all chakras to become balanced and whole for wholeness-of-being. Each balanced chakra is an awakened expression of unified consciousness and wholeness that is uninjured, unbreakable, and a particular unchanging feeling-tone of unified consciousness. It is profoundly transformative when the nature of our balanced, nondual chakras comes into whole-being embrace with our deepest injuries. Each stage that we heal, provides support for the subsequent stage. Each nondual-quality of wholeness we embody, supports our perception and awakening of the following chakra quality.

As a fractal part of a larger wholeness, each nondual-quality offers us access to unconditional love for who we are. The sense of self-acceptance and belonging that results is a game changer. It allows us to have a compassionate relationship with our injuries, and the habits or addictions that result. It also gives us access to a spiritual life, deepening our understanding of the unified wholeness of existence.

We learn to discern how our chakras are thrown off balance each time we are triggered. This happens when we are related to in a way that brings up our past injuries of feeling that we are:

Chakra 1) Not wanted/appreciated.
Chakra 2) Not respected for our choices, interests.
Chakra 3) Not given autonomy or seen for our ability and strength to manifest our interests.
Chakra 4) Not honored for our need for love, in both our contact and independence.
Chakra 5) Not witnessed, respected, and appreciated for our most genuine expressions.
Chakra 6) Not recognized for our intelligence and ability to understand and know.

Chakra 7) Not related to with the inner-peace of wholeness-of-being and the universal connectedness with all that is. (This trigger is often more subtle than others.)

Most of us can identify that we are still working through some version of the emotional issues described, that result from how our parents related to us. Understanding the emotional dynamics of the stage in which we experienced relationship trauma, can help us realize that we are not defective in any way. Realizing how vulnerable we were in each stage of development can be healing and alleviate self-criticism and self-sabotage. We understand the dynamic of how we were wounded and how that has influenced us ever since. It is helpful to keep in mind that our caregivers' limitations were due to their own injuries, limiting their ability to meet our needs.

Drawing on the nature of the nondual-qualities of self, as found in each of the balanced chakras, we can intelligently tailor our practice of healing relationship trauma, for our specific needs in the stage we need it most.

### Body Structure and the Chakras

While each chakra quality of self exists within our whole body, they are most clearly perceived where the chakra is located. *Chapter six* discusses in detail where the chakras are located, and how the body structurally has segments that correspond to each chakra. (This is a common understanding by Wilhelm Reich and in yoga.) Depending on the nature of our relationship injury, a particular chakra and part of the body are influenced most. When energy and consciousness are obstructed, our energy becomes fixated primarily, in one of the segments of our body (i.e., legs-pelvis, belly, chest, neck, mouth, eyes, forehead). (Yet, usually several other areas of the body also feel constricted, or collapsed and numb.) We potentially experience hyper or hypo fixations in the associated part/segment of the body.

For instance, when injury relates to first chakra/stage issues, our survival is threatened, and we experience hyper or hypo imbalances in our feet, legs, and body parts related to our pelvic basin (although other symptoms and body locations are also involved). When injury relates to second chakra/stage issues, involving the acceptance of our interests and choices, we experience hyper or hypo imbalances primarily in our pelvis/lower belly body segment. Relationship injury always involves some degree of emotional abandonment and/or invasion, so our heart chakra is almost always affected in some way (constriction, collapse, numbness).

An example of this can be seen in us as a child, when our fear of disappointing the people we care about most, is paralyzing. We may have been wanted and loved as an infant (stage one), and yet when we tried to assert our personal interests (stage two), our parent(s) became overwhelmed, and they shut down. Consequently, as an adult, we may quickly become excited by our contact with what feels important to us (person, situation, art project, etc.) (stage one). Yet, we may not be able to sustain the excitement, because we increasingly fixate on fears of being rejected for expressing our personal interests (stage two).

This can lead us to hyper-vigilantly look for signs of rejection, and the slightest clue feels shattering. This interrupts our ability to remain present to the direct perception of the experience of what feels important to us (person, situation, art project, etc.). We may notice how our emotions and thoughts swirl within us. It may leave us feeling, "What's the use?" or "I'm not good enough," or "You're a bad person." We may want to either simply withdraw, or angrily lash out. We may feel stuck and numb, or we simply collapse in a puddle. The following illustration depicts a first chakra/stage injury of, for example, feeling unwanted as a child, that we are not safe, or that we do not belong.

## Image #11: First Stage Obstruction

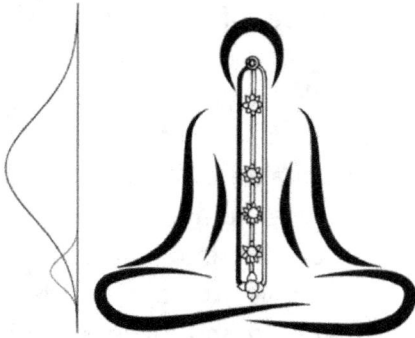

This illustrates a first-stage interruption that stops subtle energy from ascending. The energy charge shown above starts to build quickly, yet is aborted. Many variations of energy interruption in each chakra exist. Although the specific reasons for interruption in each stage are different, it always interrupts the energetic process.

It can be valuable to first attune to the balanced nondual chakra quality in the associated segment of the body. Then open to feel this attunement in the whole body. When this is deeply felt, open to feeling the nondual-quality within the environment. At this point, we can come into whole-being-embrace with the injury and the relevant balanced chakra. As we heal, we feel our own inherent goodness help us on our journey.

### Rich Blends

We can then add to this experience the chakra quality that directly precedes it. This means we feel in our body that we exist as, for instance, the second chakra quality of the essence of our "creativity." We join this with the first chakra essence of our "existence." In this way, we uncover and awaken a rich blend of qualities that is empowering. Blending qualities in this way tends to illuminate, and deepen the experience of the primary chakra quality we are attuning to, such as creativity. So, in this example, knowing, and feeling, our inherent value and our birthright to exist, (1st chakra), enhances the experience of our creative essence (2nd chakra). Awakening the essence of our creative nature in this way can improve our ability to make choices that support us as we engage with what feels important to us (person, situation, art project, etc.). Other blends can be valuable as well, such as, the essential nondual-quality of power blended together with unconditional love. Often the most meaningful blends involve reciprocal chakras.

## Reciprocal Chakras

We can benefit from the reciprocal nature of the nondual-qualities of the upper and lower chakras: Our first chakra quality (existence) relates to the fourth chakra (unconditional love) (both are gateways), the second chakra (creativity) relates to the fifth chakra (expression) (both are based on creativity), and the third chakra (power) relates to the sixth chakra (knowing) (both are about worldly manifestation and understanding). Like the first and fourth chakras, the seventh chakra quality (wholeness) is also a gateway to the nonlocal, universal/cosmic nature of unified consciousness.

Meditation upon, and embodiment of, the reciprocal chakra to the one we are primarily focusing on, like blending, tends to provide valuable support. For instance, the creative essence we uncover in the second chakra, clarifies and illuminates our perception of the fifth chakra's essence of expression. Each one has qualities that are reflected in states of consciousness that resonate with the other.

## ENERGY OBSTRUCTION & CHAKRAS & STAGES OF GROWTH

Our well-being depends on our not becoming overwhelmed. For this to happen, we need to keep the intensity of what we experience within the limits we are capable of tolerating. When a situation is too intense, we resort to automatic reactions. For instance, as an infant, we protect our self by closing down the nervous system to guard against overwhelm (habituation). The infant actively controls its body by tightening its muscles, in a kind of paralysis, to control its level of environmental stimulation. Without this ability, the infant is at the mercy of its environment (Brazelton 1989, p. 67).

Like the infant, when we protect ourselves from uncomfortable emotions as adults, we either constrict mentally, emotionally, and physically (and then sometimes collapse), or we dissociate from the situation at hand. Our constrictions help us not feel the full impact of the experience, and create a physical boundary, in the absence of an emotional boundary. Either way, our natural energy cycle of charge, discharge, balance is interrupted.

These "interruptions" are what Patanjali considered to be the life experiences that result from the "externalization" of consciousness (*vyutthana*). The more externalized we are, the more we come under the influence of duality consciousness (perception-response). Thus, Desikachar (1995) explains that a person who is troubled, has more energy (*prana*) outside the body than within. He also said that when we are suffering, the "quality of our energy in the body" is reduced.

The three-phases of energy not only relate to how our energy moves from phase to phase (Image #5), but also relate to our seven chakras and our stages of development. As mentioned, when an interruption of the cycle happens repeatedly at a certain stage of the charge or discharge phase, the associated chakra becomes imbalanced. The primary reason for the interruption is to keep us within the limits of feeling, that we can tolerate. When the intensity of our current experience is similar to an earlier wound, it can interrupt our energy from flowing and, all too often, manifest as a tight stomach, heavy heart, a pain in the neck, or a foggy mind. This has a direct impact on the accumulation and distribution of our subtle energy in each chakra of our body.

From this perspective, most emotional problems can be described in energetic terms. They result partly from not being able to build, contain, or release energy. A disrupted charge-discharge phase becomes imprinted on our mental, physical, and emotional system. Because our body and psyche are one, when an energy interruption happens, we lose awareness and skill in dealing with the relevant emotional issues associated with that developmental stage and associated chakra.

Since consciousness and energy go together, when we interrupt the three phases of energy, we either release the energy prematurely (A), simply dissociate and are not present at all, like a sleepwalker (B), or are unable to release it (C). Adi

Shankara also described a version of this when he said: "When consciousness deviates even slightly from the goal and is directed outward, then it sinks, just as an accidentally dropped ball rolls down a flight of stairs" (*Crest Jewel of Discernment,* p. 325). Below is an illustration of what happens without balance:

**Image #12:**

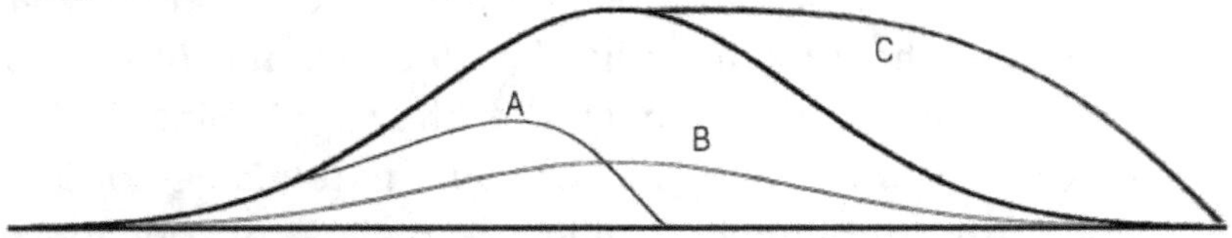

Examples of different ways energy and consciousness are obstructed: A. release the energy prematurely; B simply dissociate; C. unable to release.

In *this chapter*, we clarified the difference between indirect and direct-paths to awakening unified consciousness, and defined the nature of the nondual-qualities of self (particularly the chakras). We then examined the relationship between chakras and the stages of child development, followed by specific approaches to healing emotions. We concluded with expanding on our understanding of what happens when energy and consciousness are obstructed. In *chapter four*, we will explore whole-being-embrace in more depth, and define what it means to refine our senses. We conclude with a brief look at the nervous system's response to threat, and an overview of how this reflects our journey through life. Then, in *chapter five*, we launch into the Hero's Journey through the chakras.

# CHAPTER FOUR: MEETING PRESENT MOMENT

## WHOLE-BEING-EMBRACE & NONDUAL MIRRORING

When our interests, and our need to be witnessed, understood, and respected are honored, we receive what psychology calls "healthy mirroring."[26] When we mirror others, we reflect back (and ideally honor) what they are feeling. Just as we receive mirroring and mirror our parent's emotional expressions (that hopefully convey a feeling of openness, authenticity, and presence), we also mirror the presence of our parent's nondual consciousness. When the parent is in touch with their own unchanging-self, it awakens our pre-existing, essential ground-of-being. Mirroring activity is not limited to our evolving-self. When it involves unified consciousness, I call it "nondual mirroring."

Our unchanging-self is in an interesting position, poised between absolute pure nondual consciousness only (*atman*, *nirguna Brahman*) and our evolving-self's duality-based consciousness. It is nondual, and yet in its presence, it also has a subtle energetic resonance that is commonly referred to as nonduality with qualities, or *saguna Brahman*. This subtle energetic resonance is primarily why the nondual presence manifests in our body as lustrous illumination.

Mirroring that involves our evolving-self, is based on resonant energy that can flow between us and others, and transmits information. Nondual mirroring is based on subtle resonant energy that is an entrainment that results in us recognizing what is already interior to us.[27] Even though nondual consciousness is an innate part of us, unless it is uncovered through nondual

---

[26] This activates our brain's social engagement system (Porges) that enables us to be open and receptive to contact with other people.

[27] The basic premise of Kashmiri Shaivism's Doctrine of Recognition, pratyabhijna, is that uncovering our unchanging-self is about recognizing this pre-existent essence of our existence within us.

mirroring, it often remains submerged to varying degrees, and is never fully realized.

In the nondual mirroring process, there is a transmission of subtle feeling-tones or qualities of being, that help us develop greater self-awareness. The subtle qualities of being, are commonly transmitted in a spiritual setting.[28] Like parent-to-child transmission, "direct transmission" (*saktipata*) occurs when a spiritual teacher empowers the student by modeling a state of consciousness, so the student can attune to this same state within themselves.

While direct transmission is an exchange of energy and consciousness between our self and another awakened person (inter-personally), the transmission also happens within us (intra-personally) when our evolving-self uncovers and awakens to the unified consciousness that is already within us.[29] Simply awakening within our body, to the conscious space that is already there, timelessly present, is the most direct way to uncover a body experience of unified consciousness.

This is not a new understanding. The Kashmiri Shaivism notion of the *prakasa-vimarsa* theory (from the Pratybhijna, Trika school of Shaivism) also explored a form of whole-being-embrace. This theory asserts that existence is based on the unchanging-self, as a self-shining conscious light (*prakasa*), and its ability to sustain a reflection of itself in our evolving-self (creation, *vimarsa*). Our ability to sustain both experiences at the same time, leads to autonomy or divine sovereignty (*svātantrya*).

Awakening to our unchanging-self, happens intra-personally similarly to the way we align with a spiritual teacher, and receive direct transmission. Our unchanging-self is received by the attuned evolving-self. We perceive and open to the unchanging-self by refining our senses and attuning to the subtle embodied qualities of the unified nature of our existence. This internal meeting is a nondual mirroring experience that is revealing. In the

---

[28] This chapter section borrows heavily from my book *From Trauma to Wholeness* (2023).
[29] Via our brain's self-engagement system (Siegel).

reflective presence of embodied unified consciousness, we gain a clear, undistorted perception of our evolving-self.

As children, we see our self in the reflection of the parent's presence, and from that, we become self-aware. This is as if we have been raised in a house of mirrors. Every reflection we see gives us a distorted reflection of our self. The people we are looking at, are full of injuries and distortions that they reflect back to us. It is not that the distortions we internalize are unreal, but they are not a reflection of what is authentic to us. Only when we perceive the undistorted reflection of nondual consciousness, and experience unity and wholeness, do we gain an undistorted image of our evolving-self. When we perceive the reflection of wholeness and unity, our evolving-self realizes its true innocence. We recognize the beauty of our untraumatized, authentic nature.

Every part of our evolving-self that comes into contact with our unchanging-self's "nondual mirror," feels witnessed, understood, respected, and supported. As we awaken to the experience of unified consciousness within the tissues of our body, unified consciousness becomes a mirror that reflects our evolving-self's thoughts, emotions, and sensations, without being changed itself. This is an entangled experience where the timeless nature of the unchanging-self, eliminates all distance between our sense of existing as our evolving-self and our unchanging-self, so the reflection paradoxically, becomes us.

Our existence as the infinite nature of unity awakens through the finite nature of our body. Unity emerges as the depths of our body experiences, born not in the heart of our body but as the heart of our body. (Our evolving-self feels the unchanging-self as a self-reflective perceiving presence (self-aware), or the "nondual subjectivity" that Kashmiri Shaivism describes as "pure perceiving subjectivity" - *upalabdhrta*.)

What we receive as a child, is the content of our parent's love and their unresolved emotional issues. By contrast, the reflection we perceive in the presence of unified consciousness that pervades our body and mind, is without psychological content. It is simply wholeness, and the bliss that accompanies this. The non-abandoning, non-invasive presence of our unchanging-self, does not simply communicate ordinary knowledge. It communicates essential nondual knowing. At this depth and breadth of perception, it feels like a sacred, intimate connection (*sambandha*) between our evolving-self's ongoing process and our inherently benevolent, unchanging-self. This is whole-being-embrace.

Kashmiri Shaivism's notion of the *prakasa-vimarsa* theory explains that, as our unchanging-self "reflects" our evolving-self, we progressively become autonomous (*svatantrya*) from our injuries and come to know the "nondual bliss" (*ananda*) of our unchanging-self and our environment. Unified consciousness "reflects" duality because it ultimately contains duality within it. It can be said that this is divine entanglement. Autonomy arises from the mirror-like ability of nondual consciousness to contain and reflect all things within it.

Another way of saying this is that, as we perceive our experiences in life, nondual consciousness shines its luminosity (*prakasa*) through the "psychic instrument" of our mind-body. It is as if our mind-body "is held" within the unified field of nondual consciousness, which reveals the vibrations of the pure "I Am" (unchanging-self) within the objects of our perception. In embodied nondual meditation, this experience transforms our relationship with our unresolved injuries. It empowers us to experience various dysregulated, sensory-motor elements that compose a particular trauma, within a broader perspective

In whole-being-embrace, the changing nature of our thoughts, emotions, and sensations, feel the nondual-qualities, and entrains to the stillness of its subtle resonant feeling-tones of being. In this meeting between movement and stillness, it can seem as if the pervasive presence of stillness is inviting our evolving-self into the alignment of a divine, loving embrace. This same experience can happen with other nondual-qualities of our existence, such as timelessness, unity, and that which is pervasive, nonlocal, and universal.

Embodiment of our unchanging-self, means the nature of its nondual-qualities,  is awakened within our expressions of gesture, posture, and speech. Through this whole-being-embrace, we open and become receptive to the unchanging-self's enfolded existence within our own evolving-self.

Experiencing this kind of support that we have always wanted but never received, because of other people's limitations, is tremendously healing. The mirror reflection of each chakra's nondual-qualities, enfolded within our evolving-self, transforms everything in the way of manifesting our potential.

As wholeness, our injuries experience alternative emotional, physical, and relational cues that are subtle, still, timeless, and unified in nature. When our injury "feels felt" by wholeness, it catalyzes corrective bodily experiences that re-set the nervous system. It is able to charge, discharge, and return to balance without interruption or fixation (see *chapter seven* for details).

This integrates our mental, emotional, and physical state of fragmentation so we can complete our aborted healthy responses. Our habitual reactions and fear of those reactions, cease to be a vicious cycle that prevents us from responding to intense experiences in a healthy, empowered way. Our natural fear response to threats, stops holding us hostage and we become able to express our pre-trauma personal truth. We gain access to an alternative to having our choice taken away, being silenced, and overriding our healthy impulses for creating safety and self-protection. Our healthy responses that have been shut down are now able to be expressed authentically, and come to full completion naturally (self-paced termination).

The whole-being-embrace, is a central approach to healing and awakening that is explored here, with each of the chakras. Some of the most immediate consequences of this intimate relationship is that it gives us a feeling of belonging (1st chakra), choice (2nd chakra), confidence (3rd chakra), of being loving and lovable (4th chakra), authentic truth (5th chakra), and the completeness that accompanies knowing (6th chakra).


THE UNIFYING EFFECT OF WHOLENESS

As explained, the nondual mirror (*prakasa*) that unified consciousness provides, is a body experience of wholeness. Wholeness has an integrating and unifying influence upon us, and all of creation (*vimarsa*). It might be said that this influence moves us through evolution and partly explains evolution's speed in creating our human complexity. Quantum physics concurs with this understanding (David Bohm and Karl Pribram). It claims there is a wholeness in nature that underlies our evolution towards greater complexity and simplicity.

Bohm found that there is a quantum potential in nature that maintains an unbroken wholeness, within the ever-changing fluctuations inherent to matter. This wholeness is a "centrating" principle in nature that resists entropy and disorder (quantum coherence). In this process, our individuality is made more meaningful by our awakening to the sense of connectedness inherent to unified consciousness.

In embodied nondual meditation, we discover this vital cohesive influence in a profoundly personal way, because our body is our most personal center. It is where we heal what is injured, feel the reverence for the sacredness of life, and experience the bliss that accompanies wholeness. We feel unity acting from within by awakening a body experience of our essential ground-of-being, as an unchanging presence.

This has a deep, unifying influence that enhances our propensity towards maturity, interconnected complexity, and the beautiful simplicity of wholeness. Our personal body experience of this, is an integrating force. It draws us into a divine entanglement that invites a transformative paradigm shift. The effect this has on the collective consciousness of society is vital for our well-being and our survival as a species.


REFINING THE SENSES & ATTUNEMENT

Meditation is a way of training us to access progressively more subtle states of consciousness through refining our senses and subtle attunement. When we meditate, we tend to access experiences that progress from gross, subtle, causal, witness, to a formless nondual state of unity. As our senses become refined, we progress from perceiving the obvious to perceiving the space between the particles, to perceiving the particles themselves are pervaded by space.[30]

---

[30] Each state of consciousness shows up as a body experience: 1. waking state is accompanied by the "gross consciousness," 2. the dreaming state is accompanied by the "subtle consciousness," and 3. the formless sleep state is accompanied by the "causal consciousness." Each of these states of consciousness are modes of experience that progress from a gross experience, to a more refined subtle experience, to a very subtle or "causal" experience.

Vedanta Hinduism claims there are two more states of consciousness: 4. "nondual consciousness" (*turiya*) and 5. "nondual wholeness" (*turiyatita,* One Taste). "Nondual wholeness" is the ever-present ground of all states, which I call "whole-self." We can experience any of these five states at any stage of our emotional maturity. We simply interpret the state through the lens of the stage of development we are at.

The "unchanging-self" is, in part, an expression of causal consciousness in that it is a formless awareness. Here, it is the "with attributes" aspect of unity/Brahman (saguna Brahman) and, therefore, a more personalized experience of unity (conscious emptiness). Yet, the "unchanging-self" is most clearly experienced as "nondual wholeness" (*turiyatita*) in that our evolving-self's experiences seem to arise out of unity and wholeness, and enfolded within every particle of experience we find unified consciousness. This is in alignment with the Tantric understanding of Shiva and Shakti in divine embrace, and where *nirvana* (*purusa*) and *samsara* (*prakriti*) can be found within each other. That is, within each expression of our mundane lives we find unified consciousness, and unified consciousness contains everything (Kashmiri Shaivism, Nagarjuna).

Usually, the state of nondual wholeness (*turiyatita*) represents a state where even the sense of the "I" who is witnessing disappears. Yet when nondual wholeness is a body experience of self, a paradox emerges. The distinction between the witness and the witnessed dissolves, and yet we remain aware that these expressions of existence still exist. We do not collapse duality into nonduality, so we remain self-aware, aware that we are aware of both dimensions of our whole-self, while recognizing they are simultaneously one enfolded reality. Because the unchanging-self has traits common with several states of unified consciousness, it can be considered to truly be an integral state.

A central consequence of the unchanging-self's *embodied nondual wholeness* is the transcendent emphasis on renunciation, disidentification, and dispassion toward our evolving-self's experiences is no longer needed. Our evolving-self's experiences become the source of our transformation. Instead of only becoming an observer and not the observed, we open to both and transform passions (and injury) through recognizing that within authentic passion we always find nondual wholeness. This co-existence results in a whole-being-embrace experience.

The practice of accessing the unchanging-self as a unified dimension of existence, can only be felt if we are attuned to the most subtle level of experience. As we refine our senses in embodied nondual meditation, we come to recognize this most subtle essence-of-self as an experience in our body. Nondual body experience (*saguna Brahman*) is a "quasi-material" aspect of the human body, which is neither entirely physical or metaphysical. This contrasts with the understanding of the body that has dominated Western philosophy and psychology.

Descriptions of this quasi-material aspect of existence in yoga, became prominent with the Tantric movement in the Middle Ages. Perceiving our unchanging-self involves sensations that are not typically perceived by the normal range of sensory awareness, but with the practice of attunement it is often very easily uncovered. Uncovering it involves a very subtle, fine perception of consciousness involving opening to an atmosphere or feeling-tone of sensation.

We learn with all our senses. All of us learn in different ways and are more aware of some senses than others. Some of us learn best through hearing, and others of us through sight, touch, smell, or taste. Of course, there are the less obvious senses, including the sense of direction, balance, weight, and our "interoceptive senses," and latent sensory abilities.[31] The interoceptive senses participate with our intuition, which also receives information from unity consciousness. Our interoceptive senses play a large role in giving us access to the subtle feeling-tones of unity and wholeness.

In embodied nondual meditation, we begin to notice the nondual-qualities, such as the stillness, emptiness, openness, timelessness, unity and wholeness, that are inherent to all of the nondual-qualities of unified consciousness. We perceive this as a subtle, unchanging presence of our ground-of-being, where, due to its holographic nature, all the nondual-qualities exist

---

[31] Based on the ventral branch of the vagal nerve sending information from our viscera to the brain. It is likely that the interoceptive senses activate our self-engagement system of the brain (Siegel), facilitating our perception and communion with unified consciousness.

simultaneously. As we refine our sensory perception of this unchanging presence, often what stands out most significantly are all five layers of the aspects of self, and each of the primary chakra qualities of our self. We open to the feeling that we exist as these nondual aspects of existence.

In meditation, we notice that developing finer and finer distinctions in sensation, allows us to feel how the stillness of our unchanging presence-of-being (with no parts), differs from the movement and fixations of our thoughts and emotions (the parts of our evolving-self). We also notice patterns of how we perceive and respond, and if this involves habitual effort or effortlessness. We begin to notice that the more our effort is habitual, the less sensitivity we have to how we perceive and respond in the moment. It inhibits our ability to sense our self with accuracy. Discerning these fine distinctions refines our senses.

Our discernment of the subtle presence-of-being, allows our sense of self to be represented in finer detail in the neuronal 'maps' of the nervous system. By awakening a body experience of the stillness of our unchanging-self, we make more refined observations. This allows the map, and experience of our self and our environment, to become more detailed, and clearer to read. This is important information to have so we can learn how to grow autonomy from our source of suffering (inherent to our evolving-self). It also allows us to perceive the entangled communion between our changing and unchanging-self, in whole-being-embrace.

Refining the senses is simple, and it yet takes practice to learn about the art of attunement to the most subtle body experience of self as unity. The following brief outline offers some clues about the art of attunement. The inexperienced meditator may benefit from some initial, in-person guidance, to unpack details of what these practices actually entail.

In contemplation and meditation, we engage in practices, like the following one, based on Judith Blackstone's Realization Process® method, called "Distinction between Matter, Energy, and Fundamental Consciousness." (She appropriately calls the unchanging-self, "fundamental consciousness"):

100

Sit with support (from the ground or a chair) so your back is straight and vertical (also you can practice this as a slow walking meditation, or lying down). Take time to savor the feeling that you exist as (these experiences can take practice to feel):

1. Physical matter — such as flesh, muscle, bone, blood, nerves, etc. Savor any sense of the density and quality of each one, however briefly or deeply you need.

2. Now experience yourself as energy - such as streaming, pulsing, vibration, motion within your body... Savor feeling this inside your body: all the way through to the back, all the way down to the bottom, and all the way out to the sides... feel the movement of your breath flowing through your body...

3. Now experience yourself as the stillness of fundamental consciousness.... Savor how this is the basis of your individual wholeness, and the basis of your oneness with all of life... Notice how the constructed, imagined barrier between self and your environment naturally dissolves.

As best as you can, attune to how each of these three aspects of your self feels different in your body, and how each changes your relationship with your self and your environment. By feeling which parts of your body are easier to inhabit (physically, energetically, and as unity), you reveal your particular pattern of where you have self-contact (openness) and self-protection (constriction, frozenness, numbness, collapse).

It takes some practice to refine and awaken the subtle experience of openness, but with attunement, it becomes much more tangible. The experience of the unified field of consciousness, the essential ground of your being, as Blackstone says, arises:

"...naturally, without effort, when we reach a degree of openness. It is deeper than the physical, energetic, and conceptual levels of our being, and when we attune to it, we experience it pervading our whole body and our environment at the same time... With practice we can feel how our consciousness is becoming conscious of itself, and awakening to itself not as an object separate from our self, but as an experience of who we are."

The more we know our self as the pervasive stillness of our unified field of consciousness, she adds, the more freely, deeply and fluidly, all of the movement of life -emotion, thought, and sensation- flows through us.

One way we can notice this is through conscious breathing. Conscious breathing is about noticing the sensation of breath moving through the body. Sensation is composed of energy. When we learn to allow the energy that composes the sensation of breathing to flow freely, we set a precedent for the energy that composes our mental and emotional life to flow freely also. Our mental and emotional energy is more supported to learn to flow more authentically, without fixation. When we habitually limit our natural inhale or exhale, we feel less, and our thoughts become more fixated.

To facilitate feeling the sensation of breath moving through the body freely, close your eyes and focus inwards. Take time to practice breathing without any effort on the inhale and exhale (so there is no constriction inhaling or exhaling; not more shallowly but effortlessly, without the slightest constriction on the inhale or exhale). When this is familiar, feel the openness and space that your breath flows through. Feel the continuity of the sense of openness, and any sense of wholeness that arises...

To deepen this practice once this is familiar: without leaving your internal experience, slowly open your eyes, without looking to find the objects in your environment. Instead, find the feeling of space that is pervading you and these objects (including people) at the same time. Again, do this without leaving your sense of inward contact, through attunement to your sense of pervasive space within your body.

We can also refine our senses with the following practice (take time between sentences to savor and refine):

1. Practice relaxing. Relaxing involves four primary ingredients: 1) *Softening* habitual constrictions on the

inhale or exhale. Savoring the sense of letting go or dissolving the constrictions throughout the body (including areas that feel frozen, numb, and collapsed. Let each of these areas feel support from beneath you, and your back. Savor any sense of relaxation and opennness... 2) *Settling* the content of your experience (sensation) within the body... 3) *Rest* the content of your experience on the ground (metaphorically). Feel and let go of constrictions that lift you away from the ground, especially on your inhale... 4) *Open* to a clear perception of unobstructed inner space. Notice if you constrict and pull upward, hold your body upright, or constrict inward, away from the periphery of the body, and invite your self to relax and open. As you relax and open to the internal space of your body. Feel the continuity of the sense of openness, and any sense of wholeness that arises... (Make sure you don't collapse as you settle. Relax into the feeling openness instead). Breathe without effort...

2.  Savor the feeling of having more inner space to breathe easily and live in. Attune to the feeling of internal openness and space in your whole body. (Note: there are specific locations in the body called "functional diaphragms" that tend to accumulate more tension. *Chapter seven* offers a detailed description of these locations, which are important places to focus on relaxing, as a way to deepen the current practice.)

3.  Attune to and savor the feeling of breath flowing through any part of the body that feels open. (The more we relax, the more inner-space breath can flow through.) This can involve refining the practice of consciously breathing with the least effort possible.[32]

---

[32] We pay particular attention to the breath because the respiratory system is the only system in the body that usually is involuntary but can also be voluntarily controlled. The breath also very effectively regulates all the other autonomic systems, including brain function. Effortless breathing is a simple and powerful way to restore balance in the nervous system. It changes the chronic habit of hyperventilation (chest breathing) to diaphragmatic (belly)

4.  With very fine attunement, feel the open space through which your breath flows. The more relaxed and open you are, the more unified your body feels. (Even bones can feel open, deeper than their solidness.) Take time to attune to the feeling that this internal space is all one space. Feel the sense of uniform continuity between all the parts of your body. Deeply receive this feeling and savor any sense of unity or wholeness that may emerge.

5.  Feel how this unified inner-space is not an empty void, and is conscious. Feel that you are conscious everywhere in your body, as one body and one unchanging presence. Attune to the unchanging presence and any feeling that you are inhabiting your whole body as your essential ground-of-being. (Feel this presence as the spark of you, that you were born with, and that you still feel now. Feel the openness, pureness, and innocence of this essence and any sense of wholeness.) Savor...

Each of these steps take some practice. These practices are volitional attunements to help us open to what is an actual experience of our unchanging-self. (Don't worry if initially it is difficult to discern if you are imagining, or actually feeling something. It will become clear with practice.) In practice, we continually refine our senses to awaken awareness and uncover what is already there, deeper than the impermanent nature of our evolving experience. As mentioned, as our senses become refined, we progress from perceiving the obvious to perceiving the space between the particles, to perceiving the particles themselves are pervaded by space. (Sample meditations are available in the meditation library on my website.)

We need to open within our body to perceive the unchanging presence within the space that pervades us, in order for this self-arising realization to occur. We realize we *are* this presence. Little by little we learn to regularly stay in contact with, and then live as our inner, unwavering, self-illuminated presence.

---

breathing. It also teaches us about effortlessness (see Appendix Two, third stage).

The above practices evoke a spontaneous realization, not something we create. It appears as our basic nature that emerges as our essential ground-of-being.[33] At this most subtle level, it could be said, that this is where we can experience the electron's particle as joined with the utter stillness of the wave. At this point, our experience of self (thoughts, emotions, and sensations) enters into communion with unified consciousness, and awakens as a luminous presence in our body. Many options for healing profound emotional injuries become available at this point.

As we deepen our familiarity with this timeless, unified experience, we will find that it will change how we relate to our self and other (to people, situations, substance, etc.). With practice, we grow a sense of remaining inside the whole body, while we experience the continuity of space pervading us and everything in our surroundings. We can access a paradox of remaining internally referent, and unified with all that is, at the same time. It is experienced to be universal and cosmic, and yet it can also be felt to have specific locations in space.

Out of our experience of wholeness, valuable healing expressions spontaneously arise, such as a profound sense of belonging, compassion, and grace. We are able to express pre-trauma responses to feeling emotionally injured (explored in *chapter five*). Our authentic, spontaneous responses have the characteristic of being clear and crisp expressions that feel natural. As a result, we learn to negotiate our encounter with our present experience, without selling out what the injured part of us feels.

---

[33] I have found Mark Dyezkowski's understanding, helpful. He comments that perception of an unchanging consciousness, as a presence of our own being, is a luminous "emission" that reflects the "activity of consciousness emitting itself within and through itself. Thus, it is also quiescent "at rest within itself." In a sense, nothing is produced other than itself, nothing is taking place, and so it is in a perpetual state of absolute potential" (Tantraloka, translated by Mark Dyezkowski, 2023).

An important result of refining our senses is that our senses become unified. Our senses are conscious and communicate information that has an organizing and integrating function. Our sensory experience results in a flow of information that composes and shapes our conscious mind. As we inhabit our body as unified consciousness, all our senses increasingly function as a whole, more of the time.

This means the senses that compose our evolving sense of self's emotions, thoughts, and sensations, arise from a single source of understanding. This is a unification of our senses that allows us to experience with our whole body and mind. In this unified state, our perception is not a result of our changing experience within us or with others. Our perceptions seem to arise out of unity, stillness, conscious space, and wholeness. Our mind, emotions, sensations, and the wisdom aspects of our self all come online at the same time.

Our senses do not need to stop perceiving individual vibrational patterns. Each moment, as Blackstone (2011) says, "occurs as a single, multifaceted vibrational pattern that registers in all of our senses at once." When our senses are unified, we have a whole body, local experience of unity, which is also inherently non-local. This unified sensory awakening is an expression of how consciousness can be both local and non-local, governed by both the electron's particle and its wave. One expression of this may be how neuroscience now recognizes that consciousness depends not only on particular local region of the brain, but also on its interconnectedness and non-local unity within the whole brain. We are capable of perceiving individual experiences and also the holographic nature of, for instance, how a branch of a plant mirrors the form of the whole plant, and how each of the body's parts tell the story of the whole body.[34]

---

[34] One possible explanation for how our consciousness and senses become unified comes from quantum physics. Quantum science suggests that what increases consciousness is the relational nature of electron waves overlapping. When our experience of unity begins to emerge in embodied nondual meditation, it seems to be a result of more electron waves overlapping. One explanation for this is that our electron's overlapping energy-fields cause our

When we perceive the holographic nature of experience, our perception shifts from individual expressions, to the underlying unified essence of our nature and of the environment. Rather than only an individual creative thought or expression, we also become able to feel the essence of these aspects of our self as potentialities. We experience our self and our environment as a single continuous presence of awareness, love (or bliss), and physical sensation. Contact is inherent to this continuity of relational holism. Our conflicted emotions (state of fragmentation) are perceived within the context of this relational holism, and in the process, they are "metabolized" and integrated into our psyche.

This can suggest that a nondual-quality of self infers information to our evolving-self, about unity. This can influence how the molecules and cells in our body take shape. A central expression of this shape is that our experience of unified consciousness allows us to maintain dynamic balance and no longer respond habitually to what we experience. It allows us to have complex and intense interactions with others, without interfering with our sense of wholeness. We maintain our simplicity and integrity, so our intense thoughts and emotions do not carry the sense of emergency that they previously did.

Of central importance is how the nondual-quality of self shapes our body's senses by unifying them. As we embody the bliss layer of our being, we begin to perceive with our whole body and mind, with each layer of our self (physical, emotional, mental, wisdom). In this way, the flow of sensory information that composes and shapes our conscious mind is unified.

Before we embark on our journey through the chakras, we will explore how the nervous system participates in establishing a sense of unity and wholeness in our body and mind. In discussion of the chakras in *chapter five*, each chakra/stage begins with a brief look at how that stage correlates with how our nervous

---

consciousness to broaden to the point that it is not reducible to individual characteristics. The more the relationship between the waves of each electron is not reduced to an individual expression, or activity of the vibrating molecules of our body, our experience of unity awakens.

system responds to, and recovers from what we experience. This next section is an overview of this unfolding process, and provides a general roadmap of how this occurs.

REVIEW OF NERVOUS SYSTEM'S 7 RESPONSES TO THREAT

In the last twenty-five years, the trauma therapist Peter Levine has developed a method of healing trauma. His method describes how the nervous system works in a way that reflects the effect trauma has on us. This focus on the effects of trauma on the nervous system, lies in contrast to examining the energy dynamics (charge-discharge, balance) underlying our perceptions and responses, as found in somatic psychology and yoga.

The science behind how the brain and nervous system work is always changing, so making any definitive statements is only based on a best guess and theories about how things work. Yet, I believe that much of Levine's approach introduces very valuable information that deserves elaboration.

Levine made a fascinating discovery about the way animals in the wild recover from injuries. He noticed that because animals are able to release energy that surges through their body when in danger, they are able to move through the overwhelming event and easily release the trauma from their system. By contrast, humans have higher brain functions, which cause us to think about our trauma, stir up our emotions, and recycle or perpetuate post-trauma symptoms. In doing so, we neo-cortically override the body's natural impulse, and our system does not re-set to a dynamic state of balance as easily. Understanding how wild animals process trauma, can help us overcome how we sabotage our own recovery from emotional injuries.

Keep in mind that all of the following stages can occur on a very subtle, often unconscious level, or more overtly and dramatically. All of these survival responses are healthy ways our nervous system helps protect us. I have divided Levine's description of how we respond to challenge and threat into seven primary stages. In the following description, I depict two scenarios. One is where the stages represent how we deal with a traumatic event. The next represents how we deal with experience in general:

Trauma or distress:
1. Arrest
2. Orient
3. Flight (withdraw) Fight (resist)
4. Freeze
5. Stuck
6. Collapse
7. Death (Death in this context, refers primarily to the psychological "death" that happens when we fail to cope with what we are experiencing and, as a result, become overwhelmed and fragment.)

Generally speaking, as shown in the sequence above, after discerning what we are dealing with in the "arrest" stage, we get "oriented" with what we want to do about our experience. Then, is stage three, we apply skills to implement our strategy. Psychologically, this means we learn skills that enable us to establish the degree of contact and autonomy in relationship that we need to feel safe and supported. This can mean learning how to skillfully withdraw from contact, or resist another person's agenda and attitude (healthy boundaries). If our strategy does not work, we panic, become dumbfounded, and experience a moment of "freeze" and immobilization, in stage four.

The freeze state is associated with the residual crippling effects of trauma. It is when we dissociate and are temporarily unable to move, have a "deer in the headlights" look, and we become spaced-out or become speechless, in fear. Some of us also feel disconnected from our body. What causes humans to become fixated in trauma, is that our protective plan of action continues to occur in our brain, and is perpetuated and enhanced even when there is no actual threat. If no solution presents itself, things get worse, and we feel seriously stuck, collapse, and "die" (psychologically, this means we fail to successfully cope, lose integration, and chronically fragment).[35]

But if our coping and protective strategies, and skills (such as fleeing/withdrawing or fighting/resisting physically, emotionally, and mentally) for dealing with what we experience, are successful in stage three, it is not necessary for us to freeze, in stage four.[36] Instead, stage four becomes about effective application of our skills and releasing the energy we accumulated in stage three. We then proceed to stage five, where we further discharge the excess energy and open to the feeling of relief and satisfaction. In stage six, we fully integrate the experience and come to completion. Finally, in stage seven, we return to wholeness (more commonly well-being). This alternative sequence is as follows:

4. Climax
5. Discharge
6. Balance
7. Wholeness

Our nervous system's seven stages of responding to a challenge, such as the symptoms that result from relationship injury and trauma, is holographic or fractal in nature. Its basic

---

[35] One of the reasons why we keep encountering the same challenges in life, is that because our psyche and body are looking for ways to complete a plan of action (so we can discharge the bound energy we harbor in the body), our unconscious mind continually places us in situations that are similar to the original trauma. What we are unconsciously looking for is a way to implement our plan of action, and complete the movement back to safety. As mentioned, this is what Freud called "repetition compulsion."

Because we lose our ability to release the energy charge in our system, our body and mind become increasingly sensitive to being injured, and we tend to accumulate more and more traumas. We may switch from one abusive relationship to the next, or we have the same conflict with our partner as had with our parents. These are post-trauma symptoms of our incomplete plans of action that continue to run in our system long after the original trauma.

[36] As humans, we often override the shaking and trembling that helps us release this energy charge. This lack of release leaves us with an incomplete ability to take action and with too much bound-up energy still going round and round in our body-mind system.

expression is mirrored in all aspects of life. In *chapter five*, I introduce how this manifests in the six models, discussed in *chapter two*.

When our body-mind system becomes fixated and does not release and re-set, the residual energy persists in the body and creates a wide variety of symptoms. We all know people who seem to be trapped in one of the seven stages as a result of unresolved injuries (arrest, orient, flight-withdraw, fight-resist, freeze, stuck, collapse).

Some of us seem to always be in a state of arrest, evaluating the reality of our situation but never able to take the next step. Others of us are perpetually in a state of getting oriented, trying to discern what choices to make but always doubting our discernment. Many of us are in an ongoing state of withdrawal, hiding deep within, and are unable to take up room in our relationships. Or, we are unreceptive, resistant, assertively repulse, or push away what we experience. Then, there are those of us who continually look and feel, frozen. The state of collapse that is accompanied by an enduring sense of resignation, defeat, hopelessness, submission, and shutdown is also common.

Often, these survival responses and symptoms of injury hide out just under the surface, and rear their sabotaging power when we are distressed. The symptoms represent the way we organize our self in order to contain or control the undischarged residual energy we harbor, due to intense experiences that overwhelm us. Embodied nondual meditation helps us refine our senses, so we can clearly perceive our habitual coping strategies and injury symptoms. Then we can come into whole-being-embrace and heal our injuries.

# CHAPTER FIVE: CHAKRAS AS A HERO'S JOURNEY

UNBALANCED CHAKRA & CHILD DEVELOPMENT STRUGGLES

Many models of healing explore how chakras are a helpful roadmap for us to make sense of our experiences, and progress spiritually. When a chakra is unbalanced it reflects our evolving-self's suffering. However, the simple act of energetically balancing the chakra and experiencing nonduality falls short of resolving the emotional issues that caused the loss of balance.

Injury originally happens in relationship, and life itself is relational in nature. Consequently, drawing upon John Bowlby's (1969) "attachment theory," Margaret Mahler's (1975) model of "separation-individuation," and Murray Bowen's (1978) "family systems theory," provide us with some of the most relevant relationship guidelines for healing. What we find in these models of relationship, is that the central issue of all conflicts is the quality of contact we have (with our self and other), and how we can maintain our autonomy while in contact. This dynamic is what allows us to establish a healthy, secure bond in relationship (to our self and other).

Mahler's separation-individuation model looks at the process whereby a child separates from the caregiver, and thereby develops a sense of personal identity and autonomy with healthy interdependence. Attachment theory is based on a similar process of separation, and focuses on continuing relatedness and establishing a sense of inner security. The dynamics found in these models form the basis of family systems theory in psychology, and reveal how these emotional struggles show up in family dynamics and adult relationships. Collectively, these models go to the heart of what is involved in suffering in general, relationship trauma in particular, and the primary emotional issues involved in our recovery. What these models lack is an understanding of how the most fundamental nature of existence, and of our self, as found in unified consciousness, can contribute to the healing process.

*Chapter five* is informed by Bowlby, Mahler, and Bowen's models, in conjunction with yoga theory and meditation practice. Every strength or injury, associated with each stage of child development, is commonly revealed experientially in embodied meditation. For example, we may perceive insecurities within our thoughts, emotions, and physical sensations, about our safety and our sense of belonging. These are expressions of "symbiotic stage" issues of child development and the corresponding first chakra imbalances.

*Chapter five* describes how, in embodied nondual meditation, we do not transcend these emotional issues but instead expose them to our essential unified ground-of-being (nondual mirroring). In doing this, we honor many of the principles espoused by Bowlby, Mahler, and Bowen, yet we involve wholeness and unity in the process. This approach allows our responses to what we experience, to evolve and become less habitual and more mature, without transcending the underlying injury. In this way, our states of consciousness, that progress from gross, subtle, causal, witness, nondual, to nondual wholeness, enable us to evolve to the next stage of maturity.

We develop emotional autonomy from our injuries by listening to them with an open heart and the broader perspective, that wholeness and unity provide. Our injuries feel witnessed, understood, and respected in a way that our injured parents were unable to provide. The sensory (subtle), motor (stillness), temporal (timelessness), and spatial (unity) reality that our injury encounters (in whole-being-embrace), allows healing to prevail and awakening to occur.

## Prepping for the Journey

The descriptions of each of the chakras in *chapter five* begin with, and are placed within the context of, all the other parallel models/ontologies: 1) how the nervous system responds to intense challenges, 2) the symbolic level of employing subtle yoga practices, 3) a stage of our child development, 4) how we relate to others as an adult. Each chakra is explored in its state of imbalance (evolving-self) and balance (nondual-qualities/unchanging-self). After introducing these parallel models in each stage, a thorough description of each chakra is presented: name, location, symbolic level, emotional level, the chakra's hyper-hypo expressions, and healing suggestions.[37]

I hope to guide you, as a reader, through the descriptions in each of the chakras described in *chapter five*, while inviting you to note how any of the issues involved relate to you personally. You can then go back and explore the section in *chapter four*, "Refining the Senses & Attunement," to use the chakra description as a guide to designing your own contemplative meditation practice. Look to discern how the principles in each of the models are related to each other, and how they relate to you. The adept meditator will have little difficulty with this process, yet most of us can benefit from some initial in-person guidance.

It is fascinating to recognize how we each carry wounds in our body-mind systems that can be traced to our child development injuries. In reading the following pages, we begin to see how each chakra can support us to heal our original injuries in whole-being-embrace. It is important to remember that our caretaker's limitations were based on their own injuries, and are in no way a reflection of our true worth. Avoid getting caught up in blame. Yet, allow your self to have all your authentic feelings about what happened. With your healing, commend your self for breaking the familial legacy of limitation and injury.

### Symbolic Level Practices

The descriptions of our Hero's Journey in this chapter provide a roadmap. It orients us, helps us understand what we feel in meditation, and how it can guide us in our healing. The roadmap allows us to discern the particular stage of growth where we were injured most deeply, as well as the nondual-quality of self it is associated with. It is important to note that in the chakra descriptions offered here, much of the information about the "Symbolic Level," such as the color, visual shapes, and mantra

---

[37] The last two holographic models discussed on chapter two (5. The nervous systems stages of healing, 6. Yoga), are located in the Appendices One and Two.

sounds, varies depending upon the yoga tradition. (Hinduism's ancient scriptures, called Vedas, mention chakras, as do ancient Buddhist and Jain texts. Each one has its own unique view.)

The "Symbolic Level" offers a variety of practices, such as *mantra* sound, *yantra* visualization of a shape, and element (Earth, water, etc.). These practices provide results that can only be felt as a supportive resource, if we are attuned to the most subtle level of experience. I believe the wealth of these subtle supportive resources provided by the yoga tradition, is often misunderstood, overlooked, and considered to be irrelevant to our emotional growth in the Western mental health paradigm. This is because it does not understand the subtlety of its expression. Alternately, we too often engage in Symbolic Level practices without first refining our senses. As a result, the traits, such as the sounds, elements, or images, remain abstract symbols in our imagination only. We miss the opportunity to access their full potential as an actual supportive body-felt experience, carrying information that our specific injury can benefit from.

Symbolic Level practices can be powerful sources of support because they are designed to have a direct impact on our conscious and subconscious mind. Their true meaning and power are revealed as we refine our senses. Each of the subtle sensory experiences of Symbolic Level practices, provides supportive resources to awaken us to the nondual-qualities, such as the chakras in their balanced state.

The descriptions of the supportive resources in each chakra stage in *chapter five*, is not comprehensive. I do not address all the symbolic aspects of each chakra, such as the associated deity, mudra, mantras. These descriptions are found in most other books on chakras (sometimes superficially). Their full meaning and relevance to our growth as a source of support, is quite fascinating but goes beyond the scope of this book. When you feel drawn to the supportive resources found in practices associated with the symbols, honor this. It can contribute to the primary focus of experiencing whole-being-embrace, and awakening to the spirituality of accessing a deeper and broader experience of your self and your environment.

On our journey through evolution, keep the following progression in mind. We begin at the first chakra/stage, which involves our arrival on the planet and the affirmation of our birthright to exist and belong. This foundational sense of existence allows us to progress to the second chakra/stage, where we assert our right to take up space and make choices that resonate with us, embracing the joy this brings. Establishing this sense of security empowers us in the third chakra/stage to manifest our choices and interests, fostering confidence in our abilities. With this support, we move to the fourth chakra/stage, where we open ourselves to unconditional love for who we are. This love helps us engage in relationships that honor mutual respect. Our sense of unconditional love supports us to progress to the fifth chakra/stage where we express our most authentic truths. This expression allows us to be seen without self-doubt and shame and encourages us to view others as they are, without blame. These realizations awaken the sixth chakra/stage's deep sense of inner-knowing and acceptance of ourselves and the world around us (even if we disagree). With this heightened awareness, we enter a state of wholeness in the seventh chakra/stage, where our evolving-self is fully integrated with the bliss and expansive perspective offered by unity consciousness.

From this perspective, the end goal of our evolution is not the dissolution of our evolving-self's ego, but rather its awakening into authenticity. The tension inherent to our evolving process becomes an enfolded part of divine play.

**NERVOUS SYSTEM: Arrest stage**
**CHILD: Symbiotic stage**
**ADULT: Honeymoon phase; Self-Awareness in relationship**
**CHAKRA: "Root Chakra,"** *muladhara,* **meaning root support,**
**Unified nature of our self as "Existence"**

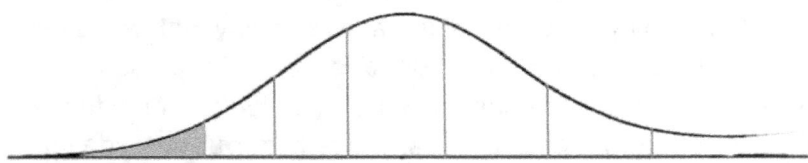

**NERVOUS SYSTEM**

**Arrest:** We initially stop in our tracks when we notice a disruption and go into a state of arrest. We can compare this to a deer in the woods who is living its mundane life. Like the wild deer, when we notice something is significantly different from our mundane life in the environment that warrants attention, we stop what we are doing (arrest) to notice what is happening. The focus here is primarily on self-awareness in relation to our environment (other).

**Energetics**

The first stage is about new beginnings of any kind. In the first stage of how we engage with the present moment, we show up, become present, and "feel into" it, so we can become familiar and understand it. Before responding, we look to understand what we are dealing with in our situation and do a reality check (with our partner/friend, the situation, or the moment). We question, "Is it real and what is its nature?" and "Where am I in this reality?" We become more grounded in the reality of the experience.

If we race through the first stage too quickly, we never have enough self-awareness to be grounded in the reality of what we are dealing with. Out of our excitement to engage with life, we might energetically charge into a project or relationship without vetting it sufficiently to see if it will meet our needs. Yet, if because of our memories of past failures, we spend too much time gathering information, we can get bogged down over analyzing and end up losing the momentum we need to proceed.

As a "Hero" on our life's journey, the first stage starts with our mundane life, which is governed by our habits of mind and body associated with our evolving-self's ego. In the movie *Star Wars* this is depicted by Luke Skywalker, as a farm boy, before he takes on the universe. From our mundane state, immersed in our habits of mind and body (including trauma), we are introduced to a new situation that can potentially interrupt our everyday life.

In *Star Wars,* Princess Leia's holographic message to Obi Wan Kenobi asks Luke to join in the quest. At this time, like Luke, in response to the call to adventure, we are faced with basic questions that range from, "do I have to deal with what is being asked of me?", "can I survive if I don't respond?", "do I belong where I am?", "am I safe?", "am I wanted here?", "can I take care of myself here?", "will I be abandoned, or attacked, if I ignore the call?" As we shall see, these are many of the same concerns we have as an infant.

When we are presented with a problem and a challenge, it is the seed for us to begin to question the life we live. This is our "call to adventure." At this point (which is the nervous system's "arrest" stage), we slow down or stop, to do a reality check and gather information. We examine who we are, how we live, and why it is we are satisfied or unsatisfied, with life as it is. We compare our habitual life to the challenge at hand and, in the process, develop self-awareness and gather information about the challenge.

118

Energy increases as we bring our attention to a situation to gather information. The image below shows what happens to our energy and consciousness when we gather information either too quickly ("A," without thoroughly vetting the situation to determine if it is suitable, accurate, or valid) and when we gather information too slowly ("B," not bringing our attention to the situation adequately to discern). (Of course, these kinds of interruptions can occur with any chakra):

**Image #13: Too Quick & Too Slow**

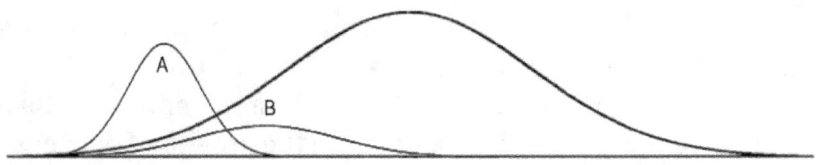

### CHILD DEVELOPMENT: The "Symbiotic" Stage, 0-5 Months

This style of relating lasts about five months (but emotionally reoccurs throughout life).[38] What this means is our experience as a child centers on internal bodily comforts, the satisfaction of needs (survival, a sense of belonging, safety, cared for, etc.) and the reduction of unpleasant tensions (self-regulation). It is out of gratification or frustration of these needs that the infant begins to differentiate pleasurable experiences from painful experiences.

As a child in the first stage, we become more self-aware in the context of our parent-child unity. The "call to adventure" for the child at this stage is the growing self-awareness that plants the seed for us to realize we are not the same as our parent. We emerge from the merged state of symbiotic unity with the parent.

As an infant, we initially alleviate concerns about our arrival and our survival by establishing a secure sense of attachment

---

[38] Since both Autistic and Symbiotic stages are based on self-other merging, I combine them (as "Symbiotic stage"), much like Mahler did in her later understanding.

with our parent. This involves the feeling of unity with the parent as a non-verbal experience of reliable connection. This is reinforced by contact between our own and other people's eyes, intimate holding, the scent of hair and skin, and tone of voice.

When this contact is not supportive for whatever reason, we constrict these aspects of sensory perception, and we fragment. We are forced from a state of comfort (symbiosis) and are faced with the call to action. This is when our nervous system engages survival responses (flight, fight, freeze, collapse). (Interestingly, in meditation, we employ some of the same senses, such as the sense of feeling held - whole-being-embrace- pleasant smells and sounds, etcetera, to help us come out of fragmentation and become more integrated and whole.)

Mutual cueing between the infant and caretaker at this stage sets up a process of relating that leads to the growth of our sense of self. If our caretakers are empathetically attuned to us, they facilitate our sense of belonging, safety, and feeling cared for. This is the stage of developing self-awareness within the context of how others relate to us. Ideally, in this process, we learn to show up and become present to our self, even in how we relate to the merged state we have with our parents. This sets the foundation for learning to have healthy boundaries in relationship, later in life.

If we do not receive empathetic attunement that gives us a sense of secure attachment, later in life, we often experience free-floating fear or panic, due to a weak sense of self and low self-esteem. We have questions such as, "Am I safe?" "Am I wanted?" "Do I have the right to be here?" "Can I be nourished?" In meditation, we learn to experience the communication between our unchanging-self's presence and our evolving-self, as a form of mutual cueing in whole-being-embrace (though our unchanging-self's presence is not an action).

Without secure attachment, later, we develop unhealthy boundaries in relationship. In our emotionally merged state, we may crave acceptance and tend to disregard or discount the differences that we have between our self and others (not show up for our own needs). Or, we may have an inability to follow rules or lack empathy for others. We may defensively grow a sense of detachment from others, and express pseudo self-sufficiency to compensate for our lack of connection. We may crave affection and yet have an inability to form lasting relationships.

## ADULT RELATIONSHIPS

The first chakra/stage correlates with the emotional issues we face at the beginning of any relationship. In an adult relationship, this occurs with our first sign of making contact with a special someone (or something) in our life. The focus is on security and establishing a secure bond in relationship, which takes a variety of forms. The "call to adventure" may be positive or not. It might be the awareness that this person is important to us, or it can be the moment we feel something about us, or the other, is wrong or painful.

To establish a secure bond as an adult, we want to know we are wanted, understood, respected, and loved or appreciated. In one sense, this involves coming to accept the life and family we incarnate into. As an adult, we want to know we are wanted, understood, respected, and loved. In one sense, this involves coming to accept the life and family we incarnate into. In this light, we attempt to resolve any issues about, for instance, being an unplanned or unwanted child. We learn to honor a deeper truth than the perception that our birth was a mistake. We learn to more fully accept that we have a birthright to exist, and that we can take up room on the planet with our presence and aliveness. This is an important feeling to have when we embark on intimate relationships.

If we realize there is trouble in paradise, or our normal way of functioning, we often fixate and can't let go of our failures, our shame, or any of the mistakes we have ever made. We face anger, sadness, and pain, and our thoughts give us the feeling that we are in a psychological neighborhood we don't want to walk in at night.

At the beginning of an adult relationship, ensuring our survival and establishing a secure bond is expressed in the falling-in-love or appreciation stage. We establish our sense of being friends or

121

a couple. Ideally, both participants are emotionally available to each other with a responsive attitude of caring and empathy. The secure bond results in a personal sense of confidence in our self and our world, and a feeling of a secure connection. This bonding phase creates a foundation that we can access as a supportive resource in times of conflict and stress.

This same bonding process occurs for us in the whole-being embrace experience of embodied nondual meditation. We establish a sense of secure ownership of the essence of our being as the unchanging presence of our existence (even though it is universal). When we feel the uninjured innocence and basic goodness of the unified dimension of our being, it feels very emotionally supportive and reliably available to us. While not responsive, its presence does feel nurturing, which can feel caring and empathetic. This support enhances confidence in our self and our world, and we feel securely connected with all that is. We experience a feeling of calm and an aura of quiet strength.

Like the child's merged boundaries in the symbiotic stage, the falling-in-love/appreciation phase of a relationship, often involves intense "merging of boundaries." When relating at this level, the "I" is not clearly differentiated from the "not I," and we either feel as if we are merged, or we feel engulfed. Emotional contagion is often rampant, and we take on our partner's emotions. Otherwise, we have more defined boundaries, yet as our friend/partner becomes more important to us over time, our experience of intimacy stirs up our unresolved childhood bonding issues. We simply end up acting out a merging of boundaries at a higher level of complexity.

Both a sense of emotional "merging" and the feeling of being "engulfed" lead to a loss of emotional bonding in relationship. As a result, we do not develop an internal sense of our self or a feeling of security as a child. When a parent fails to provide an emotional container for us by offering, for example, a place we can return to after exploring, we have no place to put our self back together. Without a sense of bonding that confirms our safety, the fear of losing the bond with our parent, or later with a partner, grows.

As an adult, one way this manifests is as a strong desire to not lose the feeling of connection to our partner. This is usually expressed in either a bold, somewhat demanding way, or we retreat, or we over-accommodate other people's needs. When our survival is threatened, the instinctual "fight for our life" and attempt to control our environment, or "flee for our freedom" and retreat response, kicks in. Just like any other relationship, we try to either control the limitations or resign our self in quiet desperation. Both strategies, of either over-accommodating or invasively controlling, are vain attempts to establish a feeling of security. These strategies never entirely get the results we want because they create problems in relationship.

In yoga philosophy, developing self-awareness in context to our relational life (merging and engulfment) and refining this, is the actual focus of the first two limbs of Ashtanga yoga (see Appendix Two).

## ROOT CHAKRA

**Name**: The first chakra is called *"muladhara"* in Sanskrit. *Muladhara* literally means "root support."

**Location**: Each chakra that is experienced as an unchanging presence-of-being, uniformly pervades our whole body and environment, on the nondual dimension. Yet, the chakra is experienced most clearly along the central-channel (*sushumna*). It is traditionally described as being located in the perineal floor at the base of the pelvis. This chakra also relates to the feet, legs, buttocks, and anus. These parts of the body have a psychological influence on us that is related to their functions and emotional experience (as explored in somatic psychology, contemplation, and meditation).

### Symbolic Level

Remember, reaping the full benefits of the Symbolic Level requires that we first refine our senses enough to perceive unified consciousness as a body experience of self (as explained in *chapter one*). The first chakra is associated with the mantra "seed" (single sound) "Lam." The Root Chakra has four petals. The square inside the circle represents solid matter, stability, and security. The square has four sides that mirror the four petals, which represent the four elements of Earth (north), air (east), fire (south), and water (west). Together, they unite to form the physical world, including our body. Yet, the primary element that we uncover and awaken as a body experience of self, in this chakra/stage, is Earth, which represents steadiness, our connection with the ground, and nourishment. Attunement and embodiment of each of these elements facilitate our embodiment and awakening of the nondual-essence of the first chakra.

The symbolic form that we visualize in meditation is a square, which represents stability. A downward-pointing triangle is depicted within the square, which represents a downward flow of energy and our sense of connection with the ground. The primary sense is smell. Smell is the most advanced sense we have at birth. It has a central role in helping us in the process of emotional bonding with our parent(s).

## Emotional Level

The first chakra, named "Root Support," is an expression of the most dense state of matter. The obvious limitation in its physical, material nature, is also its strength. Solid and heavy physical qualities can be limiting but also empowering. This density is reflected in how the first chakra is governed by the element of Earth, which is the densest level of manifestation.

If out of balance, we can get too planted and unable to move forward. The more dense an element is, the more easily we are governed by its expression in duality. Yet, as mentioned in the previous chapter, when we refine our senses, we experience first chakra traits as "essences" or as aspects of nondual (unified) wholeness. The first chakra is an experience of the essence of our "existence," that spark of self we were born with that has never changed.

When an emotion is dense, it is thick and strong. This thick, strong sensation can be powerfully passionate yet potentially overwhelming, dragging us down and limiting us. Physically we can get entrenched, unable to adapt to the reality of the situation. This can lead to habitual fear, which often shows up as anxiety, nervousness, and excessive worry. We worry about our material well-being in terms of finances and health, or our physical well-being in terms of safety and support.

The first chakra involves issues of survival and safety. When we experience injuries causing the first chakra to become unbalanced, we feel fearful and insecure about our basic survival needs. This fear can show up most prominently as a fear of loss, and a tendency to lament or regret the past and fear the future. This is similar to the concerns and fears that arise during the symbiotic stage of development (0-4 months).

When we harbor injuries leading to first chakra imbalance, small mistakes can seem like catastrophes. An almost desperate need to fill up quiet time with activities and repetitive thoughts that lead nowhere, is also a symptom of this anxiety. How this gets played out in our relationships can limit genuine intimacy in our contact with our self and others. We become so tuned-in to how each of life's interactions has an element of loss or lack of safety, that we never relax enough to receive what is fulfilling about what we experience. This can be perceived to be like the Buddhist "hungry ghost," which is a being who is driven by intense emotional needs in an animalistic way. We lack the ability to receive, feel, and savor the nourishment, safety, and support available in our experience.

## Hyper-Hypo Imbalances

The above-mentioned fears often show up as a variety of survival responses: either in a bold, somewhat demanding way (fight impulse) by invasively controlling; or we retreat (flight impulse), or we over-accommodate ("fawn"). We can also collapse into an immobility survival response (parasympathetic/discharge), where we become passive, incompetent, and unable to do anything to secure our safety and sense of belonging in life. This can manifest as a dissociative lack of self-awareness, making it very difficult for us to identify and articulate what we feel, or what we want and think. We struggle to present our self in a realistic, clear, and assertive way. Both hyper and hypo responses interfere with our ability to be in relationship in a way that is satisfying.

**Healing Focus:** In the first stage of healing, our nervous system benefits most from establishing an environment that feels relatively safe. In contemplation and meditation practice, this sense of safety begins as we discover that the physical nature of existence can be supportive. We feel how solid objects can hold us up and give us a ground to rest on for support. Emotionally, we discover the good side of the solid and heavy quality of the first chakra, the sense of inner stability and nurturing that it provides. We experience this as "grounding," and feel at home in our body and connected to the Earth, often for the first time. We have the feeling of fully belonging where we are.

When grounded, we have a settled feeling of being firmly established with a sense of place (in time and space). Support from the ground gives us a feeling of strength and resiliency, the ability to adapt to the changing dynamics of life in resourceful ways. With enough of this feeling, it becomes a vital supportive resource that helps us rebound from injury and move through it. It gives us our footing and the ground to stand on.

When we uncover the first chakra nondual-quality of self as the essence of our existence, it brings us a tremendous ability to "stand our ground." When we feel the truth of the sense of belonging, as an inner-knowing, we are able to take on negative input from others, without losing the presence of a steady presence that helps us feel safe and not go into retreat or attack. With this feeling in our body-mind system, we become like a lightning rod. We can channel the intensity of our experience into the ground.

With the physical nature of the first chakra, we are faced with the finiteness of life, which brings up life and death issues, and the fact that all things come to an end. This is a very real fact of life that has gripped the attention of all people since the beginning of time. Common suggestions that we contemplate the impermanence of life, can awaken in us the understanding of how precious our life is. We recognize that if we do not fully savor and pay attention to our life, it can quickly slip away from us. However, if we have deep abandonment issues that are so common in first-stage injuries, witnessing life and experiencing

126

its impermanence can be destabilizing. Progress is slow and difficult.

Meditation on our embodied nondual experience of our self, as that aspect of existence that is whole, is a powerful antidote because it does not change, it is unbreakable, and is always available. Uncovering the experience of inhabiting our body as this essence of our existence, supports us in clearly experiencing the subtle resonance of the first chakra as a presence of our own *being*. Since, at this dimension, existence is a holographic fractal, we can also access this as an expression of unified, unconditional love (not about love for something, but an essence of our inborn nature). When we blend this quality with our embodied sense of the unified essence of our existence, healing happens through a nurturing whole-being-embrace.

This blend inspires feelings of security, safety, and belonging. It feels like unbreakable wholeness that connects us with all that is. We feel this as an internal sense of a subtle form of what psychology might call "object constancy." In psychology, "object constancy" gives us a sense of emotional permanence. It fosters the ability to retain a bond in relationship even when we feel upset by other's actions. This experience of unity and wholeness supports us to "disentangle" our inner experience of stillness, from the movement of emotion, thought, and sensation. This implies our sense of wholeness and unity become autonomous from, and co-exist with, and thereby heal, our deepest habitual fears.

While in a contemplative state, voicing of sound (mantra, expressing our wisest personal truth), visualization (*yantra*), and the experience that we have an "energy-field that contains us" (*mandala* as "holding environment"; see Lancaster, 2023), help balance our energy, access and awaken, our nondual experience of the first chakra aspect of our self. We can chant the "seed" mantra for this chakra, "*Lam...*" or meditate on the symbolic form associated with this chakra as the solid shape of a square, which gives us a sense of inner stability. As mentioned, when meditating on the Root chakra, we are guided by the sense of smell, which is the earliest sense that we develop. We can invite pleasant smells to infuse us and provide support. The Root chakra's emotional characteristics focus on the sense of safety and trust. Meditative attunement to savoring all these first chakra expressions experientially, communicates to our deepest injuries.

It is also helpful to have a contemplative practice that awakens a sensory experience that is similar to how we establish a secure bond as a child. This is created through our experiences of contact with eyes (with our environment or via visualization of a supportive form); as well as intimate holding (via our embodiment as unity and our sense of having an energy-field that contains us); the scent of hair and skin, as an adult is replaced by receiving support from any scent we find pleasant; and the supportive tone of our voice (or a pleasant mantra). While the lack of any of these sensory experiences can be a primary source of injury, they also can potentially be conduits of learning how to fill up from the inside, with immense satisfaction and meaningful contact.

As a result of experiencing these sensations (which are involved in establishing a healthy bond), we have more support to "disentangle" from our limiting habits. This means we grow autonomy from our habitual impulse to constrict any of the various aspects/layers of our self (physical, emotional, mental, wisdom- aspects of self - "koshas"). We increasingly experience wholeness-of-being. As we uncover a body experience of our unchanging-self as a quality of our being, we can learn how to perceive each sense (smell, taste, hearing, touch, sight) with our whole body and mind. As this happens, we become able to use all our senses to imprint a healthy feeling of bonding to what gives us the sense that we exist, that we are safe, and that we belong.

Our habit of clinging to our possessions, people, and even how the people we care about behave, begins to dissolve. Then, we can take the next step of facing our fear of the unknown, with an inner sense of security, and proceed more skillfully. With practice, we begin to notice how we can enjoy the things and people in our life most, when we hold them lightly. Trying to hold on tight is like squeezing an avocado seed. It always slips away. We learn how to balance being aware of the moment as it arises, without clinging to it (sattva; sukha-sthira).

128

**NERVOUS SYSTEM: Orienting**
**ENERGY: Arousal**
**CHILD: "Differentiation" stage**
**ADULT: "Interest" or "Desire" stage**
**CHAKRA: "Sacral chakra,"** *svadhisthana,* **"self-base"**
          **Unified nature of self as "Creativity"**

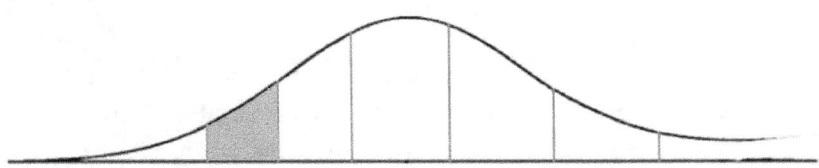

## NERVOUS SYSTEM

**Orient**: When we perceive a disruption (stage one), we orient our self in relation to the event by scanning the situation (stage 2). This means we: first, feel inside our body, second, look around, listen, and search for more clues. We then orient toward what might be causing the disruption, and we assess what we want to do about it. This involves checking in with our database of past experiences, and instincts associated with danger (this is not a mental check-in). If there is no sign of danger and there is nothing to attend to, things can go back to normal, and life goes on.

This orienting behavior correlates with how we feel about the experience. We do this by discerning our own inner experience, as well as evaluating our environment. We assess how we want to position our self in relation to what we are experiencing by discerning and evaluating our preferences, likes and dislikes, and our choices. If we do not discern anything of interest, we move on (much like the wild animal moves on at this stage if there is no danger). Yet, if it is interesting, we move on to discern why we find it interesting and how we want to be in relationship with it. These evaluations are all second-chakra issues.

**Energetics**

Energetically, this process can be graphically depicted as a moderate incline at the beginning of its ascent. This slow build of energy and consciousness is a reflection of our process of developing a clear sense of our personal truth in relationship. What is true for us is inherently enlivening. After we have checked out the situation in stage one, we may become interested in an aspect of it and want to pursue it. This interest involves an arousal of energy and an awakening of consciousness. The interest becomes a desire, that then motivates us to take action in stage three.

Developing clarity about our interests, involves understanding how we want to proceed with respect to our relationship with an other (person, situation, idea, emotion, idea, etc.). We begin to get clear about what our personal truth is, and the nature of the emotional boundaries we need to have in relationship. At this stage, we also commit to a course of action. As we take aim at defining our personal truth, we chart the course we need to take to manifest our potential. This is enacted in every moment and yet, in a larger sense, describes the process involved in making choices about how we want to proceed in life.

**THE CHILD & ADULT: "Differentiation" stage, 5-9 Months**

As a child in the first stage, we are merged with our parent(s), which ideally gave us a safe haven and a healthy bond. This bond provides the connectedness that we need to enhance our sense of self-awareness. The supportive connectedness (safety, feeling wanted, belonging) allows stage two, "differentiation," to emerge, where we develop a personal interest and an understanding of our likes and dislikes. This begins as a child

130

when we approach 5-9 months of age (but emotionally reoccurs throughout life). At this time, we start walking and begin to focus our attention away from our parent. Basically, we grow a strong desire to explore our developing interests.

Psychology calls this the "differentiation" stage, but it is also called "hatching," because it is a process of psychological birth as a distinct individual. We begin to engage in exploratory behavior with our caregiver. This shows-up in our desire to play "peek-a-boo" games of physical separation by crawling away, venturing back, and playing nearby. Throughout this process we engage in a visual "checking back" with the parent. This helps us discern what feels familiar from the unfamiliar. (As you shall see, in embodied nondual meditation we do a sensory "checking back" with our unchanging-self as a nondual essence of creativity.)

Adults can also be found engaging in a kind of "peek-a-boo" game, where in one moment we express a personal interest, and in the next we venture back to check-in with the people we care about. We also explore "playing" nearby in order to stay in contact, but with enough breathing-room, so as not to lose touch with what feels important to us.

At this point, a "transitional object" becomes important for the child. Transitional objects are things that we choose for comfort in the absence of our caretaker, such as a soft blanket. As adults, we adopt a relationship with other things and become attached to anything from food, drugs, sex, rock and roll, or even spiritual dogma. Unless we internalize the comfort this provides, we can become attached to these things in an unhealthy way. (In embodied nondual meditation at this stage, along with other relevant qualities of support, in the absence of support from others we choose the essential nondual quality of creativity for comfort. While not transitional, this serves the same purpose.)

When our parents are available to us, and supportive during our early attempts at separation, we build confident expectations and basic trust in the caregiver and in the outside world. This trust helps us activate our creative impulses. We feel initiative and desire to try new activities and experiences, without excessive fear of failure or of being abandoned. (In meditation, we build the basic trust we are so much in need of for us to express our uniqueness with confidence, through awakening an experience of our self as the uninjured essence of creativity.).

If, as a child, we could see fairies or talk to a doll, and our parents confirmed this experience by saying, "Tell me more," or "What a good imagination," we felt validated (i.e., healthy "mirroring," being witnessed, understood, respected, and supported). As an adolescent, our focus switches from family to friends. If, at this time, we are able to develop our personal interests while remaining integrated into our family system, we will not feel rejected for our decisions and behaviors. We feel a sense of initiative and a desire to try new activities.

When we leave the merged condition that characterizes the first stage, we enter the second stage where we enhance our awareness that "I am here" and that the parent is "out there." We become increasingly interested in discovering the parent as different from us. As an adult, this involves exploring our identity as a couple, or by defining the parameters of our friendship with others. We come to an understanding of what we have in common, where we differ, and what we feel about this.

If our interests are thwarted, discounted, or attacked, we feel crushed. We respond with a flight response and withdraw in fear with co-dependent tendencies. And/or we respond with a fight response and grow deep-seated resentment or anger. We may develop the rebellious vengeance of "an eye for an eye" against the world, and jealousy in general may take hold. We may also try to protect our self by expressing what we want or don't want, with little consideration for others.

We may act this out by expressing antagonism, as a way of managing the frustrations that come from the shame of not knowing our true creative power, or being able to embrace our true sexual identity. At this stage we experience chaotic internal emotions laced with feelings of frustration. We are particularly sensitive to issues of fairness, and the differentness and sameness between our self and others. This leads to power plays and push-pull interactions. When laced with frustration or anger, it can create conflict.

We test whether others will either emotionally abandon (withdraw, not show appreciation, etc.) or inundate us (with expectations or judgments). This inevitably causes our frustrations and power struggles to intensify. The question of whose reality is more real can be the underlying theme in many conversations. The roles of who is the "giver" and who is the "receiver" can become overly important, and can easily turn into a power struggle. It may be difficult to be the giver without "doing the receiver," or be the receiver and not feel "done to." (All of the above tendencies can be found in children and adults alike, involving slightly different subject matter.)

Emotional injuries emerging from this period, involve struggling with fears surrounding our expression of separation and autonomy. In our flight response, we are consumed by fear of expressing our personal truth because of how others will respond. This causes us to have unstable relationships with others and our self. It can lead to feeling unsure about our self, our choices, and our interests in relation to others. We may feel a profound sense of inner hollowness or emptiness.

We may tend to interpret our mistakes as a sign of personal failure and feel guilty that we are somehow "bad" or "not good enough." Our belief that we are not good enough, appears in a variety of ways, "I'm not good enough to express myself creatively" or "I'm not good enough to be as connected to the universe as I want." When we harbor injuries, we can be awkward about expressing our personal truth. We may simply withdraw in shame, and then try to earn our worthiness by overworking ourselves, or over committing to activities with others, or try to be all things to all people. We may subconsciously think, "If I can be more like others, I'll be better liked by them. Maybe then I'll finally feel good enough." The fear of disappointing others is a set-up for our co-dependent habits. Of course, this leaves us drained, without the energy we need for balance and renewal.

Because we can never fully meet what we imagine other people's needs are, we may carry a lot of unprocessed guilt. As a mother, we may feel the guilt of passing on to our children our own injuries, and feel shame or failure. This may be complicated by feeling the insecurity of our mother not knowing if she has what it takes to care of us. This can leave us feeling that our own existence is too much for other people. Anything we do seems to have the power to disturb and hurt, instead of the power to heal and transform. (Note, both fight and flight responses to being thwarted in the second chakra/stage can occur at the same time, causing us to oscillate between these two responses. This can then lead to collapse and a frozen immobility response. )

On the other hand, if we feel respected (seen, understood, respected, and accepted) by others ( our parents, and later by a friend or partner), we can develop our personal interests even if they disagree and want something different. (Here, being "accepted" does not always mean agreement, or not having conditions). Being treated like this makes it easier to express our personal interests to others with empathy. As adults, a primary way we explore how we are similar and different, is by learning to discern and stand by our desires to create what interests us. If we were not supported at this stage as a child, it is very important for us to learn to provide this healthy self-recognition (seen, understood, respected, and accepted) for our self as an adult.

In embodied nondual meditation, we come to recognize our fears result from other people's injuries and how they related to us. With this understanding, we focus on a deeper expression of existence and attune to the natural goodness, and uninjured innocence of our creative ground-of-being. We can feel how our essential ground of being holds space for our injuries in a way that is non-abandoning, non-invasive, and unconditionally supportive. At the heart of every nondual quality of our being lies an uninjured basic goodness and bliss that is often felt as the essence of love. With practice, this presence allows us to overcome self-doubt, and feel worthy of all the goodness life has to offer.

We begin to own that it is our birthright to express our worth creatively, without any degree of fear. This awakens a sense of worthiness and power that allows us to feel equal as we give and receive. We learn to listen to, rather than objectify, our emotions, and then to open and receive the feeling of being cared for, validated, and nurtured. This helps us let go of keeping our body and its energy as stagnant as the structure of our family of origin. We feel good enough to give and receive pleasure as the essence of co-creation of consciousness throughout the planet.

## SECOND CHAKRA

**Name**: "Sacral Chakra." The Sanskrit name "svadhisthana" means "self-base," "dwelling place of the self" or "self-sustaining." These descriptions capture the basic process of clarifying our sense of self at this stage.

**Location**: It is located within the body in its clearest presence, between the navel and the genitals, including the lower back and pelvis. Yet, it also can be felt within the whole body, allowing us to feel we are made of the creative essence of our existence.

### Symbolic Level

The mantra sound is "*Vam*." The symbolic form that we visualize is a circle (wholeness) and a crescent moon (emotion). The moon is archetypically related to our emotional life, as is the governing element water, which is all about flow, flexibility of emotional expression. Water also brings fertile creativity. The primary sense we focus on is taste.

### Emotional Level

When this chakra is balanced, we experience it as our inborn essential nature of creativity. The meaning of the name "*svadhisthana*," describes how the process of discernment involved in creativity depends on our inner sense of a "self-base," as a "dwelling place of the self," that is "self-sustaining." Its nondual expression is the essence of creativity from which our evolving-self's individual acts of creativity arise. The unified essence of creativity also provides us with the support we need to overcome the emotions related to the six lotus flower petals, associated with the Sacral chakra: anger, hatred, jealousy, cruelty, desire and pride. These emotions arise when we are not related to in a supportive manner in the second stage of our development as a child and our "acts of creativity" are thwarted.

The individual acts of creativity that we have at this stage are the internal impulses to explore our developing interests. They are acts of creation that are inspired by an underlying curiosity asking, "Who am I in relationship?" This is expressed in a variety of ways, including sexually, and our sense of gender, and the preferences that underlie the choices we make in life. As mentioned, issues concerning how we are similar and different from others, arise at this stage.

The second chakra is governed by the sense of taste. This is no coincidence, since our emotional relationship with the sense of taste is about our desire for specific experiences that we find tasteful. A tasteful life is one that reflects our distinct desires and preferences toward what we like to experientially take in. Emotionally, taste is about our desire for a specific experience that we find aesthetic. A tasteful life is one that fundamentally involves the sense of choice and entitlement to feel, sense, and discover the personal truth about our desires and aversions.

After the cloud of romantic fantasy that can exist in the first stage of a new relationship lifts, in this second stage, we often begin to understand that we are not, in all ways, on the same page. Once we are familiar with a person, we discover we do not both have the same tastes, desires, and feelings. This must be resolved in the arenas of creativity in our domestic life, including sex, pleasure, emotional expression, and control, etcetera.

All of these expressions reflect our "personal truth." The personal truth of what we want most, is for loved ones to let us be different from them, and still love and care about us. We want an environment that supports us to be different and express the personal truth of our likes and dislikes, without losing the bond.

When we experience relationship trauma at this stage, we shut down the expression of our personal truth about our preferences, because it is futile or not safe to express it. As a child, when we do not work through our differences of opinion, because we feel unsupported and disconnected, we do not learn to set achievable and reasonable parameters to explore our interests. This means we can't establish our emotional boundaries and set limits on what we want and don't want.

The balanced second chakra is an expression of the nondual-essence of our creative nature. In meditation, as we practice uncovering, clarifying, deepening, and awakening the feeling that we exist as this essence within the body, we broaden our perspective. This gives us a very different understanding of what it means to experience our fears, and struggle to define our personal truth. As adults, the embodied experience of our unchanging-self, helps us feel unconditional support due to our access to deeper expressions of existence. Much like a child in the "differentiation" stage, we are consoled by the feeling that if the differences between our self and others are not resolved, we can still feel a profound sense of connectedness and wholeness-of-being.

In embodied nondual meditation and contemplation, we experience a deep sense of self-recognition as we witness and feel witnessed, understand and feel understood, respect and feel respected. In embodied nondual meditation we embody the essential ground of our creative nature as an experience of wholeness and unity. We then meet our injuries in whole-being-embrace, so our shame and self-criticism is pervaded by our creative nature, as wholeness and unity. In the process, our creative expression is cultivated, healed, and embraced. We grow a sense of support to stand up for our personal truth, our interests, and our choices. We learn to receive the powerful support from our attunement to unchanging, unbreakable, uninjured wholeness. As we feel we exist as this wholeness-of-being, we become able to understand, respect, and address other people's needs and emotions, without giving up what is important to us. If others have different needs than we do, we are able to negotiate the differences in a way that doesn't prevent us from our main mission of discovering who we are.

Aside from the confidence we have from this whole-being embrace experience, we begin to gain access to our sense of wisdom. This gut sense is often called a gut-brain, or "enteric brain," due to its learning and discerning capacities. (Wisdom and intuition from our third eye center, comes online with the sixth chakra). This wisdom is not based on our memory of injury and the habits of mind and body that result. Wisdom is based on our evolving-self's best evaluation and intuitive senses of what we perceive to be wise. This information is a pre-trauma authenticity, that is the source of our personal truth about what we feel to be undeniably true. We discern what we need to feel safe, wanted, and creatively alive based on information that is not rooted in habitual fear. (The wisdom that begins in the second chakra appears again in the fourth chakra when we need it most, and then again in the sixth chakra, when we are bringing our journey to a close.)

The unified field of consciousness and wisdom in the second chakra, deepens our perception of what is not unified, and what needs to happen for our evolution toward wholeness. When we come to clearly recognize what we authentically feel, this naturally leads to establishing healthy emotional boundaries in relationship.

## Emotional Boundaries in Relationship

It makes developmental sense that in yoga the second chakra is commonly associated with having passionate, strong emotions. This is the stage of getting clear about what we feel and how we want to proceed. As we come to know who we are and what is meaningful to us on a deeper level, gut-felt passionate desires and aversions naturally arise. As we become equipped with a deeper emotional understanding, our desire for what we feel and want, can increase to the point of becoming a passionate conviction.

With an embodied experience of our unchanging-self, we also grow confidence in our desires. Our sense of basic trust gives us a feeling that we are supported to skillfully honor our wants, needs, and emotions with others. This provides a basis to set healthy boundaries in relationship. As we embody our unified, essential ground-of-being, the personal truth that was shut down spontaneously arises. We become able to authentically express some form of, "I have the right to have my emotions, needs, and wants," "I can choose what feels right for me," and "I can take up room on the planet with what feels authentic to me."

If we have established security in the first stage, we can rely on the feelings of security, belonging, and feeling of connection in relationship, as support for honoring our personal truth. Attuning to the innocence, purity, and unconditional nature of the essence of our self as existence (first chakra), can enhance this sense of security. This gives us the emotional fortitude to tolerate the anxiety inherent in discerning and standing by our personal interests, passions, and choices in the second chakra stage. We begin to explore our own unique nature in a more inclusive way within the relationship, and learn to stand-up for these interests. When supported in this way, our self-expression grows (fifth chakra).

Familiarity with our personal truth (healthy preferences not motivated by fear) brings with it the responsibility to make a choice or commitment to honor it. In relationship, once familiarity or intimacy is established, and we've decided to continue the relationship past the initial honeymoon stage (first chakra), we come into a deeper connection through a commitment to the other person (second chakra). We commit to a course of action together.

This process of commitment is symbolically represented by the mythic Hero who commits to "the journey." Defining what we want, think, and feel without losing our sense of support from our unchanging-self as the essence-of-creativity, gives us confidence to express our unique desires and interests to others (fifth chakra). Because our embodied sense of the essence of our creative nature includes the nondual-qualities of wholeness (unity, balance, stillness, timelessness, and conscious spaciousness), we can honor our passion. We savor and integrate the feeling of the wholeness, innocence, and inherent benevolence, of these nondual-qualities of self. This frees us to express authentically in the moment and not get tripped up in attachments, or habits of mind and body. Here we can bring the ways we doubt our interests, and are afraid to honor them, into whole-being-embrace with our unchanging-self.

Owning our authentic passions gives us more resiliency to rebound from injury and move on. We can more easily renegotiate past emotional injuries and develop the power to change the course of our automatic reactions in our current life. It provides the inner fortitude that we need to enter into chakra/stage three, where we learn to act upon our interests and passion in a way that we could not before.

In the second chakra's discernment of interests, we orient our self by understanding what we feel. Being oriented in our relationship to other people's desires and limits, naturally leads to establishing our own healthy emotional boundaries. It also leads to clarity about our sexual orientation and our relationship with pleasure.

### Sensuality & Sexuality

The second chakra is traditionally associated with our sexuality. As a child at this stage, we not only establish our emotional preferences and choices, but we also bring definition to our sexual identity. Our sexual identity is not about sexuality in terms of the genitals, but "who am I as a sexual being." This is a time when most children develop the ability to recognize the experience of their own gender. This includes recognizing gender groups, such as girl, woman, and feminine, and boy, man, and masculine, and all non-binary traits. Being in touch with the second chakra essence of our sexuality, as an experience of unity and wholeness, is a potent supportive experience to have as we affirm our gender identity.

In yoga, sexuality is associated with the second chakra's element of water. Water represents a grounding energy that follows the path of least resistance and flows downwards in the body. Water flexibly adapts to the shape of the ground, yet over time, it can have a great influence and re-shape even solid rock. The sensual and tricky crocodile-like animal named "Makara" is the vehicle of Varuna, the Vedic god of primordial waters. In this role the crocodile symbolizes fertility in watery conditions. The Hindu gods of water and sexual love rode on crocodiles and fish to fertilize the water with semen.

Our second chakra urge to explore our personal truth can lead to a healthy, strong libido. We grow a diverse repertoire of playful, passionate, sensual and/or sexual explorations. When the second chakra is balanced, we may have a lot of creative energy and sexual power, yet we are not over-run by it. This is because we are able to understand our sexual desire and the relational nature of our personal life, within the larger context of our sense of unity and wholeness.

### Pleasure

Pleasure is traditionally considered to be a central attribute of the second chakra. Pleasure plays an important role in our life.

When our personal interests are seen, heard, understood, and respected, we feel supported. We feel a sense of pleasure from honoring and choosing, or standing by what is true for us. This pleasure is the seed that supports us to manifest our interests in chakra/stage three, as a sense of power and will. We are able to manifest without crumbling under the emotional intensity of what is involved.

When our interests are not respected, trauma results. Loss of healthy interest in our preferences, causes us to lose our sense of purpose. Our actions simply lose their meaning and sense of value. When what is meaningful becomes elusive, we lose our will to engage, or attempt to discover and define our interests, choices, and passions. Healing from this involves finding a way for our personal interests to be seen, heard, understood, and respected (healthy mirroring). This is where our relationship with the presence of our unchanging-self becomes crucial.

As mentioned, our nondual unchanging-self is experienced as an uninjured wholeness. It lies deeper than our injuries and is reliably, always available when we look deeply enough. As a result, our unchanging-self is a natural source of healthy "mirroring" and non-judgmental, empathetic presence. This source of support comes from an untainted, content-free, inherently benevolent source within us, rather than an injured parent. The depth, clarity, and benevolent presence of our unchanging-self soothes and supports us, in the way we may have needed from others, for our personal growth, but never received.

When we embody our unchanging-self, we can discover that we don't need to do or be something else, in order to have value and be loved. We don't have to seek love or give love, because we can feel "I am love" (on a nondual dimension). This eventually opens us to the recognition that essentially, also, "You are love." These experiences heal the fabric of our psyche and collective consciousness. They transform how we relate to our self and others. By developing an inner-bond with the deeper, uninjured innate part of our self, our self-worth blossoms and healing happens.

The sense of wholeness, together with clarity about our personal truth, gives us a basic trust in the pleasure we get from honoring our interests and standing by our choices. Remaining present and fully open to what feels authentically pleasurable, due to its basis in personal truth, is powerfully healing. For those of us who have experienced shame or blame at this stage, trusting pleasure is a big deal. When we harbor trauma or shame, openly enjoying and expressing our well-being and pleasure, may feel as though we are tempting fate, and we withhold what we most want. We may have learned early in life, that too much well-being could upset the delicate, balanced structure of our family. We may have a history with a parent who had difficulty if we felt extremely good about our self and put a "speed limit" on our positive feelings. Consequently, we learn to associate well-being with anxiety.

Yet when we avoid our truth, clear and honest communication becomes impossible. Whether we know it or not, we choke our self off and stray from the real facts of our life as we perceive them. When these habits take charge, they drain our energy and consciousness. When we abandon awareness of our self because we are hyper-vigilantly focused on what other people do or don't want, our body's experience of personal truth stops being a source of guidance.

Without the second chakra stage's inner-strength, gained by a clear understanding of what we are feeling, we can conform to the other's (partner, group, situation, etc.) expectations or live in a perpetual state of being in reaction to them. This co-dependent and reactive behavior runs up against our second-stage desire to establish a deeper understanding and acceptance of who we are. This is also complicated by the fact that at this stage, we also begin to recognize others for who they are, and are more able to feel empathy towards them. The awareness and acceptance that we are a unique individual opens the door for us to appreciate other people's unique qualities.

In this process, we experience a desire to not hurt that which we are trying to separate from. This can be a positive force and, if not careful, it can also become a powerful force that draws us into becoming co-dependent. This leads us to either over-accommodate, or grow a phobia of accommodating the people we are close to. Either way, we lose our center of personal initiative, and our actions are motivated by fear. Resentment and anger are our most common responses to our over-accommodating behavior.

### Hyper-Hypo Imbalances

An imbalanced second chakra is expressed in a hyper way (sympathetic/charge) when we either assertively control, or we co-dependently over-accommodate, or become emotionally volatile. We can become obsessed with creativity and obsess over defining our choices, our sexuality, and our pursuit of pleasure with everything from food to sex. All of these expressions occur in an anxious, driven manner.

But we can also have a hypo response, where we feel stuck, our creativity doesn't flow, and we may feel unsure of our choices, for instance, in preparing and executing plans or projects. We often feel guilty about expressing personal truth and end-up suppressing it, along with our emotions. We may have an inability to express our emotions, and difficulty having fun, playing, or being creative. We may be unable to make choices, receive pleasure, or fully desire sexuality (often due to immobility, stuck, and collapse responses). We can have feelings of body shame, sexual guilt, and impotence/frigidity.

It is important to know that the lower abdomen, or gut, is associated with the second chakra. It is often called our "second brain," or enteric brain. Like our brain, it develops patterns of coping due to past overwhelming events. We have an emotional gut, in that the gut monitors and responds to all life events through a network of neurons that line its interior. This second brain contains 100 million neurons, which is more than either the spinal cord or the peripheral nervous system. It also contains 95% of our serotonin, which has a key role in defining our mood, sleep, digestion, nausea, wound healing, bone health, blood clotting, and sexual desire. All of these functions can become unbalanced in a hyper or hypo way.

**NERVOUS SYSTEM:** Flight-Fight
**CHILD:** "Latency" stage
**ADULT:** "Approach" stage
**CHAKRA:** "Solar Plexus" Chakra, *manipura*, meaning city of
      jewels; The unified sense of self as "Power."

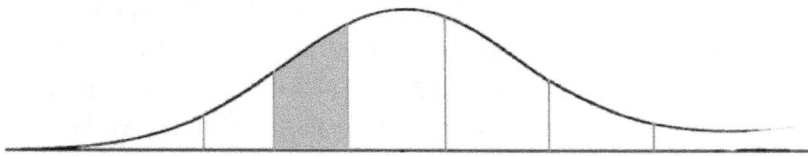

**NERVOUS SYSTEM**

If there actually is a danger, then a hardwired instinct to protect ourselves from danger, kicks in. This means the sympathetic nervous system is activated, and we go into flight (withdrawal) - fight (resist) mode. A huge amount of energy is released into the body to either evade danger in flight, or to attack in fight. When flight is expressed subtly, we commonly have symptoms of anxiety or panic, restless legs, and/or numbness in the legs, and we may resort to excessive activity or fidgeting. We may feel like withdrawing from engagement with our experience. Fight mode symptoms include bursting out crying, and feeling like we want to punch, push, rip, kick, and stomp. We also may have a desire to express anger or rage, and we may have a knotted stomach and nausea. On a more low-key level, we may simply feel irritable.

144

All of these survival responses and their symptoms, can manifest intensely or chronically on a low-grade level. We may only notice them as background impulse, moods, and slight sensations.

## Energetics

Energetically, the third stage can be graphically depicted as the steepest incline of energy and consciousness. At this point, we need enough energy and consciousness to reach, and then surmount, the climax in stage four. By embodying the experience of the essence of our existence (and the sense of security and belonging we get in the first chakra/stage), and the essence of our creative nature (and the sense of accepting our interests, choices, and personal truth in the second chakra/stage), we establish the foundation for the third chakra/stage.

In the third chakra/stage, we build the energy we need to persevere and manifest our interests. In stage two, our desires and interests align us with our goal and commitment to a course of action in our relationship to what we experience (person, emotion, situation, ideology). This sets us up for the third chakra/stage, where we find the strength, vitality, and endurance to get the "job" done.

## CHILD DEVELOPMENT: "Practicing" Stage, 9-14 Months

In the first stage of our archetypal-holographic journey, our focus is on developing self-awareness and clear perception of our environment. In the second stage we refine our discernment about, and commitment to, what is important to us, our interests.

In stage three (9-14 months), we are motivated to act on our desire. In order to do this, we learn to gather our inner-strength and personal power, so we can develop the skills to manifest our interests. Psychologically, this means we learn skills that enable us to establish the degree of contact and autonomy in relationship that we need to manifest our interests. This can mean learning how to skillfully withdraw from contact, or resist another person's agenda and attitude (healthy boundaries). While in chakra/stage three we do gather skills at maintaining our own integrity, not until the chakra/stage four do we effectively implement these skills in a way that honors the integrity of the relationships we have.

As crawlers (beginning around 7-10 months,) and beginning walkers (10-18 months), we are more able to autonomously explore our environment. As our mobility increases, we sometimes choose to separate briefly from our parent, but then we return for assurance and comfort to emotionally refuel. If our parent is able to let us independently explore while staying nearby, we learn to take pleasure in our growing world, and begin to have a basic sense of self that is not directly connected to the parent. We grow a love affair with the world, with a healthy sense of omnipotence, narcissism, and a beginning sense of self-esteem that naturally comes with newfound capabilities, skills, and functioning.

If our personal truth and interests are supported in the second stage, then we can go on to develop a sense of inner-strength and the healthy self-esteem needed to support the third stage. By developing clarity about our personal truth and interests, in the third stage we can gain the appropriate abilities and skills to manifest our interests. In the second stage, we come to recognize and honor our personal truth and the pleasure this gives us. This is what enhances our inner-strength and self-esteem enough for us to enter into the third stage of consciousness without crumbling under the emotional intensity of the associated challenges. This means when we have a third-stage injury, we can try to build inner-strength, power, and will, but without enough support. It might be better to develop clarity and respect for what our interests are before we actually can overcome doubt, shame, and build self-esteem (healthy omnipotence/narcissism).

As children at this stage, when our parents did not expect more from us than was appropriate for our age and abilities, we were supported in managing our failures. We come to understand that when we make a mistake, the behavior may not be okay, yet as a person, we are okay. This understanding allows us to develop an inner-sense of confidence that we can trust our feelings and abilities. We express power as power from within, a non-dominating "power to," instead of "power over."

Injuries at this time often involve premature loss of parental reassurance for attempting to manifest our interests. If our parents had a big agenda and expectations, our own unique traits were discouraged in favor of those that pleased them. As a result, confidence in our capacities to establish ourselves in the world and manifest what is important to us, never develops. It is difficult to take pleasure and delight in actions we take to manifest our interests and newfound skills. It sets up a pattern of low self-esteem, lack of confidence, and a sense of shame.

We often have an inordinate need for outside validation and admiration for our abilities, to feel reassured of our value. Later, we often create an inflated sense of importance and adopt the grandiosity of being "special" as a defense against not feeling valued. This sense of grandiosity decreases our need for others, yet we also crave constant admiration and reassurance. Our disappointment in others validation often leads to anger.

## ADULT RELATIONSHIPS

As an adult, we try to prove to our self and to others, that our abilities and efforts make a difference that is valuable. The third chakra/stage relates to coming face-to-face with our personal power, and the sense of inner-strength that allows us to feel capable. This inner-strength and confidence grows when the people in our life that we care about most, give us opportunities to make decisions and experience success. We feel that our actions have an impact that is recognized as valuable. We may test our abilities, knowledge, and original ideas as we participate in social situations with friends, in the workplace, and in our community. Our main question is "Who am I in the world?"

As an adult, a common third chakra/stage tendency is to either be grandiose or deflated. Grandiosity causes a sense of entitlement that reflects narcissism rather than emotional maturity. We may be obsessed with personal-power and establishing our identity in the world by getting over-attached to our work, perfectionism, exercise, money, and the clout of authority. We put on a good face to mask the real condition of our heart. On the other hand, when we are deflated, we underestimate our potential. Because of this, we can withdraw from fully interacting with significant people in our life. We withdraw from the challenge of exploring our interests and abilities in life.

Because of our quest to prove our abilities, and our sensitivity over being victimized or losing our autonomy, we commonly pull away from the relationship. We want our independence and we do not want to feel intruded upon. We want to feel that we have the control to follow our own interests in life. We can take this to an extreme by withdrawing from our close relationships to such an extent that we disregard the need for togetherness. When a friend comes to us wanting to be supported in some way, we may wish they would get their needs met separately. Even being in the company of a dear friend or our partner, may feel like a threat to our freedom. Emotional closeness can obscure our mental clarity and take a lot of effort, even when we are having fun. We may stubbornly want our own way, and be overly protective of "doing our own thing, in our own way."

To overcome the challenges that we encounter in the unbalanced third chakra/stage, as a Hero on our journey, we need to establish a relationship with our supportive resources and make "allies" (our contemplative yoga practice, self-regulation skills, and as much support from others as we can tolerate). We must also face our injuries and associated habits, such as grandiosity or underestimating our potential. In the process, we encounter certain challenges that require us to develop specific practical and emotional skills and ability to manifest our interests.

In myth and in the movies, the Hero finds supportive resources to face "enemies" (injuries) in the symbolic "saloon," where relationships are established. Of course, contemplative yoga involves an internal relationship between the evolving-self and the unchanging-self. So, going to where relationships are established is an introspective venture. The modern myth, as depicted in the iconic *Star Wars* movie's bar-scene, is an example of where these kinds of relationships are established. Once we know what our interest are (stage two), the bar is where we gather the tools to manifest our interests (a stage three activity). The bar-scene is where Luke forged an important alliance with the facilitator, Han Solo. The challenges we face (our injuries) in this stage are represented by the scene where Obi Wan teaches Luke about "the Force." In this scene, Luke is asked to learn by fighting blindfolded. The force, relates to finding the inner-power we need to get to the next stage. Fortunately, Luke passes this test successfully. In embodied nondual meditation, this involves embodying the unified essential-ground of power.

To succeed in the third stage, we need to access three primary supportive resources: 1) a sense of inner-strength, 2) skill, and, 3) endurance to manifest our interests. The capacity to endure the potential self-sabotage that we face, such as doubt, as we set out to manifest our life path, empowers us with the fortitude to succeed and persevere in life. Endurance is needed with everything from capturing an animal, to picking ourselves up after failing to score the job we wanted. Endurance is the fire that keeps us warm as we struggle with the emotional tasks of the third chakra. These emotional tasks involve our sense of self-direction, self-control, personal willpower, and energy. Endurance is at the center of each of these qualities.

Gathering emotional support and developing skills is a third chakra/stage activity. We can find this emotional support initially in meditation, by drawing upon our embodied sense of feeling we are made of "pure essence of power." Whole-being-embrace is our inner "bar scene" where we develop a secure relationship with our allies and find the supportive resources to manifest our abilities. The nondual ground of power provides the inner-strength we need to have confidence, self-discipline, and independence. These are necessary to have the control we need to take full responsibility for our actions. The challenge we face in adulthood, is the same we had as a child in this stage. It can be summarized with the question, "Am I able to explore my interests freely, without losing the relationship bond."

After committing to our interests in stage two, in stage three, we face trials and tribulations concerning our autonomy to implement our interests in a way where we do not lose contact in relationship. It can be a challenge to love somebody and not be controlling of the choices they make in their life. Emotional autonomy is not an easy thing to sustain in most relationships. In many cases, the conflicts that arise lead to doubts, fears, or personal insecurities that threaten our ability to pursue our independent interests. We wrestle with doubts and fears that are so often hidden from view.

The inner "bar-scene" in somatic psychology, involves drawing upon both talk psychotherapy and body-centered therapies, to look at the connection of mind and body. We learn how we experience our thoughts, emotions, and sensations. We learn practices to help acknowledge and release emotions that are negatively affecting us. To discern and heal our relationship injuries, we may focus on refining our personal truth in the "differentiation" stage of growth and issues of autonomy in the "latency" stage. Many of the same tools that psychology draws upon, are also used in yoga with more refinement and attention to subtlety.

In the "indirect-path" of yoga (see Appendix Two), at the second stage (called "limb three"), we practice yoga postures (*asana*) to become embodied enough to support tolerating having more energetic charge in our system. In chakra/stage three ("limb four"), we practice conscious breathing (*pranayama*) to gain control of our breath and energy system. We do practices that bring balance to our hyper and hypo energy fixations.

By contrast, embodied nondual yoga emphasizes adopting a "direct-path" to experiencing the unified dimension of existence as a resource. The practice of conscious breathing (*pranayama*) shifts from gaining control of our breath and energy system to effortless breathing (see Appendix Two, stage three), where we refine letting go of effort. Letting go of effort is a central way of releasing constrictions and accessing an internal sense of unobstructed inner space. As we refine our senses, we recognize the unified inner-space is conscious. In the third chakra we can discern this as the innate essential-ground of power.

Embodying the nondual-quality of the essence of our "inner-power" (chakra/stage three) can be tremendously healing and inspiring. The injured part of us comes into contact with the nondual attributes of the essence of power (unbreakable, timeless, conscious stillness, balance, unity, etc.) and begins to feel hope. Understanding the nature of the third chakra can help refine our access to its supportive resources.


**THIRD CHAKRA:**
**Name**: ("Solar Plexus chakra" (Manipura, means "city of jewels" or "lustrous gem.")
**Location**: It is located between the navel and the bottom of the ribs and breastbone, deep in the subtle core of the torso.

### Symbolic Level

The seed mantra is "Ram." The color is bright yellow (like the sun). The element is fire, which ignites our inner-fire and strengthens our digestion of food. It also helps us "digest" the emotional content we started having in the second chakra. In a sense, it is the "fire in the belly" needed to transform the creativity and interests we developed in the second chakra, into the positive action of manifesting our interests.

### Emotional Level

The Solar Plexus chakra is associated with our sense of inner-power. The third chakra is also considered to have a mental nature that focuses and generates willpower. This is the willpower we need to manifest our interests and realize the sense of healthy omnipotence, healthy narcissism, and a beginning sense of self-esteem that psychology talks about. It also provides the power to overcome the emotional tendencies related to the ten petals associated with the third chakra/stage: sadness, foolishness, delusion, disgust, fear, shame, treachery, jealousy, ambition, and ignorance.

Central to all of these emotional tendencies, are the issues we grapple with at the related stage of our development as a child. This chakra is developmentally related to our sense of omnipotence and is associated with the child's "practicing" stage. This omnipotence facilitates us to direct our attention (which

151

involves impulse control), manifest our sense of purpose (goals and intentions), and have the endurance to manifest our interests. When successful, this provides a sense of effectiveness in the world, self-confidence, and healthy pride. If we did not receive enough support as a child (via healthy mirroring and empathy), we will need to access alternative experiences that provide us with a sense of omnipotence.

Feeling we exist as the nondual essential-ground of power is a profound source of omnipotence. Its timeless, unbreakable nature is reassuring and supports us in accessing the sense of endurance and confidence we need to persevere. The sense of power, as an expression of our innate wholeness, helps us to naturally feel the self-confidence. It supports us to access empathy and compassion for our self. This sparks the hope and initiative to see the interests and personal truth that became clear to us in stage two, through to completion.

When this chakra is out of balance, what we do, gets confused with who we are. We identify with our job and define our self-worth by the activities of our career, or job description. To complicate this, with third-stage imbalance, we avoid processing deep, difficult emotions. We become more intolerant of the differences and diversity that we perceive in other's appearances, lifestyle choices, or political affiliations and beliefs.

The essential-ground of inner-power we embody in meditation, provides the basis for our thoughts, emotions, physical sensations, and actions to match up with integrity. We can begin to learn how to show-up in the world and reveal who we really are. We find the power to stop confusing what we do with who we are. This helps us to not feel we need to go somewhere else, do something else, or be someone else. Our actions become an expression of how we bring our true inner gifts to the world, and not just the roles we play, for how we wish to be seen by others around us.

Because in the third chakra/stage we are so focused on manifesting our interests, we often enter into a sense of urgency with time. When our third chakra is out of balance, we perceive there is not enough time to do the things we feel we need to do. Along with this, we often don't complete the things that we begin. We believe that everything we do must be extra-ordinary and exciting. As we embody the essence-of-power, our sense of inner-strength supports us in taking our time and letting this be a process we embrace. We learn to enjoy the journey of each moment, and not be so attached, preoccupied, and fixated on the destination at hand.

Nondual inner-power gives us the energy to fuel the discipline we need to manifest our interests. We grow more consistent in our actions and adopt a routine of self-care (emotionally, physically, and/or spiritually). We no longer focus on long-term lofty goals, but are more able to meet every moment as it is. This process includes learning to reconcile the tension between our personal interests and choices (associated with the second chakra) and the requirements of society. Our existence as nondual inner-power supports us to learn to navigate the relationship we have with the limits of our current situation in life.

As we engage in whole-being-embrace, we feel that our interests and goals are understood and respected, and we feel met with unconditional love. We grow a sense of pride in our interests and goals. We increasingly feel competent and that we will not be crushed by other people's expectations.

### Hyper-Hypo Imbalances

Our hypo response to a threat to our independence, sense of competence, and ability to manifest our interests, is to feel powerless, despondent, worthless, self-critical, rejected, self-conscious, and shameful. We may also have a lack of memory and ability to mentally concentrate.

A hyper response, on the other hand, is to adopt an "alpha" character style of relating. We have a need to dominate and control others, as well as our self, which can even lead to insomnia. Our feelings of rejection, self-consciousness, and shame, cause us to become overly reactive to other's judgment or evaluation of us. We also can become very judgmental towards our self and other people. We may swing between hyper and hypo responses, having a grandiose overconfidence and a depressive despondence.

153

## The Yoga & Psychology of Energy Containment: *Sthira - Sukha*

The indirect-path that uses self-regulation of energy to establish balance, is central to creating a conducive environment for accessing unified consciousness. While the primary focus of this book is the direct-path (directly attuning to wholeness), some of the principles involved in self-regulating our energy, are valuable to understand.

In the third chakra/stage, the dominant issue involves our experience of power to manifest our interests. Power can be an expression of unified consciousness, and also an expression of how we manage our energy. Energy is like money, in that it can be invested, thrown away, stingily held, or simply ignored. We are the collection of energy within a body container, which is limited in size. One of the goals in yoga and psychology, is to be able to manage more energy in our body-mind system without getting overwhelmed. We remain present, centered, and grounded. The intention is to expand our threshold for tolerating intense experiences, and to increase our resilience.

To be able to contain more of the energy in our body that accompanies troubling thoughts, emotions, and sensations, involves a process that psychology calls "containment." "Containment" happens when we do not habitually physically constrict in response to what we experience. This allows our body enough room to accommodate the surge of energy that accompanies experience of thoughts, emotions, and sensations. This is something we ideally learn to do as a child. When a caretaker scoops us up into their arms and hugs us tightly enough to provide us with the feeling that we have a container that holds us; this allows us to relax and gain access to more internal-space to hold our distressing experience. "Containment" is what gives us the resilience and endurance to survive intense experiences.

If we did not receive enough of a holding environment that contained us as a child, we need to learn how to do this as an adult. Without a sense of containment within our body vessel, energy doesn't collect properly. This means we may be left with the frustrations of not having the energy it takes to complete a task. We may also attempt to hold all our energy in, like the abusively angry person who can't contain the swell of energy, and erupts. Or, we may build-up too much energy, and have nowhere to go with it. We may discharge our energy abruptly, let it drift off, or slowly drain away.

Chakra/stage three consciousness is when the issue of "containment" is most important because we are involved in building enough energy to manifest our interests. We need to learn to face the intensity of the moment without getting triggered into our fear-based survival responses.

Containment in yoga is based on the balance of steady alertness (*sthira*) and the lightness of comfort and ease (*sukha*). In sutra 2.46 Patanjali explains the words "*sthira-sukham asanam.*" This means our posture, and how we proceed in life (*asana*), should be steady and alert without distraction (*sthira*), as well as comfortable and relaxed without dullness or heaviness (*sukha*). Variations of these expressions show-up in the yoga "*asana*" of the posture we assume, and how we respond to what we experience. For instance, if we just have steady alertness, it leads to contraction and hypervigilance. If we have comfort and ease with no alertness as we proceed through our day, it leads to various expressions of excessive release, dullness, and collapse.

A balance of the two creates an energetic and psychological container for us. It also establishes the right environment for the relaxed-alert state that accompanies a balanced nervous system. This allows us to tolerate the full range of experiences that we need to deal with in our life, without getting overwhelmed. This balance also allows our expressions to be effortless. As I emphasize In the fourth chakra/stage, in embodied nondual meditation we emphasize refining the practice of effortlessness as a means of letting go of chronic patterns of tension and collapse. Effortless perception and expression, naturally balances comfort and ease and steady alertness, in the yoga of how we proceed through life. It allows us to relax patterns of tension, and awaken areas of collapse.

Relaxing gives us more room to tolerate the intensity of experience. With practice, we are able to spread the energy that accompanies each experience, throughout our whole-body container. Attunement to what underlies our state of constriction and collapse, gives us access to a profound feeling of openness. This sense of inner-openness allows us to spread the surge of energy that accompanies experience throughout our body. We do not experience overwhelm because we can contain a larger amount of energy, and tolerate higher and deeper levels of experience and consciousness. We balance our ability to not act impulsively while not over-controlling our expressions. As our physical constrictions are released, we establish a foundation to not react automatically or habitually to what we experience.

While self-regulating our energy through comfort and ease and steady alertness is important, direct access to feeling we exist as unified consciousness is also a powerful resource. As we feel that we exist as conscious stillness and unified space within our body, we access an ultimate experience of containment. Our sense of infinite space is a game changer. When we experience an energy surge with containment, we do not feel we must do something about it. We are not tormented by the cravings that cause us to have less impulse-control, because we maintain a sense of openness and wholeness.

This ultimate containment allows us to not discharge our energy by acting upon our habitual impulses or conditioned reactions (we don't eat the candy, or grab the bottle, or video game). It also allows us to not overcontrol or hold-on too tightly. We can finally relax and let go (discharge). This balance allows us to release constrictions (*dukkha*) and spread the energy throughout the body.

Our body experience of feeling that we exist as the unlimited space of unified consciousness, facilitates containment to happen on a psychological and neurophysiological level. This directly contributes to the sense of empowerment relevant to the third chakra/stage. As mentioned, one of the most effective ways of learning to contain our energy so we can remain present, centered, grounded, and whole, is with the yoga practice of conscious breathing, "*pranayama*" (see "Effortless Breathing" in Appendix Two, and in fourth chakra).

**NERVOUS SYSTEM: Freeze versus Climax**
**CHILD : "Rapprochement" stage**
**ADULT: "Release"**
**CHAKRA: Heart center, *anahata,* meaning unstruck.**
       **Unified sense-of-self as unconditional Love**

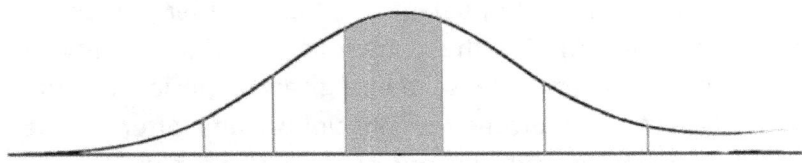

## NERVOUS SYSTEM

If we cannot engage in flight or fight successfully (stage three), our nervous system freezes into an immobility response in stage four. This is when the parasympathetic nervous system shuts down and causes us to have an immobilization experience. We can also have abrupt and disjointed alternations between sympathetic (panic) and parasympathetic (collapse) nervous system actions. Our lingering fear of being stuck can accentuate and perpetuate these experiences to varying degrees. When we feel we have no escape and we are in a frozen state, fright takes over, and we feel varying degrees of panic, dizziness, nausea, lightheadedness, tingling, numbness, and dissociation.

At this point, our life feels much like the Greek myth of the snake heads of Medusa. Confronting our suffering or trauma head-on, eye to eye, can be overwhelming and cause us to freeze and feel like we turn into stone. We are frozen in our ways, and feel trapped in self-defeating styles of relating. Peter Levine (2010) explains that a precondition for developing trauma symptoms is that we are both frightened and perceive that we are trapped, at the same time.

If we can successfully manage the surge of energy that comes with flight or fight in chakra/stage three, our system will discharge excess energy in stage four. In other words, we face the moment (stage one), get clear about what we feel about it (stage two), and act upon what we feel about it (stage three). When these stages are successful, we proceed to apply our most effective resources in stage four. This allows us to begin to discharge the excess energy we built-up in stage three. We complete this discharge in chakra/stages five and six, returning to the state of balance in the seventh stage.

As mentioned, in embodied nondual meditation, we access a more refined experience of balance and its broader perspective. We recognize it contains the conscious stillness of unity and wholeness. This healthy release of energy and experience of unity and wholeness, recalibrates our physiology and offers us new ways of resolving the suffering and trauma we harbor.

The energetics of chakra/stage four can be graphically depicted as the apex of the bell-curve of consciousness and energy flowing through the body-mind's three phases. When we manage what we experience successfully, our relationships (with self and other) become easy. This means we negotiate the balance of contact and breathing-room, or desire and aversion, as we engage with what we experience. In the process, we discover how to relate to experience in a way that is both non-invasive and non-abandoning. We don't allow our experiences to be imposing and overwhelm us, and we're not dismissive about them either.


**CHILD-ADULT DEVELOPMENT: "Rapprochement,"14-24 Months**

In the "rapprochement" stage as a child, we develop the ability for social skills (caring, cooperation, sharing, managing conflicts) (14-24 months, but emotionally reoccurs throughout life). To review how we got here, upon beginning our journey in chakra/stage one, we grow awareness of our self and our environment to confirm its nature and if we are safe and belong. As we encounter an experience in chakra/stage two, we orient our self and develop a response strategy. In chakra/stage three, we take action and respond, and then in chakra/stage four, we negotiate the consequences of our actions. In facing the consequences, we realize the limits of our abilities to manifest our interests and the consequences of doing this alone. We begin to feel the need for relationship with others.

This involves a negotiation where we join chakra/stage three's power to establish the independence we need to manifest our interests, together with chakra/stage four's ability include other people's interests. To successfully include others, we develop social skills like caring, cooperation, sharing, managing conflicts. To learn how to do this we need to face how we limit our abilities to manifest our interests alone (third chakra) and our simultaneous need for relationship (chakra four). One way we explore negotiating this dynamic is in delighting and sometimes disappointing our parents by imitating them. In this process, we refine our understanding of how our interests are different from others and our need to come to terms with how other people's interests are valid also. This can be both reassuring and/or scary. On this journey, we come to recognize that it takes self-acceptance to accept others.

From the perspective of earlier developmental stages, self-acceptance and accepting others can seem impossible. In the first stage (symbiosis), we need others to give us guidance and to reflect back to us how we feel. In the second stage, we are often guided by what interests us most and our strategies of resistance, in our struggle to define our personal truths. In the third stage, we are often inclined to leave our emotions and our relationship with others behind, so we can explore our autonomy and our independent abilities to manifest our potential.

Our self-other negotiation of autonomy and connection is depicted as the midpoint of all the stages, where we undergo death and/or rebirth. If we fail, our integration and wholeness fragments, we fixate, and we suffer in our relationship with the impermanence of life. This can ultimately cause us to get sick and die due to hyper-hypo energy imbalances. If we are successful, we experience death of the old, outdated sabotaging habits and behavior. We then experience a rebirth as we adopt a new way of being and relating. In myth, the Hero symbolically appears to die and is born again, or miraculously reappears.

Up until this point we have relied more on our sabotaging habits as a protective strategy of survival (such as flight, fight, freeze, collapse, and defensive/reactive styles of relating). This is a time that Trungpa Rinposhe described as teetering on the "threshold of magic." In this moment we face the choice of welcoming the unfamiliar sense of openness or clinging to our familiar sabotaging habits.

Letting go of habitual sabotaging strategies of responding is usually unsettling. In rites of passage and rites of initiation, we are forced to taste the unsettling nature of the death of what obstructs us. We also have the opportunity to experience the resurrection of our wholeness-of-being. This is depicted in myth when the Hero is on the brink, during a fight with a mythical beast. In *Star Wars*, this harrowing moment arises when Luke and Leia, and company, are trapped in the bowels of the Death Star's giant trash-masher.

We tend to come very alive when we think we're going to die or fail at something important. At this point, we must call upon our most powerful resources, from all our chakras/stages. These can include contemplation, spiritual practice, our personal form of yoga or meditation, and/or the help of a wise person or therapist. As a result, we deepen our relationship with the sense of autonomy and connection in relationship. We need everything we've learned in life to evolve out of our hyper-hypo fixations of mind and body, underlying our suffering and sabotaging habits due to unresolved injuries.

Embodiment of fourth chakra nondual qualities of our self, empowers us to move past our core wounds enough to be able to include other people's interests. It plays a central role in developing the social skills of caring, cooperation, sharing, and managing differences of opinion. Becoming adept at these skills help us resolve our double-bind of wanting contact and autonomy at the same time.

160

The feeling we exist as unconditional love deepens our experience of wholeness, open tenderness, and essential innocence of our self and others. We also can feel that our unchanging-self is unbreakable, reliably present, timeless, and is an experience of the inherently benevolent presence of our being. As we refine our senses, we perceive that this experience pervades our body and environment. It gives us access to our own wholeness and our unity with the environment (without leaving our body to experience this).

One way of describing how embodied unified consciousness of unconditional love influences us, is that it helps us come into "right relation with our senses" (*pratyahara*). Rather than resorting to dispassionate relationship with our senses (as is common in most spiritual traditions), we learn to open our sensory perception so we can perceive with whole body and mind through the lens of our fourth chakra's quality of unconditional love. This is an experience of whole-being-embrace that allows us to receive all the information our emotional injury has to communicate, while aware of a much broader perspective. This empowers us to know more about what is needed to heal our hurting heart, in a way that distancing our self from our evolving-self's distortions (via dispassion, disidentification, disinterest, disengagement, and withdrawal) is unable to.

Another central supportive resource that we call upon is heart wisdom. Wisdom is often depicted mythically as a Merlin-like character who is the Hero's mentor. The mentor gives wise advice that is considered to be a magical "weapon," or a divine boon that represents the exact support we need. Heart wisdom refines our understanding of key questions for each chakra/stage: 1. "who am I? (am I safe and belong)" 2. "what are my interests?" (passions, emotions) 3. "how can I manifest my interests?"(breathing room), and in the fourth chakra/stage, we refine our understanding of, 4. "how can I be true to my interests, in relationship with other people's interests?" (breathing room and connectedness).

In meditation we discover that this Merlin-like wise-one is also the wise part of our own intra-personal self. The cardiac brain's access to heart wisdom is the part of the self that is in touch with

161

our inner oracle, our most profound discernment of personal truth (*prajna*). If our interests and budding sense of our own personal truth is supported, we learn to discern and trust what we feel in our heart (cardiac brain) as a source of wisdom and personal truth. In meditation practice we learn this, not only conceptually but also experientially. Along the way, our inner-sense of wisdom can ask us to modify our personal truth, so that it reflects what is authentic (what we feel, and not just what we think).

This dynamic can be seen in the movie *Jaws*, where the mentor is the crotchety Robert Shaw character, who knows all about sharks. It can also be seen in the *Mary Tyler Moore Show* when Lou Grant takes on the role of giving advice that provides a "magical weapon." In *Star Wars*, Obi Wan Kenobi gives Luke Skywalker his father's lightsaber. Sometimes, our wise inner-guide is required to provide (our injured self) a loving, yet assertive push, to teach us the skills needed to get the "adventure" going in the right direction. The accepting (unconditional) nature of our unchanging-self does not prod or push, only our inner wisdom can do this.

In embodied nondual meditation, we can feel that our subtle discernment and wisdom, come from our deep visceral sense, felt most clearly in our heart center (fourth chakra). We attune to our heart center to refine our recognition and awaken wisdom. This sensory information becomes an inner oracle. When wisdom is joined with fourth chakra unconditional love, we profoundly support all the emotional abilities and insights we've developed in each of the earlier stages. Wisdom and unconditional love increasingly play a role in resolving our double-bind and mastering social skills of caring, cooperation, sharing, and managing conflicts.

Our unchanging-self is not fragmented, is unbreakable, reliably present, and is an experience of the inherently benevolent presence of our being. As we refine our senses, we perceive that these experiences pervade our body and environment. This gives us access to our own wholeness and our unity with the environment (without leaving our body to experience this). Having access to these attributes of the

162

deepest dimension of our existence, together with wisdom, equips us to successfully pass over the hump at the midpoint of our journey and flourish as our authentic self.

The chakra/stage four journey toward healing and spiritual awakening starts with recognizing and sizing up the reality of the challenge. We are challenged to look at what fragments our sense of integration and wholeness. This is a challenge that is symbolically depicted as the "innermost cave." This is where we find the "treasure," meaning the solution to our challenge (in each moment, or in our life in general). Within the "cave," we are challenged to look directly at what potentially obstructs us and fragments our sense of integration and wholeness.

On our approach to the cave, we are faced with the greatest potential for well-being if we succeed. We also face our greatest potential to fail and suffer even more. Our failed state is often depicted as a dragon (reptilian brain) guarding the treasure. When we fail, our energy and consciousness are obstructed, and we fragment (the reptilian brain wins). When obstructed, our immobility response to trauma makes it very difficult to discern our personal truths and create emotional boundaries in relationship. We remain limited by sabotaging habits of mind and body. When we succeed (recovering the treasure), our energy and consciousness become unobstructed. We feel authentic, integrated, and whole.

In myth, the symbolic "inner cave" that holds the solution to our challenge is often depicted as being a deep underground location, where the desired outcome, or object of our quest, is concealed. Psychologically, the desired outcome or object is to overcome our injuries and be freed from our sabotaging habits of mind and body. We also desire to experience authenticity and wholeness-of-being.

In meditation practice, recognizing and sizing up the reality of the challenge involves learning to look at our injury and suffering and not become overwhelmed. We learn to engage to the degree we can tolerate, without freezing (the nervous system is both sympathetic and parasympathetic) and becoming immobilized under Medusa's penetrating gaze. Looking directly at our suffering involves identifying the physical, mental, and emotional danger we may be in, concerning how we can be true to our interests and be in relationship with other people's interests.

The dangers we face are depicted in myth as the archetypical villain. On a personal level, the "villain" can represent our habits of mind and body, associated with our unresolved injuries. In *Star Wars*, this climactic event can be seen when Luke, Han Solo, and Obi-Wan Kenobi enter the innermost heart of the Empire, called the Death Star, to rescue Princess Leia. Luke's sacrifices at this time (saving others), change his life as they attempt to escape, and he witnesses Obi-Wan's death at the hands of Darth Vader.

In this process, we face our primary dilemma of bolstering our sense of connectedness and our simultaneous need for autonomy. We come to recognize that we often express this in "come here, go away" behaviors which lead to us assertively push away and also cling to making contact. We can struggle to reconcile the desirable and undesirable aspects of others (people, situation, substance, etc.), with our need for their loving support, caring, cooperation, and sharing. We often recognize that the consequence of our attempt to achieve autonomy and connection, is that others have misread our true desire. Because our quest for breathing-room and contact can put us in a double-bind between two divergent needs, others can misunderstand us and respond without respect. They may have responded with impatience (an invasive agenda) or unavailability (emotional abandonment). We can feel the residue of these experience in our body. When we are emotionally invaded or abandoned, we feel a loss of support or approval from others. This can lead us to have an unstable relationship with our self and others.

Facing the traumas this leaves us with head-on before we have supportive resources, can cause us to freeze and "turn to stone." When the energy underlying our sensory, emotional and mental life is obstructed in this way, our immobility response to the trauma of invasion and/or abandonment, makes it very difficult to discern our personal truth. As a result, we are unable to create healthy emotional boundaries in relationship. We may feel fragile, confused, and disorganized.

If emotional contact with others and our independence is not resolved, we will have an increased desire to simply soothe our personal insecurities in ways that can be limiting. We may co-dependently cling and over-accommodate others out of a fear of disappointing them or the loss of love. We can become our own worst critic. Or, we also may remain defensive and avoid others with shunning behavior and anger.

Our sense of vulnerability and dependency can cause us to feel aggression and anger. This can get directed towards our self and cause us to develop low self-esteem, and even collapse in sadness and regret. We also tend to emotionally separate or split what we feel are the "good" and loved aspects of our self, from the "bad" and unpleasant aspects of our self. Or, in our confusion, we can direct our anger at others. We may resort to projection to rid our self of unwanted "bad" aspects of our self, by attributing those unwanted parts to others.

All of these experiences are what we encounter in meditation. When we face these experiences while we feel that we also exist as the essential ground of unconditional love and heart wisdom, our deepest injuries gain a broader perspective and healing happens. In the fourth chakra/stage we awaken to unconditional love. With this embodied presence, we learn to remain present with our perceived experience. We monitor our self and increasingly determine the appropriate degrees of contact and distance we need from other people (and situations, ideologies, etc.), in order to feel safe and supported to manifest our interests. This awareness provides us with valuable information concerning the kinds of interactions that support us and those that do not. As a result of this clarity, starting in the fourth stage, opposing desires between us and other people can co-exist much more easily. We begin to assert our truth and accept other people's truth.

A central reason for this as children, is that we find successful ways to feel autonomous within the relationship. We know how to respectfully do what we need in order to provide our self with a sense of emotional autonomy, without waiting for other people to do the same. This gives us the ability to sustain intimacy and not get overwhelmed. Consequently, we feel safe enough to let go of the third stage focus on establishing independence, and we begin to desire more contact and closeness in relationship.

This process can be deliberately explored in an adult relationship. For instance, there is a reciprocal learning relationship between our self and others. All interactions have cycles of engagement and disengagement, each of which can have qualitative differences. When two people pay attention to each other's needs of engagement and disengagement, an experience of autonomy within the connectedness of a relationship grows. Berry Brazelton (1989) explains that a consequence of a form of contact in relationship, that honors the needed cycles of engagement and disengagement, is well-being and balance. The presence of this well-being serves as an internal guide in our contact with other people.

When doing couples therapy, in a subtle but important exercise, I guide each partner to deliberately explore a "process dance" of healthy engagement and disengagement to uncover the way they establish connectedness and breathing-room (via looking away, checking inside, expressing the desire to come back to a topic later, etc.). One way this can be explored is by guiding each partner to look at the other (or if alone, engage with an imaginary other, person, situation, etc.), noticing what this contact feels like, and when the desire to look away arises. I guide them to notice if the contact feels reassuring or imposing, and how they respond to this (such as what sensations in the body inform them, and what emotions and thoughts arise). When one partner feels the desire to look or wants to look away, we explore what impulse inspired this desire. I guide them to notice what this feels like in the body, and if there are associated thoughts and emotions. We also explore what being with a partner who disengages by looking away, feels like (what this feels like in the body and if there are associated thoughts and emotions).

In this process, information concerning how we express the need for breathing-room (often to simply check-in with what we feel individually) and how we express the need for contact, is uncovered, based on how the body responds, and what we feel. We learn about the feeling of being imposed upon, and the feeling of losing the sense of being connected (emotional

166

abandonment). We learn about how we create breathing-room. (Do we shut down, emotionally distance our self, or maintain the sense of connectedness as we create breathing-room?) We also learn about what we do, what sensations inform us, and if we desire more contact when other people want breathing-room. (Do we withdraw, become over-accommodating, or reach out and try to take control?)

The understanding that emerges about our needs and how this can be achieved skillfully, is a powerful discovery that supports healthy bonding and autonomy in relationship. (Of course, I explore a similar but slightly different process with people who are not in a romantic relationship. The results are equally profound.)

When this is practiced in a conscious manner, the learning that takes place correlates directly to Brazelton's findings with respect to how infants establish a bond and grow autonomy with their caregivers. As adults, learning how to skillfully establish a bond and autonomy in relationship, results in a desire for a deeper inner-experience of our self and with others, at the same time. Each person progressively enhances their sense of self and deepens authentic contact with the other person. In the fourth stage of our development, we have a fairly secure sense of self, and are able to learn to engage with, and disengage from others, in a non-defensive manner. This experience, in turn, grows our desire for more closeness and cultivates a profound level of mutuality and emotional intimacy in relationship.

In the fourth stage, we increasingly feel the desire to fully commit to our personal truth and to be fully in the relationship with our partner's personal truth. When we can do this successfully, we have more clarity about the capacity, nature, and purpose of our interaction with others. This provides support for us in adopting a variety of contactful yet autonomous ways of relating. We can more easily feel connected when separate and autonomous in our daily experiences of life.

As a result, our repertoire of responses to old conflicts increases, and our window of tolerance for intense experiences widens. The clarity we have about the nature of our desire for contact and autonomy, allows us to stand-up for our personal truth (healthy boundaries) from a place of inner-strength rather than fear. We learn not to respond to others in a reactive, automatic way, and yet we remain responsive and involved.

As a part of our successful negotiation of chakra/stage four dynamics, we feel a need to be recognized, and the need to recognize other people, as equal but distinct individuals. How we deal with the unresolved emotional issues that are uncovered is authentic and compassionate. Our relationship with significant others becomes more about discovering who we authentically are, and who our partner truly is, rather than behaving in a way to simply soothe our personal insecurities (over accommodate, remain defensive). We grow a basic sense that we can trust and respect our own emotional boundaries (protecting and standing up for our self), so we are less inclined to place unreasonable demands on others in an attempt to compensate for our feelings of weakness. In friendship, this allows us to relinquish our quest for the fantasy of the ideal friend or partner who will complete us and whom, in turn, we will complete. We know we are complete.


**HEART CHAKRA**
**Name**: The Sanskrit word for the fourth chakra is "*anahata,*" which means "unstruck" or "unhurt." The name is said to imply that beneath the hurts from past experiences lies nondual consciousness, where no hurt exists. It is commonly called the "Heart Chakra."
**Location**: The Heart chakra is at the center of the seven primary chakras, with three below and three above. The Heart chakra is located at the center of the chest, deep in the subtle core.

**Symbolic Level**
The seed mantra for the Heart chakra is "Yam." The corresponding element is air, which disperses and integrates the spiritual understanding of love. This is because air is within and all around us, connecting us to everything. It is most often associated with the color green, which represents transformation and love energy. The sense of touch informs the Heart chakra.

## Emotional Level

The emotions related to this chakra are love, joy, compassion, grief, and anger. The fourth chakra capacity for open, tender, unconditional love, enhances our ability to be in relationship based on mutuality that is non-abandoning and non-invasive. We gain clarity about our desire for emotional closeness and independence, yet our capacity to communicate this is not fully established until the fifth chakra/stage.

Our lack of facility to express our personal truth can have a chilling effect, and make it difficult to sustain the intensity of full contact in relationship without getting overwhelmed. We may be very sure of what we think and believe, and yet become confused about what we feel inside. Or, we may have a clear body experience of our personal truth, but still need to manage the anxiety that accompanies honestly expressing this overtly. Our oscillating needs for meaningful contact and breathing-room can become quite confusing. Our friend or partner may be unsure about when to be close and nurturing, and when to support our independence.

Yet, as we awaken to the experience of unconditional love, we quite naturally open up to experiencing acceptance, love, forgiveness, gratitude, and compassion for our self, as well as for others. These feelings help us own our desire for mutuality, as our personal truth, and soothe the anxiety about how others will respond. As a Hero at this stage, we let go of the old, outdated behavior and grow the ability to cooperate with others and manage conflicts in relationship, in an open and receptive way. This requires us to learn how to receive, to attune, to listen, as well as let out and express what is in and on our heart. We grow our ability to show-up in relationship to our self and others, with an authentic, open heart. This establishes the foundation for the fifth chakra/stage, where we communicate our personal truth while remaining open to meaningful contact in relationship.

While each chakra is an expression of nondual consciousness when balanced, often this balance does not become a stable integral part of our self and our relational life, until the fourth chakra is awakened. This is why I often attune to and embody the

Heart chakra along with awakening any of the other chakras. Unconditional love seems to illuminate all the other chakras and deepen our experience of wholeness, open tenderness, and essential innocence.

We can find symbolic clues to the fourth chakra's healing properties in the illustration at the center of the fourth chakra mandala. This mandala is composed of two superimposed triangles (as shown in the *mandala* image for the fourth chakra). One triangle is pointing up and the other down, and together, they form a six-pointed star (like the Star of David). Energetically, this is about the upward and downward movement of subtle energy (*ida*, *pingala*) (see Image #16). To gain access to the stillness of complete balance in the central-channel (*sushumna*), energy needs to flow freely in both directions. In the dimension of subtle energy, this is what brings balance (*sattva*) to our physical, emotional, and mental life, and non-attachment to the outdated habits associated with our unresolved injuries.

In terms of consciousness, the upward-facing triangle also symbolizes evolution into nondual consciousness (*Shiva, purusa*). The triangle facing downward symbolizes involution, the movement of unified consciousness incarnating within duality consciousness (*Shakti, prakriti*). In this incarnation, we experience our unity with all that is (universal or cosmic consciousness). It is in the Heart chakra that a balance can be attained between the upward and downward awakening of consciousness, as they join in harmony.

Together, unified consciousness (*Shiva*) and energy (*Shakti*), nonduality and duality, most effectively co-mingle and form the ultimate union (*yab yum*). By meeting in mutuality (without hierarchy and with equal value), this is symbolic of how unified consciousness needs duality consciousness in order to be self-aware (rather than transcendent); and how duality consciousness needs unified consciousness to evolve. In this awakening, nondual consciousness becomes a body experience that can be felt and self-reflective (aware that it is aware). Meeting in mutuality is also symbolic of unified consciousness not bypassing our duality-based habits of our personal psychology, but instead pervading (not as a verb or action) and co-existing with duality.

This communion is our whole-being-embrace. This is the essence of relational holism, as discussed.

The nondual perspective in the Heart chakra that we begin to integrate, is reflected in the meaning of the Sanskrit word for the Heart chakra, "*Anahata*," meaning "unstruck sound." The term "unstruck" metaphorically describes unified consciousness. Usually, we hear sound when two objects strike each other. These two objects are symbolic of duality consciousness. The "unstruck sound" means that the nondual dimension of the Heart Chakra is uncaused, pre-existent, and arises from itself. The heart is its own source, without a second. It is "untouched" by the drama of our life.

Our Heart chakra's expression of unity is felt as an experience of profound acceptance, connection, wholeness-of-being, and unity. The degree to which we allow our self to receive this truth is often our biggest challenge. We may mentally understand that it is true, and yet the injured part of us has another, less supportive impression. With practice, we come to recognize that we are fundamentally good, loving, and lovable. We recognize that we actually are universal, unconditional love. Many of us access unconditional love via an external female archetypal deity, such as the "Great Mother," "Mother Nature," and "Mother Mary."

Our body experience of this realization, in its communion with our broken heart, is what we must pay attention to, in order to heal. For it is in attending to the body's subtle sensory experiences of our deepest inborn nature, that we can communicate most powerfully to our reptilian brain and our emotional brain. We thereby transform our forebrain and heal the deepest wounds that we harbor in every cell of our body (Kolk, Levine).

To complete the Emotional Level associated with the fourth chakra, it is valuable to mention that the lotus in the heart chakra has twelve petals, each representing a different aspect of the heart chakra. Briefly, these aspects are: 1) Spiritual Love: is love that is not bound by physical limitations. 2) Physical Love: is the love we experience through our physical senses, such as touch, sight, and sound. 3) Friendship: is the love that we feel for our friends and our social circle. 4) Family: is the love that we feel for our family members that creates familial bonds. 5) Romantic Love: is the love that we feel towards our partners in an intimate relationship. 6) Self-Acceptance: is the love involved in accepting and loving our own strengths and weaknesses. 7) Inner Peace: is the peace and calm that comes from having access to unconditional love. 8) Compassion: This is the love that gives us the ability to feel empathy and compassion towards others. 9) Joy: This is the joy and happiness we feel when we awaken unconditional love. 10) Equilibrium: This is the sense of balance in all aspects of life that results from love. 11) Gratitude: This is the gratitude in our life we feel when we awaken unconditional love. 12) Forgiveness: is the ability to forgive our self and others for past mistakes and hurts, when we awaken unconditional love

### Hyper-Hypo Imbalances

When the Heart chakra is out of balance, we can feel heartbroken, abandoned, isolated, rejected, self-hatred, angry, and so much more. When we respond to heartbreak in a hypo way, we get fixated in the discharge phase. Symptoms include feeling depressed, ongoing grief, apathy, faithlessness, hopelessness, distrust, uncommitted, and emotionally detached.

When we respond to heartbreak in a hyper way, we get fixated in the charge phase. Symptoms include inflexible conditional love, or possessive love. We can be excessively particular about what love and appreciation from others needs to look like. We may feel unforgiving, angry, bitter, envious, or be anxiously addicted to love. Another form of an unbalanced, hyper-heart chakra, can result in overemphasizing love at the expense of rational thinking, and being unable to establish healthy boundaries in relationship.

Each moment we are faced with the choice to desperately hang on to limiting habits or let go into the freshness that accompanies dissolution and awakening. To further clarify how embodied nondual consciousness helps us overcome our deepest injuries in the fourth chakra, learning to let go of effort is a central part of responding more consciously and making choices that are not based on habit.

172

## Letting Go of Effort

To succeed, the fourth chakra/stage draws upon the understanding of self in relationship found in all the earlier chakra/stages. Moreover, the fourth chakra/stage has important "magical weapons" of its own as well, such as unconditional love, heart wisdom, and effortlessness. Our refinement of effortlessness communicates directly to the heart of what we need to deliver the final blow to our outdated sabotaging habits of emotion, thought, and sensation associated with our trauma symptoms.

Our survival responses to challenge/threat (internal or external) progress from 1) arrest (when we get clear about self in relation to other), to 2) orient (when we discern and commit to a choice in how we will respond), to 3) flight and fight (or when we try to manifest our skillful means of response), and to 4) freeze (when flight or fight did not work), or release (when our skillful means worked).

The fourth chakra/stage is a pivotal stage that determines our success or failure in how we respond to what we experience. It is a time in relationship when we have an emotional desire for divergent emotional needs (contact and independence) that can leave us in a double bind and with a sense of confusion. A central issue we deal with in the fourth chakra/stage is freezing, feeling immobilized, or in a double bind and confused.

At the heart of our injuries that makes the challenge/threat difficult is the unresolved experience of not being seen, understood, respected, and loved in a way that feels supportive. Later in life, we may notice that we have lost the flow of our creativity and responsiveness, or we are unable to think when we need to. This can leave us feeling disempowered and even trapped (or the feeling of a double bind). As a result, we can become frozen in our ways and trapped in self-defeating styles of relating.

A precondition for not being able to resolve our injuries/trauma is that we are both frightened (by the challenge/threat) and perceive that we are trapped at the same time (Levine (2010). Our feelings of overwhelm get frozen in time and, later, as adults, get switched on by experiences that remind

173

us of the original incident in some way. Yet, as Levine explains, our frozen state and immobility response can happen with fear or without fear.

For example, as Levine points out, we experience some immobility in the absence of fear during the consensual sexual act and orgasmic release. A mother cat carrying its limp kitten securely in its mouth is another example. Fear is heightened when we resist feeling paralyzed or enraged (Levine). When we allow our self to feel the trauma symptoms of immobility and emotions like rage in a safe way, we can experience them without fear or overwhelm. If we are not oriented toward fear when we experience immobility, the immobility does not last long at all. We experience what trauma therapists refer to as "self-paced termination."

It is in the fourth chakra/stage that we learn to uncouple fear from our sense of immobility by overcoming the fear we associate with our emotional injuries. We uncouple fear from our sense of immobility in a variety of ways. When nondual consciousness is a body experience, rather being dispassionate toward what we experience, we move toward disturbing beliefs and emotions so that we can move through them. With this approach, contact between our immobility (or the feeling of a double bind) and the nondual-qualities of our unchanging-self introduces our fear to a new set of subtle sensations. This offers us a broader perspective changes our relationship with our immobility response and uncouples it from fear of being trapped.[39]

Another important way we uncouple fear from our sense of immobility or double bind, is learning let go of habitual effort as we perceive and respond to the feeling of being trapped and immobilized. With this understanding, the sage Jayaratha commented, "Those that went before said that desire [suffering]

---

[39] The alternative subtle sensations, or feeling-tones, offer our interoceptive senses (ventral vagal nerve) radically new information. This activates our brain's "social-engagement system," which allows us to feel open and receptive to contact with our environment (Porges). They also activate our brain's "self-engagement system," which allows us to have open, receptive contact between our evolving-self and our unchanging-self (Siegel).

174

is checked by practice of dispassion; we teach that this is achieved by desisting from all effort." (Tantraloka, 4.257b-8a; bracket added).

In letting go of all effort, we do not collapse. Effortlessness is also not a state of inaction but rather action that is not motivated by our fear-based habits (such as flight-fight, freeze, and immobility) that live inside of us so unconsciously. With more effortlessness, the effort we do exert is pervaded by a sense of letting go and openness.

When we release any habitual constrictions in our perception and response to experience, we discover a feeling of inner openness and inner space that can be very awakening and relaxing at the same time (balance). What we also find is that the sage Jayaratha's meditation advice, of not transcending but to "desist of all effort," naturally refines our senses. It supports us in opening to the experience we are having in life, in a fuller way.

Without fear, we no longer perpetuate the immobility or intense emotion, and the injury can be released. Immobility, in the absence of unnecessary or appropriate fear, can be benign and even pleasurable. Learning to let go of all effort in embodied nondual meditation, allows us to let go of habitual effort, and have the  choice to respond to immobility differently. In the process, we heal our injuries, evolve, and awaken to the spiritual essence of life.

### The Essence of Our Physical Nature

With the broad perspective that unified consciousness provides, we can experience the physical aspect of our self as our "essence" of physicality. This essence is the fundamental, unchanging-ground of the physical dimension that pervades our whole body as a unified presence-of-being. Access to the essence of our physical nature, provides powerful support for us to skillfully manage the intensity of what we experience in life, without fragmenting.

The "essence" of our physical nature is not solid but instead it is transparent and completely permeable. When we feel that we exist as the permeable nature of this physical, conscious stillness, it fundamentally changes our physiology and our relationship

175

with suffering. One important expression of this change is that the suffering, conflict, projections, and attitudes all seem to pass through our physical form, without disturbing our sense of wholeness and unity.

As life experiences pass through the space of our body, they produce an energy current. When we feel that we exist as our unchanging-self, rather than constricting, flinching, or subtly closing against the movement of this energy, we remain open and allow it to move freely through our body's internal conscious stillness. With this experience, people's expression of emotion, such as sadness or anger, flows through the conscious stillness within, without leaving a trace. We can still respond authentically, with wisdom and compassion, because we can remain fully present, without fragmenting.

This experience is not a theoretical product of our thinking mind, but rather a matter of our own direct experience. It is an understanding of embodied nondual experience as an expression of self, that lies at the forefront of where spirituality can be integrated with our psychological process. This paradigm shift in how we perceive the physical aspect of our being, has a powerful direct influence on our psyche's transformation. Because the experience that we are notis a tangible experience in our body, it has a direct influence on our nervous system, brain , and our senses. It fundamentally changes our perception of our self and our environment. This offers us more autonomy from overwhelming experiences and more choices in how we respond to life. It is a visceral shift in perception that plays a vital role in overcoming trauma, in a way that is virtually unrecognized in spiritual communities, and in Western psychology.

What we discover in meditation is that the physical nature of self is an aspect of unified consciousness that has continuity, and a oneness with our environment due to the holographic nature of existence. We can feel this unified expression of existence even in the material plane, because we recognize that (as spiritual mystics and quantum physics understand) it all comes from the same shared source of consciousness. We also feel how the essence of our physicality is not based on any particular physical expression.

176

We may experience being in nature where we spontaneously feel we are a part of it, and it is a part of us. Our body feels a part of the same fabric that is physical in nature. While attuned to the essential nature of what is physical, we may even feel that we can reach out and actually touch the same essence of existence in nature and in other people. The separateness of the physical dimension disappears, and we feel a sense of wonder and awe. Many of us perceive this timeless quality of unity as an oceanic, deeply moving, exhilarating experience. It generates a way of perceiving reality that can seem mystical and magical, where each element is perceived together holistically, creating a moment of unity.

**NERVOUS SYSTEM: Stuck versus Discharge**
**CHIL DEVELOPMENT: Object Constancy**
**ADULT RELATIONSHIP: Satisfaction**
**CHAKRA #5: "Throat" Chakra, *vishuddha*, meaning**
      **purification. Unified sense of self as "Expression."**

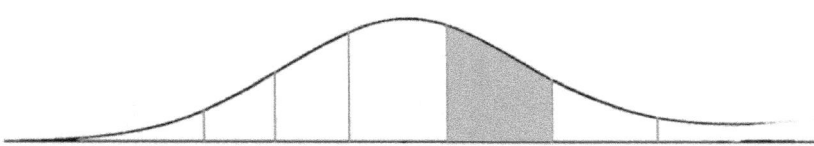

**NERVOUS SYSTEM**

As a recap, when we feel a threat, our nervous system initially goes into the 1) "arrest" phase, which enters into 2) the "orientation" phase, and this is followed up with 3) "flight-fight" phase (i.e., learning skills to be safe and supported). If we cannot succeed at either flight or fight, our system enters 4) the "freeze" phase, which is accompanied by an immobility response with dissociative symptoms. If this continues, in stage five, we feel cold, frozen, and feel stuck. But if in chakra/stage three (3), we are successful, and instead of going into a freeze state we manifest our potential, then in stage five, we feel relief and discharge the excess energy (trembling, shaking, sighing, or simply relaxing in various ways). This discharge is our focus in the fifth chakra/stage.

This success can be illustrated in a graph as a release into a post "climax" state of satisfaction (see above image). At this point, we discharge excess energy because we no longer benefit from the energy that allows us to flee, fight, or freeze. Not releasing it would actually be harmful. As mentioned, similar to other animals, we naturally physically discharge this energy through shivering, shaking, trembling, and jerking. A less dramatic form of discharge can be felt as a time of relaxing, relief, sighing, settling down, and letting go of acquired patterns of constriction.

## Energetics

In general, it is important to learn to be present with the feeling of discharging energy, and letting go of our limiting or sabotaging habits of body, emotion, and mind. Our energy discharge is accompanied by a process of dissolution and letting go of habits that interfere with our sense of integration and wholeness. This is a dissolution into wakefulness. Remaining present helps us integrate the experience psychologically, increasing our resiliency. Staying present can happen on a variety of levels (sensory, emotional, mental). In the transcendent meditation practice of neutral witnessing, we remain dispassionate towards our emotional and mental life. We narrow our focus so we experience our thoughts and emotions simply as sensory stimuli of temporal, vibratory patterns that occur. I believe that in the long run this prevents us from fully integrating the experience psychologically.

That said, when we are unable to relax (such as when it feels dangerous), narrowing our focus to only our sensations of discharging energy, as in neutral witnessing, does help us relearn how to release. Paying close attention to all the sensory nuances of what it feels like to relax, open, and awaken, facilitates this. It is important to take a moment to experience what sensations of relief and satisfaction feel like after it is clear we have successfully dealt with any situation, even small ones. Each time we recognize we are relaxing and opening, even slightly, it is important to pause to notice and savor this. In this way, we grow tolerance to feeling these body sensations without becoming overwhelmed. We begin to learn that relaxing is safe and that we can trust it, at least in the present. With practice, we can then relearn to broaden our awareness to include the mental and emotional content associated with our experience.[40]

Attending to the energetic, sensory dynamics of relaxing and receiving satisfaction are important. However, no matter how many times we release physical blocks, they will return unless we attend to the psychological reasons why we can't relax, feel safe, and open to satisfaction. The opposite is also true. Mental understanding and psychological insights alone, usually will not resolve how we harbor trauma in the body. The psychological reasons will be described in a moment, but the descriptions are only the roadmap.

The roadmap is there to be consulted as we engage in contemplation and meditation practice. This highlights how our body is involved in every aspect of the psychological dynamics that need to be dealt with. Our pain in the neck, heavy heart, and the knots in our stomach often have emotional roots. The practice of physically relaxing helps us establish a foundation from which we can recalibrate our physiology. This supports us to psychologically integrate what it means to face the source of our suffering, gain a broader perspective, and let go of the constrictions that underly all states of unbalance and fixation. Embodiment of the nondual-quality of the fifth chakra enables us to do this.

## CHILD DEVELOPMENT: Object Constancy, 24 Months plus

Growing trust that well-being and satisfaction are safe to feel happens in progressive stages. It develops emotionally through adequate bonding in the *first stage*, consistent support for our

---

[40] Another form of narrowing our attention is often found in relaxation techniques. Relaxation techniques usually involve steady alertness (*sthira*), or focused attention on something that is calming while savoring this experience in the body. Some of the details of these practices can be found in "Refining Our Senses & Attunement" (*chapter four*), developing a relationship with the ground (chair, yoga mat, earth) via, "Diaphragms as Grounding Foundation" (*chapter six*), and conscious breathing without effort, as described in "Effortless Breathing" (Appendix Two). Other simple conscious breathing practices, such as making the exhale longer than the inhale, also can be valuable. But effortless breathing stands out in its simplicity and ability to facilitate accessing unified consciousness.

unique character in the *second stage*, recognition of our autonomy and abilities to manifest our unique character in the *third stage*, and ongoing, dependable autonomy combined with loving contact in the *fourth stage*. In the *fifth stage*, there are two important emotional developments. The first is that we take the loving support that was started in the fourth stage (focused on loving our autonomy and personal interests), and we bring this to a new level. This level is about loving what we express to other people (stage three expressions were not directed at others). As a result, we learn how to communicate our deepest personal truths to others with a new sense of integrity.

In the *fifth stage*, which is prominent between two to three years of age (but emotionally reoccurs throughout life), we develop an internalized model of the parent as a means of growing a sense of self. This internalized model is based on our ability to sustain an inner-experience of what feels real that orients us ("object constancy" in psychology). With this self-identity, we ideally learn to navigate relationships and begin to establish and express the personal truth underlying our healthy boundaries in relationship.

At this stage on our Hero's Journey, we are initially still trying to escape the vengeful forces of our outdated habits. On the way out of the woods, we are being pursued by our old conditioning that enfeeble our fourth chakra/stage powers. Some of the best chase scenes occur as we escape from the grips of our sabotaging ways. The elixir or treasure that we take (in the fourth stage) from our guarded conditioning, that we defend so much, leaves our old habits devitalized.

If we have not yet managed to reconcile with the source of our injury (parents, partner, society, political foe, etc.), it/they can come raging after us. Our inner-critic can flare up, or our habitual negative emotions and thoughts try to take over. In *Star Wars*, Luke and his supportive crew flee from the Death Star with Princess Leia and plan to eliminate Darth Vader (Luke's father). In the movie *E.T.*, Elliott and E.T. take a moonlight bicycle flight to escape from governmental authority. This scene concludes with both parties reconciling their differences. The fifth stage is when we find this reconciliation.

As our self-concept as an individual develops, ideally, our self-confidence becomes fully established. This confidence is supported by chakra/stage two (the reciprocal of stage five). This is when we gain clarity about our birthright to have interests and a sense of personal truth. As a child, this is when we come to accept that we are different from our parents, which supports us in engaging with substitutes for the parents when they are absent. In embodied nondual meditation, we discover the most empowering "substitution" is our own nondual self that has always been with us (as discussed in a moment).

Ideally, in chakra/stage five, we not only learn to become clear about our own personal truth, but we also learn to express it to other people. This involves understanding other people's intentions and negotiating an arrangement that serves us. When our expressions are supported, we feel reconciled. We are able to relax and enjoy the satisfaction of shared creative projects, or meaningful interactions with people in our life.

Yet, if we do not learn to become clear about our own personal truth and our expressions are not supported, we can become fixated in the fifth chakra/stage. When our expressions of personal truth and emotional boundaries are not supported, we maintain our defensive styles of relating based on survival strategies. We can be afraid, resentful, and often vindictive. We may be unable to express our personal truth clearly, or we express our needs rigidly, passive-aggressively, or we do it in a fearful way that lacks the power of conviction.

When we first learn how to use words as children, the fifth chakra/stage's nature of open communication becomes a major dynamic in our life. When our "verbal self" develops as a child, the capacity to have an objective, self-reflective ability emerges. We ideally begin to create an independent internal narrative, reflecting the personal truth of our authentic feelings, without being overly influenced by what other people think and want.

This internal narrative of personal truth is fueled by our second chakra/stage interests, fantasies, and imagination; third chakra/stage's ability to manifest our interests and imagination; and four chakra's self-acceptance, compassion, and love. (Accessing the balanced, unified state of these chakras greatly enhances expression of personal truth.) This support for our internal narrative, inspires us in the fifth chakra/stage, to feel, think, and creatively communicate our most honest personal truth. We reconcile other people's interests with our own and negotiate an arrangement that serves us through honest communication. Honest communication honors our self and enhances our ability to relate our truth to others (people, situations, ideology, substance, etc.). It helps us go beyond mundane communication to acknowledge the deeper reality of our interactions with others.

## ADULT RELATIONSHIP

Where the fourth chakra/stage is a bridge between the lower and upper chakras, what characterizes the fifth chakra/stage is that it is infused with a broader perspective (based on reconciling other people's interests with our own and negotiating for our personal truth). This allows us to let go of limiting habits of mind and body. As mentioned, this is expressed energetically as the "discharge" or "release" phase of letting go of our limiting fixations. In the process, we emotionally bring to completion issues about autonomy and connection that we started in the fourth stage.

Yet, to reconcile other people's interests with our own and express honestly when we have unresolved relationship injuries, we need to rely heavily on our fourth chakra's unconditional love as consistent and reliable support. In meditation, we awaken to this unconditional love in communion with our inner-critic. The biggest challenge that we face as we express our deepest truths is maintaining a sense of self-love.

The ability to love as a child, arises out of the feeling of being loved and cared for by others during the fourth chakra/stage. If we did not receive love as a child, as an adult, attuning to our body experience of the essential ground-of-being as unconditional love is profoundly supportive. It can inspire a sense of the compassion, hope, and strength we need to honestly express our personal truth in relationship. When we bring what is interior to us out into the open for all to witness, the fourth chakra quality of unconditional loving support, allows us to experience relationships with others as trustworthy because we trust our self. While trusting others is important, deep trust always involves trusting our self, first. We can trust our own inner wholeness-of-being.

## Trust

The emotion that is traditionally associated with the fifth chakra is trust. Since we ideally accept the reality of who we are in the fifth chakra/stage, we naturally have access to an inner sense of self-trust. Accepting the reality of who we are is supported by trust in our connectedness, and our sovereignty. We feel this self-trust increasingly continues to exist in us, even when our needs are not met. In this way, our feeling of self-trust becomes independent from how our life events unfold or how others interact with us. This increases our ability to trust life itself.

A central trait of maintaining our personal truth is that we understand that our desire to be treated in a way that works best for us, originates, and ultimately is realized, by us. We certainly want others to fully show up, be caring, and be respectful. But we also recognize that we are personally and unilaterally responsible for fulfilling our needs for our own well-being. This does not mean we have to do it all alone. We might need a guide or guru to help us for a while. But it is up to us to find the right kind of guide, friend, situation, or even substance that works for us. It is up to us to engage, actively seek, and express our need for support from others, even if they do not offer it. Of course, if they accept, it is up to us to set the terms of engagement. If they refuse, it is also up to us to decide what we need to do to take care of our self.

There are always situations or other people who do not behave respectfully towards us. Yet, because we've internalized the feeling of unconditional love in our fourth stage, this disrespect has little impact on us. The "I love you, now change" syndrome that is so common in relationships is replaced by a personal understanding that is reflected in the statement to our self that says, "I love and believe in myself for who I am, even if others disagree with me."

184

Taking personal responsibility in this way guides us towards having a more self-referent orientation in our relationships. When we experience trauma, it is as if our system becomes locked into being externally oriented, looking for incoming injury. Our sense of autonomy is created in a reactive and defensive way. In the fifth chakra/stage, we learn how our sense of personal responsibility and ability to show up for our self, helps reverse this. This helps us get out of being hyper-vigilant and overly reactive.

We come to realize that accepting that "we are good," or that "others are trustworthy," is not something others can prove to us. As much as others reassure us, we also realize we will fully believe it when we see it. If we don't come to trust that we will show up for our self, and make room for the feeling of trust within us, no amount of wanting others to be trustworthy will work. Plus, no amount of others convincing us that we are lovable will stick. Self-acceptance is ultimately a personal affair.

Physically, the throat is a threshold and passageway into the rest of our body. Our throat muscles are closely involved in supporting oxygen to enter our body. The throat is also a threshold that serves as an emotional boundary. Any unwanted substances are turned away as we choke them off. At this stage, we learn to develop healthy emotional boundaries that are clear and yet flexible. We have a choice about what we let in, and what we expel. We make a conscious choice to selectively accept or reject food, emotions, people, and situations. We can decide to exclude what we find meaningless or hostile, while letting in affection and good intentions.

While every stage depends on developing healthy boundaries with respect to the relevant emotional issues at that stage, in the fifth chakra/stage we take responsibility to reconcile other people's interests with our own. We are able to honor other's interests more and respectfully clearly communicate our honest truth (support by power and unconditional love). The fifth chakra/stage is where we can regain our pre-trauma expression of what we need to feel we belong, and that we are accepted, respected, and loved that were shut down. These honest personal truths come back into full expression. With practice, we refine our expressions to a fine art so they effortlessly arise out of our sense of wholeness and not overwhelm.

A central part of this refinement is our ability to reach beyond our immediate interaction to a broader perspective of who we are and understand others. This ability is an important trait of the fifth chakra/stage. When we are supported by unified consciousness, rather than "reaching" for more perspective, it feels as though we let go and open to a deeper pre-existing, innate knowing of our self (discussed more soon as "*shraddha*").

This knowing supports us in developing a deeper understanding of what is actually happening in the present moment beyond our limiting habitual responses. We honor healthy emotional boundaries based on what feels undeniably true, and we relax all the habitual constrictions that result from injury and fear. Our sense of personal sovereignty supports us to open to physical, emotional, and mental contact, in a way that works for us. As a result, we easily adapt to challenges that arise while managing unexpected changes that naturally happen in life. When problems do arise, they present manageable challenges rather than crises. The impermanence of life stops causing us to clam up and solidify our outdated conditioning.


**THROAT CHAKRA**
**Name**: The Sanskrit word for the fifth chakra is "*vishuddha*," which means purification.
**Location**: The fifth chakra is located in the base of the throat at the level of the larynx.

**Symbolic Level**
The element corresponding to the fifth chakra is ether, or space. The main sense is hearing. The color is sky blue. The seed mantra is "*Ham*." The *vishuddha* Throat chakra is considered to be the purification center, where the nectar of "immortality" (*amrita*) drips down from above and infuses our body with unified consciousness. The ability for "higher discrimination" (wisdom within personal truth; *prajna*) is associated with the creative nature of the Throat chakra's nondual-essence of

186

"expression." This aspect of our wholeness is our existence as the essence of expression.

**Emotional Level**

As mentioned, our fifth chakra involves the enhanced ability to discriminate and access the nondual dimension of our existence as the essence of expression. In significant ways, this parallels the process that happens for the evolving-self in the fifth stage as we develop "object constancy." As discussed, this is when clear discernment of our sense of self orients us. We learn to navigate relationships and express our deepest personal truth. It is significant to understand that when we feel an abiding timeless experience of that which does not change in the dimension of nonduality, it takes our experience of object constancy to a whole new level of existential trust (*shraddha*) (see *chapter seven* for more on existential trust). We gain access to a sense of wholeness as an enduring, reliable, empty presence within us. This emptiness is filled with a quality-rich wholeness. This can feel enormously blissful.

Quality-rich emptiness (*sunyata*) is the experience of our body as emptiness, like an empty vessel that is a fully receptive potential. Receptive potential is paradoxical in nature. While we feel fully receptive, this emptiness is conscious and feels like the luminous presence of our own being that, as Judith Blackstone explains, shines from within each cell of the body. The receptive potential of our presence-of-being is a way of experiencing the stillness, wholeness, and unity that pervades the whole internal depth of the body and mind.

Emptiness as receptive potential, pervades our body and environment, yet when we do not leave our body as we experience this, we own and sustain this sense of emptiness as an expression of our self in our daily life. Meditation upon and feeling the emptiness and receptive potential of our luminous presence-of-being, transforms our sensory orientation to a new paradigm of existence. It broadens our perspective and changes how we relate to our self and our environment.

The fifth chakra/stage bridges the fourth chakra's unconditional love with the sixth chakra's nature of knowing, (intuition, wisdom, understanding, intelligence). Anatomically, the throat serves as a gateway between our head and chest. It psychologically discriminates and joins the two body segments. In this position, it can bring together and integrate the deep understanding inherent in both head and chest. In the dimension of unified consciousness, the ground-of-unconditional love comes together with the sixth chakra ground-of-knowing as a rich mixture of inner knowing and wisdom.

As we embody the nondual-essence of unconditional love, we can take personal responsibility to show up for our self by consciously expressing our personal truth for our self so all can hear it. Savoring the feeling that articulating truth gives us, brings great relief (discharge) and satisfaction (deepening our bliss). This naturally awakens the ground-of-knowing (wisdom, understanding, intelligence) of the sixth chakra.

Conscious expression of what feels true to us serves as a personal mantra. Mantra is a sound that carries wisdom and leaves us with a resonant feeling of truth. We awaken parts of the body with mantra (*nyasa*). Savoring what personal truth feels like in the body is profoundly healing. Noticing what part of the body relaxes and opens the most, lets us know what parts are receiving a broader perspective. Whatever part of our body relaxes, opens, and gives us more room to inhabit and fully live in. Taking time to integrate this experience of being more embodied is important.

The Throat chakra has sixteen petals. The sixteen petals depict sixteen vowels of the Sanskrit alphabet that are expressed through sixteen sacred sounds in Sanskrit.[41] Expression of these sounds, while attuned to the associated state of consciousness, facilitates overcoming the injuries associated with the fifth stage of development. With practice, we deepen our awakening of unified consciousness. The sixteen petals of the Throat chakra also represent the so-called sixteen abilities (*kalas*) related to our stages of development. They are also said to represent the

---

[41] 1) *am* – Compassion, 2) *aam* – Forgiveness, 3) *im* – Poison, 4) *eem* – Straightforwardness, 5. *um* - Self-control, 6) *oom* - Dynastical pride, 7) *rim* – Sacrifice, 8) *reem* – Pride, 9) *lrim* – Nectar, 10) *lreem* – Calmness, 11) *em* – Happiness, 12) *aim* – Vociferation, 13) *om* – Vanity, 14) *aum* - Noble nature, 15) *aam* – Truthfulness, 16) *ahm* – Knowledge.

sixteen abilities or expressions of the nondual-quality of Krishna, that become available as we awaken the nondual-essence of the fifth chakra (including dancer, singer, honesty, and truth).

When we recognize our self as the innocence and wholeness of our uninjured, nondual-essence of expression (balanced fifth chakra), we feel supported to express what is interior to us and bring it out into the open for all to witness. Any habit of withholding or lying, increasingly feels unnecessary. Spontaneously communicating our deepest personal truths that arise out of our experience of wholeness, is different from impulsive communication. It has wisdom and consciousness rather than dissociation and habit.

It takes comfort and trust in who we are, in order show up for our self and express our self openly. Embodying the experience that we exist as pure expression, together with feeling support from realizing we exist as unconditional love, gives us this comfort and trust. We feel enough self-confidence to tolerate the possible loss of connection that can result from expressing our own unique personal truth. When we add our fifth chakra's sense of discernment and wisdom to the mix, we feel the connectedness and wholeness that we need to be able to trust that expressing our self authentically, is safe and good for everybody involved (even if they don't always like it).

If other people do not like what we express, our sense of comfort and trust allows us to withstand the reality that they may withdraw their affection and appreciation, as happened to many of us as a child. Yet, in the fifth chakra, we progressively grow the ability to feel a reliable sense of deep connectedness. We feel this even when a loved one or something important to us is no longer available, leaving us with a feeling of longing and emptiness. We also grow the ability to retain a bond with another person, even if we are unhappy, angry, or disappointed by their behavior, or if they are with ours. This does not interfere with our ability to wisely discriminate and express our limits and needs.

One of the hallmarks of an evolved person is the ability to speak our truth to others with no fear of punishment or expectation of reward. In the fifth chakra/stage, we learn to communicate our truthful feelings without triggering our habitual fear. As mentioned, our attunement to the uninjured stillness, timelessness, and unified nature of our innate essence-of-expression (often experienced as the quality of our voice), offers us a much broader perspective.

Central to this broader perspective is our embodied sense that we have a birthright to exist and belong, to create and honor our interests, to be autonomous in manifesting our interests, and to have meaningful contact balanced with breathing-room. These awarenesses allows us to feel compassion, but not be responsible for other people's well-being. We may care deeply about others, but we don't make their limitations our responsibility. We understand that if we do make it our responsibility to fulfill other people's ongoing needs and feelings, it is a set-up to bypass our own needs and limits. Plus, taking responsibility may enable other people to remain weak, and our support will only be a temporary fix. Unconditional love doesn't translate into limitless giving.

The flip side of the expectation that other people need to be what we want them to be, is the understanding that being responsible for another adult's desires and aversions is not something anyone can entirely succeed at. We can feel that others are disappointed in our behavior, yet this understanding and our sense of wholeness, support us in clearly knowing we are not to blame. As a result, we are increasingly able to become known for who we authentically are, and we let go of the excessive desire for other people's approval. We become more honest and no longer selectively edit the content of our self-presentation, to elicit a positive response. We also increasingly allow others to be who they authentically are, without the need to blame or make them feel guilty. We support and allow them to take full responsibility for their life.

For instance, if we want a particular type and degree of contact in our relationship with another person, not being responsible for their emotional state can free us from a power struggle about it. We don't try to convince others that they are wrong and we are right. Instead, we give them what we honestly can, without losing our own integrity, and then let them fill in what is missing in whatever way they are capable. We then support them in finding the resources to manifest their needs in whatever way we can, again without losing our integrity. The emotional clarity and allowance for self-growth this brings to a relationship allows for tremendous levels of intimacy to grow.

When we are in touch with the inherent goodness and profound innocence of our nature, as the essence of second chakra creativity and fifth chakra expression, we access support to clearly communicate our personal truth. If we have experienced emotional abandonment and carry fear of loss, we may, for instance, need to also awaken the third and fourth chakra nondual-qualities-of-self as support. Our clarity of communication contributes to a sense of meaningful contact and even intimacy in relationship.

With enough support, our ability to communicate authentically and be known, in an uncensored way, is both soothing and enlivening. Our satisfaction only increases when others respond in a way that is empathetic. Yet, our expressions of personal truth are empowering, even if they are not received well. Open-heartedly speaking our personal truth is an open invitation for our loved ones to respond in an emotionally mature way. Maturity begets maturity.

What we find is that authentic expression can evoke an integrating effect. It is an act of reaching out and making contact that can lead to a shared way of communicating. This communication can, at first, feel much like we are talking a foreign language. Yet when we express what is undeniably true, it can integrate different cultures. Listening, voicing, writing, chanting, telepathy, and any of the arts, all have this effect. Even our gestures, postures, and facial expressions help us develop a deeper awareness of a common meaning, for what we are expressing. Our spontaneous expressions of words, song, dance, and making love, all help us discover that we have thoughts and feelings, and that others do too. The subtle nuances of other people's expressions begin to hold profound meaning for us. We increasingly recognize how clarity with our own personal truth and our ability to freely communicate this, ultimately has an integrating effect that supports mutuality and relational intimacy to grow to a new level.

## Reciprocal Nature of the Second & Fifth Chakras

Yoga recognizes there is a reciprocal relationship between the lower and upper chakras. Understanding this reciprocal relationship is helpful when it comes to healing our wounds. The second chakra is the reciprocal chakra to the fifth chakra in that they both involve similar subjects of creative self-expression. Experience of the fifth chakra's essential expressive nature is supported by embodied experience of our second chakra's essential-creative nature. In a sense, the fifth chakra's essence of expression, forms the completion of the second chakra's creative nature.

The second chakra/stage involves self-inquiry, much like how the artist reaches deep inside and makes contact with an authentic part of themselves. We gain clarity in discerning the nature of our creative impulse and discover our interests and choices. We grow self-definition and clarity about our personal truth (our best discernment of what is undeniably true for us). The fifth chakra/stage of expression, depends on this second chakra/stage's inner-discovery process about information that is deeply personal and meaningful. As we then embody the fifth chakra's essence-of-expression, we become able to express our creative impulses in relationship.

Attuning to our second chakra takes the form of uncovering an unchanging feeling of our creative-essence, in the body. The alternative spatial (unity), temporal (timelessness), sensory (subtle), and motor (stillness) experience of our self as an uninjured, innocent, wholeness of our being, gives us a broader and deeper perspective and truth. Out of these experiences, spontaneous authentic expressions arise. What is expressed involves our evolving-self's personal truth, concerning who we are as distinct individuals with unique feelings and needs. This authenticity resolves the main emotional question we have in the second stage of our emotional development as a child, which is "Who am I apart from you?" (It is no coincidence that the Sanskrit name for the second chakra, "svadhisthana," means "self-base.")

As we complete the second chakra/stage, ideally, we conclude that "I have the right to feel and understand my emotions, needs, and wants," and "I have a right to trust what I feel, and choose what feels right for me." In the third chakra/stage, we ideally learn to establish the independence and skills to manifest those choices. In the fourth chakra/stage, we uncover the unconditional love and mutuality in relationship, we need to manifest those choices. In the fifth chakra/stage, we bring our personal truth about our emotions, needs, and choices into full, authentic expression.

As a child, our answers to these second-stage questions are rarely communicated effectively. So, as an adult, we struggle to answer the fifth stage question, "How can I express who I am, to you, in an unabashed way." As mentioned, the more clearly we feel that we exist as the unified essence-of-creativity (second chakra) and expression (fifth chakra), the more we allow for a dynamic process of spontaneous expression of what is interior to us, to be shared with others. We authentically expel, draw, and dance out the subtleties and passions of our inner-life with self-acceptance.

(If we do not have third or fourth chakra/stage injuries, the path from second chakra creativity, to fifth chakra expression, happens easily. This is because we can access the confidence and endurance from the third chakra/stage, and the self-acceptance and clarity in relationship from the fourth chakra/stage, to support authentic expression.)

**Purification**

In all forms of communication, we are confronted with the conflict between communicating what we experience internally and how that experience is expressed. Our evolving-self's expressions are usually abstract representations of what we literally feel. Yet when we embody our unchanging-self (as nondual creativity and expression), the trapped energy from not expressing authentically is discharged. This purifies us because discharging trapped energy is the moment when we let go of our sabotaging habits and attachments that are our automatic reactive responses to life. The spontaneous expressions of authenticity that result are the Taoist "action in no action" moment. This is when expressions are not being motivated by our sabotaging habits but instead motivated by a bigger, broader, and deeper perspective and truth.

In the fifth chakra/stage, as our personal truth thaws out our nervous system, we exit from a sympathetic flight-fight or freeze state. As this happens, we learn to follow the sensorimotor impulses that form the expression of our wise personal truth. This level of discernment of truth supports it to be fully and honestly expressed and come to completion. It supports us to overcome the residual effects of fear and the feeling of being trapped, which remain from when it felt unsafe to express our personal truth.

As we progressively learn to do this successfully and clearly, what is interior to us is able to be brought out. This has a cleansing effect on our physical, emotional, and mental life. It is no coincidence that the Sanskrit name for the fifth chakra is "*Visuddha*," meaning purification. When we are motivated by our body's experience of unity and wholeness, and we communicate what is authentic to us, it is an act of release that purifies us. As we allow our evolving-self's profound personal truths to flow freely, we purify our body, heart, and mind. Authentic expression becomes a sort of spontaneous confessional of personal truth that is "cleansing." It is like an emotional, spiritual orgasm that opens up our body and mind. Satisfaction naturally prevails.

Resolving past emotional injuries is not only about our injured self expressing what was shut down; it is also an act of communicating the untold truth of our inborn goodness, to the injury. Yet, to make room for what we want to assimilate, we often must resolve and let go of outdated emotions and beliefs. If we feel sadness or anger without resisting it, we process it, and passing through it, we resolve our intense emotions.

In the fifth chakra/stage of embodied nondual meditation, we cleanse our body-mind system and make room for a profound awakening. What leads up to this process, as we embody our underlying unity and wholeness, is that we take time to fully savor our evolving-self's feelings. Instead of transcending desire and aversion, we attend to each expression in great detail.

When in the presence of our fifth chakra nondual-essence-of-being, our "wounded inner-child" within us is fully

194

acknowledged, understood, respected, and even experiences being unconditionally loved (whole-being-embrace). The broader perspective of subtle, conscious stillness, timelessness, and unity pervades our suffering. We feel the uninjured innocence, purity, and goodness of the essential-ground of our being. Each of these experiences is communicated to our broken heart. Through nurturing the old emotions, we gain insight and make room for accessing our authentic, deeper truth. We naturally cleanse our self of fear and the delusions and illusions that it creates. (In this way, rather than using dispassion or separation as a solution, we nourish and love our injuries, to express healthy boundaries in relationship.)

Each time we acknowledge and/or express a personal truth and pause to honor it, our body naturally lets go of the patterns of constriction we adopted to protect our self from being injured. Constricting helps us not feel our suffering so intensely, but it also keeps us locked into old patterns of emotion and thought. Our personal truth communicates an emotional boundary in relationship that naturally releases and purifies us of the associated constrictions. This provides more internal room for us to inhabit. When we savor the experience of taking up more room, that the energy associated with our emotions can flow freely through, our injury is empowered. We become able to fully honor and express the untold truth of our inborn goodness. Savoring the experience of letting go and occupying more room is so important that it warrants a little more attention here.

### Savoring Satisfaction

Savoring and sustaining the experience of the well-being and satisfaction we get from acknowledging and expressing our personal truth, is not always an easy thing to do. Venturing outside the range and depth of our preferred level of well-being, pushes the envelope of our emotional maturity. Sustaining satisfaction in the context of any relationship is a distinctly grown-up event; it is not something the immature get to explore.

Most of us can stay fully present with only a few minutes of feeling increasing levels of satisfaction inherent to well-being. We tend to interrupt it by shifting our attention to other things, such as rampant thoughts that take us away from the lived experience. Few of us can handle coming together with a friend or lover (or which may be anything, from nature, a pet, or a person) and open our heart and body to profound feelings of satisfaction, without cutting this short. Feelings of satisfaction are often accompanied by fear of losing the intimacy that we have achieved, fear of being overwhelmed by other's emotions, a sense of shame, fear of what might happen if we attract attention, or even anxiety that we will exceed other people's level of happiness.

Without the support of the innocence, purity, and wholeness of our fifth chakra's unified, essential-ground of expression as an experience of our self, it is not easy to tolerate total relaxation or feel profound satisfaction and well-being. It can feel as though we are a stranger in a strange land, or that we are experiencing another kind of puberty. As we receive the personal truth and broader perspective fifth chakra awareness makes available to us, we begin to recognize that the way we interrupt our well-being is simply resistance to going past our emotional speed limit. We have more choice to not habitually interrupt our well-being.

By taking time to trust it is safe to feel well-being and satisfaction, we can learn to open to fully receive it. With practice, we learn to stay present and grounded with the experience of satisfaction, and tolerate enhanced levels of openness and wholeness-of-being. After we have overtly expressed a personal truth, instead of focusing on lingering habitual anxiety, we are able to shift our focus to feeling any emotional fulfillment, well-being, and satisfaction we may have. This can happen spontaneously, or we feel enough inner support to deliberately take a moment to put aside any habit, such as longing or rating our self on our performance. We increasingly feel our fulfillment. We can savor the feeling of a joyful or meaningful interaction; it is complete, and we can deeply receive the experience.

## Hyper-Hypo Imbalances

One common result of an unbalanced fifth chakra/stage is excessive energy building up because we do not fully release it (charge fixation). It can also lead to a loss of energy and a state of feeling stuck (discharge fixation). In other words, when we experience injury in the fifth chakra/stage, either we do not release our energy, or we release it suddenly in an undigested way. So, if we finally begin to express our truth, it often comes out in the voice of our wounded inner-child.

When out of balance, we feel fear of being judged and find it difficult to listen to other people's opinions. Or, we are able to listen, but fear being rejected for expressing our personal truth. Hypo symptoms include feeling powerless to speak out, speechlessness, inability to express nuances of what we feel, shutting-down after we speak up, and hopelessness. Hyper symptoms include nervousness, anxiety, fear, attention deficit disorders, obsession with communicating, over-explaining what we mean, and justifying our personal truth all the time. This can feel imposing to others.

When we do not release the energy after chakra/stage four, it can lead us to act out in ways, like expressing our self too much with non-stop talking, or expressing our self recklessly. We may dump out our emotions suddenly without the attention needed to stay in touch with what we are really expressing. Excessive expression can serve as a way of not being in touch with the experience, and not listening. We may over-share what we are feeling and then anxiously clam up. Or, we may suppress what we really feel and block out input from others.

If we do not receive an experience and listen to it, this can also cause a hypo state of losing energy and awareness. We may clam up or close down and feel like the wind just got sucked out of us, and then not express our self at all. We can also withhold the one thing the people we care about want to hear most, like, "I love you," or "I respect you even when I disagree with you." We can refrain from expressing our real feelings because we are anxious that we might offend someone, or that it is not safe. Most families have a speed limit for expressing certain emotions. This is especially true when it comes to expressing anger. Whenever we don't express our personal truth, we can feel anxious and drained.

## GOING MORE SUBTLE THAN PSYCHOLOGY

At this point, the stages of development found in Western psychology come to completion. Psychology only recognizes five primary stages because it does not include more subtle, unified stages of personal evolution. Its focus is more on integrating the parts of the psyche. We can live a perfectly healthy life without going past the fifth stage of development. In fact, most individuals in Western culture do not progress past the fifth stage of development. Yet, so often, there lingers an existential emptiness where something seems to be missing, when what lies beyond the rational-emotional is not included.

Many cultures include more subtle levels of development, which in the West are regarded to be the mystical dimension of existence. Including unified consciousness in our process of maturing and evolution offers psychology a tremendously powerful supportive resource to facilitate recovery from injuries. It also opens up huge vistas of spiritual awakening to the deepest aspects of our self and of existence.

Unified consciousness allows us to reach the unseen, mystical realms of existence. The ecstatic experience of the Western mystic's union between the human and the divine, has often been represented as mental instability. Yet, including the unified dimension of consciousness is like seeing with our eyes shut. It allows us to analyze our inner-experiences beyond empirical knowledge, to the knowing of the unknowable. This introduces a deeper and more spontaneous aspect of what motivates us to grow beyond the limits of the rational and emotional mind.

Including unified consciousness in our life, introduces development with a definite direction. The various attributes of this development are not a part of what is familiar to our rational mind. These features of our development are mystical and need to be experienced as an expression of self, within the body and in our environment. This fundamentally changes our understanding of the nature of self in relationship. Based on the trajectory of our growth as a child, from symbiosis to object constancy, I have extrapolated an understanding of sixth and seventh stages of development.

198

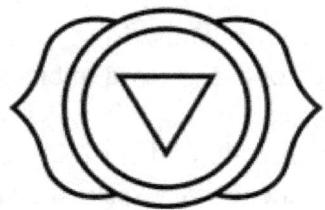

**NERVOUS SYSTEM: Collapse versus Balance**
**CHILD: Completion, Understanding**
**ADULT: Completion, Integration**
**CHAKRA: Head center; *anja*, meaning command**
          **Unified nature of self as "Knowing"**

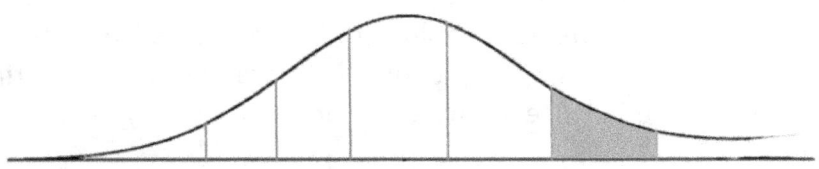

## NERVOUS SYSTEM

When we are faced with what feels like a threat or a crisis, our nervous system develops a plan of action to escape it. Usually, we respond by first running or withdrawing from a threat in flight or fight (chakra/stage three). When that does not work, we go into a freeze state (chakra/stage four). When this happens, in chakra/stage five, we remain unable to release the energy we have built up in our system to protect our self (due to how we mentally and emotionally re-trigger our self). This can cause us to go into a state of stuckness. Then, in chakra/stage six, we follow this up by going into a state of collapse, where we experience helplessness, dizziness, feel like fainting, and can even lose bowel control. The state of collapse is an excessive hypo-condition, where our body-mind system is fixated in a discharged state.

Many of us maintain an ongoing state of collapse on a low-grade level.

In healing, we learn to effectively express protective and supportive skills in chakra/stage four. This allows us to recover from our frozen and collapsed state of biological stasis and begin to recover our vital functions. It allows us to successfully release the energy we built up to defend our self in chakra/stage five, and come back into a balanced state in chakra/stage six. We return to a calm, regulated state of dynamic equilibrium, where we are more present and authentic in our responses to what we experience.

Our dynamic equilibrium in the sixth chakra/stage means we are able to repeatedly build and then release the energy in our system. The more successfully we do this, the more we broaden our perspective and become more resilient. Intense situations may elicit an authentic response to withdraw or push back in order to protect our self. We do not become fixated on these responses, so we are able to let go of them and experience a sense of resolution and completion. The more this happens with ease, the more balance we have in our body-mind system (the Gap).

In embodied nondual meditation, we refine our senses so that we can become adept at perceiving the most subtle degree of balance. In this way, our body's experience of being in a state of balance gives us direct access to the stillness of the unified ground-of-existence. With a conscious experience of unity and wholeness within us, we are much less likely to respond to intense experiences automatically, remaining stuck in our survival responses.


**CHILD & ADULT DEVELOPMENT: "Completion" Stage, 7 Years +**

The sixth stage of "Completion and Resurrection" emerges as a child after we have internalized the parent's nature in the fifth stage, and have become clear about our own individual identity. The sixth stage developmentally begins after the age of seven or eight years (but emotionally reoccurs throughout life), as we develop the self-reflective ability to have the empathetic

200

presence and discernment inherent to intuition and wisdom. At this stage, we begin to be able to look at feelings and behaviors with a clearheaded, empathetic kindness that comforts what troubles us. Our self-reflective capacity gives us access to self-aware wisdom, and intuition. In the fifth stage, we ideally develop the ability to sustain alignment with what feels true for us and a level of inner-comfort and well-being, even when our needs are not met. This is what supports us in the sixth chakra/stage to be guided by a broader understanding of our self in relationship that includes intuition and wisdom.

This takes our individual identity to a new level of clarity and understanding about our authentic nature, beyond the conditioning we internalized from childhood. (We may have access to the experience of unity before this age, but it usually does not begin to integrate cohesively until this age.) As a Hero, we emerge from the source of our suffering, our conditioning, transformed by our deeper understanding of who we really are. We are able to look at our past injuries as a process of death-and-rebirth (into wholeness). We can replay an experience from our past without feeling triggered and reinjured. As we recognize how the current ordeals we are faced with can contain some of the same challenges from the past, we gain a new level of command over our sabotaging habits of mind and body. We are transformed into a new being, liberated from our self-limitations.

Intuition and wisdom involve information about our self and others beyond our identity as a separate individual. They bridge the dimensions of duality and nondual consciousness. This means it gives us access to the sixth chakra nondual quality of inner knowing and thereby offer a broader perspective of our self and other people. It also gives us the capacity to have an understanding that provides us with much more depth and clarity about what we experience from within our self, and in our contact with other (people, situation, substance, etc.). Our access to the wisdom layer of self (*vijnana,* as described in *chapter one*) allows us to understand why other people's behavior or emotional states, such as sadness or anger, influence us the way they do. This informs us of how we can change the way we relate to this experience and what we can do about it.

Simply put, what contributes to our maturity and broader perspective at this stage is that we have a sense of continuity between our inner experience of unity, and our environment. This enhances our: 1) ability to see our self from the outside without losing our sense of being centered inside our self; and the ability to experience others from the inside without confusing it with our personal experience. It also enhances, 2) our ability to access a more refined expression of our mental self. We become able to not only think clearly, but to understand personal truth on a much deeper level in a way that is informed by our inner wisdom and intuition.

**View Self from Outside & Experience Others from Inside**:
As a child at this chakra/stage, we develop clear self-awareness. This self-awareness tends to have enhanced mental or conceptual awareness, plus enhanced capacity for intuition and wisdom. We learn how to think rationally and clearly, in a linear manner. We are also guided by a more holistic process. This holistic information is based on self-awareness that involves knowing what we are feeling. It is a result of our body's experience of the sum total of what is *actually* going on within us at the moment. In other words, at this stage, all systems are engaged: the brain in our head (cephalic brain) and what in yoga is often called our "third eye center," our heart-brain (cardiac brain), and our gut-brain (enteric brain). If we do not receive support for what we experience as a child, such as when our understanding is discounted, we shut down these aspects of our self. Later in life, we may try to rationalize away our inconvenient or uncomfortable feelings, convincing our self they are not real or valid.

At this chakra/stage, we can experience inhabiting our body as a multi-level, multi-dimensional sense of self. This includes our clear conscious awareness of our rational thought, the sensory life in our body (that informs our emotions), our intuition and wisdom, and the more subtle feeling-tones of embodied unified consciousness (*saguna* Brahman). (In the seventh chakra/stage we gain access to transcendent, universal consciousness, beyond all sensory perception, *nirguna* Brahman).

Our receptive, open experience that accompanies embodied unified consciousness, results from what the neuroscientist Daniel Siegel calls our brain's "self-engagement system." This system gives us a sense of open receptivity to experience the communication between the dual and nondual dimensions of our self. This communication is important because it allows us to keep our emotional life fully engaged and in relationship to our whole body and mind. Through our self-engagement system, our evolving-self can be in contact with, and open and receptive to, our unchanging-self. We open our perceptual system to the experience of wholeness-of-being (love, bliss, unity, etc.). Even when we are in pain and suffering, this experience is there all the time as a powerful source of support.

As a child at this stage, we ideally learn to maintain this embodied experience of self, and we do not lose this inner perspective even when focusing on other people and the environment. This self-referent orientation helps us maintain healthy relationships because it comes from knowing how we feel, and this supports us in acting with self-agency, even when we are being considerate of other people's feelings. The self-referent orientation involves the ability to objectively see our self from the outside while not losing touch with what we independently feel subjectively, from the inside. This supports the relational ability to experience others from the inside and feel empathy, while not losing touch with our own personal truth and sense of wholeness. This is a refinement of our emotional autonomy within relationship.

The integrative effect of unified consciousness and the support for us to cultivate a self-referent orientation, is enhanced in the sixth chakra/stage. This is vitally important because relationship trauma causes us to fragment our cephalic-head brain from our cardiac-heart-brain and our enteric-gut brain. When we lose our balanced state, our conceptual awareness of thinking *about* ourselves can disconnect from the realities and wisdom of what we feel or intuit, as well as our sense of wholeness. The tendency to observe our inner-experience with our mind, can keep us disconnected from the authentic personal truth of what we feel. We can disconnect from sensations that

203

form our emotions, such as fear, anger, and sadness, and what we like or dislike. We also disconnect from intuition that comes from our gut or heart-felt sense, as well as from information that lies beyond our five senses ("third-eye" intuition). Denying these sources of information and guidance, leads to disorientation, a lack of clear perception, and restricts our capacity to feel full vitality, pleasure, and joy.

As a result of unresolved injuries and trauma, we are often out of contact or numb to our inner experience. Tension, limited breathing, and not letting ourselves have certain experiences because they are overwhelming, can cause us to view ourselves from the "outside in." We mentally observe ourselves and disconnect from our experience of our bodily sensations and emotions. When perceiving from the "inside out" is lost, we objectify our self. Transcendent meditation that is non-local in nature (not a body experience), can potentially exacerbate this sixth stage fragmented condition (Lancaster 2023.)

**Thinking Clearly, Personal Truth, and Inner Wisdom**

The key forces informing us at this stage involve, 1) cognitive flexibility and integration that helps us think and, 2) combining empathy for others with a sense of our inner-reality. This combination allows us to use our imagination and our empathic abilities to step into our experience of a person or situation, and then step back out, returning our attention to our own inner experience.

This process involves more than our conceptual interpretation of an experience, because in trusting our own feelings and wisdom, we gain deeper insight. This insight is more important to us than other people's opinions or explanations of an experience. This independent perception is the basis of what I call "personal truth." Personal truth results from a level of integration that allows for full maturity and autonomous ability to perceive, understand, and know our self most authentically. We tap into clear perception based on a deeper experience of our inner-wisdom (discussed in detail soon). Our discernment of personal truth and wisdom, continues to grow throughout our life as an adult. The ability to think clearly, understand personal truth, and have access to our inner wisdom is very empowering.

Introducing wisdom into our developmental process is a novel one. For this reason, a little more reflection on what this means is warranted.

## From Rational Thinking to Wisdom

As mentioned, discerning personal truth and inner-wisdom becomes limited when we experience trauma. Awareness of body-based experience is often confusing and overwhelming, so we dissociate and become disembodied. As Winnicott observed, when we are injured, we tend to become hyper-mental and disconnect from the lived experience of our self in relationship. An expression of being hyper-mental is limiting our self to the problem-solving rational mind.

Remaining rational and keeping the frontal cortex online is an important part of overcoming trauma or the experience of overwhelm as an adult. We may try to plan, talk things out, and confirm our beliefs, as a way to rework our emotions. However, our problem-solving rational mind is very helpful at organizing our feelings and impulses, but does not rid us of overwhelming emotions and the out-of-hand impulses that no longer serve us (Damasio, 1999; LeDoux, 1996).

Joseph LeDoux (1996) taught us that the thinking brain has virtually no nerve connection with the emotional brain (limbic system). Antonio Damasio informed us about how the emotional brain learns primarily via interoceptive senses that inform us of subtle body experience. The interoceptive senses also involved in informing us about wisdom.

Wisdom is sometimes referred to, in spiritual communities, as *"prajna"* or sometimes *"buddhi."* In yoga metaphysics, this expression of self arises from the fourth layer of self, called *"vijnana kosha."* In meditation, our inner-wisdom and discernment come from a deep inner-awareness of the clues or "somatic markers" of that which feels authentic about our evolving-self (somatic markers are sensations in the body that are associated with emotions). It can be said that in meditation, we identify "subtle somatic markers" of bodily knowing. This source of wisdom includes our sense of authenticity and also our discernment of that which is beyond our evolving-self's normal range of discovery.

This means wisdom includes information that we get from the intuitive realms as well as the unified unchanging nature of existence. Wisdom lies at the threshold between duality and nonduality, and provides "homing signals" (Prendergast) or a portal for us to come to recognize and awaken to the nondual dimension of our unchanging-self. The homing signal of our subtle somatic markers is what gives us the ability to distinguish the nondual-qualities of our unchanging-self. We learn what a distortion is, and what a true reflection of a deeper expression of existence is. It also gives us access to the "aha" moment of knowing, beyond doubt, what is true for us. Wisdom is key to overcoming trauma because its refined discernment gives us access to a body experience of our unchanging-self.

At this stage, our sense of self goes beyond personal identity to include a sense of our interconnectedness. As we look around, we recognize that we are all living systems interconnected in a web of life. Our sense of self converges into a new sense of pluralities that form a planetary social web of life, where networks interact with other networks, and systems exist within systems. In this sense, we get in touch with the collective unconscious in a way that does not lose a sense of our own uniqueness within the collective. We experience the collective unconscious, which forms the archetypes of our psyche that influence us, without losing touch with the personal truth relevant to our life experience.

**From Archetypes to Wholeness**

While archetypes are broader than the finiteness of our individual self, at this stage we reach into the realm of archetypes without it defining the meaning of our personal life. We access the arena of archetypes and draw out new perspectives as we honor our personal truth. We recognize how the forms within our mind and body, and the structures of the world outside, come from the same collective source. We experience the other in our self, and our self in the other, without forgetting who we are on a personal level.

This awareness is an experience that many mystics in the East and West have commented on, yet they have emphasized the transcendent nature of this experience. As Teilhard (1980) commented, "If I am to be All, I must be fused with All." When we merge in a fused state, we forget who we are on a personal level.

Becoming aware of the collective unconscious is often when many people have their first "Aha" moment. This is when we realize the existence of a spiritual reality. This is often where the spiritual quest for something beyond our evolving-self's perspective begins. Some children never lose this awareness and are inclined to communicate with "angels" and feel connected to a deeper wisdom. Often, they end up trying to teach their parents about this dimension of existence and can be left feeling misunderstood and out of place.

The feeling of being connected by a web of consciousness and energy vibrating at different frequencies, is not always easy to maintain. This is especially true when something traumatic creates a ripple effect that disturbs the harmony of this web. We feel connected to the collective fear, anger, sadness, guilt, shame, and it can become overwhelming. This can challenge our ability to not lose a sense of our own personal truth within the collective. When this is paired with our cultural and spiritual orientation toward transcending our evolving-self (including injury and distortion), we can over emphasize discounting the personal and fixate on the transcendent state of unity.[42]

---

[42] For instance, a central theme in this book is the potential limitations of Axial Age orientation toward mind and transcendence. One of the dangers of the Christian "fall from grace" myth, is that it reinforces the belief that being on this planet is a punishment (simply being born is a sin). This implies being in a body is secondary to transcendence, and that the afterlife is our liberation. We are told the "otherworldliness" is better than being of this world, including nature, sex, pain, and pleasure. The shame and guilt that result, can leave profound scars that those of us who access the sixth stage of development with collective awareness, need support to heal.

Likewise, Eastern transcendent spiritual traditions can further confuse us by suggesting our deepest feelings are an illusion, not important for spiritual

207

Our experience of the nondual-qualities of self is almost like living as an archetype. Archetypes are organizing, slowly changing energy patterns that are a reflection of our collective unconscious as a culture or as humanity. Yet cultural collective unconscious changes, and the nondual-qualities of our self do not change. "Seeing" reflections of our collective unconscious doesn't entirely solve any of our problems. We may still be under the influence of a cultural collective psyche.

Acknowledging and understanding the impact the collective unconscious has on us, is important. Yet, we access a deeper dimension of our self and an experience of wholeness (that is not influenced by these ideologies and approaches to our suffering and a spiritual life), when we have a body experience of unified consciousness as an expression of self.

When we have an internal awareness of our unchanging-self as a stable reference, we stay in touch with the sense that our experiences and expressions arise out of stillness, unity, and wholeness, rather than the attitudes that shape the collective unconscious of archetypal existence. Our actions become self-inspired expressions from our whole body and mind, as we interact in relationship. The freedom this provides is liberating. Bringing our perceptions of collective attitudes about our body, emotions, and suffering into whole-being-embrace, with wholeness and its inherent unconditional love, is such an important part of our healing journey. Attunement to, and embodiment of the chakra qualities of self, is a powerful way to do this.


## THE ADULT IN RELATIONSHIP

Because life is full of unpredictable, ever-shifting, and ambiguous situations, anxiety naturally arises. We can't avoid it. One of the main ambiguities in life that causes stress and anxiety,

---

awakening, or secondary to the transcended state. As mentioned, the feeling that if we were sufficiently spiritual, we would not be feeling these emotions, is an easy step to make. Yet, if we can't trust our feelings, it lowers our self-esteem. We can be left feeling selfish, incompetent, and even undeserving because we have failed at living a spiritual life.

is the paradox of being connected and yet separate and independent. Having the right amount of connection yet remaining autonomous is an essential aspect of a healthy relationship with all aspects of life. Being autonomous allows us to not get lost in the emotional drama that our experience of other (people, situations, emotion, thought) always confronts us with. Because we are fundamentally social animals, being connected gives us the vital support we need to survive. As we heal our relationship injuries, we come to realize the issue is not that we are separate or united; in a healthy relationship, we are both at the same time. The issue is lack of autonomy with others (person, situation, substance, idea).

The quality of emotional support that we learned to give our self and receive in the fourth chakra/stage (rapprochement, unconditional love chakra, yoga's right relationship with the senses, *pratyahara,* as described in Appendix Two) provides us the support we need to diminish our level of unhealthy dependency on other (person, situation, substance, idea). In the fifth chakra/stage (object constancy, expression chakra, yoga's "concentration"/attunement, *dharana*), we fully integrate this feeling of support into the fabric of our relational life. This allows us to begin to let go of our unresolved bonding injuries.

Our fear that we can't trust that the people we care about will show up for us, and fear that others are trying to control us, fade. We stop being on the lookout for the smallest clues that confirm we are being betrayed. We also stop trying to get others to prove their innocence, or their love for us. One way of explaining this level of maturity is that we have a broader perspective with more unconditional regard for our own, and other people's limitations.

This doesn't mean we put up with everything others send our way. We are discerning, so we can let go of friends who are out of touch with our needs. We realize that we can attract new friends who meet our needs in a healthier way. As we feel the wholeness and innocence of the unified-ground of our self, including that we exist as unconditional love, we recognize that we can leave an unsatisfying relationship. We feel loveable and worthy of love. We begin to make decisions that are not motivated by our fear of losing other people's appreciation and attention. We also recognize that our innate nature is an essence, that does not change and is inherently innocent and pure. We feel our own basic goodness and take delight in it, in the way we always wanted to be delighted in by others.

This helps us to take responsibility for our personal weaknesses and seek situations that can provide the kind of emotional support that we need. This approach is supportive because we come to understand that there are contradictions between the expectations formed in childhood and the current reality of what is possible. We don't accept our own and other people's fear-based demands, that are based on our past. If we felt a lack of genuine love as a child, we don't have to constantly test the strength of other people's appreciation and love, now. Or, if we or other people have an expectation based on past experiences that we should be faster, slower, or have a different body type, we realize the demand disregards the reality of who we currently are as individuals. This supports us in not taking personal responsibility for other people's well-being, even though we care about them. We get over our fear of disappointing others. We accept and stand-up for who, and how, we actually are, in our dual and nondual expressions.

Our broad perspective and emotional boundaries, that come from embracing our personal truth, open the door to a whole new creative dimension in our life (especially in our most significant relationships). It gives us the strength to see through the false critical attitude we feel others have about us, or that we have for our self. We don't succumb to our partner's opinions, and we don't impose upon them either. The old complaints of, "you're so lazy," or cause-and-effect statements such as, "If you'd only change, then I'd be okay," or "you're wrong, I'm right," no longer trigger us. We also no longer feel the need to dish them out. We can let go of the limitations of cultural conditioning and personal history, to come into a more authentic perspective.

Generally speaking, when we do not integrate our earlier stages, we have a higher degree of instability. We have less emotional independence from what we experience, such as our relationship with another person, situation, emotion, thought, and sensation. As a result, we attempt to compensate, craving a higher level of predictability in our experience of other (the environment, people, situations). Things need to go a certain way or else we feel overwhelmed, fixating upon some version of desire or aversion. We may try to control the situation or loved ones, by establishing rigid rules of conduct that guarantee a certain behavioral outcome, or we withdraw into pseudo-independence (not needing others in an attempt to achieve stability).

Being related while independent is a paradox. Understanding this balance requires emotional refinement. In the sixth chakra/stage (wisdom, knowing, and yoga's state of meditation, *dhyana*), we come to understand the paradox of being connected while separate. We also come to terms with our uncertainty in the ever-shifting situations confronting relationships. At this stage, we are able to wrap our mind around these fairly difficult aspects of life, even when we are under fire from the heat of attempting to work things out in our relationship (with a situation, person, thought, emotion, and sensation). As we uncover an embodied sense of our nondual self, we come to know how to be alone and feel connected, as well as how to be together without losing our sense of autonomy. Our relationship with unified consciousness provides our highly sensitive and reactive, wounded inner-child, an ultimate degree of connectedness and breathing-room. Healthy boundaries and emotional autonomy in relationship naturally prevail.

Since the nondual-qualities of our unchanging-self are uncreated and timeless, they also give us access to a sense of our immortality. We feel that our body is mortal, but our consciousness is immortal. We recognize a timeless truth that we are a part of the consciousness that pervades the universe, which is immortal.

From a transcendent perspective, our "True Self" observes our evolving-self and remains beyond the material plane of all body sensory experience. We may feel we are a finite consciousness that emerges out of nothingness and vanishes into nothingness. I find it tragic to not recognize that we have always been, and will always be. Part of the tragedy of Western secular culture is that we are separated from our eternal divinity. This so often makes our ability to process the idea of loss or death difficult, and even traumatic. While we may have experienced unified consciousness as a body experience in prior stages, in the sixth chakra stage, we begin to accept and integrate our mortality/immortality. This gives us access to an inherently benevolent, open, unattached, and non-willful state of enduring presence-of-being. Our life becomes more than a preparation for loss and death. It also includes a celebration of eternal life. As this becomes an ongoing experience, we learn to integrate this perspective in healing the stage in which we suffered our deepest injuries and trauma.

We begin to be able to tolerate the ambiguity that naturally happens in life. We accept that our imagined "reality" is not the only show in town. We are not caught in anticipating uncertainty. We can even thrive in a life that is full of rapidly varying circumstances because we abide in a state of wholeness and eternal conscious stillness. The resilience this provides is helpful when we feel unseen, unheard, misunderstood, or not accepted by life's circumstances, or by a friend who has very different feelings and needs.

## SIXTH CHAKRA

**Name**: The Sanskrit word for the sixth chakra is *"anja,"* which means "perceive," "command," or "beyond wisdom." It is commonly called the Head center, or "third-eye" chakra. I distinguish the Forehead center from the sixth chakra Head center. The Forehead center, often called the "third eye," lies behind the forehead surface, *within* the forehead between the brows. The "Head center" lies within the center or subtle core of the head, in alignment with the central-channel. Feeling the connection between the Head center and the Forehead center, facilitates awakening the sixth chakra Head center.
**Location**: The Head center is located deep within the subtle core of the head, level with the top of the ears or middle of the eyebrows.

## Symbolic Level

The Head center chakra is associated with the color indigo; the mantra is "Om" or "Aum;" the element is light (which represents clarity, understanding, and spiritual insight). The symbolic form is a downward pointing triangle, with a vertical "*lingam*" or the symbol of nondual consciousness, "Shiva." The triangle in the sixth chakra is an expression of involution, the process of opening to awareness of unified consciousness in its universal, cosmic, purely non-local nature. Some consider the involution process to be about bringing-in unified consciousness from the cosmos into our physical form. That said, unified consciousness already exists within the body. When our intention is to heal injuries, awakening its expression within the body is vital.

Within the sixth chakra, is the final meeting point of the subtle energy channels "*ida*" and "*pingala*," which run on either side of the central-channel, "*sushumna*," (that runs from the center of the top of the head to the center of the bottom of the torso). Yoga practice (indirect) strives to balance the "*ida*" (archetypal feminine, energy discharge, yin) and "*pingala*" (archetypal masculine, energy charge, yang). The archetypal masculine, charge phase of energy inherent to *pingala,* is a more "externally" oriented, assertive, and expansive force. The archetypal feminine, discharge phase of energy inherent to *ida,* is a more internal and receptive force. These two channels come to completion and join together in the sixth chakra (and in the Forehead center). This merging creates a fully balanced state, awakening the central-channel's unified consciousness.

When the chakras are considered from a fractal or holographic perspective, nonduality exists everywhere all the time, and every chakra contains the other ones. When considered from a chronological or "sequential perspective," that informs the indirect-path, the union of opposites happens in the sixth chakra for the first time, and only becomes an enduring awakened state in the seventh chakra. This awakened state is reflected in the

Sanskrit name for the sixth chakra, *"anja,"* which means "command" or "to perceive."[43]

The sequential perspective is based on the understanding that the chakras are organized along a spectrum of density, where the first chakra is the most dense, the sixth chakra is almost the least dense, and the seventh chakra has no density. This is often the model adopted by the indirect-path. (Though, I believe the sixth chakra is almost the least dense, and the seventh chakra, as the essence of wholeness itself, is the least dense. The eighth chakra just above the head is beyond density altogether, i.e., *atman*.) By contrast, the fractal or "holographic perspective" adopted by the direct-path, is based on the premise that since unity exists everywhere, even the densest aspects of our existence, as found in the first chakra, can manifest beyond polarity, as an expression of unified consciousness, when balanced.

From a sequential perspective, the absolute freedom from the polarity of life, and the anxiety that naturally accompanies it, is symbolically depicted in the sixth chakra element of "ether." Being the lightest of elements, ether contains the essential ingredient of being free from emotional, mental, and sensory entanglement. Its ethereal nature is the least material of elements and, therefore, enables us to be unattached or not impacted by the intensity of what we experience in life. Moreover, when we are "in tune with the ethers," our psychic abilities are awake. With a balanced sixth chakra, we have a clearer intellect, wisdom, intuitive understanding, and spiritual insight into what is happening in life. We can perceive and respond to the unspoken, unexposed truth (unified consciousness).

The seed mantra for the sixth chakra is "Aum." This mantra is associated with the beginning, as experienced in pronouncing "A", middle "U", and end of all things "M." *AUM* is considered to

---

[43] Paradoxically, both sequential and holographic approaches are valid. The sequential understanding is based on the indirect-path that reflects our progressive evolution, and the holographic or embodied nondual experience, is based on a direct-path. As mentioned, the direct-path recognizes that we can access unified consciousness at any time, even though we still need to evolve so that it becomes a stable presence in our life.

214

be the sonic vibration from which all things emerge and that into which they must eventually be reabsorbed. Practically speaking, *AUM* brings an end to being controlled by our sabotaging habits, and it gives birth to our deeper wisdom that is available through unified consciousness. (The triangle and lotus flower are said to represent wisdom.)

At issue in this chakra is the right to see and understand what is really going on. This is why it is often represented by the third eye. We see clearly by using left-brain intellectual insight, and right-brain intuition, to fully see and understand the past, present, and future. With a balanced sixth chakra, this understanding gives us the ability to evaluate and discriminate on a more perceptive and subtle level. We can then behave skillfully and take "command" (as the chakra name "*anja*" implies) of our out-of-control, evolving-self's ego.

### Emotional Level

The consciousness of the sixth chakra allows us to see and understand the present moment with wisdom and spiritual (nondual) insight. Yoga, associates the sixth chakra with mind power, imagination, and intuition (mystical visions, psychic awareness, and clairvoyance). The sixth chakra allows us to receive intuitive perceptions from inside, and also from the universe. This co-creative relationship with the universe helps influence our life-direction, aligning our choices with the most insightful wisdom within us.

Because one way the sixth chakra is expressed is imagination, it is associated with both aspects of imagination: delusion and the ability to clearly observe. As delusion, our ego becomes the master of all disguises, impersonating our intuition, but gives us false guidance. When we clearly observe, this chakra is where we put our thoughts, worries, and fears to rest. Clearly observing leads to a sense of deeper understanding and inner-knowing.

This understanding and inner-knowing is, in part, informed by the wisdom of our third eye, which brings us beyond the identification with ego delusions. With refinement, we come to know the difference between our intuition and our imagination. We come to recognize how to use our imagination in the most conscious way, and to never use it against ourselves as a mischievous perpetrator of human suffering.

The third chakra is considered to be reciprocal to the sixth chakra, in that the essence of power supports awakening the sixth chakra. The third stage of our developmental life (psychology's latency stage) is a time when we develop skills to meet challenges and manifest our interests. This supports the emergence of the sixth chakra's self-reflection, intuition, and wisdom. Third chakra/stage developmental doubts about manifesting our interests come to completion in the sixth chakra/stage. We realize a sense of inner-knowing that allows us to feel solidarity with our most authentic self, even though we may fail at manifesting our interests and goals. Our inner-knowing allows us to recognize that we are equal in value to others, despite our weaknesses. This gives us the ability to be inclusive and feel harmony with others without feeling displaced.

Out of our feeling of existing as the essential-ground of pure knowing, we gain confidence in our ability to understand what we experience. In the sixth chakra/stage we integrate the reality that "I can perceive the nondual-essence of life as an expression of my self," "I can recognize and trust what feels like the evolving-self's personal truth, and not lose sight of my sense of wholeness and unty," and "I honor my intuition and wisdom as a guide." Savoring these understandings is healing and elicits a feeling of completion and clarity of insight.

We are informed by the internal vision of our mind's eye, usually called the third eye. The third eye opens, and our psychic faculties allow us to "see and know the big picture." We no longer need to strive to be more than we are, or less than we are. Along with this self-acceptance comes a deep sense of contentment, well-being, and the relaxed-alertness of complete balance.

In this balanced state, the central-channel awakens on an ongoing basis. This means the *ida* and *pingala* flow freely and awaken the *sushumna* as a luminous presence, illuminating our whole body and mind. Everything we can perceive also becomes illuminated, as the essential ground-of-existence. As we see our environment, we let go of our brain's hardwiring of only looking to see if we are safe. We also look, and see the evolving

216

dimension of life is unfolding within the wholeness, unity, and essential goodness of existence. This is a radical shift in perspective that is profoundly healing and awakening. This can be said to be the experience of an enlightened moment.

## Hyper-Hypo Imbalances

When the sixth chakra is out of balance, we are unable to listen to our inner-voice, we cannot discern the obvious, and we are unable to perceive the nondual, unified dimension of life. There is a tendency to perceive life in a polarized black-and-white way.

When this is expressed in a hyper way, our intuitive ability may be overwhelming. We over-focus on our psychic experiences. We can feel emotionally volatile and have headaches, nightmares, and neurological disorders. We may exaggerate truth and be prone to hallucinations. We may mistake the qualities of subtle psychic information, or archetypal awareness, as an ultimate "Truth." In Zen Buddhism, this is called "Zen sickness." This can lead to fundamentalism. In this case, our sensitivity to psychic information and visual images, can impede the healthy development of our personal identity. With an unbalanced sixth chakra, using insight and intuition and accessing "cosmic information" about the past, present, and future, can simply be another egotistical protective strategy.

When the sixth chakra becomes fixated in hypo mode, we are unable to self-reflect, perceive our intuition and clear insight, or perceive the nondual dimension of life. We are indecisive, and we withdraw from reaching out to connect with others. Our intelligence is muted, and we may be inclined towards a foggy mind, mental confusion, and learning difficulties. Alternately, we may be more judgmental and stuck in thought, with a brainy form of intelligence that is out of touch. Our access to psychic information is muffled and we lose clarity of vision.

In the sixth chakra, our fear of loss, or of being imposed upon, is triggered by "big picture" issues, such as our psychic experiences. When our psychic insights are not sufficiently integrated into our life, we misinterpret the information it provides us with. We may, for instance, rely on our psychic insights as the whole truth and disregard the actual situations we are facing in our life. We may discount the psychic information entirely. We may also question our authentic perceptions.

**The Mental Aspect of Self**

The *sixth chakra* is considered to be related to the mind by nature because of its location in the head and its position in the chakra system. In principle, this is in alignment with the term "mentalization" (Bentzen, 2020), which refers to, 1) The ability to see our self from outside, and experience others from the inside; 2) The ability to think clearly. The perspective that this gives us access to, enables us to begin to discern wisdom and intuition in a way that we can integrate with our evolving-self.

Mind is about the mental aspect of self in general. In the nondual dimension, the "mental aspect of self" means our general potential for understanding and awareness, as basic expressions of our nature, not a particular thought, understanding, or awareness. In the dimension of duality, mind is often related to Paul Mclean's Triune brain model, where the brain has three layers of structures. Each layer developed through evolution and, therefore, functions hierarchically.

In this hierarchy, when we are stressed our strong emotions tend to override our ability to maintain logical thought. So, processing information in times of strong emotions and stress, such as when we are fragmented, is extremely difficult. Our emotional life (limbic brain) can inhibit the maturation of our neocortex (logical thought), which is a later evolutionary development. This makes creative thinking in times of stress, unlikely. Under extreme emotional conditions, adapting to a different way of behaving is difficult, since in these times, we behave automatically and habitually (Papero, 1990).

When overwhelmed, most of us tend to fuse thinking with emotions, and thereby diminish the ability to choose between the two. Yet, when we experience right-left brain balance in the sixth chakra/stage, we balance our archetypal masculine (assertive) and feminine (receptive) energetic tendencies. We have simultaneous access to left-brain intellectual insight, and right-brain intuition.

218

In yoga, these right and left brain aspects of our self are symbolically depicted as two lotus pedals, the red one for our emotions (right brain) and the white one for our intellect (left brain). The two lotus pedals also relate to the two subtle energy channels (*ida, pingala*) on either side of the balanced state of the central-channel (*sushumna*).

In the following Image, I display the central-channel (on the left) alongside the caduceus or the "herald's wand" of the deity Hermes (on the right). Hinduism's earliest depictions of the central-channel are about 3000 years old, much like the oldest images of the caduceus from Mesopotamia are about 3000 years old. The similar imagery is striking, and the fact that they both convey information about how to heal is no coincidence:

**Image #14:**

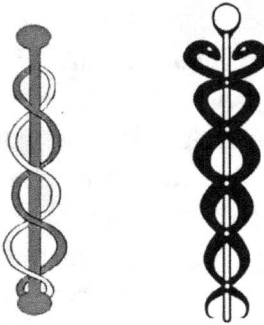

As part of the mental clarity we experience with a balanced sixth chakra, we fully establish the ability to maintain both left-brain intellectual insight, and right-brain intuition. Our strong emotions no longer override our ability to maintain logical thinking. Moreover, we can remain attuned to the experience that we exist as unified consciousness (or the expression of it that brings us the most wholeness). We are empowered to not only choose to be guided by thought or emotion, we can also choose to remain in the stillness of our unchanging-self, undisturbed by either thought or emotion.

In this way, the sixth chakra/stage allows us to be fully open and receptive to what we experience. We can fully show up in the face of intense emotions without activating our survival responses. We can behave skillfully and realize the sixth chakra power to take "command" of our habits of mind and body (as the name *anja* implies). If each moment is met with the same success, we can begin to perceive intense situations as interesting and enlivening rather than overwhelming. Challenging situations can enhance our sense of attunement to our wholeness-of-being. A balanced sixth chakra is a mind at peace.

In yoga philosophy, light is symbolically related to consciousness and our ability to see deeper truths. The Greek deity Zeus's thunderbolt is a common image for this in the West. Light travels faster than anything else. It is so fast that Einstein conjectured that if we were to travel that fast, time itself would stop. Complete balance is nondual consciousness beyond the time-space continuum because it is absolute stillness.[44] When this is a body experience, space-time seems to unfold or arise from the spacious present, which is an implicate order beyond dimensionality and mass. We experience our self simply as a conscious presence-of-being, out of which arise specific sensations, emotions, and thoughts.

A stable experience of our embodied unchanging presence-of-being, gives us the ability to sustain the paradoxical awareness that both dimensions of existence can be experienced at the same time. As mentioned, we can feel that we are both ultimately separate and fully connected at the same time. We are solid bodies with distinct thoughts and emotions, and conscious space that is the unchanging-ground of thought and emotion. Our embodied sense of our unchanging-self awakens a heightened degree of perceiving unity in our interactions with others. Our awareness of our self as separate "beings" co-exists with the awareness of being one with all that is. This paradox is fully realized in the sixth chakra/stage. As emphasized throughout this book, the paradoxical awareness of the simultaneous presence of duality and nonduality, helps us resolve our injuries from not receiving the kind of contact we want and need.

---

[44] It is said that the space consists of 3 dimensions (the three coordinates needed to determine the position of a point) and time is 1-dimensional. So the space-time continuum in which all quantities are located must, be a 4-dimensional object.

When we successfully complete the other stages of our journey and reach the sixth stage, we increasingly act from a strong understanding of our personal path. We know where we have been, and we know where we are going. We grow a sense of trust and satisfaction that comes with doing something that is deeply meaningful to us, in an inspired way, rather than out of habit. Our inner-life, depth of personality, and sense of completeness or wholeness, grow. Our superficial thoughts stop being our only reference for interpreting the present moment and situation. When we become quiet and look inside, instead of finding a body-sense of anxiety or inner-hollowness, we find a sense of self-trust and an inner-knowing at our core. We can listen to our natural body impulses and our rhythmic ebb and flow of personal truth, and our fears, in peace.

This inner-knowing in the sixth chakra is a reflection of our access to a much deeper level of understanding and inner knowing, which is a prelude to the seventh chakra attribute of unity and wholeness. Sixth chakra "knowing" is an expression of the chakra quality and its access to the intuitive nature of wisdom, which has information from both duality's authenticity and nonduality's unity and wholeness. This wisdom starts with our subtle discernment in our gut (second chakra, enteric brain), and heart (fourth chakra, cardiac brain), and becomes more intuitive and ethereal in the head center chakra (sixth chakra, cephalic brain).

**NERVOUS SYSTEM: Death versus Wholeness**
**CHILD: Knowing**
**ADULT: Wholeness**
**CHAKRA #7: Crown chakra (*sahasrara*), thousand pedals.**
       **Unified consciousness as universal wholeness**

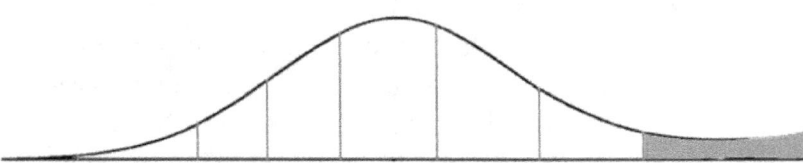

## NERVOUS SYSTEM

The ultimate failure of our survival response results in death. On a less dramatic scale, the end result of our failure to progress through all seven stages, simply obstructs our energy from flowing. This leaves us fixated on either the charge or discharge phase and leaves us with sabotaging habits of mind and body. Or, we may make it through the charge and discharge phases and yet be unable to fully embrace the balanced state of alert-relaxation. We also may experience the state of alert-relaxation and yet never refine our senses sufficiently to experience the stillness, wholeness, and unity of our unchanging presence-of-being.

With the balanced state of relaxed-alertness we are resilient and authentic, and yet are unable to find the degree of inner peace that comes with wholeness/unity. Our authenticity is based on the creative interactive act of responding to our experiences, and yet we never access spontaneous expression

222

that is self-arising our of wholeness/unity. We are able to feel connection with our environment as separate, unique individuals, yet never have the experience of entangled connectedness with all that is. We may have a sense of the finiteness of life but not the infinite and the timeless reality that also exists. And last but not least, love is still transactional and not unconditional.

On our Hero's Journey, when we return to our daily life without the knowledge and experience we need to survive and flourish, we are doomed to repeat the adventure until we do. Many tragedies and comedies have this ending, where a foolish character is unable to learn a lesson and repeats the same behavior that got him/her in trouble in the first place.

Image # 15 illustrates what happens energetically when the seventh stage is the point at which we become fully free from all our limiting habits. We become a fully liberated and enlightened person, even when our needs are not met or when we face conflict and feel stress. In the seventh stage, wholeness becomes a stable presence. We are able to transmute our evolving-self's inherent struggle as we evolve (tension-release/charge-discharge), in each moment as it arises, so it no longer feels like suffering (we return to dynamic equilibrium and the balance of unity).

Psychology's understanding of "freedom" from unresolved injuries is limited. It considers this freedom to be a state of integration of the parts of our self (mind, body, emotions). The child psychologist Donald Winnicott alluded to a deeper understanding when he said, "The alternative to Being is reacting [as apposed to responding], and reacting interrupts Being and annihilates. Being and annihilation are the two alternatives" (Winnicott, 1965, brackets added). While here Winnicott alluded to "Being" as a deeper expression of self, he failed to fully understand that when we refine our senses, we access an uninjured dimension of self that is subtle, still, timeless, and unified.

It can be said that at the seventh chakra/stage, we access a "holonomic" nervous system (Pribram, 1971). Holonomic brain theory is based on the idea that human consciousness is formed with quantum principles. Traditional neuroscience considers the brain's behavior by looking at patterns of neurons and the surrounding chemistry. By contrast, holonomic theory of quantum consciousness, describes how our consciousness is based on a global or holographic storage network (much like Teilhard's notion of "noosphere.")[45]

Karl Pribram goes so far as to suggest that this global network involves electric oscillations in the brain's fine-fibered dendritic webs, as opposed to the action potentials involving nerve axons and synapses. These oscillations are waves in which memory is encoded globally. Much like a hologram, any part of the hologram contains the whole of the stored information. This means long-term memory is uniformly distributed over our nervous system, so each part of this network contains all the information stored throughout the entire network. This is similar to what we experience in embodied nondual meditation. From every location in the body, we can experience unity, wholeness, and our universal connection to all of existence.

This non-locality of information storage within the hologram is important because when we embody a sense of unified consciousness, even if our sense of self fragments, the sense of wholeness is contained within even a single part of our body. So, if our chest constricts due to overwhelm, we may still be able to experience wholeness and unity in other parts of the body. When we experience wholeness in one part of the body, we can still access a sense of wholeness throughout (as described in *chapter six*). Our awareness is omnipresent. We are able to maintain a sense of unity and wholeness even when we feel injured.

The seventh chakra/stage is when we gain the clearest perception of the whole-being-embrace between the duality of our evolving-self, and the nonduality of our unchanging-self. We

---

[45] Teilhard proposed a future event in which we spiral toward a final point of unification. Unlike embodied nondual consciousness which co-exists with our evolving-self for eternity, Teilhard suggests the ultimate destination is complete transcendence of our evolving-self. As evolution continues, the noosphere gains coherence and ultimately reaches a final evolutionary stage of complete independence from the duality-based evolving-self, called the Omega Point.

awaken a blissful, relaxed-alert, receptive openness to what we experience. Again, this receptive, open experience is a result of what Daniel Siegel calls our brain's "self-engagement system." Based on Siegel's understanding, the "self-engagement system" is what allows our evolving-self to attune to the unified consciousness of our unchanging-self's "Buddha-Nature" (or our inner deity with qualities, *saguna Brahman*, deity of choice -*ishta-devata*, and Christ-consciousness). We open our perceptual system to the experience of wholeness-of-being (love, bliss, unity, etc.).

This allows us to keep our evolving-self's emotional life fully engaged and in relationship with the whole body and mind. It allows us to be aware of our evolving-self's own unique, authentic, individual form, while we are also in full contact with our ultimate oneness. This experience began to be integrated into our psyche in the sixth chakra/stage and comes to completion in the seventh chakra/stage. We can feel that we are a solid separate body and sovereign individual, yet also a nondual subtle experience that is part of a larger continuum as a relational holism.

With this experience, we can feel that even when we are in pain, embodied nondual experience is just there all the time as a source of support and broader perspective, so we do not suffer. Sustained attunement to the self-perceiving presence of our unchanging nature, seems to activate a state of safety and inner-peace. At this depth and breadth of perception, the brain's "self-engagement system" (Porges) activates the "social engagement system" of the brain (Siegel). This empowers us to respond to what we struggle with most in life with a sense of open receptivity to the experience, rather than defensiveness.

Non-locality of information storage, gives us a much larger capacity for storing information and making associations between different concepts and experiences. The uniformly distributed information allows for fast associative memory and understanding, so we can make connections between different pieces of stored information and non-local memory storage (where a specific memory is not stored in a specific location, i.e., a certain cluster of neurons). This is when we understand the whole picture, at once. We spontaneously access wholistic knowing in a flash of insight, rather than developing a collection of accumulated knowledge. This moves us beyond wisdom into knowing.

## CHILD DEVELOPMENT & ADULT RELATIONSHIPS:

At this stage of our Hero's Journey, when we are successful, we triumphantly return Home with the elixir that frees us from our negative conditioning. In a developmental context, this means we fully own our authenticity because we own our body experience of unified consciousness as an expression of our self (and the universe). This expression of unity contains all the attributes of the previous chakra/stages yet has a particular orientation of its own.

The seventh chakra/stage of our development as a child, is a time when we find a place in our experience of the larger collective. This includes finding our place in our culture by learning how to be a member of a larger group and community (Lizbeth Marcher, 2010). Our sense of the larger collective broadens our understanding of relationship and our role in the community. This can be expressed through social media, group activities in community, selfless service that contributes to the common good, and actions that alleviate suffering, such as caring for the disadvantaged and behavior that builds a more loving society.

This stage of development also involves the emergence of our awareness of the unified nature of relationship. In the sixth chakra/stage of development, from a sequential perspective, we can eliminate the division between a personal self and a sense of unified consciousness. We fully integrate the understanding that we are more than an individual person, and that our body is a vessel of unified consciousness. From our sense of existing as unity and wholeness, we can step away and observe our evolving-self and witness our characteristics and biases.

By contrast, in the seventh chakra/stage, we take this to the next step and recognize the experience of "I am the universe, and the universe creates everything," including the person that we

226

are and identify with. This reality is not a body-transcended state where we have ascended vertically in an "in-up-and-out" progression away from the world. At this dimension, the entire universe becomes a the "body" for our liberated being. This is the basis of our sense of unity within our self, and with all the things we perceive around us. In yoga philosophy, this experiential understanding is often called the "pure knowledge" (*suddhavidya*) that "I am all things."

This is not a superhuman or ultrahuman that only resides beyond the ego in a hyper-personal state, where "Man" is more than "Man." Rather, it is the completion of self (for all genders!) as a whole-being. As we awaken to the divine depths of our self as a human, we become our whole-self, dual and nondual. When we inhabit our body as seventh chakra unified consciousness, we recognize everything we behold is also part of a bigger, broader, and deeper perspective. Within our nondual ground-of-being, individual transient awarenesses, emotions, and sensations occur, much like particles move within the space that contains them. This is the awe-inspiring experience of the dual and nondual dimensions of our self together.

This is also not about the common feeling we have when in a transcendent state (starting with the eight chakra), of living in the world but not of this world. When the seventh chakra is a body experience, we not only live in the world while not subject to it, we are "of the world." We feel deeply, and are profoundly touched by even simple things, such as a walk in nature, or the beauty and difficulty of engaging with people. We can be moved and feel great compassion when the people we care about are suffering, and we share our response from the depths of our being, wholeness itself.

While our evolving-self emerges due to a socially interactive environment, the unchanging-self is an essential dimension of our self that is not dependent upon relationship. It is an innate, pre-existent aspect of our being. Yet, paradoxically, the unchanging-self provides a profound relational experience. It is unified and gives us access to a sense of connectedness and continuity with other people and our environment. This is a relational holism that can foster a sense of existential belonging, which is the opposite of existential angst. It is also relational in the sense that, as a child, if our caretaker is in contact with an inner-experience of wholeness, we become more able to recognize this experience in our self as well. This inner awakening also happens when we meet an awakened spiritual teacher. Their unified presence awakens us to the unified presence within us.

When we have a balanced seventh stage of growth, we not only maintain our emotional autonomy (clear personal truth/boundaries) but also our sense of self in a group of people, on the planet as a whole, and in the universe. At this stage, we feel secure inside our body, secure with our sense of evolving-self, and we have a sustained sense of wholeness-of-being. So we think about more than our immediate personal interactions, and can engage on a communal, global, or universal level.

When we awaken to unified consciousness as a relational holism, our sense of self and other changes. A central reason for this is that we balance the sense of our evolving-self and unchanging-self in whole-being-embrace, as a healing, nurturing, and empowering communion. This is not a relationship that is based on our evolving-self internalizing anything from the outside, as we learned to do as a child. Our unchanging-self is already there within us. If we look for it, we can recognize it. As a result, we can remain present with our evolving-self's suffering without losing our sense of wholeness and essential goodness. Our sense of wholeness and essential goodness, is an important part of the feeling of inner-knowing that we embody.

At this stage of our development as a child, we ideally feel secure in leading, excelling, and participating in relationship, as a member of a group, and as an aspect of the planet and universe. We feel deeply a part of a group, planet, and universe, and yet remain clear about our personal truth as an individual. We feel how the unified nature of the collective makes our sense of belonging become profoundly clear.

Later in life, the recognition that our own being is continuous with the collective and universal, while at the same time separate, helps us grow a sense of conscientiousness. Our healthy sense of inclusion and belonging, provides a feeling of a safe haven. So, when challenged, we easily maintain the intention of following our conscience, wisdom, and personal truth. We have a moral awareness of our own actions toward others, as well as how we relate to our self. It is a time when we value doing our best and showing-up fully, while honoring our honest limits, desires, and aversions. We also value helping others to be their best, while respecting their limits, desires, and aversions.

Our high level of self-worth allows us to accept when we fail or when another person is better at something than we are. We can recognize our own skills as well as other people's skills, and we can support them if they need help. We are able to easily move between leading or taking up room with our personal truth, and supporting another group or person to do the same. This transforms how we relate to our self and others. Our ability to show-up and be open to give-receive-and-take of life, grows.

We can also see the essential goodness of life because we recognize the essential ground-of-being beneath the artifices and constraints that lead to so much suffering. We perceive the radiance, fluidity, and spacious stillness that uniformly pervades everything and everybody. This gives us a warm, dynamic response of our heart, to the people in our life.

In embodied nondual meditation, we learn to sensitize our perceptions to the most subtle attunement of our self and the world around us. This is a twilight reality at the boundary of intention and effortless expression. It is the liminal edge of where Shiva and Shakti meet, the place of minimal phenomenal experience since it is felt as a feeling-tone of presence. Yet, "it is non-intentional as it is not about some content, other than itself" (Forman, 1998). At this liminal boundary between intention and effortlessness, we learn to reduce the interference of our intentional direction and will. This means we don't decide to perceive and respond. Instead, we let our experience of wholeness motivate our responses. We can feel that wholeness is eternal and we open to its truth.

When we perceive and respond, our options are relatively limited, however, our sense of inner-knowing, inherent to wholeness, is unlimited. This is a universal, and yet highly personal learning process that reinstates self-perpetuated learning. This is a process of reconnecting with the inborn intelligence of timelessness, unity, subtle conscious stillness, and chakra qualities. This expression of our self reinforces the impulse toward growth, individuation, connectedness, and creativity.

Our body's sense of unity is like a garden in which our sensations, emotions, and thoughts can mature without us rationally thinking it through. This is a sort of learning that is not intentional and happens on its own, as if out of the conscious stillness of wholeness itself. Unity consciousness creates the conditions that nurture the flowering of our individuality, as well as our self-realization as wholeness.

As mentioned in chakra/stage six, we *are* knowing, rather than the accumulation of knowledge on the road to becoming. Our body experience of unity and wholeness becomes a sophisticated biofeedback mechanism, where we feel a direct linkage to knowing. In this process, we may or may not have a conscious inkling of what is being learned. However, upon engaging in our daily life, we appreciate that our nervous system has undergone a substantial reorganization in its ability to perceive and respond.

It is as if the embodiment of unity and wholeness, or our presence as an illuminated state, has a reciprocal isomorphic (same or similar) effect on our injury. Our injury directly experiences the same sense of unity and wholeness. In this state, we elicit what the neurophysiologist, Pribram, has called the "hologramic" or "holonomic" nature of the nervous system. As mentioned, this is when each part of our being expresses an experience of the whole. Every perception and response is inscribed in a global pattern of organization in our mind and our body's nervous system.

In some ways, this is similar to the "quiet-alert" state that babies experience. As a newborn, at first, we enter a quiet-alert state, where we are cuddly and still. In this state, we are relaxed, calm, and happy. We stare contentedly into our parents' eyes, touch their hand, and listen to our parent's voice. This period is also the state in which optimal interaction, and learning through attunement occurs. All of our energy is channeled into seeing and hearing, insight, and inner listening. In the quiet-alert state, we take in our surroundings and deepen the bond we have with our most authentic expression of self.

The quiet-alert state that babies experience is similar to relaxed-alert state that yoga associates with balance/*sattva*, which, as mentioned, has the quality of goodness, purity, positivity, truth, serenity, balance, and peacefulness. *Sattva* results from the practice of steady alertness and, comfort and ease. It is the basis of what draws us towards behavior that is in harmony with our spiritual life path, cosmic order (*dharma*), and knowing (*jnana*). The baby's quiet-alert state is also similar to the relaxed-alert state the trauma therapist wants for the client recovering from severe injury. This state is precisely what we gain direct access to in embodied nondual meditation, and as an expression of self and a way of proceeding in life.

With some refinement, we begin to feel how our human expressions come from the conscious stillness of the unchanging ground-of-our-being. As this happens, we progressively eliminate all superfluous expressions from our response, and we restore our authentic human dignity. Everything that hampers, interferes with, or opposes perception and response with our whole body and mind, melts away.

By feeling the movement of expression initiating from this conscious stillness, we increasingly recruit only the muscles absolutely necessary, leaving all of the compensations and habitual defenses behind. Our expressions become light, effortless, and spontaneously arise with minimum effort and maximum efficiency. We do not seem to move through muscular strength or willfully respond, but instead, we move and respond through our sense of wholeness as if motivated by grace.

The following diagram illustrates what happens when we encounter a challenging perception while our nervous system is fully balanced in the seventh chakra/stage. This is based on the same premise first introduced in *chapter two*, that I called, The Gap. While some of what follows has been described earlier, I elaborate on it here in order to take the mystery out of the process of awakening to unified consciousness and its consequences,

## Image #15: Multiple Cycles Increasing "The Gap"

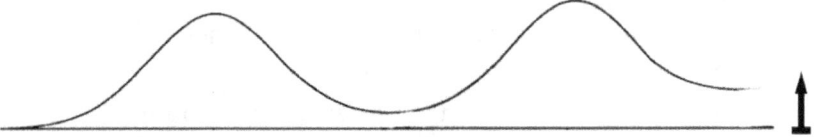

This illustrates our progressively increasing capacity for energy and consciousness in our body-mind system in a rising manner. As our body opens and our mind broadens its perspective, we increase our capacity for sustained dynamic equilibrium, integration, and unity (represented by The Gap).

### Multiple Charge-Discharge

Authenticity results from a balanced seventh chakra/stage. In energetic terms, as mentioned, this means we allow the energy underlying our thoughts, emotions, and sensations to charge, discharge, and return to balance without interruption or obstruction. This allows the charge of energy that naturally comes when we encounter a challenge, to freely spread throughout our whole body. In meditation practice, we learn that a key to doing this is "letting go of effort" in our perceptions and responses to what we experience. This allows us to let go of our habitual constrictions that lead to the fragmentation of our sense of self.[46] When we awaken a whole-body experience of the seventh chakra, we can let go of effort and sustain our experience of wholeness, even while having highly intense experiences.

This same energetic dynamic occurs every moment of the day. With each successful cycle of charge and discharge, our body and mind can let go of chronic constriction, soften, and open even more. The space we have in the body to breathe and feel, increases with each uninterrupted cycle. Thereby we increase our ability to tolerate and remain present with the higher levels of energy that accompany high-intensity experiences.

When we develop more energy charge in our body-mind system than we are used to, initially, our muscles can begin to tingle, feel a subtle resonance, or quiver and even tremble. These

---

[46] Much like how we learn to experience the immobility response without fear (see fourth chakra), we learn to experience all aspects of life without constricting and fragmenting our sense of self.

experiences are an indication of letting go of bound energy and re-energizing habitually constricted parts of the body. (As the body learns to remain open, this diminishes or becomes much more subtle.) With more energy charge in our body-mind system, we feel a sense of aliveness in the core areas of our body, often described as "streaming" current-like sensations, or a soft breeze flowing through us, as we face the challenges of daily life.

This streaming is the expression of subtle, energetic body pulsations. Body pulsations, vibration, and tingling, indicate that we are developing increasingly higher levels of energy and aliveness in the body. This energy radiates outward like the gentle ripples in a pond or the breaking of ocean waves, nourishing our tissues with an abundance of free-flowing energy. It is a dynamic process of a rhythmic, cyclic flow that is unique for each of us. This rhythm reflects the underlying pulsatory movement in all authentic expressions of nature.

In this way, we lay a foundation for our body and unconscious to stop being a reservoir of impulses that can often be overwhelming, and that we end up suppressing. Instead, the natural rhythmic flow becomes a life-sustaining activity that we learn to trust. It bypasses the mind, which can become fixated and distorted when we are injured. Our restored natural rhythms of energy flowing, allow healthy connections to form via more primitive, uninjured parts of the brain (Porges, Kolk). This bottom-up approach allows the body to inform the mind, and allows our physical, emotional, and mental life to become more integrated and whole.

As we learn to open to these body pulsations in embodied nondual meditation, we grow the ability to hold more and more energy and consciousness in our body-mind system. This becomes a vehicle for the transformation of our injuries. As bound energy is repeatedly spread throughout the body, we experience more authenticity and deeper and broader levels of consciousness throughout the whole body and mind. The energy that is no longer bound-up in the muscular holding patterns or directed at emotional and mental fixations, now enhances our sense of authenticity and the unified presence of our wholeness-of-being.

When we let go of constrictions, the original disturbing emotion that has been held in the body, is likely to come to the surface. Remaining attuned to our embodied nondual-qualities of self (such as our body's sense of conscious stillness and space, or the most soothing, integrating chakra) is important. It allows us to remain open to a profound sense of the support and nurturing experience of whole-being-embrace. In this context, the emotions that arise, open to a broader perspective with an alternative sense of time and space.

What also arises from this release are spontaneous expressions of personal truth that shape our healthy emotional boundaries in relationship. These help us resolve disturbing emotions. As this happens, core patterns of constriction are further released and remain open. We gain a deeper and broader experience of unity and openness within the body, that we can now inhabit fully. This allows us to have a deeper level of contact with our self and with other people.

As we perceive with a broader perspective and our body becomes more open, it becomes easier for us to repeatedly charge, discharge, and return to a balanced state with ease. This makes energy charge and arousal in our body-mind system feel enlivening and even pleasurable. We expand our capacity for remaining present, centered, and grounded as we have intense experiences and higher levels of energy and consciousness.

## SEVENTH CHAKRA

**Name**: The Sanskrit word for the seventh chakra is *"sahasrara,"* meaning "thousand-petaled lotus." More commonly, it is called the "Crown Center" chakra.

**Location**: The Crown Center chakra is within the center of the top of the head.

### Symbolic Level

Transcendent yoga traditions consider this chakra to be beyond form, as in the nondual consciousness of *atman* or *nirguna Brahman*. Because of this, the Crown Center chakra is associated with the color white, or no color, and silence, or no sound, since it is the most subtle of all chakra qualities of self. But, from an embodied nondual perspective, we can also experience this chakra as nonduality with qualities (*saguna Brahman, samprajnata samadhi*) within the body. For this reason, it is also described as a lotus flower with 1,000 petals of different colors. These pedals can be understood to depict the nondual-qualities of self as many expressions of wholeness, and collectively symbolize unified consciousness. These nondual-qualities can be experienced as "nondual bliss." The yoga practice of steady inner-attunement (an expression of concentration, *dharana*), and the meditative experience that results (*dhyana*), support us in awakening seventh chakra, embodied nondual consciousness.

The seventh chakra is often described as pure nondual consciousness only, beyond all qualities. From a transcendent perspective, this is graphically depicted as having no specific symbolism (color, sound, or element) connected with it (*nirguna Brahman*). Yet, the seventh chakra has also been depicted as having all qualities of wholeness (*saguna Brahman*). This is symbolically illustrated as an inverted lotus with the stem facing upward and the corolla opening downward. The one thousand flower pedals covering the top of the head are shown as all the colors of the rainbow. Each of these colors represents a nondual-quality of wholeness, signifying the pre-existent essential ground of our being (*saguna Brahman*).

Nonduality with qualities (*saguna Brahman*) is also commonly illustrated as a full moon circle that emits a luminous radiance. The luminosity bathes the subtle expression of our body in its entirety. In its form as a nondual-quality, it is an experience of pure possibility or potential, as we face our everyday limitations. The philosopher Walter Terence Stace (1960) referred to this state of a quality-rich transpersonal union as the "vacuum-plenum" paradox, an experience of a full-emptiness. As mentioned, this is much like when the Mahayana Buddhist term "*sunyata*" means a "full emptiness" (Loy, 1988) that is pregnant with the subtle qualities of our Buddha-Nature.

## Emotional Level

The seventh chakra is a "coming home" to where you have always been. Emotionally, the Crown chakra has been associated with many attributes, such as mercy, gentleness, patience, non-attachment, joy, deep love of life, humility, reflection, restfulness, effortlessness, and benevolence. These traits are the result of knowing unity and wholeness. As mentioned, the most important expression of unity and wholeness is unconditional love because it has the most power to heal our broken heart, which is at the center of our deepest relationship injuries. Paradoxically, unconditional love contains all the other chakra qualities.

What distinguishes the seventh chakra is that it is not about a particular aspect or quality of wholeness, but rather the universal nature of wholeness and unity itself. Our experience of its universal nature highlights the relational quality of unity. As mentioned, the feeling of being connected as one is particularly healing for those of us who have experienced different forms of emotional abandonment (feeling discounted, unappreciated, unloved, not included, or respected). Feeling the expansiveness, unlimited space, and spontaneity that accompanies unified consciousness, is particularly healing for those of us who feel imposed upon (by other's attitude, agenda, micro-managing). These expansive experiences enhance our sense of cohesion necessary for recovery from injury and rebuilding relationship bonds.

In a sense, from the seventh chakra, we can feel a connection to transcendent consciousness found in the eighth chakra and beyond, without rendering our body and our evolving-self irrelevant. While seventh chakra consciousness is a portal to the transcendent, with embodied unified consciousness we remain in relation to the immanent nature of our humanness. Limitation stops being a thorn in our heart, and instead becomes a divine play (pure ego; *lila*) that continually blossoms into the essence of immortality (*amrita*).

The relational quality of the universal nature of embodied unity and wholeness, can foster a broad perspective of life and our place in it. This can heighten a sense of bonding to life, the planet, and the global community. This is tremendously healing to those of us who have suffered from a sense of not belonging on the planet. It can also help us clarify the boundaries we need to have with the forces that challenge our integrity. This is because we gain a bird's-eye-view of our psychological labyrinth and see where we made supportive, or unwise choices, their consequences, and what we learned. We are more able to chart a new path with more comprehensive insight, that helps break us out of our fixated tunnel-vision, and expands our perception of the seen and unseen world.

We begin to experience how our own emotions affect the emotions of others we have never met, and we realize how important it is to become aware of how we affect the harmony of the world. We can feel how the interconnected nature of unconditional love, leads to a deeper appreciation for the emotional bonds we have with others. It can be said that our experience of quantum entanglement allows us to recognize the importance of how the intangible connectedness between humans can lead to more fulfilling interactions. We open to a sense of wonder and a deeper acceptance of the complexities of human relationships.

The completion that we experience in the sixth chakra deepens in the seventh chakra as a feeling of profound inner-peace. With all the other chakra qualities of consciousness to support us, questions concerning our sense of self and sense of other, is resolved. As mentioned, we may still have parts of our life that feel distressed, but this is felt within the context of our inner-peace, so it does not throw us off balance.

Descriptions of the psychological nature of the seventh chakra/stage have, in many ways, has already been described in earlier discussions of the nature of unity and wholeness. Some yoga practitioners include an eighth chakra located above the head. This chakra can be associated with transcendent pure "nondual consciousness only" (*atman, asamprajnata samadhi*), beyond all form and embodied nondual-qualities of self. This is the goal of many meditation approaches.

**Timelessness**

We have already considered how our experience of timelessness is healing in chakra/stage six. While in chakra/stage six we begin to get a sense of timelessness, only in chakra/stage seven do we deepen into this experience. Exploring the role timelessness plays a bit more can clarify what this means. This is important because most of us are strongly under the influence of the Axial Age hyper-focus on the mechanistic nature of existence, which eliminates our body experience of wisdom, intuition, and unified consciousness. When we are only guided only by the duality consciousness of our evolving-self, we can only perceive that which is limited.

From the perspective of our evolving-self's duality consciousness, in the absence of unified consciousness, we become fixated on the finite nature of our human mortal existence with a limited amount of time on this Earth. We may feel existential angst that we are a finite consciousness that emerges out of nothingness and vanishes into nothingness. We recognize that our solutions are ultimately limited by time, our abilities, and resources. All we know is that we can't get back time that has already passed. We are privately horrified by the reality of how our physical abilities and health decline as we age. We may fixate on how limited our resources are, including money, food, and shelter, feeling frustrated by what we will never be able to learn or experience.

By contrast, in the seventh chakra/stage, we become acutely aware of how the nondual-qualities of our unchanging-self are timeless. We feel that our body is mortal, but our consciousness, as an essential ground of our being, is immortal. We also recognize a timeless truth that we are a part of the immortal consciousness that pervades the universe. It has been with us our entire life, and has never changed and will never change. Because unified consciousness is a body experience of our self, as a subjective nonduality, it is paradoxically personal and non-personal. When timelessness is felt as an experience of our self, rather than only non-personal unity (transcendent), it communicates to our existential fears much more powerfully.

238

As mentioned, owning the experience of our immortality is a profound shift in perspective. It gives us access to an inherently benevolent, open, unattached, and non-willful state of the enduring presence-of-being. As this becomes an ongoing experience, we learn to integrate what this means in relation to our upcoming death. As we reach deeper than duality consciousness, we recognize our essence is a timeless presence-of-being. We feel it as an eternal now, where time stops, and our luminous presence is unending. We access a broader perspective that brings a sense of timeless connectedness, and belonging on a much broader level, that heals our existential fears.

**Hyper-Hypo Imbalances**

One only needs to look at child-rearing practices, family dynamics, social institutions, and politics, to see the reflection of relationship trauma acted out. Relationship trauma causes us to become fixated and creates hypo or hyper imbalances that sever us from the experience of unified consciousness.

With a hypo imbalance in the seventh chakra/stage, we distort or lose our sense of connection to universal consciousness and timelessness. We can feel alienated, lost, powerless in life, and hopeless. We remain disconnected and lack interest in spiritual subjects such as unified consciousness. In more extreme states, this can result in us having an existential crisis and apathy. We often feel low-grade anxiety and depression that saps our energy. We may suppress and mask this condition of our disheartened despondency behind a veneer of disregard and indifference.

Some of us may feel as though, somehow, we do not belong on the planet, and yet that it is up to us to save and heal the planet, in a kind of a double bind. We are responsible for it, rather than being a part of it and in harmony with it. (But with understanding the bigger picture and our interconnectedness as a part of a broad network, at this stage, we are freed from the individual responsibility for saving the planet or the need to solve everything, and yet we embody deep compassion and caring.)

Alternately, one expression of hyper imbalance of the seventh chakra/stage, is overemphasizing a transcendent approach to realizing unified consciousness. This overemphasis happens in a variety of ways (as mentioned in chapter one, "Eastern Mind Over Body"). A brief review can clarify what this means. (Keep in mind that the transcendent state is valuable, and yet on its own can be limiting). With a hyper imbalance, we often fixate upon our sense of connection to universal consciousness. Our focus may be solely on returning to the unknown of pure, nondual consciousness only (*atman, nirguna Brahman*), bypassing the evolving-self and failing to return to the inner knowing of the inborn, unified ground of our being (*saguna Brahman*).

As a culture that values the rational above the experiential and emotional, we can be detached from what we feel and remain externally oriented, disconnected from our own divinity. As discussed, this external orientation is exaggerated when we experience injuries that we don't fully recover from. When we are injured, to varying degrees, we often numb, detach from, or even leave our body, because what we experience is too overwhelming to feel. Plus, trauma always causes us to become more "externally referent" in anticipation of re-injury. This makes embodiment and accessing the experience of an internal source of guidance is very important. It is valuable to integrate the more internally referent understanding that comes with not leaving the body, and our own inner divinity, to experience our sense of being at one with all that is.

Other hyper imbalances that have already been mentioned include, over-emphasizing perception in the form of awareness only, and over-using the mental training of quieting the mind.[47] Yet, the austerity of keeping the mind concentrated on one object exclusively or eliminating thought and emotion, is usually a huge challenge, especially when we carry unresolved relationship injuries.

In embodied nondual meditation, we come to recognize the paradox that ultimately, both the experience that our evolving-self and the world are real (*sat*) and that they are not real (*maya*)

---

[47] Ongoing concentration on one object and nothing else does produce nondual consciousness. The relationship between mind and object deepens to the point at which the mind's awareness of itself concentrating diminishes. Awareness of the object of our attention begins to dominate, absorb, or consume the reflective mind.

are true. Depending on our state of consciousness and what we focus on, both transcendent and embodied states of nonduality are true. This understanding is important to heal our injuries and awaken. One understanding without the other is limiting and often sabotages our growth. For those of us with relationship trauma, that is so widespread, this can be particularly disorienting.

When we over-emphasize the transcendent state, our detachment and disidentification from our emotions, can lead us to lack understanding of our personal truth. As a result, we do not have what it takes to understand how to establish healthy boundaries in relationship. We lack a basic understanding of relationship and what it takes to negotiate and skillfully navigate its nuances.

This book combines knowledge (gnosis) and practice (praxis). Before elaborating on the conceptual details (gnosis) of the chakras in *chapter seven*, the next *chapter, six*, briefly describes some of the practical details (praxis) of what it means to awaken the chakras in practice. *Chapter six* complements *chapter four's* "Refining the Senses & Attunement" section, and serves as a practical guide for contemplation and embodied nondual meditation practice.

# CHAPTER SIX: AWAKENING THE CENTRAL-CHANNEL

This chapter begins with a consideration of the overall journey of awakening unified consciousness in the central-channel of the body, as it is expressed in myth. Then we shift focus to the practical skills that are involved in awakening the central-channel.

## THE SUBTLE CORE & THE APPLE OF KNOWLEDGE

Yoga often emphasizes balancing our energy by gently constricting the primary diaphragms of the body (*bandhas*) and directing our energy and breath in a way that creates balance. As a container is created by constricting the diaphragms for each body segment, we learn to fill it up with energy and consciousness. As a result, we wake up the sleeping "*kundalini serpent*" of *prana* in the central-channel (*sushumna*), so that it rises through each chakra of the body, releasing obstructions and awakening consciousness as it goes. In embodied nondual meditation, we do this in the most subtle, gentle way.

As mentioned, the healing staff of the medical field is a picture of two entwined serpents sliding up the staff. These two serpents represent the *ida* and *pingala*. The staff, called "*danda*," is symbolic of the central-channel. Thus, as we learn to engage the diaphragms in the body (*bandha*), we are learning to awaken this "snake" subtle energy and consciousness aspect of existence in our subtle core. The correspondence with the snake in the Garden of Eden that enticed Eve to eat the apple of knowledge, has an interesting correlation to the snake representing kundalini energy.

It is said that the myth of the Garden of Eden came from ancient Sumerians. As an allegory, the tree in the garden symbolizes the Tree of Life, which is a map of the human soul. The trunk of the tree is the central-channel, and the serpent on the tree depicts our subtle energy (Shakti) that coils around the Tree of Life. In this myth, it is said that the serpent (Enki) told

242

Adamu ("Adam," symbolizing *pingala*) and Eva ("Eve," symbolizing *Ida*) to eat from the Tree of Knowledge. As the kundalini serpent rises up the central-channel, it awakens the inner centers of unified consciousness as found in the Chakras. In the process, it informs us of the knowledge of our divine nature. Knowing (gnosis) is obtained, and one's spiritual eyes are opened. When Adamu and Eva are awakened to unified consciousness as a body experience, this symbolizes our rebirth as a divine being in a body.

## TRILOGY & CADUCEUS AS OUR DEATH-REBIRTH CYCLE

Understanding what energy is, and how it moves in the body, is important. Energy can be experienced in a variety of ways, from gross to subtle. In its most gross form, it becomes a solid object, in a less gross form, it can be experienced as the movement of sensation, emotion, and thought. The subtle energy of the kundalini serpent that rises up the central-channel and awakens unified consciousness is often described in yoga as *"prana."*

Prana energy flows through a network of channels (*nadis*) and permeates the whole body. It is especially concentrated along the midline within the central-channel, called *sushumna* in Sanskrit. The central-channel houses all the primary chakra centers of energy and consciousness (as described in the Bhagavad Gita, verse 4.29). Prana needs to be balanced to maintain our health, and to allow us to access the chakras as expressions of unified consciousness.

One way the *prana* subtle energy is expressed is in two subtle energy pathways (*nadi*) that run on either side of the central-channel. Together, they form three primary channels of subtle energy and consciousness. The nature of these three channels is like the ancient Sumerian caduceus, a short staff entwined by two serpents (the Sumerian serpent - Enki – assumes two forms). In this case, the two serpents symbolize the right (*pingala*) and left (*ida*) energy channels entwined around the staff, the central-channel. (Interestingly, this entwined pattern is like the double-helix of DNA, a primary unit of evolution and reproduction). As the yogi David Frawley explains, the right channel is associated

243

with energy's charge phase (*rajas guna*) of arousal, and the left channel is associated with energy's discharge phase (*tamas guna*). The central-channel is associated with the stillness of the balanced state (*sattva guna*).

As mentioned, these divine forms of energy and consciousness are personified as a triad of deities (*trimurti*). Brahman is the creator, Vishnu the preserver, and Shiva the destroyer. This triptych is also associated with Christianity's Holy Trilogy. As deities, they exemplify energy in its three primary forms. Here, I relate it to the fundamental three-phase nature of energy. The cyclic nature of the universe (*samsara*), where creation arises out of destruction, is a process of the death of the "ego" (limiting habits) and creating new life (habit free) out of death.

In Western myth, this eternal cycle of renewal has been depicted as the Mobius strip (the infinity symbol) or the Ouroboros serpent who eats its own tail to sustain its life. Without beginning or end, it reveals a cyclic renewal or karmic cycle of life, death, and rebirth. When this three-phase progression occurs without obstruction, balance and unity prevail in our body-mind system. This is when freedom from limiting habits emerges and the energy the underlying our mental, emotional and sensory life becomes authentic.

This perpetual eternal return cycle represents rebirth into karmic growth, yet because energy and consciousness are entangled, it also means the infinite immortality of nonduality. Like the Western myth of Ouroboros slaying itself and bringing itself to life again, it is a kind of self-fertilizing self-birthing into nondual consciousness process. The Mobius strip form of the Ouroboros snake symbolizes how nondual consciousness precedes and proceeds from the tension of opposites (charge-discharge). Opposites meet and resolve into a stage of balanced stillness, over and over. The eternal birth and death of existence describes duality and nonduality in, what is often referred to as, the "divine play of Lila."

Yet, in embodied nondual yoga we are not aspiring to transcend this eternal cycle to be free from our suffering. Symbolically, this means we do not want to slay the Sumerian serpent Enki, the Ouroboric snake, or mythic dragon. We only strive to tame the snake's renewal process by embracing it with unified consciousness. When we refine our senses and directly awaken to the energy and unified consciousness within our own body, this becomes possible. In this way, liberation and freedom from suffering in each moment (*jivanmukta*) can happen.

Because the symbolic play of Lila (spontaneous expression arising out of unified consciousness) has no capacity for self-awareness, and is therefore transcendent, I ascribe to Kashmiri Shaivism's notion of "pure ego." Pure ego is the nondual-subjectivity of embodied nondual consciousness, our self-aware unchanging-self.

Integration and assimilation of opposites that happens as we enter into whole-being-embrace with our unresolved injuries. This allows us to achieve the dynamic equilibrium and the stillness of the fully balance state. We experience this most clearly in the central-channel and the seven primary chakras (see "Ida, Pingala, Sushumna Nadi" in *chapter six*).

This cyclic process is a kind of mandala of alchemic transformation of consciousness and energy. This can be described as energy and consciousness consuming each other and turning into each other in a circulatory process of awakening. It is a "feed-back" cycle representing our evolution (toward unity) and involution (incarnation from unity) processes of personal growth and the spiritual emergence of unified consciousness. Involution is the process of the dormant nondual state becoming awakened within our incarnation, so that we can access our wholeness. Our evolution is our state of duality on its journey toward integration and nondual wholeness.

The involution cycle takes hold when we uncover and awaken a stable experience of inhabiting the body *as* our unchanging ground-of-being. It also can be the universal/cosmic nature of unity that incarnates within us upon conception, or that we awaken to within our body._Like a hologram, unity exists everywhere, all the time, all at once_.

This form of involution is not about the common practice of recognizing it as a larger cosmic unity, or an external deity being down-loaded into our body, nor about opening outward to a non-local cosmic consciousness. It is an uncovering of what is already there within our body. The awakening to the self-aware ground-of-being involves being in the world as a self-aware embodied nonduality (Buddha-Nature, Christ-consciousness, unchanging-self).

While the tail of the serpent Enki or the Ouroboric snake is a phallic symbol and the mouth a "yonic" (vulva) or womb-like symbol, it is ultimately an "all is one" expression of eternity. This is when the duality of energy's ever-changing quantum particle nature, comes into a whole-being-embrace with the quantum wave nature of energy's nondual consciousness. In embodied nondual meditation they paradoxically join as one without losing their autonomy. In this process, we experience how energy and consciousness are entangled expressions of one reality. Our openness, stillness, and wholeness, allows for the authentic movement of self-expression.

As mentioned, by healing and learning not to interrupt this cycle due to our unresolved injuries, with each cycle we experience more of the stillness of nondual consciousness in our body-mind system (referred to as "The Gap," Image #6). We progressively move from experiencing life as only the limited perception of duality consciousness, to also experiencing life as the limitless, timeless perception of nondual consciousness. With the direct-path of embodied contemplative practice, this shift in perspective becomes an ongoing, stable experience. As we uncover and awaken as the embodied experience of nondual consciousness, the fixations (hyper, hypo) we have in each of the seven-stages become increasingly pervaded with nondual consciousness.

## HOW THE PHASE-STAGE CYCLES RELATE TO THE CHAKRAS

In taking a deeper look at the chakras and their relationship with the central channel, some of what has already been explained about chakras will be mentioned again.

Too often, even therapists and meditators, do not experience the existence of a body experience of unity and wholeness. Thus, also do not recognize that this experience of wholeness can be felt as a variety of qualities that are wholenesses themselves. So,

246

clarifying what a quality-rich nondual experience is, can help clarify the focus of embodied nondual meditation. Understanding how we can uncover and awaken this as a body experience was introduced in *chapter four* ("Refining the Senses & Attunement"). In this chapter, we will refine how the central-channel (*sushumna*) participates in this awakening.

As mentioned, we can experience the unity and wholeness of our unchanging-self in a variety of ways (see "holon," p. 66). Most fundamentally, each of these ways expresses the nondual-quality of wholeness we feel as an unchanging, quality-rich presence within our body and the environment. Spiritual traditions each have their own lexicon to describe this.

The nondual-qualities of unified consciousness have been described as "emptiness," "absolute transparency," and "openness." Hinduism refers to these qualities as "truth" (*sat*), "intelligence" (*chit*), and "bliss" (*ananda*). One way these adjectives can be understood, is found in our experience of the truth of our nondual-essence (*sat*) and when we combine this with an experience of intelligence inherent in awareness (*chit*), we experience bliss (*ananda*). Buddhism calls this same trilogy "emptiness," "clarity," and "bliss." When we experience the emptiness of our nondual-essence, and combine this with an experience of clarity of perception, we experience bliss.

The Hindu and Buddhist trilogy of nondual-qualities can also be experienced as the unchanging essence of "awareness," "emotion," and physical "sensation." Tantra yoga divides these expressions of wholeness into the seven primary chakras, which is the primary focus of this chapter. Yet, each of these nondual-qualities are like holons, in that they are all expressions of unity on their own, as an expression of wholeness, that are also a part of a larger unity.[48] When we have access to the nondual unified dimension of wholeness, we access to all the chakra qualities.

---

[48] Much like how historically the immanence of embodied spirituality shifted into transcendent spirituality, the term emptiness, *sunyata*, has been interpreted in a transcendent way as well as an embodied nondual way. The root "su" means to "swell" in two ways: to "hollow" or "empty," and it also means "full," as in pregnant. The Buddhist path where "*su*" means emptiness, involves having no fixed self-nature, since our self does not exist. On the other

Chakras are commonly regarded as having a sequential nature. From this perspective, the first chakra is the densest, and the seventh chakra is the least dense. Therefore, the seventh chakra is the only one that is nondual. Yet, as we refine our senses, we discover that each chakra is an expression of unity and wholeness. This is like shining a light through a crystal to display light as a spectrum of rainbow colors. Each color is a nondual-quality that can be experienced as a wholeness unto itself (holon, Wilber).[49] The chakras are one way the plethora of nondual-qualities of existence are expressed in the body.

The vertical central axis that contains the chakras, can be said to be our "imaginal conduit" axis, or the trunk of the Tree of Life, connecting our evolving-self to unified consciousness through the central-channel.[50] Cultivating awareness of the central-channel of the body as a psycho-spiritual expression of our self (duality and nonduality), also refines our ability to clearly perceive our protective organization, and patterns of constriction, collapse, and numbness in the core of the body. As we come to inhabit this central-channel, we become more able to discern and let go of our constrictions and fragmentation, so often harbored in the deepest part of the body. This helps us get to the root of our deepest and most tightly held emotional injuries.

As we discern and let go of our fragmentation, we discover that the subtle-core of the body is a potent integrative center for

---

hand, on the Buddhist path where "*su*" means "full," we can have a diverse array of nondual experiences.

[49] The sequential understanding of the chakras is based on an indirect-path that embraces the notion that we need to evolve from the densest to the least dense. While this is true, paradoxically we also have a direct-path of attuning directly to the pre-existing unified dimension of existence

[50] The central-channel is a straight line from the center of the crown of the head to the center of the bottom of the torso (i.e., the perineum, the space between our sit-bones). While the physical body forms around the spine as a primary organizing axis, the central-channel (*sushumna*) of the subtle energy body runs vertically in front of the spine in the middle of the body. There is often a debate as to the precise location, so it is important to find it by the feel of it.

the internal space of the whole body. The central-channel is not only an integrative center but our most direct entranceway into a sense of self-other oneness. When we come to live in the core, it facilitates us to be able to think, feel, and sense at the same time.

By awakening and inhabiting the central-channel, we gain access to the deepest contact with our individual being and the deepest perspective that we can have on our environment. As we release our habitual protective constrictions in the core, we are not only becoming more open and united with all that is, but we are also deepening our inward contact with our self and the nondual, unchanging qualities of our being. By awakening and living in our body's central-channel, we find a sense of being profoundly centered and balanced. When life gets challenging, and emotions push us off balance, we feel we have an inner location, as a reference of wholeness.

While the chakras are the most potent expression of the nondual unchanging-self, they are not a physical structure in the body. As mentioned, they can only be perceived as subtle feeling-tones or qualities that are not available to the normal range of our senses. Because the central-channel and the chakra centers are the subtlest expressions of our being, they are not obvious to find and awaken. This chapter offers some suggestions that can help us do that.

With practice, we come to inhabit our whole body as the nondual-qualities of our unchanging-self, that we need most in order to awaken, and sustain our sense of wholeness-of-being. We learn to become emotionally autonomous from our habitual protective patterns, so they do not overwhelm us, while still being responsive to what we experience. Authentic responsiveness, and emotional autonomy from limiting habit, are primary aspects of living a fulfilling, enlightened life, in relationship.


IDA, PINHALA, SUSHUMNA NADI

As a psycho-spiritual expression of existence, the chakra system has a fundamental relationship with our autonomic nervous system and our subtle *prana* energy. The chakras and the nervous system both involve the three phases of energy: charge, discharge, and balance. This implies that the chakras and the nervous system have a symbiotic relationship, and influencing one affects the other. Let us take a little deeper look at what this means (some of which has already been mentioned).

Each chakra is connected to the other chakras by three channels, "*nadi,*" of subtle energy and consciousness. The *nadi* channels are much like Chinese medicine's meridians, where the acupuncture points are located. Except, instead of acupuncture points, the *nadi* channels have chakra centers. As mentioned, the primary *nadi* channels run vertically through the core of the torso, from the center of the top of the head to the center of the bottom of the torso. Each of these three energy channels is an expression of one of the three primary phases of subtle energy. So, the *nadi* energy channel on the right (*pingala*) relates to charge/*rajas*; the *nadi* channel on the left (*ida*) is discharge/*tamas*; and the central-channel *nadi* (*sushumna*) is balance/*sattva*.

The right and left channels have an ascending and descending direction in which energy flows. As Abhinavagupta explains, there is an upward-moving kundalini (*pingala/urdhva*) on the right (charge), which is allied with expansion, and a downward-moving kundalini (*ida/adha*) on the left (discharge), which is allied with contraction. Together, this forms a subtle rhythmic pulsation. This is an expression of the primordial cycle of creation (contraction) and dissolution (expansion) and the return to balance (*sattva*) as depicted in the *Trideva* myth (Brahman as the creative charge, Shiva as the destroying discharge, and Vishnu is the balancing preserver). When the right and left channels are balanced, the central-channel (*sushumna*-balance) awakens and gives us direct access to the most profound experience of unified consciousness.

We can experience the charge (*pingala*) and discharge (*ida*) subtle energy pathways as straight vertical channels on either side of the central-channel. When the subtle energy flows freely through these straight channels, they both draw in and touch base with the central-channel at certain locations along this vertical path. The places where they contact the central-channel define the locations of each of the major chakras in their nondual state.

Our subtle energy continues to flow through the charge (on the right side) and discharge (on the left side) channels in a straight line, and yet they are also connected to the central-channel at the level of each of the chakras. When unified consciousness as a body experience is awakened to the clearest degree, the *ida* and *pingala* cross over to the opposite side, while paradoxically also continuing to flow on their respective sides.[51]

These divergent models are why we see various depictions of the right and left channels. In embodied nondual meditation we do practices that focus on the first option. The second and third options arise spontaneously on their own:

1) where both channels are straight pathways on either side of the central-channel.
2) as curving channels that make contact with the central-channel.
3. the charge and discharge channels cohere and cross over to the opposite side.

---

[51] The model that represents the charge and discharge channels as crossing over to the other side of the central-channel reflects Eastern dialectics. Western dualism is commonly based on rational logic emphasizing binary opposition, where opposite poles are exclusive and cannot be integrated. Eastern nonduality is based on intuition, unity, and a dialectics of harmony. This dialectic emphasizes how two sides contrast and complement one another, and in their mutual penetration, they cohere and form a unified whole (in the central-channel). Subtle energy charge (*pingala*) transforms into discharge (*ida*), which enhances balance. Charge and discharge can be generated from each other, and transformed into each other when they reach their peak development. Opposites meet and resolve into a state of balanced stillness, over and over. When this occurs without obstruction, this establishes and maintains balance between them and awakens the unified nature of each chakra within the central-channel.

## Image #16: The Core's Three Channels

1          2          3

The practice of embodied nondual meditation helps us refine our senses enough to recognize that deeper than any experience of imbalance, solidness, and separateness, there exists the fully balanced, conscious stillness of unified consciousness. At this depth and subtlety, we experience that all our chakras are balanced and awakened as nondual-qualities of our being. When we attune to and embody the balanced nature of all the chakras, the whole central-channel is awakened, illuminating our whole body as a unified field of consciousness.

The central-channel is our most direct portal to this essential ground of our being and our environment. While descriptions of energy and consciousness in the three channels of the subtle-core of the body may seem complex, the actual process of accessing this experience is not. Attending to the transverse "diaphragms" of the body can facilitate the process.


## DIAPHRAGMS AS GROUNDING FOUNDATION

In yoga, when we think of subtle energy we commonly think of the central-channel. Our central-channel is experienced as a vertical column of consciousness through which our subtle energy (*prana*) flows. Subtle energy in Sanskrit is called "*prana.*" One interpretation of the word *prana* is "that which is infinitely everywhere." This means, that in its most refined expression, it is a form of energy that is so subtle that it is "infinite" or nondual. Energy at this level of subtlety is an expression of unified consciousness itself.

As mentioned, the chakras are composed of three subtle energy currents that flow through channels (*nadi*). The channel on the left (*ida nadi*) is a downward (*apana*), discharge current, and the one on the right (*pingala nadi*) is an upward charge current (also called *prana*). These two channels of subtle energy lie on either side of the balanced central-channel, where all the chakras are located. When the right and left channels flow freely without obstruction, we access the central-channel and all the chakras in their balanced state of unified consciousness as an experience of wholeness and unity. When we mentally, emotionally, and physically fragment due to injury or overwhelm, we constrict and obstruct the upward and downward channels of energy from flowing freely. When these channels are obstructed, they impede awakening the nondual nature of energy and consciousness inherent to the central-channel.

One of the most obvious ways we physically and energetically obstruct the central-channel is by constricting horizontal structures of the body (side to side, front to back). We automatically constrict these horizontal structures whenever we feel overwhelmed due to an unusually intense pleasant or unpleasant emotion, thought, or sensation.

The horizontal structures segment the body. *As* Wilhelm Reich explained, there are seven segments of the body where muscular tensions develop most prominently. This understanding of seven segments correlates with the locations where the seven primary chakras are located (Reich refers to the segments as: 7. ocular or eye; 6. oral; 5. cervical; 4. thoracic; 3. diaphragm; 2. abdominal; 1. pelvic). Moreover, when the neuroscientist Candace Pert (1997) describes the chakras, she explains that we are like segmented worms, and the body is a large container that is composed of several smaller containers.

What is important about this is that the segmented containers are defined by physical tissues that function like diaphragms. Our diaphragms are layers of connective tissues and interconnected fascia that run horizontally/transversely (side to side, front to back) through the body. They are sometimes referred to as called "transverse diaphragms." Most of the other myofascial tissues in our body run vertically/longitudinally (up and down). There are two kinds of transverse diaphragms: anatomical diaphragms and functional diaphragms.

There are three anatomical diaphragms that anatomists recognize: respiratory, pelvic, and laryngeal. The osteopathic doctor William Sutherland, who informed craniosacral therapy, talks about several other transverse structures that are referred to as "functional diaphragms" because they act like diaphragms: the thoracic outlet and the cranial diaphragm. The five diaphragms can be described as follows:

| Transverse Diaphragms | Location |
|---|---|
| 1. Tentorium cerebella/cranial... | Base of eyes to back of head |
| 2. Tongue/Oris | Base of tongue to back of head |
| 3. Thoracic outlet | Base of neck |
| 4. Respiratory diaphragm | Base of thoracic cavity |
| 5. Pelvic diaphragm | Pelvic basin |

Yoga practice often emphasizes three of these diaphragms: pelvic basin (*mula bhanda*), respiratory diaphragm *(uddiyana bhanda)*, base of throat (*jalandhara bhanda*). Yet, in more contemplative yoga practices, we recognize and attend to more subtle diaphragms that facilitate directly accessing unified consciousness. In the Realization Process® method, for instance, Judith Blackstone adds two more transverse structures. These two additional "functional diaphragms" serve as gateways between our body and the universe (crown) as well as the Earth (feet). When we experience them from the inside of the body in meditation, we feel them act like diaphragms, on a very subtle level:

| | |
|---|---|
| 6. Crown | Top of our head |
| 7. Feet | Soles of our feet |

Altogether, there are seven anatomical (true) and functional (act like a diaphragm) diaphragms, in our body. There are other minor ones that can come into play, especially if we have experienced some kind of emotional, physical, or mental injury that involves another part of the body. (In some Tantra yoga we include the urogenital diaphragm.)

The body is structured such that every diaphragm appears in "transitional zones" (Sutherland, 1997) or physical junctions, where the spinal column curvature changes (convex, concave). Because of this, they are places where we frequently experience weakness or constriction. While this is where we have the most fascial restriction, muscular imbalance, and accumulation of bound energy, it is also where we can most effectively self-regulate and release our bound energy.

Releasing our bound energy not only influences our emotions, body, and mind, but as we refine our senses, it gives us access to an experience of inner unified space. In embodied nondual meditation, we become familiar with all the diaphragms and learn to release the chronic tension embedded within them. In this way, we very effectively open and awaken the central-channel to gain access to a core sense of wholeness-of-being and unity.

One reason it gives us access to an experience of inner unified space is that the diaphragms function in two primary ways: 1) they separate each body segment, and yet, 2) they are also all interconnected by a large sheath of fascial body tissue and tend to respond in unison. As separate structures, they function sequentially, where the movement of one leads the others to move consecutively. As part of a larger unified, coherent, bioelectric matrix, they function simultaneously, expanding and relaxing in unison (Sills, 2001). Like a geodesic dome, when pressure is put on one part of the dome, the whole dome responds at the same time. So, if one end constricts, everything inside shifts simultaneously.

Fortunately, when we enhance the physical tone of one of the diaphragms by learning to soften, settle, and open it while meditating, we can enhance the tone in all of them. We thereby increase our access to an inner experience of integration and an internal sense of continuity between all the segments of the body. With a little refinement, what emerges is an experience of unified consciousness within the body.[52] When the unified matrix of the physical diaphragms is not habitually constricted (i.e., when they are "toned," which implies balance) we awaken the chakra centers as expressions of unity.[53]

Every diaphragm appears in "transitional zones" or physical junctions where the spine shifts from a concave to a convex curve because this is where we need the most structural support. The horizontal structure of the diaphragms support us to stand vertically. In providing this support, we do not experience excessive weakness and tissue constriction in these transitional zones. On a more subtle level, the horizontal diaphragms give the vertical central-channel the ability to remain unobstructed and unconstricted, remaining open to the natural currents of our subtle-energy (*prana*). They give us the support we need to be able to effectively soften, settle, and open patterns of tension that obstruct the central-channel. It is no coincidence that the *Hamsa Upanishad* describes the central-channel, *sushumna*, as a "hollow canal."

When a diaphragm is habitually contracted, we cannot relax the constrictions within the segment of the body it supports. In embodied nondual meditation, we can experience that if each body segment can find a sense of support from the diaphragm at its base/foundation, relaxing and accessing a core sense of openness in that part of the body becomes much easier. With practice, the diaphragms themselves also relax and open so that

---

[52] The primary content within the diaphragm is our "interstitial fluid," which some medical researchers consider to be the largest organ of the body. Our interstitial fluid surrounds all the particles of cell matter. The fascia matrix of the diaphragms has a direct influence upon the interstitial fluid of our body. When the interstitial fluid, which lies throughout our whole body, is influenced, it inherently helps us shift our consciousness from duality to nonduality.

[53] What can enhance this balanced, toned state is, rather than breathing sequentially, where we fill up the chest, then the belly, and back, we inhale and fill up the whole body at once and then we exhale everywhere at once. When we do this with the least effort possible, each of the functional diaphragms participates, and after a while, a sense of unity consciousness emerges.

256

we access the sense of open continuity between body segments, and the sense of unity and wholeness that results.

The foundational diaphragms also act as dams for fluids and subtle energy. (This is helpful since the human body is composed of 70% water.) When we fragment because we are overwhelmed by what we experience (sorrow, anger, fear, etc.), our body diaphragms are the first places we constrict, causing us to become more energetically compartmentalized. The body segments become isolated from one another, obstructing the fluids and energy from flowing through and between the major segments of the body. This is the energetic dynamic that underlies our mental and emotional fragmented state of deregulation and loss of integration.

When the dams are functional, they support the flow of body fluids and subtle energy between body segments. They become functional when they do not harbor any habitual constrictions (or the patterns of collapse that emerge as a result). We access a sense of openness and continuity between each body segment. We learn how to do this on the most subtle level so we can open each diaphragm. This allows the upward (*prana*) and downward (*apana*) flow of subtle energy to occur and awakens the central-channel.

In yoga, one of the common ways we achieve balance of the rising (*prana*) and downward (*apana*) energy currents, is by engaging our diaphragms (*bhanda*). Yoga postural and conscious breathing practices intentionally work with the understanding that the body is a physical and energetic container. As such, we self-regulate body-mind energies as well as create neuromuscular tone in the diaphragms.[54] In this way, we achieve a balanced state, which opens the central-channel and awakens unified consciousness. The emphasis on self-regulation to achieve balance is an indirect-path to unified consciousness. By

---

[54] To create balance, in coordination with conscious breathing (*ujjayi pranayama*), we repeatedly constrict and relax our diaphragms: pelvic basin (*mula bhanda*), respiratory diaphragm (*uddiyana bhanda*), base of throat (*jalandhara bhanda*). In this way, we regulate the pressure between body cavities and open the channel of energy that flows up the body (*prana*) and down the body (*apana* ). This sets the stage for awakening the central-channel.

contrast, embodied nondual meditation is a direct-path to unity that occasionally uses some very simple balancing self-regulation practices. As explored in *chapter four*, "Refining our Senses & Attunement," we attune to the openness that lies deeper than anything solid or constricted in our body. This becomes a direct portal to unified consciousness and awakening the central-channel.

## Constriction & Ground

As mentioned, one of the most obvious ways we physically and energetically obstruct the central-channel is by constricting the diaphragms whenever we feel overwhelmed. This is important to elaborate upon because constriction (and often subsequent collapse) accompanies all experiences of fragmentation due to overwhelm. In somatic psychology, Wilhelm Reich (1933) was the first to recognize that the first place the body registers emotional overwhelm is in the respiratory diaphragm. When we constrict habitually, the facia that surrounds every cell of the body, including organs and muscles, develop patterns of constriction. Moreover, the osteopath Franklyn Sills (2001) points out that all the fascia throughout the body join together where the lower back meets the upper back at the twelfth rib, the thoracolumbar fulcrum. In embodied nondual meditation, we come to recognize how all the diaphragms constrict and can be opened, on a very subtle level. At this depth of subtlety, we facilitate all the diaphragms connecting together through the myofascial connective tissue, as a unified matrix.

Meditating upon the thoracolumbar fulcrum area and feeling how it communicates to our whole respiratory diaphragm and all the other diaphragms, is an effective way to shift our physiology and our state of being. In practice, we become sensitive to such a fine level of sensory perception that we are able to clearly locate all the structures that act like diaphragms in the body. Even though the diaphragms have a shared relationship and function as a whole, depending on the specific locations we constrict most due to overwhelm, some diaphragms become less flexible than others. If we are especially constricted in any specific diaphragm,

258

we can access the experience of openness within it for a more precise influence. By first identifying where we habitually obstruct and fragment our body, and which diaphragm is most involved, it is then possible to progressively access the openness within the diaphragm that lies deeper than the constriction. In this way, the diaphragms paradoxically provide structural support and are locations of focus to uncover a sense of internal openness between body segments.

By developing a very refined awareness in meditation, we can identify the most subtle sensations of constriction in the diaphragms at their inception. Because the constriction is not fully established yet, it is easier to learn to respond to intense experiences without constricting any of the diaphragm foundations. We fine-tune the skill of effortlessness (*see chapter five, chakra four*) and not griping or constricting automatically. We learn not to lift up, pull, push, press forward or backward, or clamp down. Instead, we stay settled within each of the seven diaphragm foundations, and simultaneously open to our sense of unified space within the body. By learning to physically let go of, or disentangle from, core holding patterns of tension throughout a diaphragm (front to back and out to the sides), we gain access to our most relaxed-alert and balanced state.

Our relationship with the ground, or the sense of having a foundation we can rest upon, is important. For example, if we do not fully inhabit our legs because we were unable to stand our emotional ground as a child, we may not be able to remain present, inhabit our legs, and have a relationship with the ground as an adult. When we are healthy, our energy freely flows vertically down and up the body. Although we all have our feet on the ground, to be energetically "grounded" involves having a strong flow of energy go through the legs to our feet, and having a sense of settled contact with the ground. Like a house, we need to have a strong foundation.

When we do not have enough support from the ground, we constrict the diaphragms higher up. If our body's foundation below the waist is physically weak, numb, or lacks awareness, the upper part of the body tenses to compensate for the lack of support from below. For instance, if we are weak in our legs and not fully aware of them, we can constrict the pelvic basin or respiratory diaphragm in an attempt to establish a foundation from which we can feel support and leverage our movements.

Furthermore, when we experience emotional overwhelm, our sympathetic nervous system causes us to not only contract the diaphragm inward but also lift up away from the ground. When overwhelmed, we also can press down or pull or push our true center forward or backward. For instance, when longing for contact, we can contort our posture and energy to reach forward, and when we feel imposed upon, we can shrink inward and contort towards the back of our body. This is sometimes visible in people's posture. As we do this, we move the chakra center closest to the most affected diaphragm away from its true location. Expressions such as, "My heart dropped to the ground" or "My belly is in my throat" describe this common experience.

A good physical and emotional relationship with the ground is a primary means of accessing and maintaining our sense of unity and wholeness. In yoga practice, we recognize the importance of cultivating a sense of being present to our body experience and accessing a physical relationship with the ground. This common practice is reflected in the root of the Sanskrit word for yoga posture, "asana," which is "as," meaning "to stay, "to be," and "to be established in a particular position." When we physically establish ourselves in a position, we psychologically "take a stand." That is, we not only feel physical stability, but we also psychologically stand our ground and fully arrive in the present moment as we are. [55]

---

[55] The physical base of this grounding happens most obviously in our lower body, specifically our pelvic basin, legs, and feet. In the yoga tradition, the feet have an almost transcendent status. Touching or kissing the feet of beloved teachers is an act of reverence. The first phrase of the Ashtanga Vinyasa Yoga invocation, *vande gurunam charanaravinde* means "I honor the lotus-flower feet of all the gurus." This is an acknowledgment of the yoga that has been communicated through the path walked on the feet of the learned ones. More importantly, it also means that yoga is communicated through the path walked on the feet of the guru within, our inner knowing. This yogic veneration of the foot is a recognition of its spiritual importance as the foundation of the temple of our body.

Our autonomic nervous system's first reaction to challenge is to activate its "sympathetic" branch, which causes us to constrict. When we are fragmented, this is felt as constrictions and hyper-movement (fight-flight) or a stuck lack of movement (freeze response). As mentioned, a primary symptom of this state is constriction inward toward the core and upward away from the ground. If this is ongoing, we become fixated in a hyper-state. In some cases, our sympathetic state of constriction can then lead to a parasympathetic state of collapse. If this is ongoing, we become fixated in a hypo state. When we are fixated in either state, we obstruct the flow of subtle energy in the upward (*prana*) and downward (*apana*) channels of subtle energy.

A critical part of healing injuries is overcoming our habits of mind and body, learning to reverse this constriction response and the collapse it can lead to. In embodied nondual meditation, we learn to restore our balanced state by activating the parasympathetic branch of our nervous system in a way that prevents us from becoming fixated in either a hyper or hypo state. One important aspect of this practice is that we refine the art of opening to the downward flow (*apana*) or settling of energy, and spreading our energy outward throughout the body. This practice of softening, settling, and opening constrictions while breathing without effort (see *chapter five, chakra three*), restores the natural downward and upward flow of subtle energy (*apana*) in the charge (*pingala*) and discharge (*ida*) channels in our body. While yoga often establishes balance in very overt, willful, and intentional ways, in embodied nondual meditation, we establish balance in more subtle ways, allowing for effortless, authentic movement.

A central part of this subtlety and effortlessness involves becoming very familiar with specific sensations. We attune to what it feels like to soften our holding patterns, settling the energy and the "content of experience" (sensations associated with thoughts and emotions), rest our sensations on the foundational ground of each diaphragm, and open to our experience of inner space.

Even though we may be unable to fully perform these practices and only feel them slightly, by absorbing our self fully into what the nuances of softening, settling, resting, and openness feel like, each experience becomes a powerful resource. As we refine these supportive sensory resources and our ability to live effortlessly, we open to a natural downward flow of energy that in yoga is called "*apana*." This allows us, for instance, to settle upon the diaphragm of any segment of our body and come to a feeling of rest. In the process, we let go of our habitual core patterns of tension within each diaphragm (that obstruct and fragment the internal space of our body into segments).

The state of openness that results, is not only a relaxed state but also an experience of awakening consciousness. We have more room for our energy to flow, which loosens the grip our fixations have upon us. When we attune to the openness, we also can perceive the subtle unchanging presence of our ground-of-being. As a result, our responses to what we experience increasingly arise spontaneously out of stillness, rather than out of the willfulness of our desired goal.

When we feel the state of openness within the central-channel, we awaken the presence of our unchanging-self most clearly. To refine our perception of the central-channel, locating the center of the bottom of the torso is helpful. As we sit with support or lie down with our knees bent, we can refine the sense of fully relaxing in this specific location, at the center of the bottom of the torso. Our focus is on simply relaxing this particular area and settling down through the vertical center of the torso. We feel that we are resting on the center of this foundation without lifting away from the ground. (This can give us a sense that we are fully arriving and landing on the planet.) With practice, the core of the body opens and becomes an entryway into our central-channel. We feel our central-channel is a vertical path of openness and consciousness that illuminates our whole body and mind.

262

THE UPWARD CURRENT OF PRANA

As mentioned, when we fully settle the psychological content of our experience (physical, emotional, mental) upon the foundational diaphragms and do not lift up away from there, we experience a progressively clear sense of the open spaciousness within the whole body. A natural response arises when we let go of our habitual holding patterns (especially in the diaphragms), settle, and savor the feeling of openness that emerges. (Much as the ancient sages describe, we experience the central-channel as a "hollow canal.") This results in a spontaneous "upward-rising current," or a gentle stream of very subtle energy, rising through the central-channel of the body.

This "kundalini rising" experience is known for happening dramatically with the more forceful techniques of kundalini yoga. But in embodied nondual meditation, we access a subtle expression of this. It is felt as a gentle upward-rising current of subtle energy and consciousness, rising up through the center of the torso, from the center of the bottom of the pelvis to the center of the top of the head. We do not deliberately draw the subtle and gentle energy current up the central-channel, but instead allow it to arise on its own, spontaneously.

This is a very refined subtle energy that comes from the Earth, below the center of the bottom of the torso. It rises up through our core and out the top of the head, connecting us with the environment and the larger cosmos. The trick is not to go up with this upward-rising stream of energy, but to stay settled within the interior depths of our body as a temple of awakening. This rising current of subtle energy and consciousness awakens the luminous nature of the conscious stillness, inherent to the essential ground of our being.

The upward-rising current is available even when the nervous system has not yet achieved a homeostatic state of dynamic equilibrium. But in order for us to be able to do this, we must refine our senses so we can learn to reach deeper than our evolving-self's experiences of imbalance. Once we uncover and awaken to the stillness and openness of our unified wholeness-of-being, we can experience the upward rising current within the interior dimension of the whole body. Yet, it is most pronounced within the subtle core of the body. When the upward-rising current of subtle energy is awakened, it illuminates the whole central-channel and the nondual-essence of our being throughout the whole body. We feel our awareness of the unchanging-self as a luminous, unwavering presence, awakened by the upward-rising current, gently flowing through the body.

It often takes practice before we can experience the upward-rising current. If we have difficulty feeling the gentle, subtle energy current, taking more time to practice the nuances of simple embodiment meditations is helpful. In this way, we let go of what obstructs the natural downward flow of energy (*apana*). We also dissolve constrictions that push, pull, or shift us away from our true location, and cause us to lose our sense of center as an open channel of subtle energy and consciousness. This establishes conducive conditions for the upward-rising current to emerge through the central-channel of our body.

Also, we can facilitate awakening the upward-rising current within the central-channel, by refining our sense of the subtle energy that is flowing through the charge/*pingala* and discharge/*ida* channels (on either side of the central-channel). With our breath, in meditation, we can encourage the flow of subtle energy through these channels and feel the central-channel awaken.

For instance, the practice of alternate-nostril breathing (*nadi shodhana*) can be very helpful. It usually involves breathing through alternate nostrils, one side at a time, using fingers to close off one nostril so we can breathe exclusively through the other nostril. (YouTube has instructional videos that can be a good initial guide.) This method of alternate-nostril breathing is often a good way to start.

Yet there is also a more subtle practice first introduced to me by Judith Blackstone that is helpful. Without using fingers to close off either nostril, we can simply focus on the feeling of bringing breath gently through each of the three channels alternately. Attuning to any sense of the openness within each channel, and the feeling of breath flowing through each individual channel, can clear out constrictions and awaken the central-channel.[56] Practicing each of these steps with the intention of breathing with the least effort, deepens the experience. When the central-channel is free from obstruction (constriction, numbness, collapse), it illuminates as a conscious presence that pervades our whole body. The upward-rising current through the central-channel, that increasingly becomes available, brightens this illumination and awakens consciousness.

We can also awaken the upward-rising current with a very fine awareness of how physical support from the solid ground can be felt to extend up through the subtle core of the central-channel. This can be most clearly perceived once we refine our senses enough to feel that our body is not solid but rather an experience of openness. The feeling of receiving this support from the ground counters the downward pull of gravity. Receiving the feeling of this support from the ground moving up through the central-channel, invites it to open even more. The sense of openness extends up through the whole central-channel to the center of the top of the head. As we receive the feeling of support up through the central-channel, we often feel an upward-rising current of energy streaming through the core and feel consciousness awaken.

We can also experience this opening into the central-channel when we start at the center of the top of our head and extend downward through the core. Yet, I generally prefer to start at the foundation because it is more grounding, which is a vital feeling to sustain when overcoming injuries. The uplifting sense of support that arises, offers a profound, uplifting feeling that can replace the helplessness, which often accompanies overwhelming experiences. This spontaneously arising

---

[56] Follow the sensation of breathing in through the right nostril (as best as you can) and feel it flow through the right channel (as sensation moving through openness) to the pelvic basin. Hold the breath without strain for a short moment (*kumbhaka*), before exhaling and following the sensation of breath flowing up the left channel and out the left nostril. Repeat this in the opposite direction: down the left, briefly hold, and release up the right side and out the right nostril. Then, breathing through both nostrils, do the same with the central-channel. Repeat.

experience, provides the context and support our evolving-self needs to alight to new heights and depths of emotional maturity and spiritual awakening.

## Unified Consciousness Absorbing the Evolving-Self

The most common experience that we have when we focus inward to experience our body and sense of self, is that we are composed of physical matter, such as flesh, muscle, bone, blood, and nerves. When we refine our senses, we often perceive that we can also experience our self as energy, such as movement within our body like streaming sensations, pulsing, and vibration. Yet, with a little more refinement, we perceive that we can experience our self as the stillness of unified consciousness. As mentioned, this can be felt as an unchanging presence or conscious space pervading the body, that lies deeper than anything solid or moving.

There is a powerful phenomenon that happens when we uncover and awaken the subtle experience that the space pervading our body is a conscious presence. We can feel that the conscious space of our body, gently draws and absorbs the solid objects, the movement, and the constriction of energy, inward into the conscious space (like a vacuum or sponge). When we experience this, it helps us cultivate a sense of internal depth and we let go of our patterns of constriction that accompany our unresolved injuries, and the habits of body and mind they lead to. We let go within our body, into the space, without leaving our body as we do this.

This experience is particularly powerful when we feel this in the subtle core of our body. I first experienced this when practicing one of Judith Blackstone's Realization Process® meditations. Our deepest constrictions seem to dissolve and be consumed by the conscious space and unwavering presence within the deepest part of the body. The whole central-channel seems to awaken and illuminate the whole body, as a luminous presence-of-being. Most importantly, we feel free from the limitations that accompany our mental, emotional, and physical constrictions. We feel that we are living and breathing within the

266

core of our body, and the space that pervades the body helps us let go of our deepest limitations.

This experience becomes even more awakened and illuminating, when we feel that our whole body is breathing simultaneously. When the whole body inhales and exhales at once, it deepens our perception of our body as unified as one. When we expand this practice to feel the whole core is inhaling and then exhaling at once, it deepens this experience. The whole core expands on the inhale, and then softens, recedes, and opens on the exhale. The inhale gives us a sense of profound contact with our self, and the exhale lets go and opens, deepening contact with our conscious presence-of-being. The conscious space pervading our body absorbs our conditioned, habitual emotions, thoughts, and sensations. It lures and draws upon them to dissolve, like a sponge absorbs liquid.

This is a direct experience of the quantum potential in nature that maintains an unbroken wholeness, within the fluctuations and constrictions inherent to our body. We feel how wholeness resists the entropy and disorder, within us. We feel unity acting from within, luring us to become more integrated, to develop a cohesive sense of self, that is co-extensive and at one with our environment.

The more we practice this, the more our constructed, imagined barrier between self and other dissolves. We begin to perceive how this experience pervades our whole body and our environment at the same time. This becomes the basis of our individual wholeness as a unified presence, and our access to our evolving-self's authenticity. Our consciousness increasingly becomes conscious and awakens to itself, as a presence that is not an object separate from our self.

This chapter explored specific practices that facilitate awakening the central channel as a means of deepening embodiment of unified consciousness. The following chapter concludes with the exploration of some of the broader benefits that result from feeling that we exist as unified consciousness, in whole-being-embrace, with our injured evolving-self.

# CHAPTER SEVEN: WHAT IT IS

## FROM CONTROL & SEPARATION TO NOURISHMENT

Even when we understand the need to include the body and emotions in our healing and awakening journey, emotions can be tricky when we harbor trauma. We can easily become frozen in the headlights of our emotional drama when we have trauma in our body-mind system. It is safer for our emotions to be a guide when we recognize, uncover, and become familiar with the wholeness and unity that lies buried within our body. This recognition keeps our emotional distortions from gaining the upper-hand and overwhelming us.

In embodied nondual meditation, we are guided by the perception that we are inherently whole, and that experiences (thoughts, emotions, sensations) are doorways to our healing. Central to this perception is the understanding that the whole-being-embrace experience provides a solution to what Western psychology lacks and what Eastern spirituality discounts. It is important to highlight how our communion with wisdom and unified consciousness is nourishing and healing.

We feel nourished by listening to our desires and aversions with our sense of wisdom and the self-grace that results from whole-being-embrace. In this communion, our evolving-self is nourished by the many nondual-qualities of unified consciousness, especially the ones that give us the clearest sense of wholeness. Our wholeness and our fragmentation/injuries are in relationship based on mutuality and equity. We feel how their interconnectedness is a result of their enfolded, entangled nature.

When the sense of wisdom, wholeness, and the knowing that results, are in our body-mind system, we can "listen" to our injury symptoms attentively and with care. Our sense of innate goodness and inner benevolence shows up as a beloved presence for our injured self. Consequently, the injured part of us feels seen, heard, understood, and respected and increasingly less overwhelmed. We are also able to clearly hear the impulses of our heart, our gut, and our intuitive wisdom that guides us to follow what is right for us (our *dharma*). When we follow these guiding experiences, our wisdom grows and our wholeness awakens. These are experiences of self-grace that give us what we have always wanted, in the depths of our heart, from others. We develop a healthy perception of our self that supports the natural emergence of self-empathy and compassion, acceptance, worthiness, and love.

This self-nurturing goes straight to the heart of healing our past wounds due to dysfunctional relationships. It gives us the ability to look out for our own needs with a capacity to love and feel respected, which, in turn, inspires us to be respectful of others. It supports our body to let go of our sabotaging habits, remaining open, as we experience contact.

Any practice of learning self-regulation techniques that simply physically relax or balance our energy, is no longer just a physical or energetic practice (such as conscious breathing, asana, tai chi, or chi kung, Feldenkrais). It is supported by the nurturing, inherent to the presence of our unchanging-self, and attention to the emotional reason we became imbalanced in the first place. Because we attend to the underlying relationship issues, we can sustain our relaxed and balanced state with more ease, and in an increasingly integrated way.

Letting go of habitual constrictions, and the resulting authentic, free-flowing energy, naturally brings a broader perspective. It reveals ways of being in relationship that were hidden up until now, so we no longer need to resort to our outdated habitual strategies of self-protection. Our inner awareness gives us insight into how we can feel whole and complete, even when aspects of our life and other people are not meeting our needs.

Empathy and compassion for others arise out of self-love, self-empathy, and self-compassion. As we step into fully showing up for our self with empathy and compassion, we have more room to be supportive of other people with relative ease. Our enhanced inner-awareness is also the ground from which our heart can truly receive empathetic attunement and love from other people.

Rather than devising detailed rules of conduct and using impulse-control or willpower to change our limiting habits, the habits dissolve under the influence of the nurturing nature, and broader perspective of the unified essence of our existence. Kindness, tenderness, and gentleness towards our self and others, are no longer principles that we work to implement, because they arise spontaneously.

As the herbalist Susan Weed suggests on her "Wise Woman Tradition" web page, wholeness and injury are not polarities but are part of the continuum of life. In their communion, we are constantly renewing our mind and body, cell by cell, every moment. She explains, "Problems, by their very nature, can facilitate deep spiritual and symbolic renewal, leading us naturally into expanded, more complete ways of thinking about and experiencing ourselves."

As a result of these nourishing experiences, we increasingly uncouple fear-based associations from what we experience. This neutralizes how we fixate on the injuries that we harbor, and renews our mind and body. The vagus nerve that picks up signals from our viscera, sends signals to the part of the brain that processes emotions (limbic brain), and informs it that the danger has passed. Our fight-or-flight and immobility response turns off. Just as the animal "shakes off" the fight-flight, freeze response caused by a threat in order to recover, we do the same in meditation (and then throughout the day). We release habitual constrictions that create and sustain our chronic survival responses in our body-mind system.

This allows the quiet-alertness, inherent to the nervous system's state of dynamic equilibrium, to emerge. As mentioned, when we refine our senses in meditation, we perceive that within the balanced state of quiet-alertness exists the conscious stillness of the unified dimension of our being. As this process is repeated, we increase our resilience, and expand our capacity for energy and consciousness in our body-mind system (see The Gap in Images #6, 15).

270

WISDOM

An important source of nourishing support that often goes unacknowledged, is the guidance we receive from the wisdom layer of our self. Psychology sometimes refers to this source of guidance as the "inner-adult." It believes wisdom is simply a product of the physical, mental, and emotional aspects of our self, and does not recognize wisdom as an expression of a developmental stage or a fundamental aspect of self. Recently, some exceptions to this understanding of self, and of our development have emerged. For instance, the psychotherapist Marianne Bentzen, explains that the peak of our developmental potential can be described in terms of the many aspects of wisdom (Bentzen, 2020).

Yoga has the tendency to recognize a more subtle expression of existence, and so considers wisdom to be a distinct aspect of self. As mentioned, from this perspective, all the experiences we have are perceived through the five layers of consciousness: physical, emotional, mental, wisdom, and bliss (i.e., *anna, prana, mana, vijnana, ananda*). Our sense of wisdom, or "wise-self," draws upon our evolving-self's personal truth, as well as our unchanging-self's unified consciousness. Depending on our inclinations and limitations, some of us draw more from one end of the spectrum than the other. Wisdom can arise out of our sense of mental, emotional, and intuitive processes, but it can also serve as the guidance we need for our evolving-self to gain access to unified consciousness.

When our wounded inner-child comes into contact with our wise-self, with its mix of the evolving-self's knowledge and our unchanging-self's knowing, we feel tremendous support. In yoga, the "wisdom layer" of self (*vijnana kosha*) is considered to have the qualities of intelligence, intuition, and discernment (*prajna*). As a result of accessing our sense of wisdom, our wounded inner-child feels witnessed, understood, and respected, without leaving any part of us out. Opening to wise-self's expression of authenticity is about coming into contact with an experience of our deepest, undeniable personal truth, supported by nondual knowing. This gives us a sense of validation, fortitude, skillful means and the guidance to evolve.

In embodied nondual meditation, our senses become more refined, so we can perceive our wisdom as a distinct manifestation of self. In my experience, our subtle discernment that comes from intuition, can range from our deep visceral senses, felt most clearly in our gut (also related to second chakra), our heart (also related to fourth chakra), and the intuitive aspect of the head center chakra (also related to sixth chakra). It is no coincidence that neuroscience tells us that, aside from the brain in our head (cephalic), we also have a heart brain (cardiac) and a gut-brain (enteric).

In meditation, we attune to each one individually and all three centers of consciousness and energy at once, as a way to refine our recognition and awaken wisdom. All three "brains" are an intricate system of sensory and intuitive information that becomes our personal inner-oracle. We learn to remain present in our body and internally referent, in terms of where we get our guidance. This is an important way we strengthen our ability to reverse the externalizing consequences of trauma, culture, and religion.


## EXISTENTIAL TRUST, ACCEPTANCE, & SMELLING ROSES

When we reach beyond our evolving knowledge of life, to embody a clear sense of nondual knowing, transformation happens. Our unresolved injuries and the consequent sabotaging habits and defensive boundaries, come into whole-being-embrace with the knowing, inherent to unity and wholeness. We experience a profound sense of understanding and clarity that is tremendously healing and helps us resolve deep-seated emotions. We feel the relief of accepting who we are, and what we are, in the present moment. What underlies this acceptance of our self and life is a fundamental sense of trust.

As we embody wholeness in our body-mind system and our authenticity prevails, a powerful realization surfaces. We find that we can trust our senses, and the personal truth that this leads to. This feeds into a deep sense of existential trust, called "*shraddha*" in Sanskrit. This existential trust builds faith in what we feel, our sense of self, and our decisions based on what we authentically like and dislike. We grow a feeling of purpose that comes from deep within us, shaping our world and life. As a result, our buried choices and silenced authentic expressions resurface. The guilt, that so often comes from going against the grain and rocking the boat, evaporates. We increasingly stop taking responsibility for what is not ours, including our parent's injuries and how they treated us as a result.

The term *shraddha* is derived from two roots: *shrat,* meaning "truth," "heart," or "faithfulness," and *dha*, meaning "to direct one's mind toward" or "to hold" (sutra 1.20). *Shraddha* is more than a concept, belief, or an act of faith. It is an experience we "hold," in the sense that we harbor it in our body. The inner-knowing and wholeness that accompanies our experience of whole-being-embrace, supports us to sustain this profound experience of existential trust on an ongoing basis, even under extreme circumstances.

When we attune to our sense of existential trust, we feel less fearful and overwhelmed by experiences. Being present with the feelings in our body, gives us a reliable sense of guidance that we can trust. We more easily honor our self in relationship with life. We can increasingly let go of our habitual limiting responses and are able to go with the flow of authenticity. We find the more we trust the natural choreography of life, the more we can also trust death and all the unknowable and unseeable components of the "big picture."

Trust awakens an understanding of what the modern sage Desikachar (1995) said lies at the heart of yoga. This is the central tenet that can be described as "laying all our actions at the feet of the Divine" (i.e. *Isvara-prani-dhana*). Our focus is not only on where we want to be (state of perfection, wholeness), but also on the process of bringing wholeness to our evolving-self's trials and tribulations along the way. Rather than focusing too much on our goals, we proceed through life focusing on the unfolding divine process of our journey in life.

This allows us to not become overwhelmed when we "drop the ball" and "shit hits the fan." The direct-path of awakening unified consciousness as a body experience of self, and the existential trust that results from whole-being-embrace, enables us to live guided by the divinity within. With nondual wholeness and knowing, we take time to feel the pleasures of life and "smell the roses." Living from wholeness and knowing, and the trust that naturally accompanies it, allows us to flow with the constant changes in life and relationship. We understand the dynamic interplay with others (people, situations, substance, ideologies) free from the need to excessively control it or dissociate from it.

The luminous presence of wholeness and knowing allows us to be in touch with the true innocence of our inborn nature. As a result, our constant self-criticism evaporates. We recognize that our injuries, protective defenses, and sabotaging habits that result, are a response to coping with how other people have related to us. We come to a deep understanding that the sabotaging choices we've made, that led us in the wrong direction in life, were simply the ripple-effect of our original wounding. We feel compassion toward the habit of persistently sabotaging our self and others due to injury. We can appreciate how we all have different feelings and needs. We do not transcend our own or other people's desires and aversions in relationship (even if based on fear), nor do we fixate on them.

We feel more open to appreciating the process of life, and are more able to understand that the ebb and flow of excitement, dullness, and happiness are all natural expressions of our evolution. This broader perspective forms the ground of self-compassion and compassion for others.


FROM CREATIVITY TO SPONTANEITY

Creativity and cooperation are often considered to be the primary driving force, propelling human progress and our evolutionary development. Yet, when we introduce unified consciousness, another influence comes to play.

The philosopher Alfred North Whitehead (1929) proposed that the world is a web of interrelated processes of which we are an integral part. His intention was to help us understand how all of our choices and actions have consequences for the world

274

around us. He suggested that creativity is the primary expression that integrates the interrelated web of life. Creativity underlies our fragmented state becoming integrated. He explains that creativity is the fundamental reason why evolution leads to the changing nature of life. Creativity is the motivating force behind natural selection, adaptation, and our own growth towards self-organization. It is what underlies the energy of newness that becomes available when we let go of our limiting habits of mind, body, and emotion.

While Whitehead's understanding is astute, it does not fully recognize how unified consciousness influences the changing nature of life and our habits of mind, body, and emotion. When we have a body experience of unified consciousness, we recognize what the creative-act is more fundamentally composed of, and how this leads to a spontaneously responsive way of living.

The Tibetan Buddhist yogi poet Shabkar Rangdrol came close to this understanding when he described the liberated mind as "...a flawless piece of crystal. Intrinsically empty, naturally radiant, ceaselessly responsive."[57] The "emptiness" that Shabkar talked about is a state of receptive potential, without psychological content. The receptive potential of our luminous presence-of-being, is what allows us to let go of our attachment to habitual, or knee-jerk reactions.

When we access unified consciousness as a body experience, subject (you) and object (what you experience) are both encompassed and pervaded by the same perceptual consciousness. This frees us from being under the influence of our injuries and habits, so we exert less habitual effort in our responses to life events. With less habitual effort, life experiences that so often lead to suffering, "leave no trace" (Zen), because they do not disturb our sense of existing as wholeness and unity. This means we stay open, so our expression becomes ceaselessly responsive, spontaneous, and vitally authentic.

This spontaneity is about our responses arising out of the autonomy we gain within our unchanging-self's presence-of-

---

[57] Joseph Goldstein, p. 176, 2002

being. Spontaneous expression of this kind correlates with the Kashmiri Shaivite concept of divine sovereignty. This is traditionally called "*svatantrya*," which means self-dependency or free will. *Svatantrya* is described as an energy that emanates from unified consciousness as a wave of motion (*spanda*). This expression acts as the fundamental cosmogenesis of the world, much like the original word (logos, *paravak*). It is the first act of creation, not motivated by any other experience, and is spontaneously self-generated.

When we are in a state of emptiness as the receptive potential of our luminous presence-of-being, we embody wholeness and a deeper or broader perspective, that is beyond the drama created by our habitual mind-body tendencies. This embodiment allows us to feel the deep inter-relatedness between our ego and unified consciousness, in whole-being-embrace. This is also more than an interrelatedness of parts of our evolving-self. It is an entanglement.

It is a cosmogenesis within our body that gives the world new meaning for us, because of the broader perspective that comes with our experience of unity as a unifying force. Our actions become spontaneous expressions or nondual actions, similar to what the Daoists call "*wei wu wei*," where we are empty and free from being motivated by a "self" who "intends" and then "carries out" an "action." This is effortless action, or action born of unified consciousness. In Kashmiri Shaivism, Mark Dyczkowsky explains, it can be considered to be one's own authentic identity as the universal agent and perceiver, understood to be the universal vibration (*samanyaspanda*) of "pure ego." Pure ego functions at the universal level of cosmic subjectivity in that it is wholeness yet still self-reflective. It is "*spandasakti*," meaning it manifests as the individual ego that transmits the impulse (*samrambha*) of consciousness that activates the vital breaths, animating the mind and body (Mark Dyczkowsky, 1987).[58]

---

[58] A similar understanding is expressed in Hindu myth, where we are told that since it is impossible for the God Brahmna to have a purpose in creating the world, the world is spontaneously created out of Bliss and for Bliss through the divine play of Lila. Lila is the spontaneous sportive activity of Brahman, yet, with no self-reflective ability.

When we experience our self as a self-aware unchanging-self, we are completely spontaneous, and yet we can know we're being spontaneous. We retain our self-reflective capacity. This seems improbable because we cannot imagine being unified and whole, while maintaining a sense of self-reflection and consciousness of our self. Yet when we embody unified consciousness as a realization of self, we can reflect on the environment and on our self as a perceiver. Consciousness of self remains, because our self-aware unchanging-self is empty of psychological content, and yet it is not an absence or a void.

Spontaneous actions that arise out of unity are experienced to be uncaused, and yet we can still be aware of the self-arising experience. This is what lies at the heart of our spiritual life. This spontaneous experience is an expression of grace and living in flow, that seems to come out of nowhere. Often, grace is understood to only come from someplace "out there," such as the cosmic universal source of pure unified consciousness. When we experience that unity and wholeness is an expression of self in the body, grace can arise from within.

This is in alignment with Kashmir Shaivism's view that spiritual realization is more than transcendent pure nondual consciousness of *atman*. Full spiritual realization means to know the bliss (*ānanda*) of our unchanging-self, and thereby become free from the conditioned energies that limit our evolving-self. The root of this process is autonomy as a divine sovereignty (*svātantrya*) between our evolving-self and our unchanging-self (that results from their communion in whole-being-embrace). This is what allows our evolving-self to spontaneously express authentic truth (which is considered to be the operative, dynamic aspect of the absolute, unity). The autonomy of divine sovereignty becomes an irresistible force that allows creation (evolution) to occur authentically and spontaneously.

One form of our spontaneously arising authentic expression, is an experience that our evolving-self exists as an energy-field. This form of spontaneous expression is the energetic basis of our mental, emotional, and physical life. Our energy-field can be experienced as a container that conveys two healthy expressions that were previously shut down due to relationship trauma: the act of keeping out what is toxic (*viyoga*), and the ability to form a holding environment that contains our personal truth (*samyoga*, from an integral view) (elaborated upon in *From Trauma to Wholeness*, 2023). This underlies our fundamental need to feel connection and independence in relationship. Addressing this on the most fundamental energetic level, allows for the most profound healing and awakening.

When our energy-field arises spontaneously out of our sense of unified consciousness, it is not based on habit and fear. Thus, it forms the basis of the healthy emotional boundaries we need most in relationship. It is the energetic basis of a "pre-trauma" authentic expression, which restores or brings to completion the personal truth we were unable to communicate as a child when we were injured (and remains stuck in our body-mind as patterns of constriction). We release the trauma we harbor in our body, heal emotional injuries, and enhance our potential for intimacy, with our self and others. Understanding this dynamic lies at the forefront of a new spiritual paradigm.

RETURNING FROM TRANSCENDENCE TO SAVE THE PLANET

Experiences of unified consciousness and liberation from sabotaging habits, are usually not due to supernatural grace or special revelation, but instead are a natural process that becomes increasingly available as we embody our unchanging-self. Our liberation from our ego's projections and the emergence of authentic expression, happens in our communion with the unchanging-self in whole-being-embrace. This is a deep relationality that is stabilizing and liberating.

The orientation of spirituality and religion have a direct influence on the roots of our collective unconscious, our relationships, and the environmental problems we face today. The solutions to the problems we face must be multi-pronged, and our spiritual orientation goes to the heart of all of these issues. Our spirituality awakens and communicates with the deepest dimensions of our collective existence. In shifting our spiritual orientation, we can reshape and re-feel our reality and our destiny.

278

We must live as a holonomic person who is conscious that the wholeness of nondual-qualities of our self, like unconditional love, exist within each aspect of creation. In this way, we do not lose our self in an exclusive state of unity (transcendent spirituality) or duality (psychology). Instead, we live by the spontaneously arising opulence of our authentic self as an aspect of divinity.

The more we reconcile inwardly through communion with our unchanging-self, the more we live as the "whole-self" (dual and nondual). This is not an idea, belief, or simply a shift in perspective or mental awareness. It is a new immediate experience of inter-being in whole-being-embrace, as an interwoven relationally shared life. This is a spirituality that is a matter of the heart, not simply awareness or mind alone.

Embodied nondual meditation is also not about transcending our ego or achieving the instant enlightenment so popular with the immediatist gurus. The popular adage, "be here now" takes on a different meaning because it does not exclude our injured ego. Rather, it democratizes our life in relationship, in that both dimensions of self mutually co-exist. Whole (unchanging-self) and parts (evolving-self) have a healthy inter-dependence. We feel how every moment contains the potential to dissolve the very root of where sabotaging habit patterns are conceived.

Within the interwoven relationally shared life of our whole-self, our evolving-self is always trying to be what we are not, rather than simply, actually being. Part of the passionate nature of humankind comes from the pleasure and pains that accompany this duality-based "perception-response" orientation. Evolution is always moving toward more complexity and integrated systems that leave us with the experience of "not yet being there." Many spiritual guides tell us we need to first actively overcome the humanness of inertia, selfishness, and egoism before we can experience nondual consciousness.[59]

---

[59] Transcending duality to create freedom from suffering through separation from duality, puts unrealistic expectation on us to be completely egoless. We often feel pressure to let our humaneness dissolve completely in order to attain a permanent state of enlightenment. The "higher" state of enlightenment sets up a hierarchy because we constantly seek the

Yet, with a direct-path to wholeness, we do not need to evolve into our most mature self before we can access this essential ground-of-being. This approach is not about following moral precepts to one day create a state of wholeness. This is about getting out of our own way and uncovering what is already there. This allows wholeness to simply happen. It does not take a lifetime to become conscious of our Buddha-Nature or our Christic Reality, as a deity with qualities (*saguna Brahman*). With a very fine attunement, we can directly attune to the unchanging presence underneath our thoughts, emotions, and sensations. With a refined perception, we learn to reach deeper than the solidness of our bones, our numbness, and constrictions that limit us to feeling separate, frozen, stuck, and afraid.

On a direct-path to awakening unified consciousness, we do not craft or create, for a future result that our evolution will eventually develop. We simply uncover and learn to awaken to our own inborn nature as an unchanging, essential ground-of-being. This allows our process of evolution to not be about creating a network of associations to access a future that holds knowledge (like duality in search of a conclusion). Instead, we open to our own pre-existing knowing, in each present moment. Out of the experience of wholeness, new distinct emotions, thoughts, and sensations spontaneously arise, as if they are the expression of grace unfolding.

Whole-being-embrace allows us to feel the frustration of "not yet being there" in communion with the unity and wholeness that is "already here now." Hand in hand, our growing pains intimately resonate with our self-aware embodied wholeness, and evolves. In this dynamic, we are not only focused on the future, but rather,

---

transcendent nondual consciousness that we can't sustain. The ultimate nondual state is a place we can visit but not live from, we have to leave it in order to function. When transcendence is our goal, it perpetuates the original problem inherent in the evolution of our evolving-self's duality: trying to get to where we are not. We may feel like we're stuck in a lower state where we can't be satisfied because it's not our desired destination. We have the same orientation of being dissatisfied and always thinking our happiness or ability to rest is somewhere else, or in the future.

our focus on the future is embraced by the present, and thereby heals our trauma's hypervigilance and state of imbalance.

That our evolution and our unity are entangled, does not mean we live for a future that we are being drawn to. We can only find our existing wholeness and unity in the present moment, and it takes a direct-path of uncovering and awakening to realize this. In whole-being-embrace we exist as divine entanglement between duality and nonduality. This allows us to not feel a yearning for wholeness as we evolve, because we already *are* unity, wholeness, and unconditional love. The yearning so familiar to our evolving-self, recognizes we always have a reliable, unifying presence within us, and that we are divine.

The unifying presence as found in any nondual-quality of our existence, becomes the natural magnetism of wholeness and unity. The experience of wholeness and unity in our whole-being-embrace, is the magnetic force that draws us to evolve. We evolve simultaneously into more interrelated complexity (deeper connections), and the simplicity of our inherent unity. In this sense, we get to have the "cake" and "eat it" too. Our unified consciousness allows spontaneous expressions to be complex in their inter-relatedness, and yet simple due to our enhanced integration and sense of unity.

This approach is much like the Buddhist Bodhisattva. Bodhisattvas are enlightened beings who have put off entering the transcendent state in order to help others also attain enlightenment. Because the state of unified consciousness the Bodhisattva maintains, is not transcendent (*nirvana, atman*), they embrace more emotion, and are more engaged relationally than the transcended Buddha. Since the unified consciousness that the Bodhisattva has access to is embodied, they can live life in a way that spontaneously expresses spiritual qualities, much as we do in embodied nondual meditation. We often experience these spontaneous expressions as loving-kindness, compassion, empathy, joy, and equanimity.

The act of not transcending, in order to help others attain enlightenment, is much like the unified consciousness of our unchanging-self remaining embodied so that our evolving-self can heal. The intention is to not transcend until all aspects of our evolving-self are integrated. In our experience of whole-being-embrace, we evolve from a state of fragmentation to a new level of completion, with a new way of proceeding through life based on a new knowing. Our broader perspective brings our wholeness into a new field of conscious reality, where the divine becomes us, in our incarnation. In the process, we reconcile the darkness of trauma and its sabotaging habits, with the light of our nondual broader perspective.

There is a certain beauty in this harmony of contrasts. It is as if a myriad of fractals of light awaken our body, such that we uncover the divine nature of our own life. As unified consciousness draws the fragments of our evolving-self together, we do not sacrifice or surrender our evolving-self. We become more authentically human and realize the potential of our created existence. We live our life with spiritual qualities, such as loving-kindness, compassion, empathy, joy, and equanimity that spontaneously arise from this deeper center of unity.

What whole-being-embrace provides to each individual, becomes a way for societies to resolve conflict with compassion and acceptance. Our personal sense of unity and the healing that results, directly feeds into society's collective consciousness and forms a collective healing. Our personal contemplative practice of awakening unified consciousness, directly contributes to our global awakening.

We are in need of a collective new paradigm that is guided by unified consciousness, in a nourishing relationship with our evolving-self. As a society, we need not wait for our eventual genesis into spiritual enlightenment, to collectively realize our enfolded singularity (oneness). Directly uncovering and awakening a knowing of our self as fundamentally good and whole, allows our pre-trauma authentic expressions (of what we need to feel safe and loved), to arise spontaneously in a way that influences the collective consciousness of society. When this authenticity is played out on a global level with compassion for all, world affairs will shift.

# CONCLUSION

The path to healing and awakening consciousness based on the chakras originated in ancient Tantra yoga traditions. Tantra, like Mahayana Buddhism, describes the formula "samsara equals nirvana." This means the phenomenal world or material plane is coessential with unified consciousness. This experience of the coessential was taught in meditation practice by restoring the feminine principle of Shakti (*prakriti*), which is the force underlying the creation of our body and emotional life.[60] Yet, although the Tantra tradition held that Shiva (*atman*) without Shakti (material dimension, evolving-self) is dead or dormant, Shakti only played an instrumental role. Shakti, therefore, had a secondary, peripheral role to the ultimate transcendent state of Shiva/*atman*. In traditional Tantric practices, the male practitioner would seem to indulge in sensual pleasure (*bhoga*), but, as Feuerstein put it, in reality, he did this with the ultimate goal of transcending the body.

To this day, spiritual traditions uphold the ideal that the ultimate aim of human existence is transcendence of the earthly realm. This transcendent view upheld by the elite priests or brahmins was, as Riane Eisler (1995) explains, a way to keep oppressed people from trying to change their earthly situation. She elaborates that Tantric yoga, which emerged around the middle of the eleventh century, was a grass-roots movement originating from the casts at the bottom of the social pyramid in India. Tantra was not fully accepted by the elite casts until much later. As a result, many myths and rites about Goddess worship and sexuality have been excluded from the spiritual repertoire of mainstream Hinduism. Our body experience of our nondual self is an example of what was discounted.

---

[60] Tantra characterizes the nature of existence with a gender cosmology, where nonduality is male and duality is female. Gender infers function rather than physical sex.

Elevation of the lucidity of transcendence, as a return to a pristine state beyond the body and Earth, is based on separation from our evolving-self. Thereby, it objectifies us and minimizes our moral privilege to respect and love the material dimension of existence. It does this by either excluding, being dispassionate toward (simply witnessing), discounting, distancing, or disidentifying from what makes us human.

In a similar light, status quo Western psychology remains separate from nonduality by simply not recognizing its existence. It relies primarily upon our rational mind and our sense of being a separate, unique individual. It lacks the understanding of the unified nature of existence, and therefore, its ability to help us overcome our deepest injuries. Both Western and Eastern religion separate one dimension of existence from another by discounting the value of our human nature (body, emotion) as a viable means of spiritual awakening while overcoming suffering.

While psychology's emphasis on individuation and Eastern spirituality's transcendent practices can help, growth and spirituality are ultimately about being open to our wholeness and becoming authentic in our relational intimacy (with our self and other). Moreover, when it comes to healing trauma, the orientation of transcendent spirituality toward detachment and depersonalization, can be limiting and too often contributes to trauma symptoms, both individually and as a society.

The alternative orientation that embraces wholeness and intimacy, involves a different approach to healing and awakening. This means we contemplate, meditate, and relate to our injuries in a different way. Wholeness is understood to be the presence of unified consciousness as a body experience of self. Instead of expanding outward or downloading non-local cosmic consciousness, we uncover what already exists within us. This, in turn, gives us access to the universe as a whole, within the body. Instead of meditating to lose our ego consciousness by either collapsing it into a state of unity (Advaita Vedanta) or claiming there is no self (Buddhism), we learn to simply include unified consciousness in our ego state, so they co-exist in a healing, whole-being-embrace.

When the non-local nature of unified consciousness is a body experience, we recognize that it is an expression of all of existence and of our self at the same time. We learn that we can take personal ownership of this dimension of existence that is paradoxically universal in nature. The personal and universal do not conflict with one another. Instead, they broaden our perspective and give us access to a new experience of connectedness and breathing-room, in the relational nature of life. This paradox is reflected in how quantum physics and Eastern spirituality agree that all of existence ultimately emerges out of unified consciousness. Unified consciousness is inherent in our biological system as divine entanglement.

When unified consciousness is a body experience, we co-exist with the duality consciousness of our evolving-self. The simultaneous co-existence of both dimensions of existence as a body experience of our self, allows our desires and aversions, that underlie our suffering, to be a relevant part of our spiritual awakening. In embodied nondual meditation, we simply uncover and awaken the unified consciousness that already exists within us, so we can be in relationship with our evolving-self.

In embodied nondual meditation, we feel the emotional intensity, listen to its habitual story, and respect its psychological content within the context of our embodied wholeness (the healing relationship of whole-being-embrace.) Every thought we have, belief we nurture, and every memory we cling to, occurs within a context of the experience that we exist as unity and wholeness. When this is a felt experience, we gain a broader perspective that allows us to naturally let go of our automatic protective survival responses in relationship and habitual patterns of constriction. This is fundamental to healing trauma.

Most spiritual traditions and popular spirituality today tell us that the embodied experience of unified consciousness is not the true ultimate goal of our spiritual quest. They adamantly claim that we must still attain the superior goal of the highest stage of samadhi (*asamprajnata samadhi,* i.e., *atman*), or Buddhahood (*sambodhi*). We are told that we must continue to strive until we reach this goal. This action of transcending the material plane of existence (body, emotions, thoughts) seems equivalent to the futile idea of leaving the planet in order to save humanity. The alternative is to focus our resources on saving the planet, rather than going to Mars.

That said, transcendent nondual consciousness is an important supportive resource to have, so we can navigate life and not be overwhelmed by intense experiences. Both embodied nondual consciousness and transcendence can be a valuable resource for coming to terms with death. However, to hold transcendence as our ultimate goal for living a successful life on Earth seems counterproductive. Most of us harbor chronic injuries and trauma in our body-mind system. Our attempt to heal the planet should not be an endeavor to transcend to a pristine state beyond the body and Earth. We do not need to separate from our evolving-self's emotions, thoughts, and sensations, and objectify what is so dear to our heart. Let us behave like Bodhisattvas, remaining in our bodies and engaging in a relationship with the planet and our healing. Let us embody unified consciousness and express spiritual qualities like loving-kindness, compassion, empathy, joy, and equanimity that can heal social division and support diversity.

Embodied nondual meditation introduces a new spiritual paradigm because we do not create freedom from suffering using strategies of separation. Instead, we embrace our suffering with the unconditional acceptance inherent to the nondual essential ground-of-being (whole-being-embrace). We access the "bliss layer" of self, which is a state of unified consciousness, where we can self-reflect and be aware that we are aware. This alternative paradigm, which is based on relational holism (as found in whole-being-embrace) rather than separation, is congruent with the basic understanding of quantum physics.


## How Energy & Consciousness Are Entangled

Over the past several hundred years, Western culture has lived under the influence of a mechanistic worldview (duality) that governs our cultural outlook. The West has also been influenced by a medieval worldview that has led to our monotheistic religions that separate our human nature from the divine nature of God. Yet, this perspective has been changing with the help of science. Albert Einstein's 1905 theory of relativity introduced the notion that material things of nature are composed of energy. Matter is energy that moves slowly enough for us to see it. What was once understood to be simply solid, began to assume a more porous nature.

Quantum physics took this to another level when it explained that upon closer scientific scrutiny of the solid nature of the world, we find a unified dimension of existence. Quantum physics describes how the electrons in atoms and molecules are composed not only of little balls of matter but also of waveforms. These waveforms are not solid, so they cannot be measured, and they function as probabilities that have no mass or energy. What quantum physics made evident was that matter cannot be considered apart from unified consciousness, and both aspects of existence can be found within the nature of energy. In this sense, existence is a relational holism. This confirms the relational nature of existence that we experience as we uncover unified consciousness within the body in meditation.

As Eastern spirituality intuited thousands of years ago, Western science explains that consciousness is fundamental to the energy that composes matter. This is consistent with what we feel when we have a body experience of nondual consciousness. When we refine our senses in meditation, we can experience how the energetic nature of the material dimension of existence, as found in our thoughts, emotions, and sensations, seems to spontaneously arise out of the immaterial nature of consciousness. We feel the unified consciousness embedded within the tissues of the body.

Quantum physics adds to our understanding of the relational nature of existence with its insight that the atom's electron, inherent in energy, contains both a particle and a wave. The particle operates under the laws of duality, and a wave operates under the laws of unity. Depending on our state of consciousness, we can determine the degree to which we are under the influence of the electron's particle, or wave aspect. When unified consciousness is a body experience, we can feel how both states co-exist simultaneously.

287

David Bohm explains the relational nature of unified consciousness in his quantum model. His model shows us how everything in our evolving life (duality) is enfolded within a "mind-matter implicate order" (nondual). He explains that the movement from "enfoldment" (implicit, nonduality) into "unfoldment" (explicit, expression of duality), is an endless feedback cycle, (as in the ouroboros symbol of the serpent swallowing its own tail).

### The Three Phases & Seven Stages

In this book, I have pointed out how this endless feedback cycle is represented in the three-phases of energy and consciousness. With this understanding of the relationship between energy and consciousness, it becomes possible to see how waking-up to unified states of consciousness can influence our growing-up process. Because the stages of development have only recently been recognized, none of the spiritual traditions include this understanding. There are very few approaches that integrate states of consciousness with stages of development

Within energy, we find the electron's duality-based particle in the charge and discharge phases, and unity-based wave in the balance phase. While most spiritual traditions do not recognize that this balanced state (*sattva*) is an expression of unified consciousness, at its most refined level, we have access to the liminal edge between our evolving-self and the transcendent pure nondual consciousness of *atman* (*nirguna Brahman*; beyond sensation). Using quantum physics terms, this can be understood as an "event horizon" where local and nonlocal meet.

Although not ordinarily detected, when we refine our senses, we uncover a tangible experience of unified consciousness within the most refined state of balance. This is the quality-rich nonduality of our unchanging-self (*saguna Brahman*, Buddha-Nature, Christ-consciousness). A very significant trait is that through the unchanging-self, we have access to a non-local and universal experience without leaving the specific location of our body. From within the body, we perceive the deeply entangled fields of energy that give us access to experiencing the nature of the universe as an undivided wholeness.

In embodied nondual meditation and then in our whole life, all the physical objects we perceive appear to be non-separable. Things affect one another despite distance or space-time coordinates (entangled states). We can perceive that the consciousness inside our body is unified with the consciousness outside our body, without leaving the body as we perceive this. We experientially understand why Carl Jung spoke of the unfragmented wholeness of "unus mundus," where mind and matter complement one another. David Bohm also spoke of mind and matter as different aspects of one whole unbroken movement. Likewise, the Jesuit priest and scientist Teilhard de Chardin, once observed that our sense of the infinite, unified field of consciousness, feels like it is the "within-ness of "inside" of matter."

The divinely entangled particle-wave nature of matter can be found within the freely flowing movement of energy. That is, energy has a charge-discharge-balance cycle (with a subset of seven stages). The more energy flows freely and authentically through each of these phases, the more balance, integration, and unity we have in our body-mind system. When the particles of energy move freely, the waves become more prominent. This is why many spiritual traditions emphasize practices that balance energy to facilitate the freely flowing nature of Shakti energy as a means of awakening unified consciousness (as in Hatha yoga, neo-Tantra, etc.). Throughout this process, we increasingly evolve and become authentic until, ultimately, our authenticity spontaneously arises entirely out of our sense of wholeness and unity.

This three-phase pattern occurs in multiple ways as an underlying pattern inherent to existence, manifesting everywhere. The holographic nature of the three-phases, has seven sub-stages that are expressed in our seven chakras. This three-phase pattern bridges cultural boundaries and even our physiology. It can be found in the functioning of our nervous system and its journey back to health.

## The Body as Relational Holism

In our whole-being-embrace we find a whole new way of being in relationship to our self and others. We are informed by the spontaneous sense of connectivity, mercy, passion, and freedom. A brief review of the new ways of being in relationship can clarify the result of our Hero's Journey. These new ways are expressions of consciousness emerging from our whole-self, that evoke a revolution in our personal, social, and cosmic relations. This radical awakening is based on entangled connectedness that provides ultimate autonomy and freedom from habit. All people without exception, are invited as equals to this divine embrace to discover a new locus of sacred meaning on Earth.

When nondual consciousness is a body experience, as expressed in each of our chakra qualities, we increasingly recognize that the nondual and duality-based dimensions of our self, need each other. Pure nondual consciousness (of *atman*, or *nirguna* Brahman) on its own cannot be self-aware, express anything, or be fully known as the knower (evolving-self). Yet, we need nondual consciousness to broaden our perspective and awaken us to the spiritual nature of existence and our personal truth.

In meditation, we can recognize that our physical body is conscious. When we refine our senses, we realize the presence of consciousness in matter that science has confirmed. We can feel that our openness leads to the simultaneous awakening of our authenticity and our unity. The chakras have a powerful role in providing access to this authenticity and unity because they run parallel to each stage of our development as humans. In this process, as Julian Huxley said, we are evolution becoming conscious of itself as an evolving self.

The nondual nature of our unchanging-self is an open and ecstatic, tangible reality that transcends the moment as well as includes it. With this experience, we find that we are not just separate individuals. We can feel that we are also always embedded in the nondual consciousness from which our evolving-self emerges. In this way, our evolving-self's style of being in relationship can express itself without fixating on separation. We do not objectify our humanness nor the Earth.

Instead, we become the living expression of Earth's potential for growth and spiritual awakening.

We pass through stages of growth in the midst of our existence as unity and duality. We are in touch with a deep relationality, characteristic of not only nature's becoming, but its current existence as wholeness. Rather than only being governed by the goal of betterment, we increasingly join this with our completeness that already exists. This is a "becoming within" the form of our body, through an ongoing presence of wholeness.

As a holographic, archetypal human, our evolving-self exists along a spectrum with degrees of complexity (interrelatedness, as well as fragmentation) and simplicity (integration, unity, wholeness, and finally atman). The more clearly we embody our self as unified consciousness, the more our evolution becomes an expression of wholeness, arising out of it and unfolding within our evolving life. As we become intimate with and come to own this inner experience, we can then fully accept our divinity. We recognize that we are actors within our present biological-social-cultural system, with a sense of inner being-in-relation (evolving-self and unchanging-self) that lets us know we are part of an intrinsically connected whole.


## Unity is Not the End of Pain, But the End of Suffering

Awakening a body experience of unified consciousness is not the end of pain or the end of all "bad things." None of the great teachers have ever made a perfect place for themselves on Earth. Chasing after painless relationships will not result in freedom from pain. The "broad truth" of unified consciousness does not eliminate the mundane aspects of life. We still have our ups and downs, but we simply relate to this with a broader perspective and experience. Consequently, our intense feelings and strongest passions are experienced as an expression of the "divine."

For instance, Aurobindo explains that our impulses and instincts, such as sex and sexuality, which were believed harmful to spiritual aspirants, can be "made a cardinal condition for the spiritual seeker. The sex impulse cannot be simply ignored, suppressed or held down or put away out of sight. It is, in one of its aspects, a cosmic and even divine principle, the Shakti. Without it, there would be no world creation or manifestation…" (Aurobindo, 1953/2003, p. 49).

Relating to our passions with a different perspective is reflected in the saying, "Before enlightenment, we chop wood and carry water. After enlightenment, we chop wood and carry water." It's not what we do but how we do it that counts. The old Tibetan saying captures this: "The highest art is the art of living an ordinary life in an extraordinary manner." Our life becomes "extra-ordinary" when we are no longer motivated by underlying habitual fears. Instead, we access our wholeness as a body experience with the qualities that each chakra provides. The extra-ordinary is not based solely on ecstatic, great experiences, but on very ordinary ones. One of the most natural, joyful, and yet ordinary experiences, is being authentically who we are, while maintaining a sense of wholeness and unity in whole-being-embrace.

As a part of my life's work, compassion for the planet, and joy of sharing, I offer weekly online meditations and regular workshops on the Whole Being Embrace approach to healing and awakening. You can find me online at drzeb.com.

# APPENDIX ONE: NERVOUS SYSTEM'S SEVEN STAGES OF HEALING

## Introducing Unity to Peter Levine's Body Approach to Trauma Recovery

The use of embodied nondual experience of the chakras as a means of overcoming trauma is an unconventional approach. For this reason, it is important to position it in relation to other popular approaches to trauma. This can clarify how embodied nondual experience is relevant in the larger field of trauma therapy. This applies directly to common chronic emotional injuries in relationship that we have never fully recovered from, which is what I am calling relationship trauma.

While current trends in trauma therapy (cognitive-behavioral and exposure-based interventions) are the most common way to treat PSTD, they are quite limited. The mental nature of cognitive, language-based interventions not only needs a lot of talking with a therapist based on a top-down orientation (mind informs body), but when we suffer from traumatic experiences, our mental abilities are often reduced. Exposure-based interventions too often lack the subtly and pacing that our body provides and too easily overwhelm us.

Current Body-oriented approaches to recover from trauma (including Peter Levine's Somatic Experiencing® method) focus instead on changing our physiological and emotional processing of the traumatic experience in a way where the body informs the mind. This emphasis on a 'bottom-up' instead of 'top-down' approach, invites the body and the "body memory" (subcortical brain levels, such as the brain stem and limbic system) to change the way the body responds to trauma experiences. This information directly influences our higher cortical systems and thought processes (Levine, 1997; Van der Kolk, 2016). Yet, what is missing in this approach is an understanding of the power the unified ground-of-existence, as an expression of self, can have in this process. The role our body experience of unity and wholeness has in healing, is not recognized.

Because Peter Levine's method of Somatic Experiencing® (SE) is a body-oriented therapeutic approach to treating post-traumatic symptoms, it fills an important gap in the landscape of trauma treatments. Its bottom-up orientation has recently attracted growing interest in research and therapeutic practice. The intention of this Appendix is to contribute to the SE approach by including unified consciousness as a supportive resource. This understanding is particularly valuable for the trauma therapist, or any contemplative practitioner interested in the details of overcoming trauma.

According to Levine (1997), post-traumatic stress symptoms arise because we are unable to complete the initiated psychological and physiological defensive reaction (i.e., we have a prolonged freeze state instead of flight or fight; Levine, 1977). This leads to ongoing physical, emotional, and mental fixations and dysregulation of our nervous system. In turn, this chronically increases our "stress reaction" to what we experience (automatic survival responses: arrest, orient, flight-fight, freeze/fawn, collapse).

In order to modify our trauma-related stress response, in the contemplative approach proposed in this book, we build on supportive internal sensations, both visceral (interoception) and musculoskeletal (proprioception, kinaesthesis). In contrast to, and in compliment with, Levine's healing approach, the internal sensations focused upon in embodied nondual meditation are of a much more subtle nondual nature. Therefore, they offer a large variety of alternative benefits that give us a broader perspective.

As we learn to refine our senses in meditation, we have an increased internal (interoceptive) awareness of the innate, essential nondual ground of our being. This goes beyond simply identifying parts of the body or memories that are associated with a positive and reassuring feeling (central to practices in Levine's Somatic Experiencing). It is also a recognition of our innate, pre-existent, uninjured essence with an alternative sensory (subtle), motor (stillness), spatial (unity), and temporal (timeless) nature.

With this information, we train our self to gradually reduce our fixation on the arousal that accompanies trauma. With practice, we access nondual-qualities of self that provide a profound internal resource of support (whole-being-embrace). This increasingly allows us to learn to tolerate and accept our inner physical sensations and related emotions and thoughts. This gives us access to resilience and the sense that it is safe to live in our body and have experiences.

We naturally begin to have access to personal truth and memories that are associated with a positive and reassuring feeling. This allows us to complete the curtailed, pre-trauma psychological and physiological defensive reactions. We thereby "discharge" fixated energy and consciousness, returning to a state of dynamic equilibrium and balance. With the refined perception we access in meditation, within this balanced state, we further awaken the stillness of nondual consciousness as a whole-body experience of self. This becomes a self-perpetuating process that progressively awakens us to our divinity and ability to manifest our potential.

In contrast to exposure-based therapy, which directly guides us to relive the intensity of the whole traumatic event, we approach trauma-related memories indirectly (first cultivating a sense of wholeness and safety in the body) and very gently come into whole-being-embrace with our injuries. Uncovering and awakening a body experience of nondual consciousness, provides new corrective interoceptive experiences that physically contradict those of overwhelm and helplessness. This allows us to renegotiate our traumatic stress reactions in an adaptive and holistic manner. This bottom-up approach not only promotes our ability to self-regulate our reactions to stress and improve the quality of our life, it gives us direct access to the unity and wholeness inherent to a spiritual life.

In the following section entitled, "The Seven Stages of Healing Trauma," I describe the primary steps involved in recovering from trauma, as presented by the trauma therapist Peter Levine. Based on this understanding, this section is followed up by another section entitled "Seven Stages to Recover with Embodied Nonduality." Here, I describe the seven stages of healing from trauma that becomes possible when we include nondual consciousness as a body experience on our healing journey. This is a complementary, alternative roadmap to the one proposed by Peter Levine. It includes each of Levine's steps but changes the organization and approach to a few of his steps.

This complimentary alternative to Levine's approach has two distinct aspects: 1) It reduces Levine's nine steps to seven; 2) it includes unified consciousness. Reducing Levine's proposed nine steps to seven steps is simply a revision of how the journey is organized. In considering the principles governing each of Levine's nine step process, it is possible to understand how they also can be represented to have seven steps. This new organization correlates with the three-phases of energy and the seven-stages of our evolution. The inclusion of unified consciousness as our nondual essential ground-of-being, is a fundamental alternative to the composition of what the journey to recovery looks like. None of the content of Levine's suggested stages is rejected, but because the dimension of duality has some inherent limitations, adding the unlimited nature of unified consciousness adds valuable alternatives.

THE SEVEN STAGES OF HEALING TRAUMA

When we encounter an overwhelming experience, we initially feel fear, and either flee or fight. If that does not work, we freeze in fear, or we collapse, shut down, and dissociate or go numb. These survival responses are basically all sensations that can feel unbearable. In one way or another, we avoid and deny these experiences by constricting or dissociating in various ways. While these protective measures helped us as a child, they can become sabotaging habits and tend to limit our life in relationship as adults.

Most relevant to the subject of this book is how we recover from trauma. If we experience trauma and dysregulate our nervous system, Peter Levine proposed that we have nine stages of recovery from trauma. These stages correlate with the three-phases of energy flow when considered energetically. They also correlate with the seven-stage model presented in this book, when we consider the underlying principles involved (explained in a moment).

Peter Levine presented some biological and energetic processes that need to be considered for our survival responses to injury to release and transform. These processes are important steps in resolving trauma because, as we shall see, they also closely depict many of the experiences in our contemplative practice for health and spiritual awakening.

In Levine's 2010 book, *In an Unspoken Voice*, he describes these stages of recovery from trauma in the following way:

1) Establish an environment of relative safety.
2) Support initial exploration and acceptance of body sensation.
3) Establish skill with "pendulation" and "containment."
4) Use "titration" to create increasing stability, resilience, and organization. Titration is about carefully touching into the smallest "drop" of survival-based arousal and other difficult sensations to prevent re-traumatization.
5) Provide a corrective experience by supplanting the passive response of collapse and helplessness, with active, empowering, protective responses.
6) Separate or "uncouple" the conditioned association of fear and helplessness from the (normally time-limited but now maladaptive) biological response.
7) Resolve hyperarousal states by gently guiding the "discharge," and redistribution of the vast survival energy, to support higher level brain functioning.
8) Engage self-regulation to restore "dynamic equilibrium" and relaxed-alertness.
9) Orient to the here and now, contact the environment, and reestablish the capacity for social engagement.

I suggest that the principles involved in two of these steps have similar intentions (even though they can involve separate practices). Two of Levine's stages can be considered as part of the same stage:

1) In Levine's model, "pendulation" (Levine's stage three) and "titration" (Levine's stage four), each represent separate stages. In contrast, I propose that both "pendulation" and "titration" are forms of self-regulation of energy and consciousness, and therefore can be combined. They form what I call the "third stage." Together, they give us the primary skills needed to face the challenge in stage four.

2) In Levine's stage five, we provide a corrective experience by supplanting the maladaptive survival responses with healthy responses. Since this naturally leads to "uncoupling" the conditioned association of fear and helplessness from the maladaptive, habitual survival response (Levine's stage 6), I combine Levine's stages five and six. Together, our healthy responses and uncoupling fear from our emotions and thoughts, we gain the ability to "discharge" and redistribute our fixated energy in the next stage.

The result of combining two of Levine's steps is a sequence of seven fundamental stages, that parallel the archetypal-holographic model presented in this book. The following image is a visual depiction of the energetics involved in these interrelated models.

**Image #17: Nine versus Seven Recovery Stages**

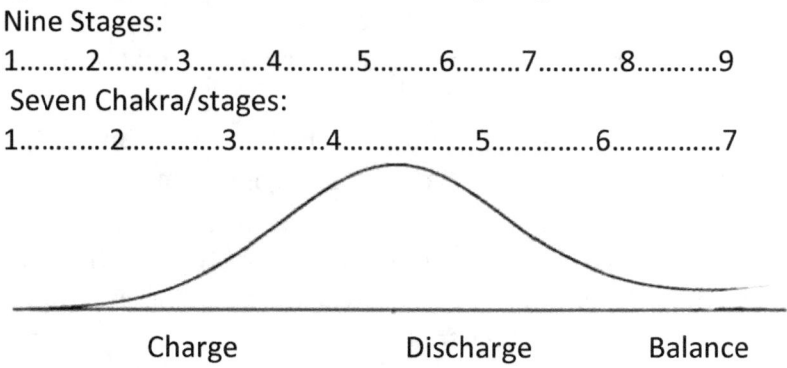

Nine Stages:
1........2.........3.........4.........5.........6.........7.........8.........9
Seven Chakra/stages:
1...........2............3...........4................5...........6............7

Charge                    Discharge                    Balance

A full elaboration of how Levine's model matches up with the seven-stage archetypal-holographic model described here, goes beyond the scope of this book. I simply suggest you consider how these two models of recovery are quite similar in principle.

SEVEN STAGES TO RECOVERY WITH EMBODIED NONDUALITY

The following description provides a brief look at the alternative approach as a roadmap to recovery from injury. It is congruent with Levine's model, yet, as mentioned, is based on seven stages. I make some suggestions of ways to include embodied nondual experience in this process. Of course, there are many more possibilities and ways to include embodied nondual experience that become available as we access the many attributes of the nondual-qualities of self.

## 1.  ESTABLISH AN ENVIRONMENT OF RELATIVE SAFETY

The first step in recovering from injury requires that we access an experience of relative safety. Depending on our injury, the following practices may only be accessible after prerequisite emotional and logistical support and healing.

Injuries are unwanted experiences that happen to us, no matter what we do to protect our self, and leave us feeling unsafe. One way to create an environment of relative safety is by gaining control of what we experience. One of the fastest ways to do this is by narrowing the focus of our attention. In trauma therapy and meditation, this is commonly done by narrowing our attention, so we are simply aware of sensations, not the associations we attach to them.

This transcendent approach is a valuable initial strategy that can help us feel that we have a choice about how we interact with those parts of our life that torment us. Simply being aware of sensations and not the associations, allows us to experience our injury differently, in part because we distance from the emotional aspect of our self. In this way, our changing experiences become objects without relevant, meaningful content. This creates safety because it allows us to remain present with the experience without becoming overwhelmed.

While this popular strategy in trauma therapy can be helpful initially, in the long run it can be limiting, for all the reasons described in this book. Briefly put, it can create a reductionist state that ultimately does not attend to the content of our emotional life and the specific dynamics of relationships. It does not adequately establish a style of being in relationship with our emotional life, that supports us to understand our personal truth or relationship dynamics. It is based on the principle of separation inherent in distancing from our injury's distortions and delusions, which reinforce our limiting cultural Axial Age mentality.

To address this shortcoming, in embodied nondual meditation the primary focus is to take a "direct-path" (p. 66) to uncover and awaken our inborn unchanging-self. This helps us in a variety of ways, some of which include:

1) When we awaken the chakra nondual-quality of self that is needed most to heal our deepest injuries, we feel safe and empowered to relate to our injuries without becoming overwhelmed. We also recognize our own inborn innocence and innate goodness.

2) Our unchanging-self is inherently non-abandoning in its contactfulness, and non-invasive in its infinite breathing-room, which communicates to our deepest bonding injuries in relationship.

3) The unchanging-self offers alternate temporal, spatial, sensory, motor experiences that restore a sense of safety and empowerment.

4) The experience of inhabiting our body as wholeness, gives us a feeling of having a location, which is a nondual "holding environment" (Winnicott) or location that holds space for us.

5) Before exploring our deepest injuries, it is very helpful to find a place in the body that feels comfortable, strong, and safe. Yet, often, when we harbor injuries and focus inward upon our body, we feel places that seem injured, constricted, numb, or vacant. When a body experience does not feel safe because of the pain we harbor there, the experience that our body is also composed of a unified, uninjured ground of our being, that lies deeper than the injury, is tremendously

relieving. We recognize the body is a safe place to live that is fundamentally supportive. Our body is not the enemy but becomes the ally in our recovery process.

As a result, when we inhabit our body as an experience of our unchanging-self, we begin to establish a foundation for uncoupling fear from our authentic experience and expression. We create safety and support so we can be in relationship with our injuries and PTSD symptoms.

## Creating Safety

Sometimes when we are severely traumatized, we might not be able to experience a palpable sense of existing in our own body at all. There are people that I have worked with for whom connecting with the body experience itself becomes re-traumatizing. Any kind of body experience is completely overwhelming, even relaxation. In this case, focusing on the trauma as a body experience is not something we would do right away. We may need to proceed very slowly and only attempt to inhabit the parts of the body that feel comfortable.

Initially, it is often important to not attune to pervasive space, or relaxation within the body, if we have a severe illness or psychological condition because it can be disorienting. Usually, with only a little practice, this changes. However, awakening the chakra qualities of our self is always safe. Being in touch with the innocent, inborn spark within us that has never changed and is still here now, is a powerful antidote to fear. The essential ground-of-being (Buddha-Nature, Christ-consciousness, or unchanging-self) allows us to feel our inherent goodness. Many of us can access this as an awareness even if it is not yet entirely a body experience.

In embodied nondual meditation, we learn to increasingly experience the feeling that we are made of this spark of "divine light," without having to seek outwardly or transcend to find it. As we experience being aligned with the nondual-quality that communicates the most support and safety to us, we naturally relax. It is important to learn to take time to recognize and then savor any sense of relaxation, and inner stability that results. This progressively uncovers a clearer sense of having a place in the body that feels safe.

## Sacred Personal Space

Yoga practice begins with cultivating clarity establishing the right size personal space to practice within (either standing, sitting, or laying down). This space can be the size of a yoga mat, the size of a room, or anything in between. Creating an intentionally supportive environment for our healing to happen creates safety. Finding a supportive place and time to practice contemplation and meditation is a basic part of creating an emotional boundary with our situation in life. This supports us to learn new skills and attune to a deeper experience of our self that is so often robbed from us as a child. Just as places of worship create a safe place to practice using a variety of sensory experiences (visual, auditory, olfactory, etc.), we need to do this also. Once a safe and supportive location is established, we can then learn to practice anytime, anywhere.

The process of establishing a safe and supportive location to practice, psychologically provides us with a sense of having personal space that we have a birthright to occupy. This experience deepens when we refine our senses, so we perceive that on a fundamental level, our existence is energetic in nature.

## Our Evolving-Self's Energy-Field

Attuning to embodied nondual experience helps us become clear about our pre-trauma personal truth. One important expression of our pre-trauma personal truth is the nature of the space we occupy as a human. Familiarity with the nature of this authentic (non-defensive) energy-field is important. When we experience trauma, we lose clarity about where we physically, emotionally, and mentally end, and others begin (Kolk, Levine, Ogden). We also lose clarity about how much room we can take up with the energy underlying our personal truth in a relationship, and the degree to which we are okay with other people taking up room. Lack of clarity about these things, with all its psychological ramifications, is a primary source of conflict and the loss of emotional autonomy and intimacy in relationship.

302

In meditation, we can feel how our physical emotional, and mental existence has a radiant, energetic presence. We can feel how our energy is always moving (unless stuck) and is radiant in nature, extending, like a lightbulb or an aura, beyond our skin. The space it occupies when it is authentic (not based on habitual defensiveness), is an energy-field that contains expressions of our ever-changing evolving-self's physical, emotional and mental presence. We can feel variations of this in how some people occupy the whole room (often narcissists), and others barely exist (often co-dependents). When afraid, our radiant energy-field usually constricts, and when happy, it usually expands. Our healthy, authentic energy-field is naturally resilient and flexibly adapts to what we experience in life.

As mentioned, awakening a body experience of our self as unified consciousness, puts us in touch with our essential goodness, innocence, and unbreakable, timeless nature. This provides the safety and support we need for us to rediscover healthy, authentic expressions of our energy-field. Out of our experience of wholeness and unity, our energy-field, as a personal space that we have a birthright to occupy, arises spontaneously_and effortlessly, out of our experience of wholeness. Our authentic energy-field is experienced as a personal truth in relationship, that we were never able to communicate as a child, concerning our safety and support.

In practice, take time to define the size and shape of this personal space. Feel how its radiance creates a safe container that serves as a physical, emotional, and mental "holding environment" (Winnicott), often in a way your parents were unable to. It provides the kind of support an ideal, healthy parent would have given you as a child. This experience contributes to a sense of belonging and that you are "at home" within your body. This "home" becomes a place from which you can own your personal truth (pre-trauma feelings, wisdom and discernment), which can then reinforce your ability to negotiate your conflicts in relationship more skillfully.

## 2. SUPPORT EXPLORING & ACCEPTING SENSATION

When we feel safe, we begin to feel curious about what was shut down as a result of injury. This expression involves inquiry into our personal truth about our injured inner child's repressed initial, authentic, pre-trauma feelings about feeling injured. We begin to discover that nature of our personal truth about any of our survival responses, or other significant issues concerning our relationship with our self and others. This discovery process is what supports our initial exploration beyond our habitual ways of responding, defensive boundaries, and our fixations. In the process of discovery, we increase our acceptance of all sensations: challenging and supportive. This increases our resilience.

Accepting the sensations that inform us of our personal truth about feeling emotionally abandoned or imposed upon, is important. We become more able to manage sensations of guilt, grief, and anger that have been tearing us apart. It shifts the focus from fear, helplessness, and stuckness into an act of self-respect. We come to establish that it is safe to show up for our self, and honor the personal truth of what we need to feel safe and supported. We begin to own that our personal truth is undeniably right for us, valid, and not too much to ask for.

The sense of existential trust that results from knowing our personal truth as an expression that arises out of unified consciousness, is profound. The trust and respect we develop for what our senses communicate to us is empowering, even when they tell us stories about our experience of being injured. It provides us with the sense of security to feel our unpleasant emotions, like helplessness and anger, and not be overwhelmed. We increasingly feel that we belong and have a birthright to honor what feels true to us.


## 3. SELF-REGULATION: PENDULATION TITRATION
### (Levine's stage 3-4)

In the last stage the focus was primarily on exploring what feels true for us and learning to accept what we feel. In this third stage, we learn more about managing the intensity of the injuries we still harbor in our body and mind.

To help us overcome our natural tendency to avoid pain and fear, we need to be able to trust that if we feel them, we will not be overwhelmed or hijacked by them. To establish this trust, we must have access to something that gives us a feeling of support. Ideally, initially this was our parent's supportive way of relating to us. But as adults, we have internalized these expressions, and ideally find this support within our own inner experience and identity. One way we can find this internally, is by cultivating a secure bond with a physically and/or emotionally pleasant and supportive internal experience within the body. In order to discern what pleasant internal experience to establish a secure bond with, Peter Levine suggests we begin by simply choosing an opposite sensory experience in the body to the unpleasant one (if we can find this).

This process can be accelerated by attunement to our embodied nondual experience, so that it communicates support to our injury. The nature of our injury always lets us know what nondual-quality we need most, to overcome our fragmentation (see nondual mirroring, *chapters four and five*). Having access to the chakra quality that brings us the most wholeness-of-being is a powerful supportive resource. By maintaining a sense of the whole-being-embrace between our evolving-self's injuries and our unchanging-self, a secure bond between the chosen nondual chakra quality, and our injury develops.

When our memory of a past injury is activated due to a current event, we tend to automatically become overwhelmed and resort to our habitual survival responses and defensive boundaries. In these moments, we call on our body experience of our most relevant chakra of embodied wholeness to support us through the experience.[61] This natural state gives us a sense of

---

[61] To deepen our experience of the chakra quality or any nondual attribute, we can explore bringing our nondual experience into movement in walking meditation. This supports our expressions to be a result of our "pure ego" (p. 259). We can also explore certain postures that seem to express the particular chakra feeling-tone. In the process, we learn from our experience of movement and stillness, which is fundamental to our learning process.

living more effortlessly and reinforces the important experience that our suffering will not last forever. We learn to move through difficult sensations and open to natural feelings of expansion and a sense of relief and flow. The more we perceive that movement and flow are a possibility, the more we accept and integrate sensations that were once overwhelming.

As we come out of the habit pattern associated with trauma, we get in touch with experiences and emotions that we had at the time of the injury. This is our personal truth showing up progressively more clearly. Without access to our ground-of-being, letting go, and the appearance of our personal truth could be overwhelming. Yet, when we feel that we are made of the nondual-qualities of self, the magnitude of feeling our personal truth does not overwhelm us. Our intense sensations and powerful emotions of fear and rage can move through us without fragmenting our ground of wholeness.

The enduring presence of our unchanging-self enables us to pace our self or "titrate" the experience. In whole-being-embrace with our most relevant chakra quality of self, we feel empowered to slowly and incrementally come into contact with the intensity of what we feel. The sense that we exist as an alternative sensory-motor, temporal-spatial experience, allows us to renegotiate our trauma. For instance, we learn to repeatedly go in and out of the experience of panic or immobility, returning to a state of equilibrium with relative ease.

We increasingly learn to go into the feeling of fragmentation while supported by wholeness and our nondual-quality. We learn to not become stuck in fragmentation, because our symptoms of fragmentation do not elicit as much fear. With practice, our panic or immobility feels like it is pervaded by the unifying force of wholeness. The contraction, that naturally comes with overwhelm, and the expansion, that comes with letting go and opening to a deeper truth, begin to become uncoupled from fear and stop fragmenting us.

In practice and then in our whole life, we get better at self-regulating our energy (with practices such as conscious breathing, mantra, yantra, asana, "inclusive *pratyahara*," wisdom, etcetera). Our sense of wholeness and unity helps us to deliberately moderate the scale and pace of the contraction expansion rhythm. Plus, in whole-being-embrace, we learn to allow the feeling of fragmentation to occur without disturbing our attunement to our unchanging-self (nondual relational autonomy). We grow a secure bond with our inner reliable reference of support (i.e., wholeness, our "subtle object constancy"). This kind of moderation and pacing helps us to not become retraumatized in our daily life, and as we deepen in our contemplation and meditation practice.

## 4. HEALTHY RESPONSES & UNCOUPLE FEAR
   (Levine's stage 5-6)

In stage one we establish a sense of safety (also Levine's stage one). We begin to learn it is okay for us to feel what we experience. As a result of feeling safe, in stage two we begin to feel that we belong and have a birthright to honor what feels true to us (also Levine's stage two). We learn to trust and develop respect for what our senses communicate to us. In stage three (Levine's stage three and four), this supports us to grow the ability to manage the intense feelings of our injuries. We grow the inner fortitude needed to experience our personal truth about our healthy emotional boundaries (that we were unable to fully acknowledge and honor for our self as a child).

This leads to stage four, where we provide a corrective experience by supplanting the maladaptive survival responses with active, empowering, protective responses (Levine's stage 5). As mentioned, since this naturally leads to "uncoupling" the conditioned association of fear and helplessness from the maladaptive, habitual survival response (Levine's stage 6), I combine Levine's stages five and six. They support each other in a cyclic manner that is self-perpetuating.

By providing a corrective experience for our self, we begin to restore our healthy pre-trauma responses to being injured. This naturally leads to a sense of inner stability, being settled and grounded, as well as a sense of being lighter and brighter. We incrementally learn that it is safe to receive sensations of support, to relax, feel relief, and to open into a deeper experience of our self in relationship with a new way of resolving conflicts.

Restoring our pre-trauma, authentic responses is an incremental process. Understanding how relationship trauma occurs and how this influences us, can clarify what needs to happen to heal. As infants, we picked up on the often subtle parental cues that communicated how acceptable our behavior was. We adapted our response in order to receive love. We repressed and forgot that which was not supported or mirrored positively, and we enhanced those kinds of behaviors that made us pleasing to others.[62]

Relationship traumas are often the most difficult to detect because the trauma usually involves low to moderate levels of nervous system activation. It usually happens over a long period of time as exposure to multiple, cumulative traumatic events, in a slow trickle of injuries. Many of us are not fully aware of it (Kolk, 2005). We often do not recognize that those aspects of life that easily trigger our knee-jerk responses, have roots in our childhood trauma. These automatic and often unconscious reactions are irrational and usually outside of most people's control or awareness. So, when we feel hyper-sensitive or react strongly to certain aspects of life, such as how somebody is behaving, we often blame ourselves for feelings of anger, terror, or heartbreak that spring up, seemingly out of nowhere.

When we give up an authentic expression, and our energy becomes obstructed in constriction or collapse, we feel helpless and defeated. Yet, underneath our constriction, collapse, and defeat, we are still poised to carry out our authentic expression, and our muscles are still receiving the signals to do so. At this point, the depth and clarity of our interoceptive awareness that

---

[62] Philip Bromberg explains how all attachment figures, such as a parent, have imperfections that influence the child, "through relating to their child as though he is "such and such" and ignoring other aspects of him as if they don't exist, the parents "disconfirm" the relational existence of those aspects of the child's self that they perceptually dissociate (2011 p. 57). In this way, our wholeness becomes fragmented, and our evolving-self is unable to express easily and authentically.

we cultivate in embodied nondual meditation, becomes a powerful antidote.[63]

The experience of reinhabiting (uncovering and awakening) unified consciousness as a body experience of self, provides a broader perspective and experience. We develop autonomy between our injury and our chakra quality, so both can co-exist. Our injuries and fragmentation are informed by the uninjured and whole, in whole-being-embrace. This increasingly supports our energy to flow through charge, discharge, and balance phases more freely and naturally. With practice, we increasingly uncouple fear from what we experience. We let go of our automatic constriction response to disturbing experiences. This allows us to discharge the bound energy that participates in our survival response and defensive boundaries (patterns of constriction and collapse).

When the energy underlying our physical, emotional and mental sense of self flows more authentically, it empowers us to express the personal truth honestly. We express what we wanted to before we got overwhelmed and shut down. The subtle nondual-qualities, such as timelessness, stillness, wholeness, and space, give us the ability to express our self authentically, so that we complete the unfinished experience that lies frozen, or in a state of collapse, within us. In the process, we begin to skillfully renegotiate the relationship we have with our self and others.

An important experience that we gain access to in embodied nondual meditation, is that we can feel how we live in our body as conscious stillness. This puts us in an excellent position to notice the most subtle fluctuation of sensations, and shifts in perception. It helps us recognize our habits of mind and body at their inception, before they gain power over us. Our subtlety of perception is important for recognizing and healing our most camouflaged traumas. It allows us to more easily track body sensations, and the meaning we attach to what we experience.

---

[63] Embodied nondual experience is an important part of what addresses Levine's stage five (Provide a corrective experience by maladaptive responses); also his stage six (uncouple" the conditioned association of fear and helplessness from the maladaptive) biological response).

The experience of our self as conscious stillness, allows us to become aware of the most subtle sensations of the ways in which we constrict by lifting away from the ground, or how we push, pull, or withdraw. When we are attuned to the stillness of embodied nondual experience, we can more clearly hear, see, feel, and understand our body-voice that expresses our emotions. Moreover, as we inhabit our body and sense of self as presence-of-being or conscious spaciousness, our orientation shifts from feeling solid and separate, to feeling open and connected. Our interoceptive experience begins to give us hints about what kind of movement and emotion is not being expressed.

At first, these empowering, protective expressions usually arise in small micro-movements. When we feel this, we can then revisit this small expression with an open mind and heart. This supports it to expand into a full-blown expression. These subtle sensations of our existence, like conscious stillness and conscious spaciousness, enables those parts of our self, that previously had been unconscious, to awaken. We can experience the activation of muscle fibers as our body prepares for authentic expression. As we embody our sense of stillness, spaciousness, and wholeness, this healthy expression (initially as micro-expressions) dissolves our constrictions. It also dissolves any symptoms of fragmentation, such as resignation, guilt, shame, and helplessness. Instead, we begin to feel resourceful, empowered, and even elated.

Each moment we consciously feel our way through the nuances of our previously abandoned authentic expressions, we have a body-based epiphany that broadens our perspective. We increasingly experience varying degrees of integration and wholeness. We begin to gain a sense of empowerment from a sense of agency, mastery, and satisfaction. We feel how our meaningful psychological self-expression is being restored.

Managing the intensity of what we experience through "titration," (in Levine's stage four), involves slowing things down when our experience of trauma is "too much, too fast, too soon." We do this by working with only small bits of difficult experiences at a time. In embodied nondual meditation, we add to slowing things down, by also learning to access a much broader perspective and experience. We access a deeper, more subtle part of our being that is inherently uninjured, unbreakable, unchanging, and universal. These nondual body sensations directly balance our nervous system (ventral vagal) and empower us to restore our capacity for authentic expression.

**Energy-field as Container and Protector**

As we have learned, the most important healthy pre-trauma response to feeling emotionally abandoned or invaded, is to establish our personal truth concerning the healthy relationship boundaries we need to feel safe and supported. When we experience our personal truth in the form of an energy-field (that arises out of unity), we feel how our healthy relationship boundaries serve two basic functions: 1) a container of energy and consciousness that we can fill up with our mental, emotional, and physical pre-trauma personal truth, and 2) a protective container of energy and consciousness that shields us by keeping out negative influences.

(This an important part of what addresses Levine's stage five (provide a corrective experience by supplanting maladaptive responses with active, empowering, protective responses); and stage six (uncouple" the conditioned association of fear and helplessness from the maladaptive survival response).)

It can be said that these two expressions lie at the center of two fundamental yoga practices: *samyoga* (container) and *viyoga* (separation). *"Viyoga,"* is the practice of cultivating autonomy through separating, to protect our self from influences that interfere with our ability to realize nondual consciousness. Typically, from an "exclusive nondual" transcendent path, this means separating from the evolving-self's perceived experiences in general. However, on an integral yoga perspective or "inclusive nondual" path, this involves allowing our evolving-self to spontaneously express pre-trauma authentic actions of protection and separation, without losing our body experience of unity.

*Samyoga* practice, from an integral yoga perspective, is a process of "linking together" and connecting to, or aligning with, whatever feels supportive, positive, and productive about our self. We bring together aspects of our "healthy ego-self" that feel integrated and cohesive.

Of course, every yoga tradition has a different interpretation of what *samyoga* means.[64] It must be said that the understanding of *samyoga* adopted here, is oriented towards principles not based on separation, transcendence, or the view that our evolving-self is an illusion (*mayavada*). I emphasize that everything is real (*satvada*) and that liberation from suffering involves our whole-being, dual and nondual.

It is said that *viyoga* and *samyoga* become tools for receiving "deeper knowledge" of the qualities of an "object." In embodied nondual meditation, this "object" is our evolving-self. The "deeper knowledge" we gain about the qualities of our evolving-self, involves reaching deeper than our injuries. We contemplatively inquire and "listen" to our pre-trauma, personal truth concerning what our wounded self feels. This involves being in touch with the wisdom aspect of our self. We listen with the brain in our head (cephalic), heart (cardiac brain), and gut (enteric brain). Since we are "listening" while attuned to the state of unity and wholeness, listening is also a result of the communion our evolving-self has with our unchanging-self in whole-being-embrace (via the brain's self-engagement system, Siegel).

As mentioned, when we inhabit our body as our unchanging-self, we can discern what our evolving-self feels much more clearly. We perceive our evolving-self's habitual survival

---

[64] From the traditional, transcendent orientation of classical yoga, *"viyoga"* means separating from the evolving-self's perceived experiences in general. However, on an embodied nondual path, this involves allowing our evolving-self to spontaneously express actions of protection and separation authentically, without losing our body experience of unity. In classical yoga (Ashtanga), *"samyoga"* means the combined simultaneous practice of focused attention (*dharana*), effortless meditation (*dhyana*), and the state of unity (*samadhi*). *Samyoga* can also be understood as falsely associating unified consciousness with our evolving-self. But the word *"samyoga"* itself means "holding together," "tying up," "binding," and "integration." *Samyoga* practice is a process of "linking together," which can have a positive expression in connecting to whatever feels positive about our self and our life.

responses, but we also perceive the pre-trauma responses of our authentic personal truth. Our healthy, authentic responses to being hurt arise spontaneously out of the woodwork of our careworn heart. This informs us of the supportive and protective boundaries we need to skillfully manage our life in relationship.

With practice, we grow a vivid experience of our personal space and feel how it provides a "holding-environment" container that holds us and protects us. These contemplative practices are a powerful means of re-discovering these two fundamental healthy responses (energy-field as container and protector) that are crucial for overcoming the central ingredients in relationship trauma: emotional abandonment and invasion.


## 5. NONDUAL RELATIONAL AUTONOMY: (Levine's stage seven)

At this stage, we progressively master our ability to not become overwhelmed by the intensity of what we experience. We also experience varying degrees of visceral sensations of triumph from successfully expressing what we had buried. (This can be considered to correlate with Levine's stage seven (Resolving hyperarousal states by gently guiding the "discharge," and redistribution of the vast survival energy, to support higher level brain functioning.)

The more we inhabit our body as nondual attributes, as mentioned, we increasingly can develop autonomy between the evolving-self and unchanging-self. This way, both dimensions of self can exist at the same time. This autonomy provides us with the mastery we need to have more choices in how we respond to what we perceive, ultimately providing freedom from our injuries.

As you know, in embodied nondual meditation, we uncover our unchanging-self as a body experience. We grow a sense of having a calm, secure center that feels relaxed and alert. When we reach stage four (Levine's 5-6), we refine our ability to then bring this feeling into contact with our injured self in whole-being-embrace. We do this by practicing repeatedly going into, and then coming out of, our injury and sense of panic or immobility. As we repeat this, the back and forth stops, and our

313

panic or immobility is continually accompanied by an underlying wholeness. Becoming very familiar with this process is important for avoiding the lingering debilitating effects of trauma. It establishes a foundation for recovering from the most entrenched trauma symptoms. The main reason why this is important is that it enables us to separate our sense of fear and helplessness (inherent to having experienced trauma) from our immobility and habitual survival responses.

It is scary to "go into" our experience of panic or immobility because of how powerful the sensations and accompanying feelings of vulnerability and helplessness can be. It is especially terrifying when we feel detached from our body, which is an experience that often accompanies immobility. Yet, that which we resist, persists and gets entrenched and more powerful. This makes the wise saying "time heals our wounds" lose credibility. This is why in stage four we must fully feel the intense fear and anger that we've buried.

Because we believe in feeling our emotions we risk the possibility of feeling more abandoned or invaded, we often will initially be unable to sustain our contact with the sensations of trauma for long. We also won't be able to sustain contact with other people or situations that stimulate painful feelings. To expand our potential in embodied nondual yoga meditation, we attune to the nondual attribute of our unchanging-self that we need most. We establish a bond with this experience to the point where we feel that we exist as this attribute (without submerging our evolving-self).

"Pendulation" (shuttling back and forth between feeling support and feeling our injuries; Levine's stage three) and "titration" (incremental exposure to our pain; Levine's stage four) provides safety and support. While we embody the nondual-qualities of self and also engage in pendulation and titration, we increasingly expose the injured part of our self (as an experience in the body) to the feeling of support. The inherently benevolent nature and broader perspective that accompanies our nondual-qualities of self, as an experience of wholeness, is transformative. We "uncouple" the conditioned association we have with what we experience, such as fear and helplessness, from our habitual survival response, such as flight and fight.

This supports the injured part of us to not feel overwhelmed. We learn to tolerate the intensity of our suffering incrementally, at a pace that is congruent with our ability to cope. In embodied nondual meditation, we practice going into, and then coming out of, our panic, freeze, and immobility response. Our injured emotions increasingly become permeated by the pervasive space of our unchanging-self, and we gain relational autonomy between our injury and our unchanging-self nondual attributes, so they co-exist at all times.

With this information, we begin to learn that we are not helpless victims and that we are intact and alive all the way through to the core of our being. When we do feel overwhelmed by disturbing emotional content, we learn to remain open and receptive to what we experience, without becoming fixated, dissociating, or getting stuck in limiting ways of behaving. This uncoupling of fear from our experience of injury is critical for trauma recovery. Even if we feel fear, it is not habitual fear but rather a realistic response to the present moment. Gradually, the evolving-self is allowed to regain healthy, authentic functioning.

## 6. DISENTANGLING ENERGY & CONSCIOUSNESS
### (Levine's stage 8)

When we successfully uncouple fear from our injury symptoms (Levine's stage 6) this naturally leads to letting go of our fixations. The energy that was involved in sustaining our fixations is released (Levine's stage 7). When we fully release bound energy, we return to a balanced state, which is our goal in this sixth stage (Levine's stage 8).

Peter Levine explains that as we let go of our habitual protective physical patterns of organization, associated with our injuries, the potential energy bound in the patterns is set free to become kinetic energy in motion. The energy that underlies our authentic expressions, that lay dormant as potential energy bound up in our fixations, is liberated. The energy that is released from letting go of our old injury habit patterns, can be relieving and enlivening (*tapas*). We begin to feel that we have more choices in how we respond to what we perceive, which feels energizing. When this happens, our truncated authenticity is replaced by healthy, authentic self-expression.

When the energy that is released is too much for the limited space available in our body due to constrictions, we usually experience varying degrees of involuntary micro-movements, like shaking, trembling, shuddering, and vibrating. We can also repeatedly yawn, cry, or laugh. This is accompanied by spontaneous irregular changes in breathing. These experiences can be quite dramatic when our trauma is severe. All these expressions help discharge the excessive energy that we mobilized for our protection at the time of the injury.[65]

Embodied nondual experience can dramatically reduce the involuntary micro-movements and associated expressions. This is because we are attuned to, and embody, what lies deeper than our constrictions and sense of collapse. At this depth, the sense of unified conscious space draws in and absorbs the released energy like a sponge (chapter six). Our constrictions simply dissolve within our sense of unified conscious space.

Furthermore, our embodiment brings us into a state of whole-being-embrace with nondual-qualities of our existence, such as unconditional love, knowing, and wholeness. This can be tremendously reassuring and help us let go of physical constrictions and open. Moreover, what lies deeper than our

---

[65] The sage Patanjali has a similar understanding of what happens when an experience becomes too intense. This is reflected in *Yoga Sutra* 1.31 with the aphorism, "Suffering, depression, physical restlessness, and disturbed breathing accompany mental dispersion" (Bouanchaud, 1997). Here Patanjali tells us that the two most apparent symptoms of suffering are the hypo state of depression and the hyper state of physical restlessness, much like what we feel with anxiety. Freud's student Wilhelm Reich (grandfather of somatic psychology) also claimed that in either state of disruption, our breathing will be disturbed and irregular and our mind will be dispersed in a state of dissociation, much like Patanjali's understanding of "mental dispersion." Even though they proposed different solutions, the similarity between Patanjali and Reich's views is worth noticing. At this stage, the involuntary shaking, trembling, and irregular breathing are a result of bound energy becoming kinetic energy in motion.

316

constrictions and sense of collapse is the experience of having an infinite amount of space. Our feeling of having an infinite amount of space, allows us to manage the huge volume of energy that is released.

Our energy does is not stuck or concentrated in one part of the body (as when our breathing becomes chronically shallow or when we feel habitually anxious, angry, or sad). Rather than constricting our belly, chest, throat, or head, we have much more space within the body for the energy that accompanies these emotions, to move freely (an experience psychology calls containment). It is dispersed and spread out within our experience of the stillness and conscious space that pervades the body.

As a result, the shudders and shakes are much less intense. We breathe easily, and our energy flows more freely. Because this energy is more dispersed, we feel less physically, emotionally, and mentally overwhelmed. We have less of a tendency to dissociate or constrict when intense experiences arise. We can tolerate what we feel and remain present and whole. As we spread the energetic charge that accompanies our emotions, we have a heightened sense of relief, integration, and authentic aliveness, even as the drama of our life unfolds.

Along with the energy discharge comes the potential for expressing and owning the aborted self-protection we needed to feel safe and supported. We gradually become able to physically, emotionally, and mentally express the personal truths that define the emotional boundaries of what works for us and what does not. We increasingly express our authentic desire for meaningful contact or desire for independence and breathing-room, with wisdom and discernment.

### Restoring Self-Regulation & Dynamic Equilibrium

As mentioned, when we let go of our habitual protective physical patterns and the potential energy bound in the patterns is set free, authentic expression prevails. We feel that we can let go of our sabotaging habits and have more choices, which is relieving and energizing. What this means in terms of our energy and nervous system is we increasingly sustain a balanced state of

317

"dynamic equilibrium." This means our nervous system becomes charged in response to a challenge/threat and then resiliently discharges and returns to a pre-threat state of balance or homeostasis (before repeating this energy cycle.

As we continue to release our holding patterns, and experience this cycle without obstructing it, we restore the pre-threat level of arousal, and open to a state of relaxed-alertness. In this state our perceptions are enhanced and, like the quiet-alert infant who "takes it all in" and remains calm. This is a time when we most effectively absorb new information that provides alternative ways of responding to challenge, stress, and our injuries. This is enhanced as we refine our senses.

As described throughout this book, the state of balance, uncovered and awakened in nondual meditation, is more subtle than the state of balance or "dynamic equilibrium" that Levine talks about. As we refine our senses, the stillness of balance can be felt as a body experience of unified consciousness. At this depth and breadth, we open to quantum learning, where we experience learning with our whole body and mind simultaneously. This broadens our perspective and transforms how we respond to our perceptions. This increasingly builds resilience, and we grow existential trust. This is a visceral sense that whatever we are dealing with, we will never lose our internal milieu of balance, stillness, spaciousness, and wholeness. This body and perception of self becomes a reliable and secure home base.

In returning to the pre-threat level of dynamic balance and wholeness, the nervous system reintegrates the excess energy back into the body. We experience each of our physiological survival responses to being overwhelmed (alert, orient, fight, flight, freeze, stuck, collapse), and release the energy involved. The pre-trauma self-protective responses we harbor in our body and mind come to expression and begin to resolve. As these protective responses are released, we feel less fragmented and can more completely let go of our ego entanglements (such as fear and helplessness). We recognize our conditioning (the meaning, associations, and distortions that we have about the past and present painful experiences), yet we increasingly are

318

able to experience this from the perspective of our state of wholeness-of-being. As we let go of our defenses and increasingly realize this nondual-essence of our self, our senses become more subtle and expose the nurturing spacious stillness that pervades the material world and all of our experiences.

## 7. ORIENT TO THE HERE AND NOW (Levine's stage 9)

In stage seven, we experience each moment as a fresh newness, as if we are perceiving the miracle of life for the first time. What we touch, smell, see, and hear, feel like a vibrant living experience. Our capacity for social engagement is transformed, and we are able to connect in relationship with our self and with others, more authentically and with more ease.

We grow our potential for generating energy and consciousness to establish satisfying relationship experiences. Our internal, intrapersonal self-engagement system of the brain (that allows for communication between the dual and nondual dimensions of our self) is activated. The divine whole-being-embrace between our evolving-self and our unchanging-self, provides relational autonomy from the overwhelming drama of our life. At this point, there is no need to transcend. Our sense of wholeness prevails and as we engage with what troubles us in a way where we are fully present and yet free from its limiting influences.

The more we practice the seven stages for renegotiating and transforming trauma in relationship, we release fixated energy, so it flows freely and our consciousness remains unified. We increasingly regain our sense of authenticity, emotional resilience, and we expand our window of tolerance for facing the biggest challenges in our life. We feel like Dorothy in the Wizard of Oz, who, at the beginning of her journey, is itching to go somewhere to help her manage life. As she sings, she fantasizes about being able to fly over the rainbow to an ideal world, like birds do. Then, towards the end of her Hero's Journey, she repeatedly taps her heals together and says, "There's no place like Home," and is transported back to Kansas, much more able to appreciate her life and make the ordinary extraordinary (The Gap).

# APPENDIX TWO: INTEGRAL APPROACH TO PATANJALI'S YOGA

When yoga is only equated to postures (*asanas*) and a form of exercise, it is not "yoga" by definition. Yoga is based on the fact that the body affects the mind (bottom-up), and the mind affects the body (top-down). This bottom-up and top-down relationship is vital for helping us become resilient to face stress and heal our chronic injuries. Yoga also includes unified consciousness in the healing process, which adds powerful supportive resources for awakening and overcoming our suffering. Because the value of this approach is so obvious, many of its practices are gaining recognition in psychology, medicine, and our own personal contemplative practice.

In the classical yoga text Yoga Sutra (200 BCE), Patanjali laid out central tenets of the method of Raja yoga called "Ashtanga," meaning the "eight-fold path." It is commonly referred to as "Ashtanga yoga." (Just to be clear, the Ashtanga yoga of Patanjali is distinct from the *vinyasa* postural yoga, also commonly called Ashtanga yoga.) While yoga has roots that go back thousands of years, the Patanjali Yoga Sutras is the oldest known text on the theory and practice of yoga (200 BCE). The Yoga Sutras describe eight elements of practice that culminate in unified consciousness. It is the basis of almost all yoga taught in the West today.

To understand the breadth and depth of yoga and its healing potential, becoming familiar with Patanjali's perspective is important. Ashtanga Yoga is a very effective way to enhance our resilience. It combines relationship skills, physical postures, breath control, and meditation to create a transformative system of self-discovery and self-realization.

Ashtanga yoga of Patanjali is an approach that is primarily transcendent in orientation, with some exceptions. Yet, I believe we are entering into an age where transcendence need not be the only method and goal in our tool bag. This *Appendix Two* examines each of the stages involved in Ashtanga yoga, and proposes an alternative approach that is not transcendent in nature. As a result, its potential for healing relationship trauma is greatly enhanced. *Appendix Two* is intended to inform those familiar with the classical approach of Ashtanga yoga, of an alternative application of its practices from an embodied nondual perspective. It is also for those unfamiliar with yoga, who can benefit from understanding its intelligence and potential for awakening and overcoming injuries in an integral way that does not lead to spiritual bypass.[66]

This alternative approach gives us a roadmap for using yoga to heal and awaken in a way that nurtures our body and mind rather than transcends them. It provides insight into why the stages of yoga practice are arranged sequentially (such as why our focus on relationship precedes focus on postures, and why the postures come before conscious breathing). The discussion of yoga practices also sheds light on valuable steps involved in learning the contemplative aspect of yoga practice (inner/*antar* yoga).

In this appendix, I point out that when we awaken unified consciousness as an expression of self, we can integrate the nondual-qualities found in each chakra with each of the stages/"limbs" in Patanjali's Ashtanga yoga. These stages are: right relationship to other (*yamas*), right relationship to self (*niyamas*), postures (*asanas*), conscious breathing (*pranayama*), right relationship with the senses (*pratyahara*), concentration (*dharana*) or attunement to the unified dimension of experience, and meditation (*dhyana*).

---

[66] The Buddhist spiritual tradition has many similarities to Ashtanga yoga philosophy. Particularly the Mahayana school of Buddhism, in its use of conscious breathing practices (*pranayama*), conscious vocal expression (*mantra*), conscious visualizations (*yantra*), and deities (*deva*). (Here the term "conscious" implies that it is practiced while in a contemplative, meditative state.) While the eight-fold path of Ashtanga and the noble eight-fold path of Buddhism have similar three-phase, seven-stage underlying principle at play, I limit my observations to Ashtanga because it is what I am personally most familiar with.

Embodied nondual meditation is a direct-path to awakening unified consciousness (*samadi*). As a body experience, we are able to gain direct access to nondual awareness even when our evolving-self is still suffering. This allows us to include unified consciousness in each of the steps of Ashtanga yoga (rather than mastering all the steps beforehand). This clarifies and deepens our ability to awaken embodied nondual consciousness as a body experience (*samprajnata samadhi*) on an ongoing basis, so we can heal our injuries in a nurturing manner.

In this book, I combine the first two stages (commonly called limbs) of Ashtanga yoga's "eight-fold path." This is because the first two stages have a similar focus involving observances in relationship, either to others (*yama*) or to ourselves (*niyama*). While each of these stages is distinct, they are fundamentally based on the same principle: relationship. What this leaves us with are seven stages, which correlate with the basic principles of the holographic Hero's Journey. This appendix describes how these two models compare.

In this book, I correlate each of the stages/limbs of Ashtanga yoga to the principles involved in the stages of child development and the holographic nature of our evolution. With this understanding, when we are injured at a particular stage of development, we can choose the correlating stage/limb of Ashtanga yoga practice to attend to the specific emotional issues for that stage of development. This diagnostic and prescriptive approach helps us include, rather than distance from, our evolving-self's process of awakening to a broader perspective and overcoming self-sabotaging limitations.

(Because of the language used in this appendix and the references that are made, it is most likely important to first read the book.)


YOGA'S FIRST STAGES OF PRACTICE (limbs 1-2)

The Hero's "call to journey" is a request for us to address the issues concerning our relationship with others and our self. Self-awareness and awareness of our contact with other (person, place, situation, substance, etc.) is the central attribute of this stage. Developmentally this is a time of establishing a bond and self-awareness in the autistic-symbiotic stage as a child.

Self-awareness correlates with what we encounter in the first two limbs of Ashtanga yoga. It is central to how we grapple with the desires and aversions inherent in our practice of dealing with our relationship with others (*yama*) and our self (*niyama*). While the specific practices involved in these two stages/limbs are distinct to the Ashtanga approach, they are both involved in establishing our self in relationship. As a child, we first learn about our sense of self via the nature of our relationship with our parents (other). So, it makes sense that understanding our self in relation to others is the primary focus of the first limb of Ashtanga (*yama*). Understanding the relationship we have with our self is the primary focus of the second limb (*niyama*) of Ashtanga. The attention we give to the relationship we have with others/*yama* and our self/*niyama* in Ashtanga yoga, basically establishes the conditions for us to create a secure bond (with other and our self) based on the most supportive form of relationship.

In yoga, our most supportive form of relationship is based on healthy morals and intentions/observances. These morals and intentions are effectively based on mental and emotional conditions (boundaries in relationship) that we need to establish (with other and with our self) for us to be able to have "right living." What underlies "right living" is the capacity to form a healthy bond with other and with our self.[67] The boundaries and healthy bond support us not to become engulfed or merge in relationship. The specific practices proposed in Ashtanga yoga are not intentionally directed at developing a sense of security and belonging, as we try to do in the first stage of child development (symbiosis). However, the net effect of boundaries and healthy bonding, effectively provides a relational foundation for this to happen.

---

[67] *Yama: Ahimsa* (non-harming/violence in thought, word, and deed); *Satya* (truthfulness); *Asteya* (non-stealing); Brahmacharya (celibacy/right use of sexual energy); *Aparigaha* (non-greed). *Niyama*: Saucha (cleanliness); *Santosha* (contentment); *Tapas* (discipline, burning enthusiasm); *Svadhyaya* (self-awareness and of text); *Isvara Pranidhana* (awakening our wholeness as we face our goals).

More than any other limb, in the first and second limbs of Ashtanga, the primary focus is on how to manage our desires and aversions in our relationship to others and our self. Likewise, in the autistic/symbiotic stages of child development (and later, in how we grapple with this stage as an adult), concern with the right amount and kind of contact is a central issue in our relationship to the parent (other, self). Understanding how to negotiate our desires and aversions allows us to have "right living." Most relevantly, it helps us become grounded and clear about the orientations of our contemplative practice, so we can manifest our potential in life most effectively.

As adults, we need to have enough self-awareness mentally, emotionally, and physically to have an intimate relationship with our self and others. Without self-awareness in relation to others, we may not have enough presence to build genuine interest and desire (traits related to stage two/limb three) to engage with life in a way that provides depth of meaning and authentic contact. (Patanjali explains, the way to overcome the lack of presence is with: 1) practice, sutra 1:13; and 2) self-awareness, sutra II.44). Self-awareness in relation to others and our self is the central attribute of this first stage of the Hero's Journey.

As a "Hero," we may balk or hesitate at the threshold of a new "adventure"/experience because we realize we are facing the unknown. Concerns of being alone on the journey, or of being imposed upon and inundated, are common. These concerns are expressed as resistance or as hesitation. This is often what we face in the first two limbs of Ashtanga as we grapple with the guidelines for supportive conduct in relationship with others (*yama*) and our self (*niyama*). We may believe we are in some way unworthy, unable to face the challenge, or we may initially feel duty-bound to stay where we are in life and not change how we relate to what we experience. An example of this is in the movie Star Wars when Luke refuses Obi Wan's call to adventure because he feels duty-bound to his aunt and uncle. This refusal represents our attachment to outdated habits of mind and body that keep us stuck in our limited perspective.

Luke then goes back to his aunt and uncle's farmhouse and finds they (or that part of his own psyche) have been killed by the

Emperor's stormtroopers (i.e., the habitual forces in Luke's life). This changes his mind and heart, and he becomes motivated and even eager to undertake the "call to adventure." Like Luke, after initially hesitating or even declining the call, we can change our minds and hearts. As the consequences of our outdated habits of mind and body increase, we are compelled to "journey."

As a Hero, this is when we pass the first threshold and enter the "special world" of our new perspective, for the first time. As the adventure gets going, at this point, we commit to our path (practice, project, process, interaction) to healing and awakening, and there's no turning back. As our engagement with this new path begins, we take the first step on the new adventure, much like Dorothy does in *The Wizard of Oz* when she sets out on the yellow brick road.

Patanjali's words *"atha yoga anushasanam"* (meaning "now yoga") invites us to experience our inner essential nature in the present moment. Of course, "Now" always has implications to the life we are living right at the moment. Our individual experience of the moment can teach us of the innermost essence of life only if we want to know its true nature. When we recognize the gravity of our situation and how it is upheld by outdated habits of mind and body, we increasingly let go of our resistance to embarking on a new "adventure"/experience on the yellow brick road.

Wanting to know the innermost essence of life, in our relationship with others and our self, is based on self-awareness (the central trait of the "arrest" phase when facing a challenge). We come to understand that the innermost essence of life only becomes a fully clear, tangible experience, if we volitionally embark on a new adventure of looking under the surface. (Sometimes the volition is inspired when we receive a dramatic wakeup call or flash of insight.) In embodied nondual meditation we discover this by observing our inner experience carefully and discovering the obscured and concealed nondual presence-of-being in our body. This discovery opens doorways of limitless possibilities in the here and now.

As we become familiar with our self in Ashtanga's guidelines for relationship (with others and our self), we naturally become inspired to pursue some of our most meaningful experiences or interests. As described in the second chakra, exploration of our interests, discerning our choices, and our creative nature, are all traits of stage two behavior. To know and understand what these preferences are, we learn to become present to what we feel in the moment. This fundamentally orients us (the central trait of the "orient" phase when facing a challenge). It is based on discernment that comes from our body as a general felt-sense.

In Ashtanga, yoga postures (*asana*) help us to become aware of what we feel. The postures also lay the foundation for self-regulating our hyper (*rajas*) and hypo (*tamas*) energy tendencies (as found in balancing *sukha-sthira,* see third chakra). The embodied awareness we develop as we practice our own personalized form of "*asana*," helps us develop a physical foundation and body awareness from which to understand our self and our interests. As we become present to what we feel and are more embodied, we naturally become discerning. We discover our personal interests, passions, likes, and dislikes and establish the inner stability to support this.

This sense of postural "*asana*" is not merely a static pose, but from an Ayurvedic perspective, it is about how we move through life (David Frawley). This is when our life becomes a living expression of "*vinyasa*," the linking of movement with breath. We begin to naturally use our breath as a guide that supports our movement through life. The energy and attention that we bring to each step along the way, determines the form and rhythm of the asana of moving through our life. In this respect, our *asana* becomes a kind of meditation of form in movement, that refines the condition of our energy and consciousness.

The root of the word "*asana*," Sanskrit for posture, is "*as*," meaning "to stay, "to be," or "to be established in a particular position." In a broad sense, yoga posture is how we proceed and move through life. Doing this with equipoise (*sukha-sthira*) and with authentic freedom of expression (uninfluenced by habitual fear), is the essence yoga "*asana*" posture practice. When our yoga practice is contemplative in nature, our yoga posture involves dealing with life in a way that is balanced. This lies at the center of our yoga postural "*asana*" practice.[68]

The heart of our postural yoga *asana* practice is our embodiment (*devata*). Embodiment, in one sense, is about sustaining a sensory awareness of what we feel in our body, in regard to our emotions, thoughts, and sensations. We feel a pattern or form of aliveness in our body that becomes clear when we are embodied. This is about sensing the presence of what feels authentic to us. We have a sense of becoming real and experiencing life as it really is.

Awakening to this ever-changing authenticity is about opening to an experience of our deepest wisdom and undeniable personal truth. This body experience is a reality-check that is affirming and leaves us with a sense of validation. It provides the fortitude to move through life authentically. This helps us move from the first stage, involving self-awareness in relationship, of simply recognizing "I exist," to answering the second stage question, "Who am I?"

Another experience of embodiment is uncovering our sense of self as a unified field of consciousness in the body. This is the primary goal of embodied nondual meditation. When we move through life in a state of unity and wholeness, authenticity prevails.[69] Our mental, emotional, and physical life is in its most

---

[68] The process of establishing a yoga posture involves practices that help us 1. let go of habitual constrictions, 2. spread out the bound energy that is then released. As a part of these practices, we 3. attend to sensations of comfort, ease (*sukha*), alertness and steadiness (*sthira*). We notice when we begin to strain or if the effort we are exerting is automatic or authentic. In meditation, effort (*sthira*) in part involves focusing on being present, and ease (*sukha*) involves letting go, spreading out habitually constricted or bound energy, and not attaching to what we experience. For instance, taking time to explore each experience of softening constrictions, settling sensations, resting experience, and opening to an internal sense of openness and space.

[69] The principles of "*sukha*" (ease and comfort) and "*sthira*" (steady alertness) underly maintaining the state of balance. This practice, in one form or another, is a part of every limb of Ashtanga yoga until we reach unified consciousness of "*samadi*."

328

integrated state. The energy and consciousness underlying our evolving-self is unobstructed.

When we are authentic, our energy flows freely. We are in our most open and unfragmented state when the charge-discharge-balance of energy (*gunas*) underlying our body and mind flows freely. As mentioned, when we refine this state of balance in meditation, the feeling of unobstructed openness gives us direct access to a sense of unity. The space that our energy flows through becomes unified and we feel at one with everything around us, in coexistence with the authentic movement of life.

The recognition of our embodiment of unobstructed authenticity, and embodiment of the conscious stillness of our essential ground-of-being, arises spontaneously in embodied nondual meditation practice. This is based on the direct-path to accessing unified consciousness. Yet, to refine the subtlety and depth of our embodiment, we also benefit from the indirect-path of self-regulating our energy. Because we have a body, some degree of self-regulation is necessary, especially when we are overwhelmed and fragment our sense of wholeness. The next stage of this process is what we find in the third level of yoga practice (limb four).

YOGA'S THIRD STAGE (Limb 4)

**Conscious Breathing *Pranayama***
The third chakra is known to govern digestion and metabolism. In Tantra yoga, much like the fourth limb of Ashtanga yoga, we can easily regulate both digestion and metabolism with conscious breathing exercises. Conscious breathing is also one of the more direct ways of gaining control over our flight-fight (sympathetic; the "accelerator") and relaxation (parasympathetic; the "brake") responses of the nervous system. The element of fire inherent to the third chakra is considered to be the "flame of life" that is regulated via conscious breathing (*pranayama*).

Fire is an active element that facilitates transformation. This element shows up in our hot passions (lust, rage, or intense desire) or the heat that cleanses and purifies us on our path. It is said that this fire is the heat that helps us digest both physical food and emotional life experiences. Fire is the fuel that gives us the endurance to make it to stage four. Fire also provides the actual fuel for the momentum we need to move forward and realize our personal desires, our direction in life, and our intentions in the world to reach our goals (fire in the belly).

It is no coincidence that the central quality of self, associated with the third chakra, is the essence of power and inner-strength. Fire is the heat that gives us the power to express our interests autonomously. It is also no coincidence that these traits associated with fire in ancient myth, parallel the child's "latency stage" of development. (This is when we strive to find the autonomy, inner confidence, endurance, and strength to manifest our interests and abilities.)

In Ashtanga yoga, we find the same dynamics. In stage one (limb #1 and #2) we come to recognize the nuances of how we can exist and be safe in the world. We become familiar with the reality of being alive by negotiating our relationship with other(s) and with self (*yamas, niyamas*). In stage two (limb #3, *asana*) we build the physical ground to manifest our motivation (posture, *asana*). In stage three (limb #4, *pranayama*), we build the energetic steam so that our desires and actions have the gumption it takes to be truly effective. This stage is about managing our energy so we can gain the inner-strength and endurance to sustain our efforts and persevere. When our inner fire of purification (*agni*) is ignited, it burns through limiting habits, physical obstructions, and emotional hang-ups. This allows us to know firsthand the empowering self-knowledge that is the essence of yoga.

In yoga literature, the third chakra is commonly called the "solar plexus chakra," and its location spans from the bottom of the ribs to the belly button, including the respiratory diaphragm. The third chakra plays a central physiological role in establishing emotional and energetic balance. Aside from governing our digestion and metabolism, congruent with other yoga literature, it is said that this chakra balances our nervous system. By consciously guiding our breath, we can very directly affect changes in our autonomic nervous system. Through its proximity to the diaphragm, the third chakra is intimately associated with breathing.

Neuroscience has now concurred that conscious breathing (*pranayama*) is one of the most effective ways of managing our nervous system and psycho-physiology. It gives us the inner-strength to sustain our efforts so they can come to maturity and fruition in the next stage. Guiding how we breathe has a powerful role in developing the control we need to accomplish this. The somatic psychologist Wilhelm Reich noticed that a person with unresolved emotional conflict, always contracts the respiratory diaphragm muscle. We now know the respiratory diaphragm communicates to the autonomic nervous system via the vagus nerve situated in the solar plexus.

The third chakra's relationship with breath is symbolically illustrated in a mandala. This mandala has triangles that represent three "doors" to facilitate entrance into the diaphragm. We enter the diaphragm energetically and with consciousness. These "doors" have also been interpreted as T-shaped "svastikas," which is one of the Hindu symbols for fire. As mentioned, fire represents light, warmth, protection, drive, creation, rebirth, destruction, and purification, and is symbolically associated with our nervous system.

It is said that the nervous system enables us to control our thoughts, which in turn determines our behavior. Thus, the emphasis in yogic practices such as conscious breathing *pranayama* and yoga postures of *asana* is to create balance of the fire element of the nervous system and of the subtle body. In applying this to our life, by becoming conscious of our diaphragms, we tend to temper the fire and thereby access support to moderate our response to intense experiences.

Desikachar (1995) explains that when we have unresolved emotional issues and our chakras are not balanced, we collect "rubbish" in the abdomen. A central aim of yoga practice is to burn off the waste product by raising it up and submitting it to the fire manifest from the diaphragm. The flame changes direction as we breathe, so when we inhale, the breath moves toward the belly, directing the flame downward. During exhalation, the breath moves the flame upwards, releasing the waste out of our system. So, if we can exhale longer, then when we inhale, we have more time to release the body from its blockages.

While energetically releasing the "rubbish" in the abdomen through conscious breathing does create more balance (*sattva*) in the body-mind complex, it is still important to address the relationship issues that are very involved in the original cause of the obstructed energy. At this stage, we gather the skills we need to become adept. As mentioned, often mythology depicted this as a time when we form alliances to gather support for the Hero's Journey. The emotional autonomy we gain in the latency stage as a child and as an adult, as well as the confidence, inner-strength, and energy that we gain in the third stage, are a prelude to bearing the fruit of our actions in stage four.

## Effortless Breathing

The classical yoga tradition of Patanjali employs conscious breathing as a way to prepare the mind and body for meditation and nondual consciousness (sutra 2.52). Here, conscious breathing is a self-regulation practice that establishes balance. Most conscious breathing establishes balance by engaging the body in certain ways to serve as a kind of control valve to regulate the flow of breath and balance our hyper and hypo energy fixations and habits. As mentioned, when the energy that accompanies the sensation of our breath can flow freely, the energy underlying our emotional and mental life also flows more authentically.

A common way to create this control valve is to create a sealed pressurized container in the torso, within which we release the holding patterns that create imbalance. We create a sealed pressurized container by engaging the physical body and working with the main "functional diaphragms" or (*bandhas*). The primary ones include in the pelvic basin, respiratory diaphragm, and the bottom and top of the throat. We also gain control by engaging other parts of the body, like the tongue or monitoring breath flow through the nostrils. These are all instruments that regulate the flow of breath and energy.

By contrast, in embodied nondual meditation, rather than emphasizing breathing in a measured way or deliberately doing something to manipulate and regulate the breath, we breathe effortlessly. We refine our ability to not constrict on the inhale or exhale. As we do this, we directly attune to the stillness and spaciousness of unified consciousness pervading our whole body. Effortless breathing naturally allows energy underlying our mental, emotional, and sensory life to move freely through the space in the body. To facilitate this, in meditation and conscious breathing, we focus on our inner experience of unified space pervading the body and the movement of breath flowing through it.

The more we let go of any way we constrict in response to the movement of breath, the more freely energy flows and the more autonomy we have from the energy inherent in the content of our experience. With practice, we can tolerate more energy in our body-mind system, even unpleasant experiences, without disturbing our sense of unity and without interrupting our sensory, mental, and emotional energy from flowing naturally and authentically. This is what helps us overcome habit and the automatic reactions that result from unresolved injuries.

As mentioned, in embodied nondual meditation we attune directly to the experience of balance and awaken as balance itself. So, rather than having the primary intention of self-regulating to balance energy in the body, we access a whole-body experience of unified consciousness. Out of this unity, the state of balance naturally arises spontaneously from unified consciousness. This is much like what happens in embodied nondual meditation practice when regular, balanced, and even breathing arises out of not constricting on the inhale and exhale so that we don't obstruct and fragment our internal space of the body.

In this way, being non-judgmental, non-responsive, authentic expression of our healthy desires and aversions that form our personal truth and relationship boundaries, all can arise spontaneously out of our experience of unity. It arises out of the stillness and spaciousness of nondual consciousness rather than arising out of memories of past experiences that make us fear the future.

To access a whole-body experience of unified consciousness, we let go of effort. As mentioned, Abhinavagupta explains, "...rather than practicing dispassion, we let go of all effort." In yoga, this means we cycle through the three phases of energy that are the building blocks of all existence: *rajas* (which involves energy charge), *tamas* (involving energy release), and balance, *sattva*. The intention of conscious breathing and meditation is to increase the state of balance/sattva. Neurologically, this means our autonomic nervous system (ANS) is able to go through a cycle of sympathetic energy charge, followed by a parasympathetic discharging release and a state of homeostatic balance. In Somatic psychology and yoga this means freely building, releasing (spreading) energy in order to create more balance (*sattva*) in the body-mind system.

Effort results in habits of mind, emotion, and behavior. Chronic constriction is an expression of effort. Emotions are organized by the mind, but they are harbored and physically felt in the body. So, we need to unleash the harbored unresolved injuries and the associated constrictions. Since every unresolved injury leads to habitual constrictions of our mental, emotional, and physical self, we engage in refining effortlessness. We learn to disentangle our sense of stillness (as a conscious presence) and "letting go" of the constrictions that we harbor whenever we have unresolved injuries. We let go of effort and attune to the stillness of the unchanging ground of our being.

Conscious breathing is a primary way we "let go" of effort and constrictions. With each breath, we cycle through the three phase cycle: we inhale (build charge), exhale (discharge), and pausing (energetic balance). We then repeat this repeating without interruption, which causes our breath to become limited to one part of the body, shallow, or stuck. Where we interrupt that cycle is also reflected in our nervous system and mental, emotional, and sensory fixations. This can be a valuable self-diagnostic discovery process. So, taking time to notice the fine nuances of how we breathe without changing anything is an important place to start our personal conscious breathing practice. Psychologically, we learn to breathe without effort so that we stay present, un-constricted, and open within, even as we come into contact with our disturbing thoughts and intense emotions. This allows us to not lose touch with our wholeness as we deal with what disturbs us in life.

Consciously breathing without effort allows us to breathe freely and experience the natural rhythm of our breath and evolving-self's energy moving freely. Access to the natural rhythm of breathing is important because, as neuropsychology now tells us, breath is what gets obstructed with unresolved injuries and the resulting habits of mind and body. The authentic rhythm of our breath and our whole body-mind system regains its natural rhythm (charge-discharge-balance). The authentic, biological rhythm of our body-mind system is the basis of our evolving-self's authentic expression. Breath is a fundamental way we reestablish this rhythm.

Conscious breathing pranayama has many elaborate ways of breathing to achieve unified consciousness. But the simplest is often the most powerful. Smooth and even breathing is the simplest form of conscious breathing and is perhaps the foundation of all conscious breathing practices.

## YOGA'S FOURTH STAGE (Limb 5)

In Ashtanga yoga, the fourth stage (limb #5) involves managing how we relate to our senses (*pratyahara*). Our senses are the medium through which we have a relationship with what we experience. At this stage on our journey, we learn to not become attached to what our senses perceive. In yoga practice, we can do this through resorting to either a transcendent, or embodied nondual practices. Clarifying the difference can help us understand the embodied nondual approach to practice. Briefly put, the transcendent approach taken by Patanjali's Raja yoga, emphasizes pure nondual consciousness (*atman*). The embodied nondual approach recognizes nondual consciousness can be an experience in the body.

A central tenet of Patanjali's approach (sutra I-2), describes the self-regulation process of yoga as *"chitta vritti nirodha,"* meaning control of the whirlpools or changes of the "mind." In this case, mind refers to the key ingredients of what our mind perceives: impulses of thought, emotion, and body sensation. The primary way we control the "whirlpools of our mind" is with a practice called *"pratyahara."*

The traditional goal of *"pratyahara"* is to gain voluntary control of these impulses by withdrawing our attention from each of our senses. A common way this is practiced is by keeping our senses open, perceiving them but withdrawing attention and energy from them while directing our attention internally. This cultivates distance through indifference or dispassion towards our sensory perceptions. If this is the only goal of our *pratyahara* practice, we remain transcendent, and this is ultimately limiting.

When overwhelmed, it is important that we narrow our focus to what we can assimilate. Separating through distance (indifference, dispassion) narrows our focus, in that our emotions and thoughts become insignificant occurrences. In this way, it puts us back in control, so we are not hijacked by intense or disturbing experiences. But, once we have some degree of control, if we do not follow this up by opening the senses, so we are seeing, hearing, and sensing with our whole body and mind, we create limitations.

A complementary alternative "inclusive" way of managing the senses is to practice an embodied nondual form I call "inclusive *pratyahara"* (Lancaster 2023). Rather than separating from the meaning of what we experience through the withdrawal of our energy or our attention from our senses, we open to what we experience, developing an intimate relationship with our senses.

This way of developing relationship with our senses enables us to let go and disentangle from the emotional projections (with the accompanying thoughts and constrictions or collapse), inherent in our fragmented state. This is a relational form of autonomy. Disentangling is an opening of our senses and our whole body and mind in a way that allows us to engage and embrace our habits of mind and body, that result from trauma. Disentangling supports autonomy between movement and stillness within us. This allows for ultimate union between both dual and nondual dimensions of existence. Our senses can still be significant, but we let go of our habitual, automatic grip on them. We learn to respect the information our senses provide without being attached to the distortions and delusions this leads to. This gives us access to a sense of safety, choice, inner-strength, and existential trust.

A central reason we can disentangle from what our senses perceive, has to do with developing the skill of effortlessness (as described in chakra four). As mentioned in chapter five, sage Jayaratha explains the importance of effortlessness in this way: "Those that went before said that desire [suffering] is checked by the practice of dispassion; we teach that this is achieved by desisting from all effort." Effortlessness plays a central role in helping us to not be motivated by our sabotaging habits. In the fourth stage, we learn to apply effortlessness in how we engage each of our senses, rather than dispassion.

The other important reason our senses let go of habitual defensive responses is because of the "direct-path" to awakening our nondual-qualities of self. Our direct embodiment of a quality-rich unified consciousness "holds space" for our sabotaging habits in whole-being-embrace. Through whole-being-embrace, and the influence of nondual mirroring (chapter four), we access powerful support. This allows us to master awakening and opening our senses, so they perceive with our whole body and mind, nurturing our self to health. This approach is what allows the injured heart to recover and blossom.

In practice, our embodied sense of wholeness allows each of our senses (smell, taste, touch, hearing, sight) to develop autonomy from the intensity of what we experience without constricting, fragmenting, and losing its ability to perceive and receive. Our senses develop autonomy from sensation in a variety of ways, such as: between the movement of the movement or stuckness of our evolving-self's experiences and the stillness of our unchanging-self; between the time bound limitations of our evolving-self's feelings, such as longing and inundation, and the timelessness of the unified ground-of-being; the fragileness of our evolving-self and the unbreakable nature of the unchanging-self; the distance between our self and others and the unity that connects all that is. Autonomy from our senses opens a whole new level of possibilities for growth, and a new way of dealing with the potential intensity of what we experience.

When stage four is viewed from a developmental context, the first stage (symbiosis) is about the quality of our bond and sense of connection; the second stage (differentiation) is about being accepted for our differences; the third stage (latency) is about manifesting our autonomy as an individual independent from what other people want. In this fourth stage (rapprochement), we have enough emotional autonomy to seek a "right relationship" between the senses that participate in forming our desire for contact, and for breathing-room in relationship.

For the first time, in stage four, we have the breadth of understanding to support both desire for close contact, and a desire for autonomy, simultaneously. They both play an equally important role in our relationship with our own internal process concerning our senses (and the emotions and thoughts they lead to). We also seek this from other people. Understanding of the nondual nature of the fourth chakra clarifies how this happens.

Like the archetypal Hero at this stage, we achieve this balance by attending to our desires with our newly learned skills. Yet our most potent support comes from opening to our innate wholeness, and its expression as unconditional love. Unconditional love is an open, tender expression of the innate ground of our being, as found most clearly in the heart center of the fourth chakra. The subtle, timeless nature of unconditional love serves as a grounding and unifying force for each of our senses, so they function in unison and inform our whole body, heart, and mind.

This provides the needed support for us to become adept at cultivating contact and independence between our unchanging-self and what our evolving-self senses. In whole-being-embrace and nondual mirroring, we do not simply consume our evolving-self in a state of unconditional love, but we bring this experience of unity into profound communion with our personal relationship injuries and trauma. It is a time when we most clearly discern how

338

both dimensions can meet in harmony and discover a new way of being in relationship. What becomes available is a tremendous potential for remaining present with our lived experience in relationship. In brief, at this stage, there is a potential for a great birth (awakening) but also a great death (of limiting habits).

As our attunement to embodied nondual experience becomes a stable experience, we gain clarity about our desires concerning contact and autonomy. This sets us up for clearly expressing our personal truth as healthy boundaries in relationship in the fifth stage, supported by the throat chakra's nondual-essence of expression.

## YOGA'S FIFTH STAGE (Limb 6)

At this stage, from a sequential perspective, we begin to introduce much more subtle experiences that are not entirely recognized in Western psychology.

In the classical yoga of the eight-fold path of Ashtanga, each stage naturally leads to the next stage, and yet collectively, they are divided into two primary categories. The first four limbs of the eight-fold path (here turned into three) are called "*bahiranga*" yoga (like *yama, niyama, asanas, pranayama*), meaning the external aspect of yoga. The next four limbs represent *Antaranga,* meaning the internal or intimate aspect of yoga (concentration, meditation, and nonduality). Sometimes, the fourth stage (limb five-*pratyahara*) is included as well. Stage four (limb #5, developing autonomy from our senses, *pratyahara*) is a bridge connecting the external to the internal aspect of yoga.

In stage four (limb #5), we use all the abilities and awareness learned earlier to get past the apex of the charge-discharge cycle. In yoga, as described, this means we develop a specific orientation with our senses and what we perceive (inclusive *pratyahara*). Having the appropriate relationship with our senses in stage four, makes stage five possible. Stage four enables us to not be overwhelmed by our sensory perceptions and enhances our ability to show up and sustain our focus and concentration. Learning to show up fully in stage four, allows us to be undistracted and more present to the moment as it is happening.

This newfound focus of attention to the present, is the basis of Ashtanga yoga's stage five practice of "concentration" (limb #6, *dharana*).

Concentration often takes the form of focusing the mind on a single point or subject with intense willpower, so that our thinking mind becomes quiet of thought. By contrast, in embodied nondual meditation, "concentration" becomes less about focusing the mind on stilling thoughts, and more about effortless opening to perception and attunement. This is because experience includes more than our mental faculties. When we effortlessly open and attune to the subtle experience of our unchanging-self, we feel with all our senses. We attune to the subtle stillness, unity, timeless reality that is already inside of us, even though thoughts may still be present.

Attunement in relationship, normally helps us feel the internal world of other people's experience. We then can learn to fully receive and feel more fully received by others. When we attune to the subtle level of existence, we perceive the transpersonal dimension of self as a body experience, beyond the limits of personal identity. Through attunement we uncover and awaken an unwavering presence ("subtle object constancy") as an experience of our innate self, that is a pre-existent essence of our own being. We don't create it or discover it from relating to others. It is not a transitional comfort object, security blanket, or external deity. We discover it from opening to what is already there.

## YOGA'S SIXTH STAGE (limb 7)

Attunement naturally leads us to stage six, called "meditation" (limb #7; *dhyana*). Meditation arises when a deeper level of ongoing effortless attunement develops. That is, when we sustain our concentration/attunement to embodied experience of unity and wholeness (as a "subtle object constancy") in stage five long enough, we enter the state of "meditation" in stage six (limb #7, *dhyana*). This is when we become effortlessly present to our self and our environment as an expression of unified consciousness.

At this point, all our insights and reflections, behavior, and emotions are always grounded in the present moment and our sense of unity and wholeness. As we engage with our reflections of the past and future, we don't lose the felt reality of the embodied presence of nondual experience. We are able to fully receive the feeling of fulfillment and wholeness-of-being, as a stable ongoing experience. Because we are free from perceiving and responding in automatic habitual ways (reacting), we feel content, relaxed, and have a sense of well-being, even if we have disturbing emotions and thoughts. We are able to experience whole-being-embrace with authentic difficult emotions without becoming overwhelmed and acting out. Our enduring ability to attune to the nature of our existence and sense of self, as unified consciousness, leads to a shift in perspective and understanding. Putting this into the context of our overall psychological development can be helpful.

Psychologically speaking, as we move through each of the stages as a child (and again as an adult), we progress from establishing a bond and self-awareness in the autistic-symbiotic stage (limb #1-2), to defining our differences and preferences in the "differentiation" stage two (limb #3), to establishing freedom/autonomy to manifest our differences/preferences in the "latency" stage three (limb #4), to balancing desire and aversion to contact in the "rapprochement" stage four (limb #5). In stage five, called "object constancy," we grow a profound sense of the enduring presence of a parent, even in their absence. This involves internalizing the parent to form our own self-identity. This sense of self is described by Winnicott as a sense of 'going-on-being' at the most basic level.

In stage six, we access a more subtle experience of self. Our subjective sense of self increasingly emerges out of our innate essential ground-of-being, wholeness, and unity. The domain of interpersonal relations involving the 'social matrix of the psyche', shifts from being an interaction between separate interrelated entities, to an experience of radically open and unified beings in simultaneous and immediate contact with each other.

As mentioned, when attunement becomes an effortless ongoing experience, we enter into stage six (meditation, limb #7),

341

which is a time of refining and deepening our experience of meditation and unified consciousness. Through effortless attunement to the unchanging-self's embodied attributes of nondual experience (subtle stillness, unity, timelessness, wholeness, etc.), as found in all the chakras, we perceive a presence that supports us at all times. Attunement to the sixth chakra, the essence of knowing and understanding, is particularly relevant to the sixth stage (limb #7).

On a most basic level, unity consciousness and embodiment of the essence of knowing and understanding, supports us even when we are aware of simultaneously being separate from our most desired goal, hope, or wish in life. Our essential ground-of-being, begins to come into whole-being-embrace with our evolving-self, more consistently and effortlessly. With this depth and breadth of perspective and understanding, our "whole-self," dual and nondual, can heal in whole-being-embrace. We feel stable and unharmed, despite the presence of setbacks, conflicts, or disagreements we have in relationship (with self, other, situation, substance, etc.).

In terms of our yoga practice, at this point, embodiment of our unchanging-self provides a much deeper experience than the Western conception of self. We experience our unchanging-self as a deep sense of inner knowing. This unchanging ground gives us access to a profound level of resolution of our unfinished and unresolved emotions, beliefs, and actions. With this understanding, our pre-trauma, inner wisdom, and personal truth (healthy emotional boundaries) spontaneously arise within us and come into authentic expression. The result of this is a profound sense of completion, inherent to the sixth stage (limb #7).

Stage six arises after we experience the release of bound energy and consciousness as we let go of our habits of mind and body (in stage five). While we may experience the inner heat and awakening (*tapas*) from stages one through five, not until stage six is this fully an integral part of our being. In yoga practice, this is a time when we can master the ability to consistently engage with the present moment, without fragmenting our wholeness.

After we, as the Hero, successfully survive the great ordeal at the apex of our journey in stage four, and receive our just reward (freedom from unsupportive habit), we release our bound energy and set out for "home" (attunement to unity) in stage five. While we may have fulfilled our original objective of sustaining attunement to our embodied state in stage six ("meditation," *dhyana*), we still need to integrate the new perspective and experience. This sets us up for stage seven (*samadhi*), where our wholeness is a fully integrated as an ongoing stable experience.

In stage six, we integrate the discord between our former self and our current sense of wholeness-of-being. We complete the letting go of old sabotaging habits of mind and body, due to our access to a sense of understanding, knowing, and wholeness. It takes adjustment for our life to match the new perspective we have. We may still need to resolve mistakes we made earlier in life and integrate the new understanding we have. These final adjustments, so we can fully come to completion, are what is involved in stage six. In our meditation practice, attunement to, and embodiment of our sense of existing as understanding, knowing, and wholeness can facilitate our journey toward completion.

These final adjustments show up in popular hero myths as some of the best chase scenes. The Hero is pursued by the vengeful forces (sabotaging injury/ego) from whom we have stolen the object of desire (in stage four). In Star Wars, this is the chase as Luke and Princess Leia escape from the Death Star with the plans to bring down Darth Vader.

In our contemplative practice, as we integrate the new perspective, and forge a new normal in which to thrive, we may feel a sense of inner heat and energy (*tapas*), much like we began to feel in stage five. (In Star Wars, this inner energy is called the "the Force").

The act of changing a limiting habit, releases an inner heat and awakens vitality. As a Hero, we feel a sense of celebration, a moment of great self-realization, or the feeling that we have recovered the parts of our self that we had to give up, in order to survive. As we integrate our experience of changing a limiting habit, we win new command over our life. This is one reason the sixth chakra is called "command." We are transformed into a new being by this experience. Equipped with a new perspective and a new normal, we reaffirm the meaning and value of the journey we took. We fully experience how our journey has not only improved our life but also the quality of our relationships.

As mentioned, steady attunement in stage five brings us to the fruition of awakening in stage six. Out of meditation (stage six, *dhyana*) spontaneously arises stage seven, our perception of all of existence as unified consciousness, "*samadhi*" (limb #8).

## YOGA'S SEVENTH STAGE (Limb 8)

In embodied nondual meditation our focus is on awakening unified consciousness as an experience of self. This is a self-reflective unified consciousness, in that we are aware of being aware. The intention in Ashtanga yoga is to sustain a state where, for example, we are the tree we are hugging, and we are not aware of a self in contact with a tree. The knower (self) and the known (tree) become one. This goal of traditional Ashtanga yoga is called, "*asamprajnata samadhi*."

While this can be tremendously relieving and lead us toward overcoming our injuries and suffering, it can be limiting on its own. We cannot effectively function in this state and we do not learn about our personal truth or important relationship skills, needed to live life in relationship. For this reason, in embodied nondual meditation, our intention is to experience our self as an expression of unified consciousness that is able to be aware of being aware. This makes it possible to be in communion with the tree we are hugging, rather than become the tree itself.

In yoga, this self-reflective unified consciousness is called, "*samprajnata samadhi*." Self-reflective unified consciousness is characterized by its ability to co-exist with thought, deliberation, joy and an unqualified ego (Yoga sutra I.17); or in Kashmiri Shaivism, "pure ego" (*asmad; aharri*; ahambhava; a pure expression of Siva/consciousness "resting in itself"). In this state, we acquire the ability to be free from our sabotaging habits, yet are still self-conscious. In self-reflective unified consciousness,

344

the mind remains identified with the object of meditation, our unchanging-self (it is sometimes called "*savikalpa samadhi*"). In yoga terms, this means our state of unified consciousness is with "seed" (*sabija*) or quality of being (Yoga sutra, I.44-46). This allows us to co-exist with our evolving-self.

To be more specific, our self-reflective unified consciousness (*samprajnata samadhi*) has four expressions. All of these expressions arise spontaneously, so it is not necessary to dwell too much on these details. Yet, the details also serve as a roadmap and help us make sense of what we are experiencing.

In the first expression (*vitarkanugata samadhi*), we recognize the nondual-qualities of our self as tangible experiences (i.e., we are aware of being aware). The nondual-qualities are considered to be "objects" or "props," of sorts. This means experiencing our self as a quality-rich expression of unity, is a tool or "prop" for accessing ultimate transcendent unified consciousness (*atman*). (In embodied nondual meditation, we do not aspire to the goal of the transcendent state (*atman*) only.) There are two types of props: 1) we have the perception, experience its meaning, and have ideas about the experience of unified consciousness (*savitarka*); 2) the meaning and ideas are eclipsed, while we simply notice our self as luminous unified consciousness (*nirvitarka*).

The second expression of self-aware unified consciousness (*vicharanugata samadhi*) is experienced as consciousness that is accompanied by thoughts. There are two types of thoughts (Yoga sutra, I.44, 47): 1) Our thoughts are varied due to not being inhibited (*savichara*); 2) our thoughts are experienced as an expression of unified consciousness (*nirvichara*).

In the third expression of self-aware unified consciousness (*anandanugata samadhi*), we have a sense of joy and contentment as we can discern the substratum of phenomena. The element of purity and goodness (*sattva guna*) pervades our being in communion with our ego-self (*aham*).

As we deepen to the fourth expression of self-aware unified consciousness (*asmitanugata samadhi*), we come to realize our divine entanglement. We experience that our sense of evolving-self and our unchanging-self, are both rooted in the same energy and consciousness (Yoga sutra II.6). Sustaining our self-reflective awareness allows us to be aware of this divine entanglement, as we come into whole-being-embrace and nurture our self to health, and awaken.

# BIBLIOGRAPHY

Aurobindo, 1976/2003, *Questions and Answers 1953*, published by Sri Aurobindo Ashram Publication

Bentzen, Marianne, 2020, *Neureffective Meditation*; published by Healing Arts Press.

Bishop, Scott, et al., 2004, *Mindfulness: A Proposed Operational Definition*, online article.

Blackstone, 2011, *The Intimate Life: Awakening to the Spiritual Essence in Yourself and Others*; published by Sounds True.

_____, 2018, *Trauma and the Unbound Body: The Healing Power of Fundamental Consciousness*; published by Sounds True.

Bohm, David, 1980, *Wholeness and the Implicate Order*, published by Routledge.

Bowen, Murray, (1978), *Family Therapy in Clinical Practice*; published by New York Jason Aronson.

Bowlby, John, (1969). *Attachment*; published by New York: Basic Books.

_____, (1973), *Separation: Anxiety and Anger*, New York: Basic Books.

Brazelton, 2001, Stanley I. Greenspan, *The Irreducible Needs of Children: What Every Child Must Have to Grow*; published by Da Capo Lifelong Books.

_____, 1989, *Families: Crisis and Caring*; published by Random House.

Bouanchaud, Bernard, 1997, *The Essence of Yoga: Reflections on the Yoga Sutras of Patanjali*; published by Rudra Press.

Bromberg, Philip, 2011, *The Shadow of the Tsunami*, published by Routledge.

Bucknell, Roderick, Stuart-Fox, Martin, 1986, *The Twilight Language*; published by Routledge.

Joseph Campbell, 1949, *The Hero with a Thousand Faces*, 2008; published by New World Library

Delio, Ilia, 2020, *Re-Enchanting the Earth, Why AI Needs Religion*; published by Obis Books.

_____, 2023, The Not-Yet God: Carl Jung, Teilhard de Chardin, and the Relational Whole, published by Obis Books

Damasio, Antonio, 1999, *The Feeling Of What Happens: Body and Emotion in the Making of Consciousness*; published by Heinemann.

Desikachar, 1995, *The Heart of Yoga*; published by Inner Traditions.

Dyczkowski, Mark S. G., 2023, *Tantraloka: The Light On and Of the Tantras*, translated with commentary by Dyczkowski, independently published.

Eisler, Riane, 1988, *The Chalice and The Blade: Our History, Our Future*; published by Harper One.

_____, 1995 *Sacred Pleasure: Sex, Myth, and the Politics of the Body*, New Paths to Power and Love; published by HarperCollins

Eliade, Mircea, 1957, *The Sacred and the Profane, The Nature of Religion*, 1987; published by Harper Collins.

Feuerstein, George, 1989, *The Yoga-Sutra of Patanjali: A New Translation and Commentary*; published by Inner Traditions.

Frawley, David, 1999, *Yoga for Your Type: An Ayurvedic Approach to Your Asana Practice*, published by Lotus Press.

Hart, Susan, 2018, *Brain, Attachment, Personality: An Introduction to Neuroaffective Development*; published by Routledge.

Jaspers, Karl, 1949 *The Origin and Goal of History*; published 2021 by Routledge.

_____, 1966, Socrates, Buddha, Confucius, Jesus: From The Great Philosophers, Volume I, published by Harper Collins.

Feuerstein, George, 1989, *The Yoga-Sutra of Patanjali: A New Translation and Commentary*; published by Hohm Press, U.S.

Josipovic, Zoran, Science Direct, 2019, *Progress in Brain Research*, volume 244, Pages 273-298

_____, 2013, *Freedom of the Mind*, Contemplative Science Lab, Department of Psychology, New York University, New York, NY.

Jaynes, Julian, 1976 *The Origin of Consciousness in the Breakdown of the Bicameral Mind*, 2000; published by Houghton Mifflin.

Jung, Carl, 1958 *Psychology & Religion, East & West*, vol. XI of the Collected Works, Vol. 11; second printing 1972; published by Princeton University Press.

Kabat-Zinn, 2003, *Mindfulness-based interventions in context: Past, Present, and Future*. Clinical Psychology: Science and Practice, 10(2), 144–156. Brain, Mind, and Body in the Healing of Trauma,

Kahn, Matt, 2022, *All for Love: The Transformative Power of Holding Space*, published by Sounds True.

_____, 2020, *Whatever Arises Love That: A Love Revolution That Begins with You*, published by Sounds True.

Kolk, Bessel, van der, 2014, *The Body Keeps the Score: Brain, Mind, and Body in the Healing of Trauma*; published by Penguin Publishing Group.

Maclean, Paul D., 1990, *The Triune Brain in Evolution: Role in Paleocerebral Functions*, published by Springer.

Lancaster, Zeb, 2023, *From Trauma to Wholeness: Embodied Nondual Meditation*, Yoga Therapy, Somatic Psychology, published by Whole Being Books.

LeDoux, Joseph, 1996, *The Emotional Brain: The Mysterious Underpinnings of Emotional Life*, published by Simon Schuster.

Levine, Peter, 1997, *Waking the Tigger: Healing Trauma*; published by North Atlantic Books.

_____, 2010, *In an Unspoken Voice: How the Body Releases Trauma and Restores Goodness*; published by North Atlantic Books.

Lizbeth Marcher, Fich, Sonja, 2010, *Body Encyclopedia: A Guide to the Psychological Functions of the Muscular System*; published by North Atlantic Books.

Loy, David R., 1988, *Nonduality: In Buddhism and Beyond*; published by Wisdom Publications.

Mahler, Margaret S., 1975, *Psychological Birth Of The Human Infant Symbiosis and Individuation*: Mahler, Margaret S., Pine, Fred, Bergman, Anni; published by Basic Books.

Ogden, Pat, 2006, *Trauma and the Body: A Sensorimotor Approach to Psychotherapy*; published by W.W Norton.

Papero, D.V., 1990, *Bowen family systems Theory*. Boston: Allyn & Bacon.

Pert, Candace, 1997, *Molecules of Emotion, The Science Behind Mind-Body Medicine*; published by Simon & Schuster.

Prendergast, John J., 2015, *In Touch: How to Tune In to the Inner Guidance of Your Body and Trust Yourself*, Sounds True publishing.

Pribham, Karl H., 1991, *Brain and Perception: Holonomy and Structure in Figural Processing*; published by Psychology Press.

Reich, Wilhelm, 1933, *Character Analysis*, Farrar, Straus & Giroux.

Roche, Lorin, 2014, *The Radiance Sutras: 112 Gateways to the Yoga of Wonder and Delight*; published by Sounds True

Rosenberg, Jack, Kitaen-Morse, Beverly, 1996, *The Intimate Couple: Reaching New Levels of Sexual Excitement Through Body Awakening and Relationship Renewal*; published by Turner Publishing

Sable, Pat, 2000, *Attachment and Adult Psychotherapy*; published by Jason Aronson, inc..

Shankara, Adi, 1978, *Crest Jewel of Discernment*: Timeless Teachings on Nonduality - The Vivekachudamani; published by Vedanta Press.

Siegel, Daniel, 2012, *The Developing Mind; Second Edition: How Relationships and the Brain Interact to Shape Who We Are*; published by Guilford Press.

Sills, Franklyn, 2001, *Craniosacral Biodynamics, Volume One: The Breath of Life, Biodynamics, and Fundamental Skills*; published by North Atlantic Books.

Sutherland, William Garner, 1997, *Contributions of Thought: The Collected Writings of William Garner Sutherland*; published by Rudra Press.

Teilhard de Chardin, Pierre, 1978, *The Heart of Matter*; published by Harper Collins.

Versluis, Arthur, 2014, *The American Gurus: From Transcendentalism to New Age Religion*; published by Oxford University Press.

Welwood, John, 2000, *Toward a Psychology of Awakening: Buddhism, Psychotherapy, and the Path of Personal and Spiritual Transformation*; published by Shambhala Publications.

Winnicott, Donald, 1965, *The Maturational Processes and The Facilitating Environment*; published by New York International Universities Press.

Whitehead, Alfred North, 1929, *Process and Reality*; published by Simon and Schuster.

www.ingramcontent.com/pod-product-compliance
Lightning Source LLC
Chambersburg PA
CBHW071704120626
46550CB00001B/105